Mirror for Humanity

Seventh Edition

Mirror for Humanity

A Concise Introduction to Cultural Anthropology

Conrad Phillip Kottak

University of Michigan

The McGraw-Hill Companies

Mc Graw Hill **Connect Learn Succeed**™

Published by McGraw-Hill, an imprint of The McGraw-Hill Companies, Inc., 1221 Avenue of the Americas, New York, NY 10020. Copyright © 2010, 2008, 2007, 2005, 2003, 1999, 1996 by The McGraw-Hill Companies. All rights reserved. No part of this publication may be reproduced or distributed in any form or by any means, or stored in a database or retrieval system, without the prior written consent of The McGraw-Hill Companies, Inc., including, but not limited to, in any network or other electronic storage or transmission, or broadcast for distance learning.

This book is printed on acid-free paper.

1 2 3 4 5 6 7 8 9 0 DOC/DOC 0 9

ISBN: 978-0-07-353104-5
MHID: 0-07-353104-9

Editor in Chief: Michael Ryan
Publisher: Frank Mortimer
Sponsoring Editor: Gina Boedeker
Managing Editor: Meghan Campbell
Developmental Editor: Kate Scheinman
Marketing Manager: Leslie Oberhuber
Media Project Manager: Vivek Iyer
Text Permissions Coordinator: Karyn L. Morrison
Production Editor: Leslie LaDow
Manuscript Editor: Patricia Ohlenroth
Designer: Allister Fein
Photo Research Coordinator: Nora Agbayani
Photo Researcher: Barbara Salz
Production Supervisor: Louis Swaim
Composition: 10/12 Times by Aptara®, Inc.
Printing: 45 # New Era Matte Plus by R.R. Donnelley & Sons
PMS: 1815

Credits: The credits section for this book begins on page 313 and is considered an extension of the copyright page.

Library of Congress Cataloging-in-Publication Data

Kottak, Conrad Phillip.
  Mirror for humanity : a concise introduction to cultural anthropology/
  Conrad Phillip Kottak.—7th ed.
    p. cm.
  Includes bibliographical references and index.
  ISBN-13: 978-0-07-353104-5 (alk. paper)
  ISBN-10: 0-07-353104-9 (alk. paper)
  1. Ethnology. I. Title.
  GN316.K66 2009
  306—dc22

                                    2009031733

The Internet addresses listed in the text were accurate at the time of publication. The inclusion of a website does not indicate an endorsement by the authors or McGraw-Hill, and McGraw-Hill does not guarantee the accuracy of the information presented at these sites.

www.mhhe.com

To My Daughter,
Dr. Juliet Kottak Mavromatis

Ordinarily we are unaware of the special lens through which we look at life. It would hardly be fish who discovered the existence of water. Students who had not yet gone beyond the horizon of their own society could not be expected to perceive custom which was the stuff of their own thinking. Anthropology holds up a great mirror to man and lets him look at himself in this infinite variety.

(Kluckhohn 1944, p. 16—his emphasis)

Also available from McGraw-Hill by Conrad Phillip Kottak

Anthropology: The Exploration of Human Diversity, 13th ed. (2009)

Cultural Anthropology, 13th ed. (2009)

Windows on Humanity: A Concise Introduction to Anthropology, 4th ed. (2010)

On Being Different: Diversity and Multiculturalism in the North American Mainstream, 3rd ed. (2008) (with Kathryn A. Kozaitis)

Physical Anthropology and Archaeology, 2nd ed. (2006)

Assault on Paradise: The Globalization of a Little Community in Brazil, 4th ed. (2006)

Brief Contents

Table of Contents

Anthropology Today Boxes

About the Author

Conrad Phillip Kottak (A.B. Columbia College, 1963; Ph.D. Columbia University, 1966) is the Julian H. Steward Collegiate Professor of Anthropology at the University of Michigan, where he has taught since 1968. He served as Anthropology Department Chair from 1996 to 2006. In 1991 he was honored for his teaching by the university and the state of Michigan. In 1992 he received an excellence in teaching award from the College of Literature, Sciences, and the Arts at the University of Michigan. In 1999 the American Anthropological Association (AAA) awarded Professor Kottak the AAA/Mayfield Award for Excellence in the Undergraduate Teaching of Anthropology. In 2005 he was elected to the American Academy of Arts and Sciences and in 2008 to the National Academy of Sciences.

Professor Kottak has done ethnographic fieldwork in Brazil (since 1962), Madagascar (since 1966), and the United States. His general interests are in the processes by which local cultures are incorporated—and resist incorporation—into larger systems. This interest links his earlier work on ecology and state formation in Africa and Madagascar to his more recent research on global change, national and international culture, and the mass media.

The fourth edition of Kottak's popular case study *Assault on Paradise: The Globalization of a Little Community in Brazil,* based on his continuing field work in Arembepe, Bahia, Brazil, was published in 2006 by McGraw-Hill. In a research project during the 1980s, Kottak blended ethnography and survey research in studying "Television's Behavioral Effects in Brazil." That research is the basis of Kottak's book *Prime-Time Society: An Anthropological Analysis of Television and Culture* (Wadsworth 1990)—a comparative study of the nature and impact of television in Brazil and the United States.

Kottak's other books include *The Past in the Present: History, Ecology and Cultural Variation in Highland Madagascar* (1980), *Researching American Culture: A Guide for Student Anthropologists* (edited 1982) (both University of Michigan Press), and *Madagascar: Society and History* (edited 1986) (Carolina Academic Press). The most recent editions (thirteenth) of his texts *Anthropology: The Exploration of Human Diversity* and *Cultural Anthropology* were published by McGraw-Hill in 2008. He also is the author of *Mirror for Humanity: A Concise Introduction to Cultural Anthropology* (7th ed.—this book), and *Window on Humanity: A Concise Introduction to Anthropology* (4th ed. 2010). With Kathryn A. Kozaitis, he wrote *On Being Different: Diversity and Multiculturalism in the North American Mainstream* (3rd ed., McGraw-Hill, 2008). His newest book, with Lara Descartes (Descartes and Kottak 2009), is *Media and Middle Class Moms: Images and Realities of Work and Family* (published by Routledge/Taylor and Francis)

Conrad Kottak's articles have appeared in academic journals, including *American Anthropologist, Journal of Anthropological Research, American Ethnologist, Ethnology, Human Organization,* and *Luso-Brazilian Review*. He also has written for more popular journals, including *Transaction/SOCIETY, Natural History, Psychology Today,* and *General Anthropology*.

In recent research projects, Kottak and his colleagues have investigated the emergence of ecological awareness in Brazil, the social context of deforestation and biodiversity conservation in Madagascar, and popular participation in economic development planning in northeastern Brazil. Professor Kottak has been active in the University of Michigan's Center for the Ethnography of Everyday Life, supported by the Alfred P. Sloan Foundation. In that capacity, for a research project titled "Media, Family, and Work in a Middle-Class Midwestern Town," Kottak and his colleague Lara Descartes have investigated how middle-class families draw on various media in planning, managing, and evaluating their choices and solutions with respect to the competing demands of work and family. That work is the basis of *Media and Middle Class Moms*.

Conrad Kottak appreciates comments about his books from professors and students. He can be readily reached by e-mail at the following address: ckottak@bellsouth.net.

Preface

Mirror for Humanity is intended to provide a concise, readable, relatively low-cost, introduction to cultural anthropology. The combination of shorter length and lower cost increases the instructor's options for assigning additional reading—case studies, ethnographies, readers, and other supplements—in a semester course. *Mirror* also works well in a quarter system; traditional cultural anthropology texts often are too long for a one-quarter course.

As a college student, I was drawn to anthropology by its breadth and because of what it could tell me about the human condition. Cultural anthropology has compiled an impressive body of knowledge about human similarities and differences. I'm eager to introduce that knowledge in the pages that follow. I believe strongly in anthropology's capacity to enlighten and inform. Anthropology's subject matter is intrinsically fascinating, and its focus on diversity helps students understand and interact with their fellow human beings in an increasingly interconnected world and an increasingly diverse North America.

Anthropology remains exciting, even as profound changes affect the people and societies ethnographers study. In cultural anthropology it's increasingly difficult to know when to write in the present tense and when to write in the past tense. Yet many texts ignore change—except maybe with a chapter tacked on at the end—and write as though cultural anthropology and the people it studies were the same as they were decades ago. While any competent text must present cultural anthropology's core, it should also demonstrate anthropology's relevance to today's world.

Anthropology, reflecting the world itself, seems to change at an increasing rate—hence this edition's new chapter titled "Global Issues Today." An introductory text should not, I believe, restrict itself to subject matter defined more than a generation ago, ignoring the pervasive changes affecting the peoples, places, and topics traditionally studied by anthropologists. *Mirror* thus includes discussions of ethnicity and nationalism in a global context and of diversity and multiculturalism in North America. Also highlighted are anthropology's increasingly transnational, multilocal, and longitudinal perspectives.

Rapid change notwithstanding, anthropology has a core—the subject matter, perspectives, and approaches that first attracted me when I was an undergraduate. Even the briefest text must expose anthropology's nature, scope, and roles as a science, a humanities field, and a mirror for humanity. Anthropology is a science—a "systematic field of study or body of knowledge that aims, through experiment, observation, and deduction, to produce reliable explanations of phenomena, with reference to the material and physical world" (Webster's *New World Encyclopedia*, 1993, p. 937). Clyde Kluckhohn called anthropology "the science of human similarities and differences." His statement of the need for such a science still stands: "Anthropology provides a scientific basis for dealing with the crucial dilemma of the world today: how can peoples of different appearance, mutually unintelligible languages, and dissimilar ways of life get along peaceably together?" (Kluckhohn 1944, p. 9).

Anthropology also has strong links to the humanities. Cultural anthropology may well be the most humanistic of academic fields because of its fundamental respect for human diversity. Anthropologists listen to, record, and represent voices from a multitude of nations and cultures. We strive to convince our students of the value of local knowledge, of diverse worldviews and perspectives. Cultural anthropology brings a comparative and nonelitist perspective to forms of creative expression, including art, narratives, music, and dance. Cultural anthropology is influenced by and influences the humanities. Adopting a view of creativity in the context of cultural, social, and power differentials, recent approaches in the humanities have mirrored anthropology in paying greater attention to mass and popular culture and to local and subaltern creative expressions.

Anthropology's final basic role is as a mirror for humanity—a term derived from a Clyde Kluckhohn metaphor, in his book *Mirror for Man* (1944), which suggested the title of this text. By looking at other cultures we can see ourselves more clearly:

> Ordinarily we are unaware of the special lens through which we look at life. It would hardly be fish who discovered the existence of water. Students who had not yet gone beyond the horizon of their own society could not be expected to perceive custom which was the stuff of their own thinking. Anthropology holds up a great mirror to man and lets him look at himself in his infinite variety. (Kluckhohn, 1944, p. 16)

Kluckhohn's point and quotation, which I chose to open this book, remind me of one of my own teachers, Margaret Mead, who is remembered for her unparalleled success in demonstrating anthropology's value and relevance in allowing Americans to reflect on cultural variation and the plasticity of human nature. Mead represented anthropology so effectively because she viewed it as a humanistic science of unique value in understanding and improving the human condition. This book is written in the belief that anthropologists should remember and emulate Dr. Mead's example.

Content and Organization

No single or monolithic theoretical perspective orients this book. My e-mail, along with reviewers' comments, confirms that instructors with a wide range of views and approaches have been pleased with *Mirror* as a teaching tool.

The chapters are organized to place related content close together—although they are sufficiently independent of one another to be assigned in any order the instructor might select. Culture, ethnography, and language are covered in Chapters 2–4. "Political Systems" (Chapter 6) logically follows "Making a Living" (Chapter 5). Chapters 7 and 8 ("Families, Kinship, and Marriage" and "Gender," respectively) also form a coherent unit.

The chapter on religion (9) covers not just traditional religious practices but also contemporary world religions and religious movements. It is followed by four chapters (10–13) that form a natural unit exploring sociocultural transformations and expressions in today's world. This concluding unit represents one of the key differences between this text and others. Several important questions are addressed in these four chapters: How and why did the modern world system emerge? How has world capitalism affected patterns of stratification and inequality within and among nations? What were colonialism, imperialism, and Communism, and what are their legacies? How are race and ethnicity socially constructed and handled in different societies, and how do they generate prejudice, discrimination, and conflict? How do economic development, globalization, and climate change affect the peoples, societies, and communities among which anthropologists traditionally have worked? How do people today actively interpret and confront the world system and the products of globalization? What factors threaten continued human diversity? How can anthropologists work to ensure the preservation of that diversity?

Let me focus here as well on two chapters present in *Mirror for Humanity* but not found consistently in other anthropology texts: "Ethnicity and Race" (Chapter 11) and "Gender" (Chapter 8). I believe that systematic consideration of race, ethnicity, and gender is vital in an introductory anthropology text. Anthropology's distinctive four-field approach can shed special light on these subjects. Race and gender studies are fields in which anthropology always has taken the lead. I'm convinced that anthropology's special contributions to understanding the biological, social, cultural, and linguistic dimensions of race, ethnicity, and gender should be highlighted in any introductory text. So significant do I consider the anthropological approach to issues of race that this topic is introduced in the very first chapter of this book. Even since the writings of Franz Boas, a founder of American anthropology, issues of race, language, and culture have been central to anthropology. I make every attempt to illuminate them in this book.

NEW IN THE SEVENTH EDITION

One slight change in chapter order is the shift of "Culture" from Chapter 3 to Chapter 2. I did this to highlight the centrality of the culture concept in anthropology. Also, I have added to that chapter a new section on "Culture's Evolutionary Basis." The other major change is in Chapter 13. I have combined parts of old Chapter 13 ("Cultural Exchange and Survival") with new material on global issues to make this chapter "Global Issues Today."

All chapters of *Mirror* have been updated, with charts, tables, and statistics based on the most recent information available. Of the thirteen end-of-chapter boxes, nine are new to this edition. These "Anthropology Today" boxes are intended to bring home anthropology's relevance to current issues and events, including, for example, the election of an anthropologist's son as president of the United States. With the new chapter "Global Issues Today" and other changes, the focus on global themes, trends, and issues has been strengthened even further in this edition.

Chapter By Chapter Changes

Chapter 1: What Is Anthropology?

A substantially revised Chapter 1 introduces anthropology as a four-field, integrated, biocultural discipline that focuses on human biological and cultural diversity in time and space. Anthropology is discussed as a comparative and holistic science, with links to the natural and social sciences and the humanities. Chapter 1 includes an expanded and updated discussion of problems with the race concept. A new "Anthropology Today" box about Stanley Ann Dunham Soetoro, Barack Obama's anthropologist mother, concludes the chapter.

Chapter 2: Culture

This chapter has been moved up a bit, from Chapter 3 in the last edition. This new placement responds to users' and reviewers' comments that because the culture concept is so central, it should be presented as early in the text as possible. Chapter 2 examines the anthropological concept of culture, including its symbolic and adaptive features. A major new section on "Culture's Evolutionary Basis" discusses the role culture has played in human evolution, along with differences and similarities between humans and the apes. There is a new "Anthropology Today" box on the emergence of behavioral modernity.

Chapter 3: Ethics and Methods

An updated Chapter 3 focuses on ethical issues and research methods. The ethical issues anthropologists increasingly confront are highlighted. Students learn how anthropologists do their work and how that work is relevant in understanding ourselves.

Chapter 4: Language and Communication

Chapter 4 introduces methods and topics in linguistic anthropology, including nonverbal communication, descriptive and historical linguistics, sociolinguistics, and language and culture. There is a new discussion of the genetic basis of language and a new section on language loss. The chapter concludes with a new "Anthropology Today" box on linguistic diversity and the Internet.

Chapter 5: Making a Living

Chapter 5 surveys economic anthropology, including changing adaptive strategies (systems of food production), industrial alienation, and exchange systems. The concluding box on scarcity has been updated based on the author's most recent revisit to Madagascar.

Chapter 6: Political Systems

Using case material from various societies, Chapter 6 discusses political systems in terms of scale and types of conflict resolution. The chapter concludes with a new "Anthropology Today" section that illustrates the various levels of political regulation (local, regional, national, and international) that determine how contemporary people such as the Yanomami of Venezuela and Brazil live their lives and strive to maintain their health, autonomy, and cultural traditions.

Chapter 7: Families, Kinship, and Descent

Chapter 7 discusses families, households, descent groups, and marriage cross-culturally, and also with reference to updated U.S. and Canadian census data. Various definitions of *family* are considered. The discussion of marriage examines exogamy, endogamy, the incest taboo, caste, postmarital residence rules, marital exchanges, replacement marriage, and plural marriage cross-culturally. Also covered are divorce and same-sex marriage, updated to reflect recent events and legal decisions. The new "Anthropology Today" box shows how customs involving plural marriage are changing in the contemporary world and in the context of nation-states and globalization.

Chapter 8: Gender

A thoroughly updated Chapter 8 examines cross-cultural similarities and differences in male and female roles, rights, and responsibilities. Systems of gender stratification and multiple genders are examined. There is information on contemporary gender roles and issues, including the feminization of poverty. The latest relevant census data is included. The new "Anthropology Today" box describes changes in work patterns and gender roles in contemporary India, where women increasingly are entering the work force after college and deferring marriage.

Chapter 9: Religion

Chapter 9 surveys time-honored anthropological approaches to religion, while also discussing contemporary world religions and religious movements. The section on contemporary world religions has been updated. The new "Anthropology Today" box focuses on France's Musée du Quai Branly, inspired by, and site of events honoring, a famed anthropologist of religion, Claude Lévi-Strauss. That museum, which has become one of Paris's key tourist destinations, is a tribute to the arts, beliefs, and cosmology of non-Western peoples.

Chapter 10: The World System and Colonialism

This chapter examines the emergence and nature of the modern world system, including industrial and postindustrial systems of stratification and their impact on nonindustrial societies. Also discussed are colonial systems and development policies that have impinged on the people and societies anthropologists traditionally have studied. Covered as well are neoliberalism, Communism and its fall, postsocialist transitions, and global energy consumption. This chapter's new "Anthropology Today" box reports on a conundrum facing a major university. Is a firm whose operations have destroyed the landscapes and livelihoods of indigenous peoples a proper advisor for an institute devoted to ecological sustainability?

Chapter 11: Ethnicity and Race

This chapter focuses on the social construction of race and ethnicity and offers cross-cultural examples of variation in racial classification and ethnic relations. Discussed as well are discrimination and ethnic conflict. A new section on "Race in the Census" is based on the most recent sources and census data for the United States and Canada.

Chapter 12: Applying Anthropology

Applied anthropology is presented here as anthropology's second dimension, rather than as a fifth subfield. Examples of applying anthropology are provided from all four subfields. Development anthropology is discussed as an important subtopic within applied anthropology.

Chapter 13 Global Issues Today

This chapter begins with sections on global climate change and environmental anthropology. Using recent examples, it shows how local people actively confront the world system and the products of globalization. All chapter material, including that on the political mobilization of indigenous peoples, has been revised so as to highlight globalization. Using a case study from contemporary Alaska, Chapter 13's new "Anthropology Today" section describes some of the first climate change refugees in the United States—true victims of global warming. This chapter also considers the role of the anthropologist in ensuring the continuance and preservation of cultural diversity.

Pedagogy

This seventh edition incorporates suggestions made by users of my other texts as well as reviewers of previous editions of *Mirror for Humanity*. The result, I hope, is a sound, well-organized, interesting, and "user-friendly" introduction to cultural anthropology.

 Mirror contains "Anthropology Today" boxes (nine new ones) at the end of each chapter, intended to give students a chance to consider anthropology's relevance to today's world and to their own lives. Some boxes examine current events or debates. Others are more personal accounts, which add human feeling to the presentation of cultural anthropology's subject matter. Many boxes illustrate a point with examples familiar to students from their enculturation or everyday experience.

 A glossary defining key terms presented in each chapter is found at the end of the book, along with a bibliography of references cited.

 End-of-chapter summaries are numbered, to make major points stand out.

Supplements

Visit our Online Learning Center website at www.mhhe.com/kottak for robust student and instructor resources.

For Students

Student resources include self-quizzes (multiple-choice, true or false, essay), Internet exercises, and additional chapter study aides.

For Instructors

The password-protected instructor portion of the website includes the instructor's manual, a comprehensive computerized test bank, PowerPoint lecture slides, and a variety of additional instructor resources.

CourseSmart e-Book

Course

CourseSmart is a new way find and buy eTextbooks. At CourseSmart you can save up to 50% off the cost of a print textbook, reduce your impact on the environment, and gain access to powerful Web tools for learning. CourseSmart has the largest selection of eTextbooks available anywhere, offering thousands of the most commonly adopted textbooks from a wide variety of higher education publishers. CourseSmart eTextbooks are available in one standard online reader with full text search, notes and highlighting, and e-mail tools for sharing notes between classmates. For further details contact your sales representative or go to www.coursesmart.com.

Tegrity Campus

Tegrity Campus is a service that makes class time available all the time by automatically capturing every lecture in a searchable format for students to review when they study and complete assignments. With a simple one-click start and stop process, you capture all computer screens and corresponding audio. Students replay any part of any class with easy-to-use, browser-based viewing on a PC or Mac.

Educators know that the more students can see, hear, and experience class resources, the better they learn. With Tegrity Campus, students quickly recall key moments by using its unique search feature. This search helps students find what they need, when they need it across, an entire semester of class recordings. Help turn all your students' study time into learning moments immediately supported by your lecture.

To learn more about Tegrity, watch a 2-minute Flash demo at http://tegritycampus.mhhe.com.

Acknowledgments

I'm grateful to many colleagues at McGraw-Hill. Gina Boedeker has been supportive and enthusiastic as McGraw-Hill's sponsoring editor for anthropology. As developmental editor, Kate Scheinman once again did an excellent job synthesizing the reviews, helping me plan and implement the revision, working with me to complete and turn over the manuscript, and keeping things moving. I also enjoy working with Frank Mortimer, McGraw-Hill's publisher of anthropology and other social sciences, and Marketing Manager Leslie Oberhuber.

I would like to thank Leslie LaDow for her excellent work as production editor (for this and my other books), guiding the manuscript through production and keeping everything moving on schedule. Louis Swaim, production supervisor, worked with the printer to make sure everything came out right. It's always a pleasure to work with Barbara Salz, freelance photo researcher, with whom I've worked for two decades. I want to thank Victoria Springer for her work on the Instructor's Manual and Test Bank, Gerry Williams for his work on the PowerPoints, and Maria Perez for her work on the student supplements located on the Online Learning Center website. I also thank Patricia Ohlenroth for her copyediting, George F. Watson for proofreading, and Allister Fein for conceiving and executing the design.

Nora Agbayani also deserves thanks as photo research coordinator for this and other books of mine. Thanks, too, to Vivek Iyer, media producer, for creating the OLC. I also thank Karyn Morrison, who has handled the literary permissions.

I'm very grateful to the following prepublication reviewers of this and previous editions of *Mirror for Humanity:*

Sue L. Aki, *University of Texas at San Antonio*
Linda Allen, *Kirkwood Community College*
Robyn Andrews, *Massey University*
Diane Everett Barbolla, *San Diego Mesa College*
Linda Bender, *Cerritos College/College of the Canyons*
Sharla Blank, *Washburn University*
Beau Bowers, *Central Piedmont Community College*
Jim Brady, *California State University, Los Angeles*
Christina Brewer, *Saddleback Community College*
Larisa Lee Broyles, *California State University, San Bernardino*
Monica Cable, *Franklin & Marshall College*
William L. Coleman, *University of North Carolina, Greensboro*
Lawrence W. Crissman, *Griffith University*
Sheilah Clarke-Ekong, *University of Missouri*
Barbra E. Erickson, *California State University–Fullerton*
Les W. Field, *University of New Mexico*
Martin Forsey, *University of Western Australia*
Elizabeth Fortenbery, *Pierce Community College*
Ted Fortier, *Seattle University*

Liesl L. Gambold, *Dalhousie University*
Mathias Guenther, *Wilfrid Laurier University*
Tracey Smith-Harris, *Cape Breton University*
Mark J. Hartmann, *University of Arkansas at Little Rock*
Christopher Hays, *University of Wisconsin–Washington County*
Katherine Hirschfeld, *University of Oklahoma*
David Julian Hodges, *CUNY Hunter College*
Donald S. Johnson, *Mesabi Range Community and Technical College*
Hilary Kahn, *Indiana University–Indianapolis*
Jami Leibowitz, *East Carolina University*
William Leons, *University of Toledo*
James MacKenzie, *University of Lethbridge*
Daniel Maher, *University of Arkansas–Fort Smith*
Karen McGarry, *York University*
Thomas McIlwraith, *Douglas College*
Garry Morgan, *Northwestern College*
John Napora, *University of South Florida*
Sharlotte Neely, *Northern Kentucky University*
Kevin Neuhouser, *Seattle Pacific University*
Aihwa Ong, *University of California–Berkeley*
Martin Oppenheimer, *Kansas State University*
Patricia Ann Owens, *Wabash Valley College*
Benjamin Purzycki, *University of Connecticut*
Gerald F. Reid, *Sacred Heart University*
Carolyn Rock, *Valdosta State University*
Eugene E. Ruyle, *California State University–Long Beach*
Priscilla Schulte, *University of Alaska Southeast*
Andris Skreija, *University of Nebraska–Omaha*
Betty A. Smith, *Kennesaw State University*
Shannon Speed, *University of Texas at Austin*
Karen Stocker, *California State University, Bakersfield*
Emily Stovel, *Ripon College*
Ted Swedenburg, *University of Arkansas*
Tom Thompson, *Northland Pioneer College, University of the Incarnate Word*
Jack Thornburg, *Benedictine University*
Mark Tromans, *Broward Community College*
Adam Wetsman, *Rio Hondo College*
Raelene Wilding, *The University of Western Australia*
Thomas Williamson, *St. Olaf College*
Marty Zelenietz, *St. Mary's University*

Students, too, regularly share their insights about *Mirror* via e-mail. Anyone—student or instructor—with access to e-mail can reach me at the following address: ckottak@bellsouth.net.

As usual, my family has offered me understanding, support, and inspiration during the preparation of *Mirror for Humanity*. Dr. Nicholas Kottak regularly shares his insights with me, as does Isabel Wagley Kottak, my companion in the field and in life for four decades. This book is dedicated to my daughter, Dr. Juliet Kottak Mavromatis, who continues our family tradition of exploring human diversity and diagnosing and treating the human condition.

During my long teaching career, I've benefited from the knowledge, help, and advice of so many friends, colleagues, teaching assistants (graduate student instructors–GSIs), and students that I can no longer fit their names into a short preface. I hope they know who they are and accept my thanks. Feedback from students, faculty, and GSIs keeps me up to date on the interests, needs, and views of the people for whom *Mirror* is written, as does my ongoing participation in workshops on the teaching of anthropology. I continue to believe that effective textbooks are based in the enthusiastic practice of teaching. I hope this product of my experience will continue to be helpful to others.

Conrad Phillip Kottak
Ann Arbor, Michigan
and Johns Island, South Carolina
ckottak@bellsouth.net

What Is Anthropology?

❖ **Human Adaptability**

Adaptation, Variation, and Change

❖ **General Anthropology**

❖ **Human Biological Diversity and the Race Concept**

Explanatory Approaches

❖ **The Subdisciplines of Anthropology**

Cultural Anthropology

Archaeological Anthropology

Biological, or Physical, Anthropology

Linguistic Anthropology

❖ **Anthropology and Other Academic Fields**

❖ **Applied Anthropology**

Anthropology Today: Anthropologist's Son Elected President

"That's just human nature." "People are pretty much the same all over the world." Such opinions, which we hear in conversations, in the mass media, and in a dozen scenes in daily life, promote the erroneous idea that people in other countries have the same desires, feelings, values, and aspirations that we do. Such statements proclaim that because people are essentially the same, they are eager to receive the ideas, beliefs, values, institutions, practices, and products of an expansive North American culture. Often this assumption turns out to be wrong.

Anthropology offers a broader view—a distinctive comparative, cross-cultural perspective. Most people think that anthropologists study nonindustrial societies, and they do. My research has taken me to remote villages in Brazil and Madagascar, a large island off the southeast coast of Africa. In Brazil I sailed with fishers in simple sailboats on Atlantic waters. Among Madagascar's Betsileo people I worked in rice fields and took part in ceremonies in which I entered tombs to rewrap the corpses of decaying ancestors.

However, anthropology is much more than the study of nonindustrial peoples. It is a comparative science that examines all societies, ancient and modern, simple and complex. Most of the other social sciences tend to focus on a single society, usually an industrial nation such as the United States or Canada. Anthropology offers a unique cross-cultural perspective, constantly comparing the customs of one society with those of others.

To become a cultural anthropologist, one normally does *ethnography* (the first-hand, personal study of local settings). Ethnographic fieldwork usually entails spending a year or more in another society, living with the local people and learning about their way of life. No matter how much the ethnographer discovers about the society, he or she remains an alien there. That experience of alienation has a profound impact. Having learned to respect other customs and beliefs, anthropologists can never forget that there is a wider world. There are normal ways of thinking and acting other than our own.

Human Adaptability

Anthropologists study human beings wherever and whenever they find them—in a Turkish café, a Mesopotamian tomb, or a North American shopping mall. Anthropology is the exploration of human diversity in time and space. Anthropology studies the whole of the human condition: past, present, and future; biology, society, language, and culture. Of particular interest is the diversity that comes through human adaptability.

Humans are among the world's most adaptable animals. In the Andes of South America, people wake up in villages 16,000 feet above sea level and then trek 1,500 feet higher to work in tin mines. Tribes in the Australian desert worship animals and discuss philosophy. People survive malaria in the tropics. Men have walked on the moon. The model of the starship *Enterprise* in Washington's Smithsonian Institution symbolizes the desire to "seek out new life and civilizations, to boldly go where no one has gone before." Wishes to know the unknown, control the uncontrollable, and create order out of chaos find expression among all peoples. Creativity, adaptability, and flexibility are basic human attributes, and human diversity is the subject matter of anthropology.

Students often are surprised by the breadth of **anthropology,** which is the study of the human species and its immediate ancestors. Anthropology is a uniquely comparative and **holistic** science. Holism refers to the study of the whole of the human condition: past, present, and future; biology, society, language, and culture.

People share *society*—organized life in groups—with other animals, including baboons, wolves, and even ants. Culture, however, is more distinctly human. **Cultures** are traditions and customs, transmitted through learning, that form and guide the beliefs and behavior of the people exposed to them. Children learn such a tradition by growing up in a particular society, through a process called enculturation. Cultural traditions include customs and opinions, developed over the generations, about proper and improper behavior. These traditions answer such questions as: How should we do things? How do we make sense of the world? How do we tell right from wrong? What is right, and what is wrong? A culture produces a degree of consistency in behavior and thought among the people who live in a particular society.

The most critical element of cultural traditions is their transmission through learning rather than through biological inheritance. Culture is not itself biological, but it rests on certain features of human biology. For more than a million years, humans have had at least some of the biological capacities on which culture depends. These abilities are to learn, to think symbolically, to use language, and to employ tools and other products in organizing their lives and adapting to their environments.

Anthropology confronts and ponders major questions of human existence as it explores human biological and cultural diversity in time and space. By examining ancient bones and tools, we unravel the mysteries of human origins. When did our ancestors separate from those remote great-aunts and great-uncles whose descendants are the apes? Where and when did *Homo sapiens* originate? How has our species changed? What are we now, and where are we going? How have changes in culture and society influenced biological change? Our genus, *Homo,* has been changing for more than 1 million years. Humans continue to adapt and change both biologically and culturally.

Adaptation, Variation, and Change

Adaptation refers to the processes by which organisms cope with environmental forces and stresses, such as those posed by climate and *topography* or terrains, also called landforms. How do organisms change to fit their environments, such as dry climates or high mountain altitudes? Like other animals, humans use biological means of adaptation. But humans are unique in also having cultural means of adaptation. Table 1.1 summarizes the cultural and biological means that humans use to adapt to high altitudes.

Mountainous terrains pose particular challenges, those associated with high altitude and oxygen deprivation. Consider four ways (one cultural and three biological) in which humans may cope with low oxygen pressure at high altitudes. Illustrating cultural (technological) adaptation would be a pressurized airplane cabin equipped with oxygen masks. There are three ways of adapting biologically to high altitudes: genetic adaptation, long-term physiological adaptation, and short-term physiological adaptation. First, native populations of high-altitude areas, such as the Andes of Peru and the Himalayas of Tibet and Nepal, seem to have acquired certain genetic advantages

TABLE 1.1

Forms of Cultural and Biological Adaptation (to High Altitude)

Form of Adaptation	Type of Adaptation	Example
Technology	Cultural	Pressurized airplane cabin with oxygen masks
Genetic adaptation (occurs over generations)	Biological	Larger "barrel chests" of native highlanders
Long-term physiological adaptation (occurs during growth and development of the individual organism)	Biological	More efficient respiratory system, to extract oxygen from "thin air"
Short-term physiological adaptation (occurs spontaneously when the individual organism enters a new environment)	Biological	Increased heart rate, hyperventilation

for life at very high altitudes. The Andean tendency to develop a voluminous chest and lungs probably has a genetic basis. Second, regardless of their genes, people who grow up at a high altitude become physiologically more efficient there than genetically similar people who have grown up at sea level would be. This illustrates long-term physiological adaptation during the body's growth and development. Third, humans also have the capacity for short-term or immediate physiological adaptation. Thus, when lowlanders arrive in the highlands, they immediately increase their breathing and heart rates. Hyperventilation increases the oxygen in their lungs and arteries. As the pulse also increases, blood reaches their tissues more rapidly. All these varied adaptive responses—cultural and biological—achieve a single goal: maintaining an adequate supply of oxygen to the body.

As human history has unfolded, the social and cultural means of adaptation have become increasingly important. In this process, humans have devised diverse ways of coping with the range of environments they have occupied in time and space. The rate of cultural adaptation and change has accelerated, particularly during the past 10,000 years. For millions of years, hunting and gathering of nature's bounty—*foraging*—was the sole basis of human subsistence. However, it took only a few thousand years for **food production** (the cultivation of plants and domestication of animals), which originated some 12,000–10,000 years ago, to replace foraging in most areas. Between 6000 and 5000 B.P. (before the present), the first civilizations arose. These were large, powerful, and complex societies, such as ancient Egypt, that conquered and governed large geographic areas.

Much more recently, the spread of industrial production has profoundly affected human life. Throughout human history, major innovations have spread at the expense of earlier ones. Each economic revolution has had social and cultural repercussions. Today's global economy and communications link all contemporary people, directly or indirectly, in the modern world system. People must cope with forces generated by progressively larger systems—region, nation, and world. The study of such contemporary adaptations generates new challenges for anthropology: "The cultures of world peoples need to be constantly rediscovered as these people reinvent them in changing historical circumstances" (Marcus and Fischer 1986, p. 24).

General Anthropology

The academic discipline of anthropology, also known as **general anthropology** or "four-field" anthropology, includes four main subdisciplines or subfields. They are sociocultural, archaeological, biological, and linguistic anthropology. (From here on, the shorter term *cultural anthropology* will be used as a synonym for "sociocultural anthropology.") Of the subfields, cultural anthropology has the largest membership. Most departments of anthropology teach courses in all four subfields.

There are historical reasons for the inclusion of four subfields in a single discipline. The origin of anthropology as a scientific field, and of American anthropology in particular, can be traced to the nineteenth century. Early American anthropologists were concerned especially with the history and cultures of the native peoples of North America. Interest in the origins and diversity of Native Americans brought together

Early American anthropology was especially concerned with the history and cultures of Native North Americans. Ely S. Parker, or Ha-sa-no-an-da, was a Seneca Indian who made important contributions to early anthropology. Parker also served as Commissioner of Indian Affairs for the United States.

studies of customs, social life, language, and physical traits. Anthropologists still are pondering such questions as, Where did Native Americans come from? How many waves of migration brought them to the New World? What are the linguistic, cultural, and biological links among Native Americans and between them and Asia? (Note that a unified four-field anthropology did not develop in Europe, where the subfields tend to exist separately.)

There also are logical reasons for the unity of American anthropology. Each subfield considers variation in time and space (that is, in different geographic areas). Cultural and archaeological anthropologists study (among many other topics) changes in social life and customs. Archaeologists use studies of living societies to imagine what life might have been like in the past. Biological anthropologists examine evolutionary changes in physical form, for example, anatomical changes that might have been associated with the origin of tool use or language. Linguistic anthropologists may reconstruct the basics of ancient languages by studying modern ones.

The subfields influence each other as anthropologists talk to each other, read books and journals, and meet in professional organizations. Anthropologists share certain key assumptions. Perhaps the most fundamental is the idea that sound conclusions about "human nature" cannot be derived from studying a single population, nation, society, or cultural tradition. A comparative, cross-cultural approach is essential.

General anthropology explores the basics of human biology, society, and culture and considers their interrelations. The four-field approach has been particularly effective in examining the relation between biology (e.g., "race"—see below) and culture. About 70 years ago, the famed anthropologist Ruth Benedict realized, "In World history, those who have helped to build the same culture are not necessarily of one race, and those of the same race have not all participated in one culture" (Benedict 1940, Ch. 2). This statement is even truer in today's globalizing world. How do contemporary anthropologists deal with issues of human biological diversity and race?

Human Biological Diversity and the Race Concept

The photos in this book offer only a glimpse of the range of human biological variation. Additional illustration comes from your own experience. Look around you in your classroom or library, or at the mall or multiplex. Inevitably you'll see people whose ancestors lived in many lands. The first (Native) Americans had to cross a land bridge that once linked Siberia to North America. For later immigrants, perhaps including your own parents or grandparents, the voyage may have been across the sea or overland from nations to the south. They came for many reasons. Some came voluntarily, while others were brought here in chains. The scale of migration in today's world is so vast that millions of people routinely cross national borders or live far from the homelands of their grandparents. Now meeting every day are diverse human beings whose biological features reflect adaptation to a wide range of environments other than the ones they now inhabit. Physical contrasts are evident to anyone. Anthropology's job is to explain them.

Historically, scientists have approached the study of human biological diversity in two main ways: (1) racial classification (now largely abandoned) versus (2) the current explanatory approach, which focuses on understanding specific differences. First we'll consider problems with **racial classification** (the attempt to assign humans to discrete categories [purportedly] based on common ancestry). Then we'll offer some explanations for specific aspects of human biological diversity (in this case light versus dark skin color). *Biological differences are real, important, and apparent to us all.* Modern scientists find it most productive to seek *explanations* for this diversity, rather than trying to pigeonhole people into categories called races.

What is race anyway? In theory, a biological race would be a geographically isolated subdivision of a species. (A *species* is a population whose members can interbreed to produce offspring that can live and reproduce.) Such a *subspecies* would be capable of interbreeding with other subspecies of the same species, but it would not actually do so because of its geographic isolation. Some biologists also use "race" to refer to "breeds," as of dogs or roses. Thus, a pit bull and a Chihuahua would be different races of dogs. Such domesticated "races" have been bred by humans for generations. Humanity (*Homo sapiens*) lacks such races because human populations have not been isolated enough from one another to develop into such discrete groups. Nor have humans experienced controlled breeding like that which has created the various kinds of dogs and roses.

A race is supposed to reflect shared *genetic* material (inherited from a common ancestor), but early scholars instead used *phenotypical* traits (usually skin color) for human racial classification. **Phenotype** refers to an organism's evident traits, its "manifest biology"—anatomy and physiology. Humans display hundreds of evident (detectable) physical traits. They range from skin color, hair form, eye color, and facial features (which are visible) to blood groups and enzyme production (which become evident through testing).

Racial classifications based on phenotype raise the problem of deciding which traits are most important. Should races be defined by height, weight, body shape, facial features, teeth, skull form, or skin color? Like their fellow citizens, early European and American scientists gave priority to skin color. Many school books and encyclopedias still proclaim the existence of three great races: the white, the black, and the yellow. This overly simplistic classification was compatible with the political use of race during the colonial period of the late 19th and early 20th centuries. Such a tripartite scheme kept white Europeans neatly separate from their African, Asian, and Native American subjects. Colonial empires began to break up, and scientists began to question established racial categories, after World War II.

The photos in this chapter illustrate only a small part of the range of human biological diversity. Shown above is a woman from Guangzhou province, People's Republic of China.

A young man from the Marquesas Islands in Polynesia.

A Native American: a Chiquitanos Indian woman from Bolivia.

A Native Australian.

Politics aside, one obvious problem with such racial labels is that they don't accurately describe skin color. "White" people are more pink, beige, or tan than white. "Black" people are various shades of brown, and "yellow" people are tan or beige. These terms also have been dignified by more scientific-*sounding* synonyms— Caucasoid, Negroid, and Mongoloid—which actually have no more of a scientific basis than do white, black, and yellow.

It's true also that many human populations don't fit neatly into any one of the three "great races." For example, where does one put the Polynesians? *Polynesia* is a triangle of South Pacific islands formed by Hawaii to the north, Easter Island to the east, and New Zealand to the southwest. Does the bronze skin color of Polynesians place them with the Caucasoids or the Mongoloids? Some scientists, recognizing this problem, enlarged the original tripartite scheme to include the Polynesian race. Native Americans present an additional problem. Are they red or yellow? Again, some scientists add a fifth race—the red, or Amerindian—to the major racial groups.

Many people in southern India have dark skins, but scientists have been reluctant to classify them with black Africans because of their Caucasoid facial features and hair form. Some, therefore, have created a separate race for these people. What about the Australian aborigines, hunters and gatherers native to the most isolated continent? By skin color, one might place some Native Australians in the same race as tropical Africans. However, similarities to Europeans in hair color (light or reddish) and facial features have led some scientists to classify them as Caucasoids. But there is no evidence that Australians are closer genetically or historically to either of these groups than they are to Asians. Recognizing this problem, scientists often regard Native Australians as a separate race.

Finally, consider the San ("Bushmen") of the Kalahari Desert in southern Africa. Scientists have perceived their skin color as varying from brown to yellow. Those who regard San skin as yellow have placed them in the same category as Asians. In theory, people of the same race share more recent common ancestry with each other than they do with any others; but there is no evidence for recent common ancestry between San and Asians. More reasonably, the San are classified as members of the Capoid (from the Cape of Good Hope) race, which is seen as being different from other groups inhabiting tropical Africa.

Similar problems arise when any single trait is used as a basis for racial classification. An attempt to use facial features, height, weight, or any other phenotypical trait is fraught with difficulties. For example, consider the Nilotes, natives of the upper Nile region of Uganda and Sudan. Nilotes tend to be tall and to have long, narrow noses. Certain Scandinavians also are tall, with similar noses. Given the distance between their homelands, to classify them as members of the same race makes little sense. There is no reason to assume that Nilotes and Scandinavians are more closely related to each other than either is to shorter (and nearer) populations with different kinds of noses.

Would it be better to base racial classifications on a combination of physical traits? This would avoid some of the problems just discussed, but others would arise. First, skin color, stature, skull form, and facial features (nose form, eye shape, lip thickness) don't go together as a unit. For example, people with dark skin may be tall or short and have hair ranging from straight to very curly. Dark-haired populations may have light or dark skin, along with various skull forms, facial features, and body sizes and shapes. The number of combinations is very large, and the amount that heredity (versus environment) contributes to such phenotypical traits is often unclear.

There is a final objection to racial classification based on phenotype. The phenotypical characteristics on which races are based supposedly reflect genetic material that is shared and that has stayed the same for long periods of time. But phenotypical similarities and differences don't necessarily have a genetic basis. Because of changes in the environment that affect individuals during growth and development, the range of phenotypes characteristic of a population may change without any genetic change. There are several examples. In the early 20th century, the anthropologist Franz Boas (1940/1966) described changes in skull form among the children of Europeans who had migrated to the United States. The reason for this wasn't a change in genes, since the European immigrants tended to marry among themselves. Some of their children had been born in Europe and merely raised in the United States. Something in the new environment, probably in the diet, was producing this change. We know now that changes in average height and weight produced by dietary differences in a few generations are common and have nothing to do with race or genetics.

Anthropology's comparative, biocultural perspective recognizes that environmental factors, including customary diet and other cultural forces, constantly mold human biology. (**Biocultural** refers to the inclusion and combination of both biological and cultural perspectives and approaches to comment on or solve a particular issue or problem.) Culture is a key environmental force in determining how human bodies grow and develop. Cultural traditions promote certain activities and abilities, discourage others, and set standards of physical well-being and attractiveness.

Bodies—ideal, and actual—vary from culture to culture and within one culture over time. Ideal bodies change from generation to generation and, with the influence of the mass media, even from decade to decade. Old movies make it easy for us to study bodies and clothing over time. Such movie stars of the past as Humphrey Bogart and Barbara Stanwyck wore stylish hats and smoked cigarettes. Contemporary American men and women wear baseball caps and lift weights. When asked how he recognized Americans in the street, one European mentioned lifting (of weights, and its effects on the body) and tennis shoes (an item of dress considered inelegant in Europe, but a mainstay of hard-core American touring).

Explanatory Approaches

Traditional racial classification assumed that biological characteristics were determined by heredity and were stable (immutable) over long periods of time. We know now that a biological similarity doesn't necessarily indicate recent common ancestry. Dark skin color, for example, can be shared by tropical Africans and Native Australians for reasons other than common ancestry. It is not possible to *define human races* biologically. Still, scientists have made much progress in *explaining* variation in skin color, along with many other expressions of human biological diversity. We shift now from classification to *explanation,* in which natural selection plays a key role.

Before the 16th century, almost all the very dark-skinned populations of the world lived in the tropics, as does this Samburu woman from Kenya.

Very light skin color, illustrated in the photo above, maximizes absorption of ultraviolet radiation by those few parts of the body exposed to direct sunlight during northern winters. This helps prevent rickets and osteoporosis.

First recognized by Charles Darwin and Alfred Russel Wallace, **natural selection** is the process by which the forms most fit to survive and reproduce in a given environment—such as the tropics—do so in greater numbers than others in the same population do. Over the years, the less fit organisms die out and the favored types survive by producing more offspring. The role of natural selection in producing variation in skin color will illustrate the explanatory approach to human biological diversity. Comparable explanations have been provided for many other aspects of human biological variation.

Melanin, the primary determinant of human skin color, is a chemical substance manufactured in the epidermis, or outer skin layer. The melanin cells of darker-skinned people produce more and larger granules of melanin than do those of lighter-skinned people. By screening out ultraviolet (UV) radiation from the sun, melanin offers protection against a variety of maladies, including sunburn and skin cancer.

Before the 16th century, most of the world's very dark-skinned populations lived in the **tropics,** a belt extending about 23 degrees north and south of the equator, between the Tropic of Cancer and the Tropic of Capricorn. The association between dark skin color and a tropical habitat existed throughout the Old World, where humans and their ancestors have lived for millions of years. The darkest populations of Africa evolved not in shady equatorial forests but in sunny open grassland, or savanna, country.

Outside the tropics, skin color tends to be lighter. Moving north in Africa, for example, there is a gradual transition from dark brown to medium brown. Average skin color continues to lighten as one moves through the Middle East, into southern Europe, through central Europe, and to the north. South of the tropics skin color also is lighter. In the Americas, by contrast, tropical populations don't have very dark skin. This is because the settlement of the New World, by light-skinned Asian ancestors of Native Americans, was relatively recent, probably dating back no more than 18,000 years.

How, aside from migrations, can we explain the geographic distribution of human skin color? Natural selection provides an answer. In the tropics, intense UV radiation poses a series of threats that make light skin color an adaptive disadvantage. First, UV radiation can cause severe sunburn, which aside from discomfort can lead to vulnerabilities in the body. By damaging sweat glands, sunburn reduces the body's ability to perspire and thus to regulate its own temperature (thermoregulation). Sunburn also can increase susceptibility to disease. Yet another disadvantage of having light skin color in the tropics is that exposure to UV radiation can cause skin cancer (Blum 1961). Melanin, nature's own sunscreen, confers a selective advantage (i.e., a better chance to survive and reproduce) on darker-skinned people living in the tropics because it helps protect them from sunburn and skin cancer.

Another selective factor in the geographic distribution of human skin color relates to the manufacture (synthesis) of vitamin D in the body. Years ago, W. F. Loomis (1967) focused on the role of UV radiation in stimulating the manufacture of vitamin D by the human body. The unclothed human body can produce its own vitamin D when exposed to sufficient sunlight. However, in a cloudy environment that also is so cold that people have to dress themselves much of the year (such as northern Europe, where very light skin color evolved), clothing interferes with the body's manufacture of vitamin D. The ensuing shortage of vitamin D diminishes the absorption of calcium in the intestines. A nutritional disease known as rickets, which softens and deforms the bones, may develop. In women, deformation of the pelvic bones from rickets can interfere with childbirth. In cold northern areas, light skin color maximizes the absorption of UV radiation and the synthesis of vitamin D by the few parts of the body that are exposed to direct sunlight. There has been selection against dark skin color in northern areas because melanin screens out UV radiation.

This natural selection continues today: East Asians who have migrated recently from India and Pakistan to northern areas of the United Kingdom have a higher incidence of rickets and osteoporosis (also related to vitamin D and calcium deficiency) than the general British population. A related illustration involves Eskimos (Inuit) and other indigenous inhabitants of northern Alaska and northern Canada. According to Nina Jablonski (quoted in Iqbal 2002), "Looking at Alaska, one would think that the native people should be pale as ghosts." One reason they aren't is that they haven't inhabited this region very long in terms of geological time. Even more important, their traditional diet, which is rich in seafood, including fish oils, supplies sufficient vitamin D so as to make a reduction in pigmentation unnecessary. However, and again illustrating natural selection at work today, "when these people don't eat their aboriginal diets of fish and marine mammals, they suffer tremendously high rates of vitamin D-deficiency diseases such as rickets in children and osteoporosis in adults" (Jablonski quoted in Iqbal 2002). Far from being immutable, skin color can become an evolutionary liability very quickly.

According to Jablonski and George Chaplin (2000), another key factor explaining the geographic distribution of skin color involves the effects of UV on folate, an essential nutrient that the human body manufactures from folic acid. Folate is needed for cell division and the production of new DNA. Pregnant women require large amounts of folate to support rapid cell division in the embryo, and there is a direct connection between folate and individual reproductive success. Folate deficiency causes neural tube defects (NTDs) in human embryos. NTDs are marked by the incomplete closure of the neural tube, so the spine and spinal cord fail to develop completely. One NTD, anencephaly (with the brain an exposed mass), results in stillbirth or death soon after delivery. With spina bifida, another NTD, survival rates are higher, but babies have severe disabilities, including paralysis. NTDs are the second-most-common human birth defect after cardiac abnormalities. Today, women of reproductive age are advised to take folate supplements to prevent serious birth defects such as spina bifida.

Natural sunlight and UV radiation destroy folate in the human body. Because melanin, as we have seen, protects against UV hazards, such as sunburn and its consequences, dark skin coloration is adaptive in the tropics. Now we see that melanin also is adaptive because it conserves folate in the human body and thus protects against NTDs, which are much more common in light-skinned than in darker-skinned populations (Jablonski and Chaplin 2000). Studies confirm that Africans and African Americans have a low incidence of severe folate deficiency, even among individuals with marginal nutritional status. Folate also plays a role in another process that is central to reproduction, spermatogenesis—the production of sperm. In mice and rats, folate deficiency can cause male sterility; it may well play a similar role in humans.

Today, of course, cultural alternatives to biological adaptation permit light-skinned people to survive in the tropics and darker-skinned people to live in the far north. People can clothe themselves and seek shelter from the sun; they can use artificial sunscreens if they lack the natural protection that melanin provides. Dark-skinned people living in the north can, indeed must, get vitamin D from their diet or take supplements. Today, pregnant women are routinely advised to take folic acid or folate supplements as a hedge against NTDs. Even so, light skin color still is correlated with a higher incidence of spina bifida.

Jablonski and Chaplin (2000) explain variation in human skin color as resulting from a balancing act between the evolutionary needs to (1) protect against all UV hazards (favoring dark skin in the tropics) and (2) have an adequate supply of vitamin D (favoring lighter skin outside the tropics). This discussion of skin color shows that common ancestry, the presumed basis of race, is not the only reason for biological similarities. Natural selection, still at work today, makes a major contribution to variations in human skin color, as well as to many other human biological differences and similarities.

The Subdisciplines of Anthropology

Cultural Anthropology

Cultural anthropology is the study of human society and culture, the subfield that describes, analyzes, interprets, and explains social and cultural similarities and differences. To study and interpret cultural diversity, cultural anthropologists engage in two kinds of activity: ethnography (based on field work) and ethnology (based on cross-cultural comparison). **Ethnography** provides an account of a particular community, society, or culture. During ethnographic fieldwork, the ethnographer gathers data that he or she organizes, describes, analyzes, and interprets to build and present that account, which may be in the form of a book, article, or film. Traditionally, ethnographers have lived in small communities and studied local behavior, beliefs, customs, social life, economic activities, politics, and religion (see Wolcott 2008).

The anthropological perspective derived from ethnographic field work often differs radically from that of economics or political science. Those fields focus on national and official organizations and policies and often on elites. However, the groups that anthropologists traditionally have studied usually have been relatively poor and powerless. Ethnographers often observe discriminatory practices directed toward such people, who experience food shortages, dietary deficiencies, and other aspects of poverty. Political scientists tend to study programs that national planners develop, while anthropologists discover how these programs work on the local level.

Cultures are not isolated. As noted by Franz Boas (1940/1966) many years ago, contact between neighboring tribes always has existed and has extended over enormous areas." Human populations construct their cultures in interaction with one another, and not in isolation" (Wolf 1982, p. ix). Villagers increasingly participate in regional, national, and world events. Exposure to external forces comes through the mass media, migration, and modern transportation. City and nation increasingly invade local communities with the arrival of tourists, development agents, government and religious officials, and political candidates. Such linkages are prominent components of regional, national, and international systems of politics, economics, and information. These larger systems increasingly affect the people and places anthropology traditionally has studied. The study of such linkages and systems is part of the subject matter of modern anthropology.

Ethnology examines, interprets, analyzes, and compares the results of ethnography—the data gathered in different societies. It uses such data to compare and contrast and to make generalizations about society and culture. Looking beyond the particular to the more general, ethnologists attempt to identify and explain cultural differences and similarities, to test hypotheses, and to build theory to enhance our understanding of how social and cultural systems work. Ethnology gets its data for comparison not just from ethnography but also from the other subfields, particularly from archaeological anthropology, which reconstructs social systems of the past. (Table 1.2 summarizes the main contrasts between ethnography and ethnology.)

TABLE 1.2

Ethnography and Ethnology—Two Dimensions of Cultural Anthropology

Ethnography	Ethnology
Requires field work to collect data	Uses data collected by a series of researchers
Often descriptive	Usually synthetic
Group/community specific	Comparative/cross-cultural

Archaeological Anthropology

Archaeological anthropology (more simply, "archaeology") reconstructs, describes, and interprets human behavior and cultural patterns through material remains. At sites where people live or have lived, archaeologists find artifacts, material items that humans have made, used, or modified, such as tools, weapons, camp sites, buildings, and garbage. Plant and animal remains and ancient garbage tell stories about consumption and activities. Wild and domesticated grains have different characteristics, which allow archaeologists to distinguish between gathering and cultivation. Examination of animal bones reveals the ages of slaughtered animals and provides other information useful in determining whether species were wild or domesticated.

Analyzing such data, archaeologists answer several questions about ancient economies. Did the group get its meat from hunting, or did it domesticate and breed animals, killing only those of a certain age and sex? Did plant food come from wild plants or from sowing, tending, and harvesting crops? Did the residents make, trade for, or buy particular items? Were raw materials available locally? If not, where did they come from? From such information, archaeologists reconstruct patterns of production, trade, and consumption.

Archaeologists have spent much time studying potsherds, fragments of earthenware. Potsherds are more durable than many other artifacts, such as textiles and wood. The quantity of pottery fragments allows estimates of population size and density. The discovery that potters used materials that were not available locally suggests systems

An archaeological team works at Harappa, one site from an ancient Indus River civilization dating back some 4,800 years.

of trade. Similarities in manufacture and decoration at different sites may be proof of cultural connections. Groups with similar pots may be historically related. Perhaps they shared common cultural ancestors, traded with each other, or belonged to the same political system.

Many archaeologists examine paleoecology. *Ecology* is the study of interrelations among living things in an environment. The organisms and environment together constitute an *ecosystem,* a patterned arrangement of energy flows and exchanges. Human ecology studies ecosystems that include people, focusing on the ways in which human use "of nature influences and is influenced by social organization and cultural values" (Bennett 1969, pp. 10–11). *Paleoecology* looks at the ecosystems of the past.

In addition to reconstructing ecological patterns, archaeologists may infer cultural transformations, for example, by observing changes in the size and type of sites and the distance between them. A city develops in a region where only towns, villages, and hamlets existed a few centuries earlier. The number of settlement levels (city, town, village, hamlet) in a society is a measure of social complexity. Buildings offer clues about political and religious features. Temples and pyramids suggest that an ancient society had an authority structure capable of marshaling the labor needed to build such monuments. The presence or absence of certain structures, like the pyramids of ancient Egypt and Mexico, reveals differences in function between settlements. For example, some towns were places where people came to attend ceremonies. Others were burial sites; still others were farming communities.

Archaeologists also reconstruct behavior patterns and lifestyles of the past by excavating. This involves digging through a succession of levels at a particular site. In a given area, through time, settlements may change in form and purpose, as may the connections between settlements. Excavation can document changes in economic, social, and political activities.

Although archaeologists are best known for studying prehistory, that is, the period before the invention of writing, they also study the cultures of historical and even living peoples (see Sabloff 2008). Studying sunken ships off the Florida coast, underwater archaeologists have been able to verify the living conditions on the vessels that brought ancestral African Americans to the New World as enslaved people. In a research project begun in 1973 in Tucson, Arizona, archaeologist William Rathje has learned about contemporary life by studying modern garbage. The value of "garbology," as Rathje calls it, is that it provides "evidence of what people did, not what they think they did, what they think they should have done, or what the interviewer thinks they should have done" (Harrison, Rathje, and Hughes 1994, p. 108). What people report may contrast strongly with their real behavior as revealed by garbology. For example, the garbologists discovered that the three Tucson neighborhoods that reported the lowest beer consumption actually had the highest number of discarded beer cans per household (Podolefsky and Brown 1992, p. 100)! Rathje's garbology also has exposed misconceptions about how much of different kinds of trash are in landfills: While most people thought that fast-food containers and disposable diapers were major waste problems, in fact they were relatively insignificant compared with paper, including environmentally friendly, recyclable paper (Rathje and Murphy 2001).

Biological, or Physical, Anthropology

The subject matter of **biological,** or **physical, anthropology** is human biological diversity in time and space. The focus on biological variation unites five special interests within biological anthropology:

1. Human evolution as revealed by the fossil record (paleoanthropology).
2. Human genetics.
3. Human growth and development.
4. Human biological plasticity (the body's ability to change as it copes with stresses, such as heat, cold, and altitude).
5. The biology, evolution, behavior, and social life of monkeys, apes, and other nonhuman primates.

These interests link physical anthropology to other fields: biology, zoology, geology, anatomy, physiology, medicine, and public health. Osteology—the study of bones—helps paleoanthropologists, who examine skulls, teeth, and bones, to identify human ancestors and to chart changes in anatomy over time. A paleontologist is a scientist who studies fossils. A paleoanthropologist is one sort of paleontologist, one who studies the fossil record of human evolution. Paleoanthropologists often collaborate with archaeologists, who study artifacts, in reconstructing biological and cultural aspects of human evolution. Fossils and tools often are found together. Different types of tools provide information about the habits, customs, and lifestyles of the ancestral humans who used them.

More than a century ago, Charles Darwin noticed that the variety that exists within any population permits some individuals (those with the favored characteristics) to do better than others at surviving and reproducing. Genetics, which developed later, enlightens us about the causes and transmission of this variety. However, it isn't just genes that cause variety. During any individual's lifetime, the environment works along with heredity to determine biological features. For example, people with a genetic tendency to be tall will be shorter if they are poorly nourished during childhood. Thus, biological anthropology also investigates the influence of environment on the body as it grows and matures. Among the environmental factors that influence the body as it develops are nutrition, altitude, temperature, and disease, as well as cultural factors, such as the standards of attractiveness we considered previously.

Biological anthropology (along with zoology) also includes primatology. The **primates** include our closest relatives—apes and monkeys. Primatologists study their biology, evolution, behavior, and social life, often in their natural environments. Primatology assists paleoanthropology, because primate behavior may shed light on early human behavior and human nature.

Linguistic Anthropology

We don't know (and probably never will) when our ancestors acquired the ability to speak, although biological anthropologists have looked to the anatomy of the face and the skull to speculate about the origin of language. And primatologists have described the communication systems of monkeys and apes. We do know that well-developed, grammatically complex languages have existed for thousands of years. Linguistic anthropology offers further illustration of anthropology's interest in comparison, variation, and change. **Linguistic anthropology** studies language in its social and cultural context, across space and over time. Some linguistic anthropologists make inferences about universal features of language, linked perhaps to uniformities in the human brain. Others reconstruct ancient languages by comparing their contemporary descendants and in so doing make discoveries about history. Still others study linguistic differences to discover varied perceptions and patterns of thought in different cultures.

Historical linguistics considers variation in time, such as the changes in sounds, grammar, and vocabulary between Middle English (spoken from approximately A.D. 1050 to 1550) and modern English. **Sociolinguistics** investigates relationships between social and linguistic variation. No language is a homogeneous system in which everyone speaks just like everyone else. How do different speakers use a given language? How do linguistic features correlate with social factors, including class and gender differences (Tannen 1990)? One reason for variation is geography, as in regional dialects and accents. Linguistic variation also is expressed in the bilingualism of ethnic groups. Linguistic and cultural anthropologists collaborate in studying links between language and many other aspects of culture, such as how people reckon kinship and how they perceive and classify colors.

Anthropology and Other Academic Fields

As mentioned previously, one of the main differences between anthropology and the other fields that study people is holism, anthropology's unique blend of biological, social, cultural, linguistic, historical, and contemporary perspectives. Paradoxically, while distinguishing anthropology, this breadth is what also links it to many other disciplines. Techniques used to date fossils and artifacts have come to anthropology from physics, chemistry, and geology. Because plant and animal remains often are found with human bones and artifacts, anthropologists collaborate with botanists, zoologists, and paleontologists.

As a discipline that is both scientific and humanistic, anthropology has links with many other academic fields. Anthropology is a **science**—a "systematic field of study or body of knowledge that aims, through experiment, observation, and deduction, to produce reliable explanations of phenomena, with references to the material and physical world" (*Webster's New World Encyclopedia* 1993, p. 937). The following chapters present anthropology as a humanistic science devoted to discovering, describing, understanding, and explaining similarities and differences in time and space among humans and our ancestors. Clyde Kluckhohn (1944) described anthropology as "the science of human similarities and differences" (p. 9). His statement of the need for such a field still stands: "Anthropology provides a scientific basis for dealing with the crucial dilemma of the world today: how can peoples of different appearance, mutually unintelligible languages, and dissimilar ways of life get along peaceably together?" (p. 9). Anthropology has compiled an impressive body of knowledge that this textbook attempts to encapsulate.

Besides its links to the natural sciences (e.g., geology, zoology), and social sciences (e.g., sociology, psychology), anthropology also has strong links to the humanities. The humanities include English, comparative literature, classics, folklore, philosophy, and the arts. These fields study languages, texts, philosophies, arts, music, performances, and other forms of creative expression. Ethnomusicology, which studies forms of musical expression on a worldwide basis, is especially closely related to anthropology. Also linked is folklore, the systematic study of tales, myths, and legends from a variety of cultures. One might well argue that anthropology is among the most humanistic of all academic fields because of its fundamental respect for human diversity. Anthropologists listen to, record, and represent voices from a multitude of nations and cultures. Anthropology values local knowledge, diverse worldviews, and alternative philosophies. Cultural anthropology and linguistic anthropology in particular bring a comparative and nonelitist perspective to forms of creative expression, including language, art, narratives, music, and dance, viewed in their social and cultural context.

Applied Anthropology

Anthropology is not a science of the exotic carried on by quaint scholars in ivory towers. Rather, anthropology has a lot to tell the public. Anthropology's foremost professional organization, the American Anthropological Association (AAA), has formally acknowledged a public service role by recognizing that anthropology has two dimensions: (1) academic or general anthropology and (2) practicing or **applied anthropology.** The latter refers to the application of anthropological data, perspectives, theory, and methods to identify, assess, and solve contemporary social problems. As Erve Chambers (1987, p. 309) states it, applied anthropology is the "field of inquiry concerned with the relationships between anthropological knowledge and the uses of that knowledge in the world beyond anthropology." More and more anthropologists from the four subfields now work in such "applied" areas as public health, family planning, business, economic development, and cultural resource management.

Applied anthropology encompasses any use of the knowledge and/or techniques of the four subfields to identify, assess, and solve practical problems. Because of anthropology's breadth, it has many applications. For example, applied medical anthropologists consider both the sociocultural and the biological contexts and implications of disease and illness. Perceptions of good and bad health, along with actual health threats and problems, differ among societies. Various ethnic groups recognize different illnesses, symptoms, and causes and have developed different health-care systems and treatment strategies.

Applied archaeology, usually called *public archaeology*, includes such activities as cultural resource management, contract archaeology, public educational programs, and historic preservation. An important role for public archaeology has been created by legislation requiring evaluation of sites threatened by dams, highways, and other construction activities. To decide what needs saving, and to preserve significant information about the past when sites cannot be saved, is the work of **cultural resource management (CRM).** CRM involves not only preserving sites but also allowing their destruction if they are not significant. The "management" part of the term refers to the evaluation and decision-making process. Cultural resource managers work for federal, state, and county agencies and other clients. Applied cultural anthropologists sometimes work with the public archaeologists, assessing the human problems generated by the proposed change and determining how they can be reduced. Table 1.3 relates anthropology's four subfields to its two dimensions.

TABLE 1.3

The Four Subfields and Two Dimensions of Anthropology

Anthropology's Subfields (General Anthropology)	Examples of Application (Applied Anthropology)
Cultural anthropology	Development anthropology
Archaeological anthropology	Cultural resource management (CRM)
Biological or physical anthropology	Forensic anthropology
Linguistic anthropology	Study of linguistic diversity in classrooms

ANTHROPOLOGY TODAY

Anthropologist's Son Elected President

It is widely known that Barack Obama is the son of a Kenyan father and a White American mother from Kansas. Less recognized is the fact that the 44th president of the United States is the son of an anthropologist— Dr. Stanley Ann Dunham Soetoro (usually called simply Ann Dunham). This account focuses on her life and her attraction to diversity, which led her to a career in anthropology. A sociocultural anthropologist by training, Dunham's work on microfinance and socioeconomic issues affecting Indonesian women illustrates the application of anthropology to identify and solve contemporary problems. In other words, she was both a cultural and an applied anthropologist.

Anthropologists study humanity in varied times and places and in a rapidly changing world. By virtue of his parentage, his enculturation, and his experience abroad, Barack Obama provides an excellent symbol of the diversity and interconnections that characterize such a world. As well, his election is a tribute to an ever more diverse United States of America.

Young Barack Obama with his mother, anthropologist Ann Dunham.

In the capsule version of the Barack Obama story, his mother is simply the white woman from Kansas. . . . On the campaign trail, he has called her his "single mom." But neither description begins to capture the unconventional life of Stanley

Continued

ANTHROPOLOGY TODAY   *Continued*

Ann Dunham Soetoro, the parent who most shaped Mr. Obama. . . .

In Hawaii, she married an African student at age 18. Then she married an Indonesian, moved to Jakarta, became an anthropologist, wrote an 800-page dissertation on peasant blacksmithing in Java, worked for the Ford Foundation, championed women's work and helped bring microcredit to the world's poor.

She had high expectations for her children. In Indonesia, she would wake her son at 4 a.m. for correspondence courses in English before school; she brought home recordings of Mahalia Jackson, speeches by the Rev. Dr. Martin Luther King Jr. And when Mr. Obama asked to stay in Hawaii for high school rather than return to Asia, she accepted living apart—a decision her daughter says was one of the hardest in Ms. Soetoro's life.

"She felt that somehow, wandering through uncharted territory, we might stumble upon something that will, in an instant, seem to represent who we are at the core," said Maya Soetoro-Ng, Mr. Obama's half-sister. "That was very much her philosophy of life—to not be limited by fear or narrow definitions, to not build walls around ourselves and to do our best to find kinship and beauty in unexpected places.". . .

Mr. Obama . . . barely saw his father after the age of 2. Though it is impossible to pinpoint the imprint of a parent on the life of a grown child, people who knew Ms. Soetoro well say they see her influence unmistakably in Mr. Obama. . . .

"She was a very, very big thinker," said Nancy Barry, a former president of Women's World Banking, an international network of microfinance providers, where Ms. Soetoro worked in New York City in the early 1990s. . . .

In a Russian class at the University of Hawaii, she met the college's first African student, Barack Obama. They married and had a son in August 1961, in an era when interracial marriage was rare in the United States. . . .

The marriage was brief. In 1963, Mr. Obama left for Harvard, leaving his wife and child. She then married Lolo Soetoro, an Indonesian student. When he was summoned home in 1966 after the turmoil surrounding the rise of Suharto, Ms. Soetoro and Barack followed. . .

Her second marriage faded, too, in the 1970s. Ms. Soetoro wanted to work, one friend said, and Mr. Soetoro wanted more children. He became more American, she once said, as she became more Javanese. "There's a Javanese belief that if you're married to someone and it doesn't work, it will make you sick," said Alice G. Dewey, an anthropologist and friend. "It's just stupid to stay married.". . .

By 1974, Ms. Soetoro was back in Honolulu, a graduate student and raising Barack and Maya, nine years younger. . . . When Ms. Soetoro decided to return to Indonesia three years later for her field work, Barack chose not to go. . . .

Fluent in Indonesian, Ms. Soetoro moved with Maya first to Yogyakarta, the center of Javanese handicrafts. A weaver in college, she was fascinated with what Ms. Soetoro-Ng calls "life's gorgeous minutiae." That interest inspired her study of village industries, which became the basis of her 1992 doctoral dissertation.

"She loved living in Java," said Dr. Dewey, who recalled accompanying Ms. Soetoro to a metalworking village. "People said: 'Hi! How are you?' She said: 'How's your wife? Did your daughter have the baby?' They were friends. Then she'd whip out her notebook and she'd say: 'How many of you have electricity? Are you having trouble getting iron?' "

She became a consultant for the United States Agency for International Development on setting up a village credit program, then a Ford Foundation program officer in Jakarta specializing in women's work. Later, she was a consultant in Pakistan, then joined Indonesia's oldest bank to work on what is described as the world's largest sustainable microfinance program, creating services like credit and savings for the poor.

Visitors flowed constantly through her Ford Foundation office in downtown Jakarta and through her house in a neighborhood to the south, where papaya and banana trees grew in the front yard and Javanese dishes . . . were served for dinner. Her guests were leaders in the Indonesian human rights movement, people from women's organizations, representatives of community groups doing grass-roots development. . . .

Ms. Soetoro-Ng . . . remembers conversations with her mother about philosophy or politics, books, esoteric Indonesian woodworking motifs. . . .

"She gave us a very broad understanding of the world," her daughter said. "She hated bigotry. She was very determined to be remembered for a life of service and thought that service was really the true measure of a life." Many of her friends see her legacy in Mr. Obama—in his self-assurance and drive, his boundary bridging, even his apparent comfort with strong women. She died in November 1995, as Mr. Obama was starting his first campaign for public office. After a memorial service at the University of Hawaii, one friend said, a small group of friends drove to the South Shore in Oahu. With the wind whipping the waves onto the rocks, Mr. Obama and Ms. Soetoro-Ng placed their mother's ashes in the Pacific, sending them off in the direction of Indonesia.

Summary

1. Anthropology is the holistic, biocultural, and comparative study of humanity. It is the systematic exploration of human biological and cultural diversity across time and space. Examining the origins of, and changes in, human biology and culture, anthropology provides explanations for similarities and differences among humans and their societies.

2. The four subfields of general anthropology are (socio)cultural, archaeological, biological, and linguistic. All consider variation in time and space. Each also examines adaptation—the process by which organisms cope with environmental stresses.

3. Anthropology's biocultural perspective is a particularly effective way of approaching the topics of human biological diversity and "race." Because of a range of problems involved in classifying humans into racial categories, contemporary scientists focus on specific differences, such as in skin color, and try to explain them. Biological similarities between groups—rather than common

ancestry (the assumed basis of race)—may reflect similar but independent adaptation to similar natural selective forces. Cultural forces mold human biology, including our body types and images.

4. Cultural anthropology explores the cultural diversity of the present and the recent past. Archaeology reconstructs cultural patterns, often of prehistoric populations. Biological anthropology documents diversity involving fossils, genetics, growth and development, bodily responses, and nonhuman primates. Linguistic anthropology considers diversity among languages. It also studies how speech changes in social situations and over time.

5. Concerns with biology, society, culture, and language link anthropology to many other fields—natural sciences, social sciences, and humanities.

6. Anthropology has two dimensions: general and applied. The latter uses anthropological perspectives, theory, methods, and data to identify, assess, and solve social problems. The fields in which applied anthropologists work include business, government, economic development, education, and social services, action, and outreach. Applied anthropologists come from all four subfields.

Key Terms

adaptation (p. 3)
anthropology (p. 2)
applied anthropology (p. 18)
archaeological anthropology (p. 14)
biocultural (p. 9)
biological (or physical)
    anthropology (p. 16)
cultural anthropology (p. 12)
cultural resource management
    (CRM) (p. 18)
cultures (p. 2)
ethnography (p. 12)

ethnology (p. 13)
food production (p. 4)
general anthropology (p. 4)
holistic (p. 2)
linguistic anthropology (p. 17)
natural selection (p. 10)
phenotype (p. 6)
primates (p. 16)
racial classification (p. 6)
science (p. 17)
sociolinguistics (p. 17)
tropics (p. 10)

Go to our Online Learning Center website at **www.mhhe.com/kottak** for Internet resources directly related to the contents of this chapter.

Culture

In Chapter 1 we saw that humans share *society,* organized life in groups, with other animals—social animals, such as monkeys, wolves, and ants. Other animals, especially the great apes, have rudimentary cultural abilities, but only humans have fully elaborated cultures—distinctive traditions and customs transmitted over the generations through learning and through language.

The concept of culture has long been basic to anthropology. Well over a century ago, in his book *Primitive Culture,* the British anthropologist Edward Tylor proposed that cultures, systems of human behavior and thought, obey natural laws and therefore can be studied scientifically. Tylor's definition of culture still offers an overview of the subject matter of anthropology and is widely quoted.

"Culture . . . is that complex whole which includes knowledge, belief, arts, morals, law, custom, and any other capabilities and habits acquired by man as a member of society" (Tylor 1871/1958, p. 1). The crucial phrase here is "acquired . . . as a member of society." Tylor's definition focuses on attributes that people acquire not through biological inheritance but by growing up in a particular society in which they are exposed to a specific cultural tradition. **Enculturation** is the process by which a child *learns* his or her culture.

What Is Culture?

Culture Is Learned

The ease with which children absorb any cultural tradition rests on the uniquely elaborated human capacity to learn. Other animals may learn from experience, so that, for example, they avoid fire after discovering that it hurts. Social animals also learn from other members of their group. Wolves, for instance, learn hunting strategies from other pack members. Such social learning is particularly important among monkeys and apes, our closest biological relatives. But our own *cultural learning* depends on the uniquely developed human capacity to use **symbols,** signs that have no necessary or natural connection to the things they stand for or signify.

On the basis of cultural learning, people create, remember, and deal with ideas. They grasp and apply specific systems of symbolic meaning. Anthropologist Clifford Geertz defined culture as ideas based on cultural learning and symbols. Cultures have been characterized as sets of "control mechanisms—plans, recipes, rules, instructions, what computer engineers call programs for the governing of behavior" (Geertz 1973, p. 44). These programs are absorbed by people through enculturation in particular traditions. People gradually internalize a previously established system of meanings and symbols, which helps guide their behavior and perceptions throughout their lives.

Every person begins immediately, through a process of conscious and unconscious learning and interaction with others, to internalize, or incorporate, a cultural tradition through the process of enculturation. Sometimes culture is taught directly, as when parents tell their children to say "thank you" when someone gives them something or does them a favor.

Culture also is transmitted through observation. Children pay attention to the things that go on around them. They modify their behavior not just because other people tell them to do so but as a result of their own observations and growing awareness of what their culture considers right and wrong. Culture also is absorbed unconsciously. North Americans acquire their culture's notions about how far apart people should stand when they talk not by being told directly to maintain a certain distance but through a gradual process of observation, experience, and conscious and unconscious behavior modification. No one tells Latins to stand closer together than North Americans do; they learn to do so as part of their cultural tradition.

Culture Is Symbolic

Symbolic thought is unique and crucial to humans and to cultural learning. A symbol is something verbal or nonverbal, within a particular language or culture, that comes to stand for something else. Anthropologist Leslie White defined culture as

> dependent upon symbolling. . . . Culture consists of tools, implements, utensils, clothing, ornaments, customs, institutions, beliefs, rituals, games, works of art, language, etc. (White 1959, p. 3)

For White, culture originated when our ancestors acquired the ability to use symbols, that is, to originate and bestow meaning on a thing or event, and, correspondingly, to grasp and appreciate such meanings (White 1959, p. 3).

There need be no obvious, natural, or necessary connection between the symbol and what it symbolizes. The familiar pet that barks is no more naturally a *dog* than it is a *chien, Hund,* or *mbwa,* the words for "dog" in French, German, and Swahili, respectively. Language is one of the distinctive possessions of *Homo sapiens.* No other animal has developed anything approaching the complexity of language, with its multitude of symbols.

Symbols often are linguistic. There also are myriad nonverbal symbols, such as flags, which stand for various countries, and the arches that symbolize a particular hamburger chain. Holy water is a potent symbol in Roman Catholicism. As is true of all symbols, the association between a symbol (water) and what is symbolized (holiness) is arbitrary and conventional. Water probably is not intrinsically holier than milk, blood, or other natural liquids. Nor is holy water chemically different from ordinary water. Holy water is a symbol within Roman Catholicism, which is part of an international cultural system. A natural thing has been associated arbitrarily with a particular meaning for Catholics, who share common beliefs and experiences that are based on learning and that are transmitted across the generations.

For hundreds of thousands of years, humans have shared the abilities on which culture rests—the abilities to learn, to think symbolically, to manipulate language, and to use tools and other cultural products in organizing their lives and coping with their environments. Every contemporary human population has the ability to use symbols and thus to create and maintain culture. Our nearest relatives—chimpanzees and gorillas—have rudimentary cultural abilities. However, no other animal has elaborated cultural abilities to the extent that *Homo* has.

Culture Is Shared

Culture is an attribute not of individuals per se but of individuals as members of *groups.* Culture is transmitted in society. Don't we learn our culture by observing, listening, talking, and interacting with many other people? Shared beliefs, values, memories, and expectations link people who grow up in the same culture. Enculturation unifies people by providing us with common experiences.

People in the United States sometimes have trouble understanding the power of culture because of the value that American culture places on the idea of the individual. Americans are fond of saying that everyone is unique and special in some way. However, in American culture individualism itself is a distinctive shared value. Individualism is transmitted through hundreds of statements and settings in our daily lives. From the late Mr. Rogers on TV to parents, grandparents, and teachers, our enculturative agents insist that we are all "someone special."

Today's parents were yesterday's children. If they grew up in North America, they absorbed certain values and beliefs transmitted over the generations. People become agents in the enculturation of their children, just as their parents were for them. Although a culture constantly changes, certain fundamental beliefs, values, worldviews, and child-rearing practices endure. Consider a simple American example of enduring shared enculturation. As children, when we didn't finish a meal, our parents may have reminded us of starving children in some foreign country, just as our grandparents might have done a generation earlier. The specific country changes (China, India, Bangladesh, Ethiopia, Somalia, Rwanda—what was it in your home?). Still, American culture goes on transmitting the idea that by eating all our brussels sprouts or broccoli, we can justify our own good fortune, compared to a hungry child in an impoverished or war-ravaged country.

Culture and Nature

Culture takes the natural biological urges we share with other animals and teaches us how to express them in particular ways. People have to eat, but culture teaches us what, when, and how. In many cultures people have their main meal at noon, but most North Americans prefer a large dinner. English people eat fish for breakfast, but North Americans prefer hot cakes and cold cereals. Brazilians put hot milk into strong coffee, whereas many North Americans pour cold milk into a weaker brew. Midwesterners dine at five or six, Spaniards at ten.

Cultural habits, perceptions, and inventions mold "human nature" into many forms. People have to eliminate wastes from their bodies. But some cultures teach people to defecate standing, while others tell them to do it sitting down. Peasant women in the Andean highlands squat in the streets and urinate, getting all the privacy they need from their massive skirts. All these habits are parts of cultural traditions that have converted natural acts into cultural customs.

Our culture—and cultural changes—affect how we perceive nature, human nature, and "the natural." Through science, invention, and discovery, cultural advances have overcome many "natural" limitations. We prevent and cure diseases such as polio and smallpox, which felled our ancestors. We use Viagra to enhance or restore sexual potency. Through cloning, scientists have challenged the way we think about biological identity and the meaning of life itself. Culture, of course, does not always protect us from natural threats. Hurricanes, floods, earthquakes, and other natural forces regularly overthrow our wishes to modify the environment through building, development, and expansion. Can you think of other ways in which nature strikes back at culture?

Culture Is All-Encompassing

For anthropologists, culture includes much more than refinement, good taste, sophistication, education, and appreciation of the fine arts. Not only college graduates but all people are "cultured." The most interesting and significant cultural forces are those that affect people every day of their lives, particularly those that influence children during enculturation.

Culture, as defined anthropologically, encompasses features that are sometimes regarded as trivial or unworthy of serious study, such as those of "popular" culture. To understand contemporary North American culture, we must consider television, fast-food restaurants, sports, and games. As a cultural manifestation, a rock star may be as interesting as a symphony conductor (or vice versa); a comic book may be as significant as a book-award winner.

Culture Is Integrated

Cultures are not haphazard collections of customs and beliefs. Cultures are integrated, patterned systems. If one part of the system (the overall economy, for instance) changes, other parts change as well. For example, during the 1950s most American women planned domestic careers as homemakers and mothers. Most of today's college women, by contrast, expect to get paying jobs when they graduate.

What are some of the social repercussions of this particular economic change? Attitudes and behavior regarding marriage, family, and children have changed. Late marriage, "living together," and divorce have become more common. The average age at first marriage for American women rose from 20 in 1955 to 26 in 2007. The comparable figures for men were 23 and 28 (U.S. Census Bureau 2007). The number of currently divorced Americans quadrupled from 4 million in 1970 to about 23 million in 2007 (U.S. Census Bureau 2008). Work competes with marriage and family responsibilities and reduces the time available to invest in child care.

Cultures are integrated not simply by their dominant economic activities and related social patterns but also by sets of values, ideas, symbols, and judgments. Cultures train their individual members to share certain personality traits. A set of characteristic **core values** (key, basic, central values) integrates each culture and helps distinguish it from others. For instance, the work ethic and individualism are core values that have integrated American culture for generations. Different sets of dominant values influence the patterns of other cultures.

Culture Can Be Adaptive and Maladaptive

Humans have both biological and cultural ways of coping with environmental stresses. Besides our biological means of adaptation, we also use "cultural adaptive kits," which contain customary activities and tools that aid us. Although humans continue to adapt biologically, reliance on social and cultural means of adaptation has increased during human evolution and plays a crucial role.

Sometimes, adaptive behavior that offers short-term benefits to particular subgroups or individuals may harm the environment and threaten the group's long-term survival. Economic growth may benefit some people while it depletes resources needed for society at large or for future generations. Thus, cultural traits, patterns, and inventions can also be *maladaptive,* threatening the group's continued existence (survival and reproduction). Air conditioners help us deal with heat, as fires and furnaces protect us against the cold. Automobiles permit us to make a living by getting us from home to workplace. But the by-products of such "beneficial" technology often create new problems. Chemical emissions increase air pollution, deplete the ozone layer, and contribute to climate change. Many cultural patterns such as overconsumption and pollution appear to be maladaptive in the long run. Can you think of others?

Cultures are integrated systems. When one behavior pattern changes, others also change. During the 1950s, most American women expected to have careers as wives, mothers, and domestic managers. As more and more women have entered the workforce, attitudes toward work and family have changed. On the top, mom and kids do the dishes in 1952. On the bottom (taken in January 2005), nuclear expert and Deputy Director of ISIS (Institute for Science & International Security) Corey Hinderstein uses her office in Washington, D.C., to monitor nuclear activities all over the globe.

Culture's Evolutionary Basis

The human capacity for culture has an evolutionary basis that extends back at least 2.5 million years to early toolmakers. Evidence for these toolmakers exists in the archeological record. However, based on observation of tool use and manufacture by apes, scientists believe the evolutionary basis for culture may extend even further back.

Similarities between humans and apes, our closest relatives, are evident in anatomy, brain structure, genetics, and biochemistry. Most closely related to us are the African great apes: chimpanzees and gorillas. *Hominidae* is the zoological family that includes fossil and living humans, as well as chimps and gorillas. We refer to members of this family as **hominids.** The term **hominins** is used for the group that leads to humans but not to chimps and gorillas and that encompasses all the human species that ever have existed.

Many human traits reflect the fact that our primate ancestors lived in the trees. These traits include grasping ability and manual dexterity (especially opposable thumbs), depth and color vision, learning ability based on a large brain, substantial parental investment in a limited number of offspring, and tendencies toward sociality and cooperation. Like other primates, humans have flexible, five-fingered hands and *opposable thumbs:* each thumb can touch all the other fingers on the same hand. Like monkeys and apes, humans also have excellent depth and color vision. Our eyes are placed forward in the skull and look directly ahead, so that their fields of vision overlap. Depth perception, impossible without overlapping visual fields, proved adaptive—e.g., for judging distance—in the trees. Having color and depth vision also facilitates the identification of various food sources, as well as mutual grooming—picking out burrs, insects, and other small objects from hair. Such grooming is one way of forming and maintaining social bonds.

The combination of manual dexterity and depth perception allows monkeys, apes, and humans to pick up small objects, hold them in front of their eyes, and appraise them. Our ability to thread a needle reflects an intricate interplay of hands and eyes that took millions of years of primate evolution to achieve. Such dexterity, including the opposable thumb, confers a tremendous advantage in manipulating objects and is essential to a major human adaptive capacity: tool making. In primates, and especially in humans, the ratio of brain size to body size exceeds that of most mammals. Even more important, the brain's outer layer—concerned with memory, association, and integration—is relatively larger. Monkeys, apes, and humans store an array of images in their memories, which permits them to learn more. Such a capacity for learning is another tremendous adaptive advantage. Like most other primates, humans usually give birth to a single offspring rather than a litter. Receiving more parental attention, that one infant has enhanced learning opportunities. The need for longer and more attentive care of offspring places a selective value on support by a social group. Humans have developed considerably the primate tendency to be social animals, living and interacting regularly with other members of their species.

What We Share with Other Primates

There is a substantial gap between primate *society* (organized life in groups) and fully developed human *culture,* which is based on symbolic thought. Nevertheless, studies of nonhuman primates reveal many similarities with humans, such as the ability to learn from experience and change behavior as a result. Apes and monkeys, like humans, learn throughout their lives. In one group of Japanese macaques (land-dwelling monkeys), for example, a three-year-old female started washing sweet potatoes before she ate them. First her mother, then her age peers, and finally the entire troop began washing sweet potatoes as well. The ability to benefit from experience confers a tremendous adaptive advantage, permitting the avoidance of fatal mistakes. Faced with environmental change, humans and other primates don't have to wait for a genetic or physiological response. They can modify learned behavior and social patterns instead.

Although humans employ tools much more than any other animal does, tool use also turns up among several nonhuman species, including birds, beavers, sea otters, and especially apes (see Mayell 2003). Humans are also not the only animals that make tools with a specific purpose in mind. Chimpanzees living in the Tai forest of Ivory Coast make and use stone tools to break open hard, golfball-sized nuts (Mercader, Panger, and Boesch 2002). At specific sites, the chimps gather nuts, place them on stumps or flat rocks, which are used as anvils, and pound the nuts with heavy stones. The chimps must select hammer stones suited to smashing the nuts and carry them to where the nut trees grow. Nut cracking is a learned skill, with mothers showing their young how to do it.

In 1960, Jane Goodall (1996) began observing wild chimps—including their tool use and hunting behavior—at Gombe Stream National Park in Tanzania, East Africa. The most studied form of ape tool making involves "termiting," in which chimps make tools to probe termite hills. They choose twigs, which they modify by removing leaves and peeling off bark to expose the sticky surface beneath. They carry the twigs to termite hills, dig holes with their fingers, and insert the twigs. Finally, they pull out the twigs and dine on termites that were attracted to the sticky surface. Given what is known about ape tool use and manufacture, it is almost certain that early hominins shared this ability, although the first evidence for hominin stone tool making dates back only 2.5 million years. In addition, bipedalism (moving around upright on two legs) would have permitted the carrying and use of tools and weapons against predators and competitors in an open grassland habitat.

The apes have other abilities essential to culture. Wild chimps and orangs aim and throw objects. Gorillas build nests, and they throw branches, grass, vines, and other objects. Hominins have elaborated the capacity to aim and throw, without which we never would have developed projectile technology and weaponry—or baseball.

Like tool making, hunting once was cited as a distinctive human activity not shared with the apes. Again, however, primate research shows that other primates, especially chimpanzees, are habitual hunters. For example, in Uganda's Kibale National Park chimps form large hunting parties, including an average of 26 individuals (almost always adult and adolescent males). Most hunts (78 percent) result in at least one prey item being caught—a much higher success rate than that among lions (26 percent), hyenas (34 percent), or cheetahs (30 percent). Chimps' favored prey there is the red colobus monkey (Mitani and Watts 1999).

Archaeological evidence suggests that humans hunted by at least 2.5 million years ago, based on stone meat-cutting tools found at Olduvai Gorge in Tanzania.

Given our current understanding of chimp hunting and tool making, we can infer that hominids may have been hunting much earlier than the first archaeological evidence attests. However, because chimps typically devour the monkeys they kill, leaving few remains, we may never find archaeological evidence for the first hominin hunt, especially if it was done without stone tools.

How We Differ from Other Primates

Although chimps often share meat from a hunt, apes and monkeys (except for nursing infants) tend to feed themselves individually. Cooperation and sharing are much more developed among humans. Until fairly recently (12,000 to 10,000 years ago), all humans were hunter-gatherers who lived in small social groups called bands. In some world areas, the hunter-gatherer way of life persisted into recent times, permitting study by ethnographers. In such societies, men and women bring resources back to the camp and share them. Everyone shares the meat from a large animal. Nourished and protected by younger band members, elders live past reproductive age and are respected for their knowledge and experience. Humans are among the most cooperative of the primates—in the food quest and other social activities. As well, the amount of information stored in a human band is far greater than that in any other primate group.

Another difference between humans and other primates involves mating. Among baboons and chimps, most mating occurs when females enter estrus, during

Tool use by chimps. These chimps in Liberia are using stone tools to crack palm nuts, as described in the text.

which they ovulate. In estrus, the vaginal area swells and reddens, and receptive females form temporary bonds with, and mate with, males. Human females, by contrast, lack a visible estrus cycle, and their ovulation is concealed. Not knowing when ovulation is occurring, humans maximize their reproductive success by mating throughout the year. Human pair bonds for mating are more exclusive and more durable than are those of chimps. Related to our more constant sexuality, all human societies have some form of marriage. Marriage gives mating a reliable basis and grants to each spouse special, though not always exclusive, sexual rights in the other.

Marriage creates another major contrast between humans and nonhuman primates: exogamy and kinship systems. Most cultures have rules of exogamy requiring marriage outside one's kin or local group. Coupled with the recognition of kinship, exogamy confers adaptive advantages because it creates ties between the spouses' different kin groups. Their children have relatives, and therefore allies, in two kin groups rather than just one. The key point here is that ties of affection and mutual support between members of different local groups tend to be absent among primates other than *Homo*. Other primates tend to disperse at adolescence. Among chimps and gorillas, females tend to migrate, seeking mates in other groups. Humans also choose mates from outside the natal group, and usually at least one spouse moves. However, *humans maintain lifelong ties with sons and daughters.* The systems of kinship and marriage that preserve these links provide a major contrast between humans and other primates. Table 2.1 lists differences in the cultural abilities of humans and chimpanzees, our nearest relatives.

TABLE 2.1

Cultural Features of Chimpanzees (Rudimentary) and Humans (Fully Developed)

	Chimpanzees	Humans
Cultural Learning	Rudimentary	Fully developed
Tool Use	Occasional	Habitual
Tool Manufacture	Occasional: hammer stones, termiting	Habitual and sophisticated
Aimed Throwing	Occasional objects, not tools	Projectile technology
Hunting	Significant, but no tools	Basic hominin subsistence strategy, with tools
Food Sharing	Meat sharing after hunt	Basic to human life
Cooperation	Occasional in hunting	Basic to human life
Mating and Marriage	Female estrus cycle, limited pair bonds	Year-round mating, marriage, and exogamy
Kin Ties	Limited by dispersal at adolescence	Maintained through sons and daughters

Universality, Generality, and Particularity

Anthropologists agree that cultural learning is uniquely elaborated among humans and that all humans have culture. Anthropologists also accept a doctrine termed in the 19th century "the psychic unity of man." This means that although *individuals* differ in their emotional and intellectual tendencies and capacities, all human *populations* have equivalent capacities for culture. Regardless of their genes or their physical appearance, people can learn *any* cultural tradition.

To understand this point, consider that contemporary Americans and Canadians are the genetically mixed descendants of people from all over the world. Our ancestors were biologically varied, lived in different countries and continents, and participated in hundreds of cultural traditions. However, early colonists, later immigrants, and their descendants all have become active participants in American and Canadian life. All now share a common national culture.

To recognize biopsychological equality is not to deny differences among populations. In studying human diversity in time and space, anthropologists distinguish among the universal, the generalized, and the particular. Certain biological, psychological, social, and cultural features are **universal,** found in every culture. Others are merely **generalities,** common to several but not all human groups. Still other traits are **particularities,** unique to certain cultural traditions.

Universals and Generalities

Biologically based universals include a long period of infant dependency, year-round (rather than seasonal) sexuality, and a complex brain that enables us to use symbols, languages, and tools. Among the social universals is life in groups and in some kind of family (see Brown 1991). Generalities occur in certain times and places but not in all cultures. They may be widespread, but they are not universal. One cultural generality that is present in many but not all societies is the *nuclear family,* a kinship group consisting of parents and children. Although many middle-class Americans ethnocentrically view the nuclear family as a proper and "natural" group, it is not universal. It was absent, for example, among the Nayars, who live on the Malabar Coast of India. Traditionally, the Nayars lived in female-headed households, and husbands and wives did not live together. In many other societies, the nuclear family is submerged in larger kin groups, such as extended families, lineages, and clans.

Societies can share the same beliefs and customs because of borrowing or through (cultural) inheritance from a common cultural ancestor. Speaking English is a generality shared by North Americans and Australians because both countries had English settlers. Another reason for generalities is domination, as in colonial rule, when customs and procedures are imposed on one culture by another one that is more powerful. In many countries, use of the English language reflects colonial history. More recently, English has spread through *diffusion* (cultural borrowing) to many other countries, as it has become the world's foremost language for business and travel.

Particularity: Patterns of Culture

A cultural particularity is a trait or feature of culture that is not generalized or widespread; rather it is confined to a single place, culture, or society. Yet because of cultural borrowing, which has accelerated through modern transportation and communication systems, traits that once were limited in their distribution have become more widespread. Traits that are useful, that have the capacity to please large audiences, and that don't clash with the cultural values of potential adopters are more likely to be borrowed than others are. Still, certain cultural particularities persist. One example would be a particular food dish (e.g., pork barbeque with a mustard-based sauce available only in South Carolina, or the pastie—beef stew baked in pie dough characteristic of Michigan's upper peninsula). Besides diffusion which, for example, has spread McDonald's food outlets, once confined to San Bernadino, California, across the globe, there are other reasons why cultural particularities are increasingly rare. Many cultural traits are shared as cultural universals and as a result of independent invention. Facing similar problems, people in different places have come up with similar solutions. Again and again, similar cultural causes have produced similar cultural results.

At the level of the individual cultural trait or element (e.g, bow and arrow, hot dog, MTV), particularities may be getting rarer. But at a higher level, particularity is more obvious. Different cultures emphasize different things. *Cultures are integrated and patterned differently and display tremendous variation and diversity.* When cultural traits are borrowed, they are modified to fit the culture that adopts them. They are reintegrated—patterned anew—to fit their new setting. MTV in Germany or Brazil isn't at all the same thing as MTV in the United States. As was stated in the earlier section "Culture Is Integrated," patterned beliefs, customs, and practices lend distinctiveness to particular cultural traditions.

Consider universal life-cycle events, such as birth, puberty, marriage, parenthood, and death, that many cultures observe and celebrate. The occasions (e.g., marriage, death) may be the same and universal, but the patterns of ceremonial observance may be dramatically different. Cultures vary in just which events merit special celebration. Americans, for example, regard expensive weddings as more socially appropriate than lavish funerals. However, the Betsileo of Madagascar take the opposite view. The marriage ceremony is a minor event that brings together just the couple and a few close relatives. However, a funeral is a measure of the deceased person's social position and lifetime achievement, and it may attract a thousand people. Why use money on a house, the Betsileo say, when one can use it on the tomb where one will spend eternity in the company of dead relatives? How unlike contemporary Americans' dreams of home ownership and preference for quick and inexpensive funerals. Cremation, an increasingly common option in the United States, would horrify the Betsileo, for whom ancestral bones and relics are important ritual objects.

Cultures vary tremendously in their beliefs, practices, integration, and patterning. By focusing on and trying to explain alternative customs, anthropology forces us to reappraise our familiar ways of thinking. In a world full of cultural diversity, contemporary American culture is just one cultural variant, more powerful perhaps, but no more natural, than the others.

Culture and the Individual: Agency and Practice

Generations of anthropologists have theorized about the relationship between the "system," on one hand, and the "person" or "individual" on the other. The system can refer to various concepts, including culture, society, social relations, or social structure. Individual human beings always make up, or constitute, the system. But, living within that system, humans also are constrained (to some extent, at least) by its rules and by the actions of other individuals. Cultural rules provide guidance about what to do and how to do it, but people don't always do what the rules say should be done. People use their culture actively and creatively, rather than blindly following its dictates. Humans aren't passive beings who are doomed to follow their cultural traditions like programmed robots. Cultures are dynamic and constantly changing. People learn, interpret, and manipulate the same rule in different ways—or they emphasize different rules that better suit their interests. Culture is *contested:* Different groups in society struggle with one another over whose ideas, values, goals, and beliefs will prevail. Even common symbols may have radically different *meanings* to different individuals and groups in the same culture. Golden arches may cause one person to salivate while another plots a vegetarian protest. The same flag may be waved to support or oppose a given war.

Even when they agree about what should be done, people don't always do as their culture directs or as other people expect. Many rules are violated, some very often (for example, automobile speed limits). Some anthropologists find it useful to distinguish between ideal and real culture. The *ideal culture* consists of what people say they should do and what they say they do. *Real culture* refers to their actual behavior as observed by the anthropologist.

Culture is both public and individual, both in the world and in people's minds. Anthropologists are interested not only in public and collective behavior but also in how *individuals* think, feel, and act. The individual and culture are linked because human social life is a process in which individuals internalize the meanings of *public* (i.e., cultural) messages. Then, alone and in groups, people influence culture by converting their private (and often divergent) understandings into public expressions (D'Andrade 1984).

Conventionally culture has been seen as social glue transmitted across the generations, binding people through their common past, rather than as something being continually created and reworked in the present. The tendency to view culture as an entity rather than as a process is changing. Contemporary anthropologists now emphasize how day-to-day action, practice, or resistance can make and remake culture (Gupta and Ferguson, eds. 1997*b*). *Agency* refers to the actions that individuals take, both alone and in groups, in forming and transforming cultural identities.

The approach to culture known as *practice theory* (Ortner 1984) recognizes that individuals within a society or culture have diverse motives and intentions and different degrees of power and influence. Such contrasts may be associated with gender, age, ethnicity, class, and other social variables. Practice theory focuses on how such varied individuals—through their ordinary and extraordinary actions and practices—manage to influence, create, and transform the world they live in. Practice theory appropriately recognizes a reciprocal relation between culture (the system—see above) and the individual. The system shapes how individuals experience and respond to external events, but individuals also play an active role in how society functions and changes. Practice theory recognizes both constraints on individuals and the flexibility and changeability of cultures and social systems.

Levels of Culture

We distinguish between different levels of culture: national, international, and subcultural. In today's world these distinctions are increasingly important. **National culture** embodies those beliefs, learned behavior patterns, values, and institutions that are shared by citizens of the same nation. **International culture** extends beyond and across national boundaries. Because culture is transmitted through learning rather than genetically, cultural traits can spread through borrowing or diffusion from one group to another.

Because of diffusion, migration, colonialism, and globalization, many cultural traits and patterns have acquired international scope. The contemporary United States, Canada, Great Britain, and Australia share cultural traits they have inherited from their common linguistic and cultural ancestors in Great Britain. Roman Catholics in many different countries share beliefs, symbols, experiences, and values transmitted by their church. The World Cup has become an international cultural event, as people in many countries know the rules of, play, and follow soccer.

Cultures also can be smaller than nations (see Jenks 2005). Although people who live in the same country share a national cultural tradition, all cultures also contain diversity. Individuals, families, communities, regions, classes, and other groups within a culture have different learning experiences as well as shared ones. **Subcultures** are different symbol-based patterns and traditions associated with particular groups in the same complex society. In large or diverse nations such as the United States or Canada, a variety of subcultures originate in region, ethnicity, language, class, and religion. The religious backgrounds of Jews, Baptists, and Roman Catholics create subcultural differences between them. While sharing a common national culture, U.S. northerners and southerners also differ in their beliefs, values, and customary behavior as a result of national and regional history. French-speaking Canadians sometimes pointedly contrast with English-speaking people in the same country. Italian Americans have ethnic traditions different from those of Irish, Polish, and African Americans.

Nowadays, many anthropologists are reluctant to use the term *subculture*. They feel that the prefix *sub-* is offensive because it means "below." Subcultures thus may be perceived as "less than" or somehow inferior to a dominant, elite, or national culture. In this discussion of levels of culture, I intend no such implication. My point is simply that nations may contain many different culturally defined groups. As mentioned earlier, culture is contested. Various groups may strive to promote the correctness and value of their own practices, values, and beliefs in comparison with those of other groups or the nation as a whole.

Ethnocentrism, Cultural Relativism, and Human Rights

Ethnocentrism is the tendency to view one's own culture as superior and to apply one's own cultural values in judging the behavior and beliefs of people raised in other cultures. We hear ethnocentric statements all the time. Ethnocentrism contributes to social solidarity, a sense of value and community, among people who share a cultural tradition. People everywhere think that the familiar explanations, opinions, and customs are true, right, proper, and moral. They regard different behavior as strange, immoral, or savage. Often other societies are not considered fully human. Their members may be castigated as cannibals, thieves, or people who do not bury their dead.

Among several tribes in the Trans-Fly region of Papua New Guinea homosexuality was valued over heterosexuality (see the chapter in this book on gender). Men who grew up in the Etoro tribe (Kelly 1976) favored oral sex between men, while their neighbors the Marind-anim encouraged men to engage in anal sex. (In both groups heterosexual coitus was stigmatized and allowed only for reproduction.) Etoro men considered Marind-anim anal sex to be disgusting, while seeing nothing abnormal about their own oral homosexual practices.

Opposing ethnocentrism is **cultural relativism,** the viewpoint that behavior in one culture should not be judged by the standards of another culture. This position also

The notion of indigenous intellectual property rights (IPR) has arisen in an attempt to conserve each society's cultural base, including its medicinal plants, which may have commercial value. Shown here is the hoodia plant, a cactus that grows in the Kalahari Desert of southern Africa. Hoodia, which traditionally is used by the San people to stave off hunger, is used now in diet pills marketed on the Internet.

can present problems. At its most extreme, cultural relativism argues that there is no superior, international, or universal morality, that the moral and ethical rules of all cultures deserve equal respect. In the extreme relativist view, Nazi Germany would be evaluated as nonjudgmentally as Athenian Greece.

In today's world, human rights advocates challenge many of the tenets of cultural relativism. For example, several societies in Africa and the Middle East have traditions of female genital modification (FGM). *Clitoridectomy* is the removal of a girl's clitoris. *Infibulation* involves sewing the lips (labia) of the vagina, to constrict the vaginal opening. Both procedures reduce female sexual pleasure, and, it is believed in some cultures, the likelihood of adultery. Such practices have been opposed by human rights advocates, especially women's rights groups. The idea is that the tradition infringes on a basic human right—disposition over one's body and one's sexuality. Some African countries have banned or otherwise discouraged the procedures, as have Western nations that receive immigration from such cultures. Similar issues arise with circumcision and other male genital operations. Is it right for a baby boy to be circumcised without his permission, as has been done routinely in the United States? Is it proper to require adolescent boys to undergo collective circumcision to fulfill cultural tradition, as has been done in parts of Africa and Australia?

Some would argue that the problems with relativism can be solved by distinguishing between methodological and moral relativism. In anthropology, cultural relativism is not a moral position, but a methodological one. It states: To understand another culture fully, you must try to see how the people in that culture see things. What motivates them—what are they thinking—when they do those things? Such an approach does not preclude making moral judgments or taking action. When faced with Nazi atrocities, a methodological relativist would have a moral obligation to stop doing anthropology and take action to intervene. In the FGM example, one only can understand the *motivations* for the practice by looking at the situation from the point of view of those who engage in it. Having done this, one then faces the moral question of whether to intervene to stop it. We should recognize as well that different people and groups living in the same society— for example, women and men, old and young, the more and less powerful—can have widely different views about what is proper, necessary, and moral (see Hunt 2007).

The idea of **human rights** invokes a realm of justice and morality beyond and superior to the laws and customs of particular countries, cultures, and religions (see R. Wilson, ed. 1996). Human rights include the right to speak freely, to hold religious beliefs without persecution, and not to be murdered, injured, or enslaved or imprisoned without charge. Such rights are seen as *inalienable* (nations cannot abridge or terminate them) and international (larger than and superior to individual nations and cultures). Four United Nations documents describe nearly all the human rights that have been internationally recognized. Those documents are the U.N. Charter; the Universal Declaration of Human Rights; the Covenant on Economic, Social and Cultural Rights; and the Covenant on Civil and Political Rights.

Alongside the human rights movement has arisen an awareness of the need to preserve cultural rights. Unlike human rights, **cultural rights** are vested not in individuals but in *groups,* such as religious and ethnic minorities and indigenous societies. Cultural rights include a group's ability to preserve its culture, to raise its children in the ways of its forebears, to continue its language, and not to be deprived of its economic base by the nation in which it is located (Greaves 1995). The related notion of indigenous **intellectual property rights (IPR)** has arisen in an attempt to conserve each society's cultural base—its core beliefs, knowledge, and practices (see Merry 2006). Much traditional cultural knowledge has commercial value. Examples include ethnomedicine (traditional medical knowledge and techniques), cosmetics, cultivated plants, foods, folklore, arts, crafts, songs, dances, costumes, and rituals (see Nazarea 2006). According to the IPR concept, a particular group may determine how indigenous knowledge and its products may be used and distributed and the level of compensation required.

The notion of cultural rights is related to the idea of cultural relativism, and the problem discussed previously arises again. What does one do about cultural rights that interfere with human rights? I believe that anthropology's main job is to present accurate accounts and explanations of cultural phenomena. The anthropologist doesn't have to approve infanticide, cannibalism, or torture to record their existence and determine their causes and the motivations behind them. However, each anthropologist has a choice about where he or she will do fieldwork. Some anthropologists choose not to study a particular culture because they discover in advance or early in fieldwork that behavior they consider morally repugnant is practiced there. Anthropologists respect human diversity. Most ethnographers try to be objective, accurate, and sensitive in their accounts of other cultures. However, objectivity, sensitivity, and a cross-cultural perspective don't mean that anthropologists have to ignore international standards of justice and morality. What do you think?

Mechanisms of Cultural Change

Why and how do cultures change? One way is **diffusion** or borrowing of traits between cultures. Such exchange of information and products has gone on throughout human history because cultures never have been truly isolated. Contact between neighboring groups has always existed and has extended over vast areas (Boas 1940/1966). Diffusion is *direct* when two cultures trade with, intermarry among, or wage war on one another. Diffusion is *forced* when one culture subjugates another and imposes its customs on the dominated group. Diffusion is *indirect* when items or traits move from group A to group C via group B without any firsthand contact between A and C. In this case, group B might consist of traders or merchants who take products from a variety of places to new markets. Or group B might be geographically situated between A and C, so that what it gets from A eventually winds up in C, and vice versa. In today's world, much international diffusion is indirect—culture spread by the mass media and advanced information technology.

Acculturation, a second mechanism of cultural change, is the exchange of cultural features that results when groups have continuous firsthand contact. The cultures of either or both groups may be changed by this contact (Redfield, Linton, and Herskovits 1936). With acculturation, parts of the cultures change, but each group remains distinct. One example of acculturation is a *pidgin,* a mixed language that develops to ease communication between members of different cultures in contact. This usually happens in situations of trade or colonialism. Pidgin English, for example, is a simplified form of English. It blends English grammar with the grammar of a native language. Pidgin English was first used for commerce in Chinese ports. Similar pidgins developed later in Papua New

Guinea and West Africa. In situations of continuous contact, cultures have also exchanged and blended foods, recipes, music, dances, clothing, tools, and technologies.

Independent invention—the process by which humans innovate, creatively finding solutions to problems—is a third mechanism of cultural change. Faced with comparable problems and challenges, people in different societies have innovated and changed in similar ways, which is one reason cultural generalities exist. One example is the independent invention of agriculture in the Middle East and Mexico. Over the course of human history, major innovations have spread at the expense of earlier ones. Often a major invention, such as agriculture, triggers a series of subsequent interrelated changes. These economic revolutions have social and cultural repercussions. Thus in both Mexico and the Middle East, agriculture led to many social, political, and legal changes, including notions of property and distinctions in wealth, class, and power (see Naylor 1996).

Globalization

The term **globalization** encompasses a series of processes, including diffusion, migration, and acculturation, working to promote change in a world in which nations and people are increasingly interlinked and mutually dependent. Promoting such linkages are economic and political forces, as well as modern systems of transportation and communication. The forces of globalization include international commerce and finance,

Globalization includes the internationalization of people and cultures through transnational migration and developments in commerce, transportation, and communication. This photo of Chinese youth in an Internet café was taken in Prato, Tuscany, Italy, on July 21, 2006. For what purposes do you think these teenagers use these computers?

travel and tourism, transnational migration, the media, and various high-tech information flows (see Appadurai, ed. 2001; Friedman and Friedman 2008; Scholte 2000). During the Cold War, which ended with the fall of the Soviet Union, the basis of international alliance was political, ideological, and military. More recent international pacts have shifted toward trade and economic issues. New economic unions (which have met considerable resistance in their member nations) have been created through the North American Free Trade Agreement (NAFTA), the World Trade Organization (WTO), and the European Union (EU).

Communication systems and the media play a significant role in today's process of globalization. Long-distance communication is easier, faster, and cheaper than ever, and extends to remote areas. I can now e-mail or call families in Arembepe, Brazil, which lacked phones or even postal service when I first began to study the community. The mass media help propel a globally spreading culture of consumption. Within nations and across their borders, the media spread information about products, services, rights, institutions, lifestyles, and the perceived costs and benefits of globalization. Emigrants transmit information and resources transnationally, as they maintain their ties with home (phoning, faxing, e-mailing, making visits, sending money). In a sense such people live multilocally—in different places and cultures at once. They learn to play various social roles and to change behavior and identity depending on the situation (see Cresswell 2006).

The effects of globalization are broad and not always welcome. Local people must cope increasingly with forces generated by progressively larger systems—region, nation, and world. An army of outsiders now intrudes on people everywhere. Tourism has become the world's number one industry (see Holden 2005). Economic development agents and the media promote the idea that work should be for cash rather than mainly for subsistence. Indigenous peoples and traditional societies have devised various strategies to deal with threats to their autonomy, identity, and livelihood (Maybury-Lewis 2002). New forms of political mobilization and cultural expression, including the rights movements discussed previously, are emerging from the interplay of local, regional, national, and international cultural forces (see Ong and Collier, eds. 2005).

ANTHROPOLOGY TODAY

The Advent of Behavioral Modernity

Scientists agree that (1) around six million years ago, our hominin ancestors originated in Africa, and as apelike creatures they became habitual bipeds; (2) by 2.5 million years ago, still in Africa, hominins were making crude stone tools; (3) by 1.7 million years ago, hominins had spread from Africa to Asia and eventually Europe; and (4) sometime after 200,000 years ago, anatomically modern humans (AMHs) evolved from ancestors who had remained in Africa. Like earlier hominins (*Homo erectus*), AMHs spread out from Africa. Eventually they

Continued

ANTHROPOLOGY TODAY   *Continued*

replaced—perhaps in some cases interbreeding with—nonmodern human types, such as the Neandertals in Europe and the successors of *Homo erectus* in the Far East.

There is disagreement, however, about when, where, and how early AMHs achieved *behavioral modernity*—relying on symbolic thought, elaborating cultural creativity, and as a result becoming fully human in behavior as well as in anatomy. Was it as much as 165,000 or as little as 45,000 years ago? Was it in Africa, the Middle East, or Europe? What triggered the change: a genetic mutation, population increase, competition with nonmodern humans, or some other cause? The traditional view has been that modern behavior originated fairly recently, perhaps 45,000–40,000 years ago, and only after *Homo sapiens* pushed into Europe. This theory of a "creative explosion" is based on finds such as the impressive cave paintings at Lascaux, Chauvet Cave, and other sites in France and Spain (Wilford 2002). However, recent discoveries outside Europe suggest a much older, more gradual evolution of modern behavior.

Anthropologist Richard G. Klein of Stanford University is a leading advocate for the idea that human creativity dawned suddenly, in Europe around 45,000 years ago. Prior to this time, Klein thinks *Homo* had changed very slowly in anatomy and behavior. After this "dawn of culture," human anatomy changed little, but behavior started changing dramatically (Klein with Edgar 2002). Indeed, by 40,000 years ago AMHs in Europe were making varied tools that display a pattern of abstract and symbolic thought. Their modern behavior included burying their dead with ceremonies, adorning their bodies with paints and jewelry, and making figurine images of fertile females. Their cave paintings displayed im-

ages from their minds, as they remembered the hunt, and events and symbols associated with it.

To explain such a flowering of creativity, Klein proposes a neurological hypothesis. About 50,000 years ago, he thinks, a genetic mutation acted to rewire the human brain, possibly allowing for an advance in language. Improved communication, in Klein's view, could have given people "the fully modern ability to invent and manipulate culture" (quoted in Wilford 2002). Klein thinks this genetic change probably happened in Africa and then allowed "human populations to colonize new and challenging environments" (quoted in Wilford 2002). Reaching Europe, the rewired modern humans met and replaced the resident Neandertals. Klein recognizes that his genetic hypothesis "fails one important measure of a proper scientific hypothesis—it cannot be tested or falsified by experiment or by examination of relevant human fossils" (quoted in Wilford 2002). AMH skulls from the time period in question show no change at all in brain size or function.

Questioning Klein's views are discoveries made in Africa and the Middle East during the last 30 years. These finds provide substantial evidence for earlier (than in Europe) modern behavior, in the form of finely made stone and bone tools, self-ornamentation, and abstract carvings. Surveying African archaeological sites dating to between 300,000 and 30,000 years ago, Sally McBrearty and Alison Brooks (2000) conclude that what might appear to be a sudden event in Europe actually rested on a slow process of cultural accumulation within Africa, where *Homo sapiens* became fully human long before 40,000 years ago. At South Africa's Blombos Cave, for example, an archaeological team led by

Christopher Henshilwood found evidence that AMHs were making bone awls and weapon points more than 70,000 years ago. Three points had been shaped with a stone blade and then finely polished. Henshilwood thinks these artifacts indicate symbolic behavior and artistic creativity—people trying to make beautiful objects (Wilford 2002).

In 2007 anthropologists reported the discovery of even earlier evidence (dating back to 164,000 B.P.) for behavioral modernity in a cave site at Pinnacle Point, South Africa. The cave yielded small stone bladelets, which could be attached to wood to make spears, as well as red ochre, a pigment often used for body paint. Also significant is the ancient diet revealed by remains from this seaside site. For the first time, we see early representatives of *H. sapiens* subsisting on a variety of shellfish and other marine resources. According to paleoanthropologist Curtis Marean, who led the discovery team, once early humans knew how to make a living from the sea, they could use coastlines as productive home ranges and move long distances (Guyot and Hughes 2007).

Cultural advances would have facilitated the spread of AMHs out of Africa. Such advances had reached the Middle East by 43,000 years ago, where, in Turkey and Lebanon, Steven Kuhn, Mary Stiner, and David Reese (2001) found evidence that coastal people made and wore beads and shell ornaments (see also Mayell 2004). Some of the shells were rare varieties, white or brightly colored. Body ornaments could have been part of a system of communication, signaling group identity and social status. Such communication through ornamentation implies "the existence of certain [modern] cognitive capacities" (Stiner and Kuhn, quoted in Wilford 2002; Kuhn, Stiner, and Reese 2001).

According to archaeologist Randall White, early personal adornment in Africa and the Middle East shows that the capacity for human creativity existed among AMHs long before they reached Europe (Wilford 2002). AMHs honed their cultural abilities, which enabled them to maintain a common identity, communicate ideas, and organize their societies into "stable, enduring regional groups" (quoted in Wilford 2002). Symbolic thought and cultural advances were expressed most enduringly in artifacts, ornamentation, and art.

The origin of behavioral modernity continues to be debated. We see, however, that archaeological work in many world areas suggests strongly that neither anatomical modernity nor behavioral modernity was a European invention. Africa's role in the origin and development of humanity has been prominent for millions of years of hominin evolution.

Summary

1. Culture, which is distinctive to humanity, refers to customary behavior and beliefs that are passed on through enculturation. Culture rests on the human capacity for cultural learning. Culture encompasses rules for conduct internalized in human beings, which lead them to think and act in characteristic ways.

2. Although other animals learn, only humans have cultural learning, dependent on symbols. Humans think symbolically—arbitrarily bestowing meaning on things and events. By convention, a symbol stands for something with which it has no necessary or natural relation. Symbols have special meaning for people who share memories, values, and beliefs because of common enculturation.

3. Cultural traditions mold biologically based desires and needs in particular directions. Everyone is cultured, not just people with elite educations. Cultures may be integrated and patterned through economic and social forces, key symbols, and core values. Cultural rules don't rigidly dictate our behavior. There is room for creativity, flexibility, diversity, and disagreement within societies. Cultural means of adaptation have been crucial in human evolution. Aspects of culture also can be maladaptive.

4. The human capacity for culture has an evolutionary basis that extends back at least 2.5 million years—to early tool makers whose products survive in the archaeological record (and most probably even further back—based on observation of tool use and manufacture by apes). Humans share with monkeys and apes such traits as manual dexterity (especially opposable thumbs), depth and color vision, learning ability based on a large brain, substantial parental investment in a limited number of offspring, and tendencies toward sociality and cooperation.

5. Many hominin traits are foreshadowed in other primates, particularly in the African apes, which, like us, belong to the hominid family. The ability to learn, basic to culture, is an adaptive advantage available to monkeys and apes. Chimpanzees make tools for several purposes. They also hunt and share meat. Sharing and cooperation are more developed among humans than among the apes, and only humans have systems of kinship and marriage that permit us to maintain lifelong ties with relatives in different local groups.

6. Using a comparative perspective, anthropology examines biological, psychological, social, and cultural universals and generalities. There also are unique and distinctive aspects of the human condition (cultural particularities). North American cultural traditions are no more natural than any others. Levels of culture can be larger or smaller than a nation. Cultural traits may be shared across national boundaries. Nations also include cultural differences associated with ethnicity, region, and social class.

7. Ethnocentrism describes judging other cultures by using one's own cultural standards. Cultural relativism, which anthropologists may use as a methodological position rather than a moral stance, is the idea of avoiding the use of outside standards to judge behavior in a given society. Human rights are those based on justice and morality beyond and superior to particular countries, cultures, and religions. Cultural rights are vested in religious and ethnic minorities and indigenous societies, and IPR, or intellectual property rights, apply to an indigenous group's collective knowledge and its applications.

8. Diffusion, migration, and colonialism have carried cultural traits and patterns to different world areas. Mechanisms of cultural change include diffusion, acculturation, and independent invention. Globalization describes a series of processes that promote change in a world in which nations and people are interlinked and mutually dependent.

Key Terms

acculturation (p. 39)
core values (p. 27)
cultural relativism (p. 37)
cultural rights (p. 38)
diffusion (p. 39)
enculturation (p. 23)
ethnocentrism (p. 37)
generality (p. 33)
globalization (p. 40)
hominid (p. 29)

hominins (p. 29)
human rights (p. 38)
independent invention (p. 40)
intellectual property rights (IPR) (p. 39)
international culture (p. 36)
national culture (p. 36)
particularity (p. 33)
subcultures (p. 36)
symbol (p. 24)
universal (p. 33)

 Go to our Online Learning Center website at **www.mhhe.com/kottak** for Internet resources directly related to the contents of this chapter.

C H A P T E R **3**

Ethics and Methods

❖ **Ethics and Anthropology**
❖ **Research Methods**
❖ **Ethnography: Anthropology's Distinctive Strategy**
❖ **Ethnographic Techniques**
   Observation and Participant Observation
   Conversation, Interviewing, and Interview Schedules
   The Genealogical Method
   Key Cultural Consultants
   Life Histories

Local Beliefs and Perceptions, and the Ethnographer's
The Evolution of Ethnography
Problem-Oriented Ethnography
Longitudinal Research
Team Research
Culture, Space, and Scale
❖ **Survey Research**
Anthropology Today: Even Anthropologists Get Culture Shock

In Chapter 1, we learned about anthropology and its subfields, and in Chapter 2 we focused on culture. Chapter 3 begins with a consideration of the ethical dimensions of anthropology, then turns to a discussion of research methods in cultural anthropology.

As the main organization representing the breadth of anthropology (all four subfields, academic, and applied dimensions), the American Anthropological Association (AAA) believes that generating and using knowledge of the peoples of the world, past and present, is a worthy goal. The mission of the AAA is to advance anthropological research and encourage the spread of anthropological knowledge through publications, teaching, public education, and application. Part of that mission is to help educate AAA members about ethical obligations and challenges (http://www.aaanet.org).

Ethics and Anthropology

Anthropologists increasingly are mindful of the fact that science exists in society, and in the context of law and ethics. Anthropologists can't study things simply because they happen to be interesting or of value to science. As anthropologists conduct research and engage in other professional activities, ethical issues inevitably arise. Anthropologists typically have worked abroad, outside their own society. In the context of international contacts and cultural diversity, different value systems will meet, and often compete. To guide its members in making decisions involving ethics and values, the AAA offers a Code of Ethics.

The most recent revision of the code, adopted in 2009, recognizes that anthropologists have obligations to their scholarly field, to the wider society and culture, and to the human species, other species, and the environment. This code's aim is to offer guidelines and to promote discussion and education, rather than to investigate allegations of misconduct. The AAA code addresses several contexts in which anthropologists work. Its main points may be summarized.

> Anthropologists should be open and honest about . . . their research projects with all parties affected by the research. These parties should be informed about the nature, procedures, purpose(s), potential impacts, and source(s) of support for the research. Researchers should not compromise anthropological ethics in order to conduct research. They should . . . pay attention to proper relations between themselves as guests and the host nations and communities where they work. The AAA does not advise anthropologists to avoid taking stands on issues. Indeed, . . . seeking to shape actions and policies may be as ethically justifiable as inaction.

The full Code of Ethics is available at the AAA website (http://www.aaanet.org/issues/policy-advocacy/Code-of-Ethics.cfm).

Most ethnographers (field workers in cultural anthropology) work outside their nations of origin. In the host country (the nation where the research takes place), the ethnographer seeks permissions, cooperation, and knowledge from government officials, scholars, and many others, most importantly the people of the community being studied. Cultural sensitivity is paramount when the research subjects are living people into whose lives the anthropologist intrudes. Anthropologists need to establish and maintain appropriate, collaborative, and nonexploitative relationships with colleagues and communities in the host country.

To work in a host country and community, researchers must inform officials and colleagues there about the purpose and funding, and the anticipated results and impacts, of the research. Researchers have to gain the informed consent of all affected parties— from the authorities who control access to the field site to the members of the community to be studied. Before the research begins, people should be informed about the purpose, nature, and procedures of the research and its potential costs and benefits to them. **Informed consent** (agreement to take part in the research, after having been so informed) should be obtained from anyone who provides information or who might be affected by the research.

According to the AAA code, anthropologists have a debt to the people they work with in the field, and they should reciprocate in appropriate ways. For example, it is highly appropriate for North American anthropologists working in another country to (1) include host country colleagues in their research plans and funding requests, (2) establish collaborative relationships with those colleagues and their institutions, and (3) include host country colleagues in publication of the research results. Of course, in cultural anthropology, as in all the subfields, anthropologists' primary ethical obligation is to the people being studied. Their welfare and interests come first.

Research Methods

Cultural anthropology and sociology share an interest in social relations, organization, and behavior. However, important differences between these disciplines arose from the kinds of societies each traditionally studied. Initially sociologists focused on the industrial West; anthropologists, on nonindustrial societies. Different methods of data collection and analysis emerged to deal with those different kinds of societies. To study large-scale, complex nations, sociologists came to rely on questionnaires and other means of gathering masses of quantifiable data. For many years sampling and statistical techniques have been basic to sociology, whereas statistical training has been less common in anthropology (although this is changing somewhat as anthropologists work increasingly in modern nations).

Traditional ethnographers studied small, nonliterate (without writing) populations and relied on ethnographic methods appropriate to that context. "Ethnography is a research process in which the anthropologist closely observes, records, and engages in the daily life of another culture—an experience labeled as the fieldwork method—and then writes accounts of this culture, emphasizing descriptive detail" (Marcus and Fischer 1986, p. 18). One key method described in this quote is **participant observation**—taking part in the events one is observing, describing, and analyzing.

World famous anthropologist Margaret Mead in the field in Bali, Indonesia, in 1957.

Anthropology started to separate from sociology around 1900. Early students of society, such as the French scholar Émile Durkheim, were among the founders of both sociology and anthropology. Comparing the organization of simple and complex societies, Durkheim studied the religions of Native Australians (Durkheim 1912/2001), as well as mass phenomena (such as suicide rates) in modern nations (Durkheim 1897/1951). Eventually anthropology would specialize in the former, sociology in the latter.

Ethnography: Anthropology's Distinctive Strategy

Anthropology developed into a separate field as early scholars worked on Indian (Native American) reservations and traveled to distant lands to study small groups of foragers (hunters and gatherers) and cultivators. Traditionally, the process of becoming a cultural anthropologist has required a field experience in another society. Early ethnographers lived in small-scale, relatively isolated societies, with simple technologies and economies.

Ethnography thus emerged as a research strategy in societies with greater cultural uniformity and less social differentiation than are found in large, modern, industrial nations. Traditionally, ethnographers have tried to understand the whole of a particular culture (or, more realistically, as much as they can, given limitations of time and perception). To pursue this goal, ethnographers adopt a free-ranging strategy for gathering information. In a given society or community, the ethnographer moves from setting to setting, place to place, and subject to subject to discover the totality and interconnectedness of social life. By expanding our knowledge of the range of human diversity, ethnography provides a foundation for generalizations about human behavior and social life. Ethnographers draw on varied techniques to piece together a picture of otherwise alien lifestyles. Anthropologists usually employ several (but rarely all) of the techniques discussed here (see also Bernard 2006; Wolcott 2008).

Ethnographic Techniques

The characteristic *field techniques* of the ethnographer include the following:

1. Direct, firsthand observation of behavior, including *participant observation.*
2. Conversation with varying degrees of formality, from the daily chitchat, which helps maintain rapport and provides knowledge about what is going on, to prolonged *interviews,* which can be unstructured or structured.
3. The *genealogical method.*
4. Detailed work with *key consultants,* or *informants,* about particular areas of community life.
5. In-depth interviewing, often leading to the collection of *life histories* of particular people (narrators).
6. Discovery of local (native) beliefs and perceptions, which may be compared with the ethnographer's own observations and conclusions.
7. Problem-oriented research of many sorts.
8. Longitudinal research—the continuous long-term study of an area or site.
9. Team research—coordinated research by multiple ethnographers.

Observation and Participant Observation

Ethnographers must pay attention to hundreds of details of daily life, seasonal events, and unusual happenings. They should record what they see as they see it. Things never will seem quite as strange as they do during the first few weeks in the field. The ethnographer eventually gets used to, and accepts as normal, cultural patterns that initially were alien. Staying a bit more than a year in the field allows the ethnographer to repeat the season of his or her arrival, when certain events and processes may have been missed because of initial unfamiliarity and culture shock.

Many ethnographers record their impressions in a personal *diary,* which is kept separate from more formal *field notes.* Later, this record of early impressions will help point out some of the most basic aspects of cultural diversity. Such aspects include distinctive smells, noises people make, how they cover their mouths when they eat, and how they gaze at others. These patterns, which are so basic as to seem almost trivial, are part of what Bronislaw Malinowski called "the imponderabilia of native life and of typical behavior" (Malinowski 1922/1961, p. 20). These features of culture are so fundamental that natives take them for granted. They are too basic even to talk about, but the unaccustomed eye of the fledgling ethnographer picks them up. Thereafter, becoming familiar, they fade to the edge of consciousness. Initial impressions are valuable and should be recorded. First and foremost, ethnographers should try to be accurate observers, recorders, and reporters of what they see in the field.

Ethnographers strive to establish *rapport,* a good, friendly working relationship based on personal contact, with our hosts. One of ethnography's most characteristic procedures is participant observation, which means that we take part in community life as we study it. As human beings living among others, we cannot be totally impartial and detached observers. We take part in many events and processes we are observing and trying to comprehend. By participating, we learn why local people find such events meaningful, as we see how they are organized and conducted.

In Arembepe, Brazil, I learned about fishing by sailing on the Atlantic with local fishers. I gave Jeep rides to malnourished babies, to pregnant mothers, and once to a teenage girl possessed by a spirit. All those people needed to consult specialists outside the village. I danced on Arembepe's festive occasions, drank libations commemorating new births, and became a godfather to a village girl. Most anthropologists have similar field experiences. The common humanity of the student and the studied, the ethnographer and the research community, makes participant observation inevitable.

Conversation, Interviewing, and Interview Schedules

Participating in local life means that ethnographers constantly talk to people and ask questions. As their knowledge of the native language and culture increases, they understand more. There are several stages in learning a field language. First is the naming phase—asking name after name of the objects around us. Later we are able to pose more complex questions and understand the replies. We begin to understand simple conversations between two villagers. If our language expertise proceeds far enough, we eventually become able to comprehend rapid-fire public discussions and group conversations.

One data-gathering technique I have used in both Arembepe and Madagascar involves an ethnographic survey that includes an interview schedule. In 1964, my fellow field-workers and I attempted to complete an interview schedule in each of Arembepe's 160 households. We entered almost every household (fewer than 5 percent refused to participate) to ask a set of questions on a printed form. Our results provided us with a census and basic information about the village. We wrote down the name, age, and gender of each household member. We gathered data on family type, religion, present and previous jobs, income, expenditures, diet, possessions, and many other items on our eight-page form.

Although we were doing a survey, our approach differed from the survey research design routinely used by sociologists and other social scientists working in large, industrial nations. That survey research, discussed below, involves sampling (choosing a small, manageable study group from a larger population). We did not select a partial sample from the total population. Instead, we tried to interview in all households in the community (that is, to have a total sample). We used an interview schedule rather than a questionnaire. With the **interview schedule,** the ethnographer talks face to face with people, asks the questions, and writes down the answers. *Questionnaire* procedures tend to be more indirect and impersonal; often the respondent fills in the form.

Our goal of getting a total sample allowed us to meet almost everyone in the village and helped us establish rapport. Decades later, Arembepeiros still talk warmly

Dr. Amity Doolittle (center) interviews in Bundu Tuhan, Malaysia, in 1996, on how rural people use natural resources. Does this strike you as a formal or informal interview?

about how we were interested enough in them to visit their homes and ask them questions. We stood in sharp contrast to the other outsiders the villagers had known, who considered them too poor and backward to be taken seriously.

Like other survey research, however, our interview schedule did gather comparable quantifiable information. It gave us a basis for assessing patterns and exceptions in village life. Our schedules included a core set of questions that were posed to everyone. However, some interesting side issues often came up during the interview, which we would pursue then or later.

We followed such leads into many dimensions of village life. One woman, for instance, a midwife, became the key cultural consultant we sought out later when we wanted detailed information about local childbirth. Another woman had done an internship in an Afro-Brazilian cult (*candomblé*) in the city. She still went there regularly to study, dance, and get possessed. She became our candomblé expert.

Thus, our interview schedule provided a structure that *directed but did not confine* us as researchers. It enabled our ethnography to be both quantitative and qualitative. The quantitative part consisted of the basic information we gathered and later analyzed statistically. The qualitative dimension came from our follow-up questions, open-ended discussions, pauses for gossip, and work with key consultants.

The Genealogical Method

As ordinary people, many of us learn about our own ancestry and relatives by tracing our genealogies. Various computer programs now allow us to trace our "family tree" and degrees of relationship. The **genealogical method** is a well-established ethnographic technique. Early ethnographers developed notation and symbols to deal with kinship, descent, and marriage. Genealogy is a prominent building block in the social organization of nonindustrial societies, where people live and work each day with their close kin. Anthropologists need to collect genealogical data to understand current social relations and to reconstruct history. In many nonindustrial societies, kin links are basic to social life. Anthropologists even call such cultures "kin-based societies." Everyone is related, and spends most of his or her time with relatives. Rules of behavior attached to particular kin relations are basic to everyday life (see Carsten 2004). Marriage also is crucial in organizing nonindustrial societies because strategic marriages between villages, tribes, and clans create political alliances.

Key Cultural Consultants

Every community has people who by accident, experience, talent, or training can provide the most complete or useful information about particular aspects of life. These people are **key cultural consultants,** also called *key informants*. In Ivato, the Betsileo village in Madagascar where I spent most of my time, a man named Rakoto was particularly knowledgeable about village history. However, when I asked him to work with me on a genealogy of the fifty to sixty people buried in the village tomb, he called in his cousin Tuesdaysfather, who knew more about that subject. Tuesdaysfather had survived an epidemic of influenza that ravaged Madagascar, along with much of the world, around 1919. Immune to the disease himself, Tuesdaysfather had the grim job of burying his kin as they died. He kept track of everyone buried in the tomb. Tuesdaysfather helped me with the tomb genealogy. Rakoto joined him in telling me personal details about the deceased villagers.

Life Histories

In nonindustrial societies as in our own, individual personalities, interests, and abilities vary. Some villagers prove to be more interested in the ethnographer's work and are more helpful, interesting, and pleasant than others are. Anthropologists develop likes and dislikes in the field as we do at home. Often, when we find someone unusually interesting, we collect his or her **life history.** This recollection of a lifetime of experiences provides a more intimate and personal cultural portrait than would be possible otherwise. Life histories, which may be recorded or videotaped for later review and analysis, reveal how specific people perceive, react to, and contribute to changes that affect their lives. Such accounts can illustrate diversity, which exists within any community, since the focus is on how different people interpret and deal with some of the same problems. Many ethnographers include the collection of life histories as an important part of their research strategy.

Local Beliefs and Perceptions, and the Ethnographer's

One goal of ethnography is to discover local (native) views, beliefs, and perceptions, which may be compared with the ethnographer's own observations and conclusions. In the field, ethnographers typically combine two research strategies, the emic (native-oriented) and the etic (scientist-oriented). These terms, derived from linguistics, have been applied to ethnography by various anthropologists. Marvin Harris (1968/2001) popularized the following meanings of the terms: An **emic** approach investigates how local people think. How do they perceive and categorize the world? What are their rules for behavior? What has meaning for them? How do they imagine and explain things? Operating emically, the ethnographer seeks the "native viewpoint," relying on local people to explain things and to say whether something is significant or not. The term **cultural consultant,** or *informant,* refers to individuals the ethnographer gets to know in the field, the people who teach him or her about their culture, who provide the emic perspective.

The **etic** (scientist-oriented) approach shifts the focus from local observations, categories, explanations, and interpretations to those of the anthropologist. The etic approach realizes that members of a culture often are too involved in what they are doing to interpret their cultures impartially. Operating etically, the ethnographer emphasizes what he or she (the observer) notices and considers important. As a trained scientist, the ethnographer should try to bring an objective and comprehensive viewpoint to the study of other cultures. Of course, the ethnographer, like any other scientist, is also a human being with cultural blinders that prevent complete objectivity. As in other sciences, proper training can reduce, but not totally eliminate, the observer's bias. But anthropologists do have special training to compare behavior between different societies.

What are some examples of emic versus etic perspectives? Consider our holidays. For North Americans, Thanksgiving Day has special significance. In our view (emically) it is a unique cultural celebration that commemorates particular historical themes. But a wider, etic perspective sees Thanksgiving as just one more example of the postharvest festivals held in many societies. Another example: Local people (including many Americans) may believe that chills and drafts cause colds, which scientists know are caused by germs. In cultures that lack the germ theory of disease, illnesses are emically explained by various causes, ranging from spirits to ancestors to witches. *Illness* refers to a culture's (emic) perception and explanation of bad health, whereas *disease* refers to the scientific—etic—explanation of poor health, involving known pathogens.

Ethnographers typically combine emic and etic strategies in their fieldwork. The statements, perceptions, categories, and opinions of local people help ethnographers understand how cultures work. Local beliefs are also interesting and valuable in themselves. However, people often fail to admit, or even recognize, certain causes and consequences of their behavior. This is as true of North Americans as it is of people in other societies.

The Evolution of Ethnography

The Polish anthropologist Bronislaw Malinowski (1884–1942), who spent most of his professional life in England, is generally considered the founder of ethnography. Like most anthropologists of his time, Malinowski did *salvage ethnography,* in the belief that the ethnographer's job is to study and record cultural diversity threatened by Westernization. Early ethnographic accounts (*ethnographies*), such as Malinowski's classic *Argonauts of the Western Pacific* (1922/1961), were similar to earlier traveler and explorer accounts in describing the writer's discovery of unknown people and places. However, the *scientific* aims of ethnographies set them apart from books by explorers and amateurs.

The style that dominated "classic" ethnographies was *ethnographic realism.* The writer's goal was to present an accurate, objective, scientific account of a different way of life, written by someone who knew it firsthand. This knowledge came from an "ethnographic adventure" involving immersion in an alien language and culture. Ethnographers derived their authority—both as scientists and as voices of "the native" or "the other"—from this personal research experience.

Malinowski's ethnographies were guided by the assumption that aspects of culture are linked and intertwined. Beginning by describing a Trobriand sailing expedition, the ethnographer then follows the links between that entry point and other areas of the culture, such as magic, religion, myths, kinship, and trade. Compared with Malinowski, today's ethnographies tend to be less inclusive and holistic, focusing on particular topics, such as kinship or religion.

According to Malinowski, a primary task of the ethnographer is "to grasp the native's point of view, his relation to life, to realize *his* vision of *his* world" (1922/1961, p. 25—Malinowski's italics). This is a good statement of the need for the emic perspective, as was discussed earlier. Since the 1970s, *interpretive anthropology* has

Bronislaw Malinowski (1884–1942), who was born in Poland but spent most of his professional life in England, did fieldwork in the Trobriand Islands from 1914 to 1918. Malinowski is generally considered to be the father of ethnography. Does this photo suggest anything about his relationship with Trobriand villagers?

considered the task of describing and interpreting that which is meaningful to natives. Interpretivists such as Clifford Geertz (1973) view cultures as meaningful texts that natives constantly "read" and ethnographers must decipher. According to Geertz, anthropologists may choose anything in a culture that interests them, fill in details, and elaborate to inform their readers about meanings in that culture. Meanings are carried by public symbolic forms, including words, rituals, and customs.

A current trend in ethnographic writing is to question traditional goals, methods, and styles, including ethnographic realism and salvage ethnography (Clifford 1982, 1988; Marcus and Cushman 1982). Marcus and Fischer argue that experimentation in ethnographic writing is necessary because all peoples and cultures have already been "discovered" and must now be "*re*discovered . . . in changing historical circumstances" (1986, p. 24).

In general, experimental anthropologists see ethnographies as works of art as well as works of science. Ethnographic texts may be viewed as literary creations in which the ethnographer, as mediator, communicates information from the "natives" to readers. Some experimental ethnographies are "dialogic," presenting ethnography as a dialogue between the anthropologist and one or more native informants (e.g., Behar 1993; Dwyer 1982). These works draw attention to ways in which ethnographers, and by extension their readers, communicate with other cultures. However, some such ethnographies have been criticized for spending too much time talking about the anthropologist and too little time describing the local people and their culture.

The dialogic ethnography is one genre within a larger experimental category—that is, *reflexive ethnography*. Here the ethnographer puts his or her personal feelings and reactions to the field situation right in the text. Experimental writing strategies are prominent in reflexive accounts. The ethnographer may adopt some of the conventions of the novel, including first-person narration, conversations, dialogues, and humor. Experimental ethnographies, using new ways of showing what it means to be a Samoan or a Brazilian, may convey to the reader a richer and more complex understanding of human experience.

Linked to salvage ethnography was the idea of the *ethnographic present*—the period before Westernization, when the "true" native culture flourished. This notion often gives classic ethnographies an unrealistic timeless quality. Providing the only jarring note in this idealized picture are occasional comments by the author about traders or missionaries, suggesting that in actuality the natives were already part of the world system.

Anthropologists now recognize that the ethnographic present is a rather unrealistic construct. Cultures have been in contact—and have been changing—throughout history. Most native cultures had at least one major foreign encounter before any anthropologist ever came their way. Most of them already had been incorporated in some fashion into nation-states or colonial systems.

Contemporary ethnographies usually recognize that cultures constantly change and that an ethnographic account applies to a particular moment. A current trend in ethnography is to focus on the ways in which cultural ideas serve political and economic interests. Another trend is to describe how various particular "natives" participate in broader historical, political, and economic processes (Shostak 1981).

Problem-Oriented Ethnography

We see, then, a tendency to move away from holistic accounts toward more problem-focused and experimental ethnographies. Although anthropologists are interested in the whole context of human behavior, it is impossible to study everything. Most ethnographers now enter the field with a specific problem to investigate, and they collect data relevant to that problem (see Chiseri-Strater and Sunstein 2001; Kutsche 1998). Local people's answers to questions are not the only data source. Anthropologists also gather information on factors such as population density, environmental quality, climate, physical geography, diet, and land use. Sometimes this involves direct measurement—of rainfall, temperature, fields, yields, dietary quantities, or time allocation (Bailey 1990; Johnson 1978). Often it means that we consult government records or archives.

The information of interest to ethnographers is not limited to what local people can and do tell us. In an increasingly interconnected and complicated world, local people lack knowledge about many factors that affect their lives. Our local consultants may be as mystified as we are by the exercise of power from regional, national, and international centers.

Longitudinal Research

Geography limits anthropologists less now than in the past, when it could take months to reach a field site, and return visits were rare. New systems of transportation allow anthropologists to widen the area of their research and to return repeatedly. Ethnographic reports now routinely include data from two or more field stays. **Longitudinal research** is the long-term study of a community, region, society, culture, or other unit, usually based on repeated visits.

One example of such research is the longitudinal study of Gwembe District, Zambia. This study, planned in 1956 as a longitudinal project by Elizabeth Colson and Thayer Scudder, continues with Colson, Scudder, and their associates of various nationalities. Thus, as is often the case with longitudinal research, the Gwembe study also illustrates team research—coordinated research by multiple ethnographers (Colson and Scudder 1975; Scudder and Colson 1980). In this study, four villages in different areas have been followed for five decades. Periodic village censuses provide basic data on population, economy, kinship, and religious behavior. Censused people who have moved are traced and interviewed to see how their lives compare with those of people who have stayed in the villages.

A series of different research questions have emerged, while basic data on communities and individuals continue to be collected. The first focus of study was the impact of a large hydroelectric dam, which subjected the Gwembe people to forced resettlement. The dam also spurred road building and other activities that brought the people of Gwembe more closely in touch with the rest of Zambia. In subsequent research Scudder and Colson (1980) examined how education provided access to new opportunities as it also widened a social gap between people with different educational levels. A third study then examined a change in brewing and drinking patterns, including a rise in alcoholism, in relation to changing markets, transportation, and exposure to town values (Colson and Scudder 1988).

Team Research

As mentioned, longitudinal research often is team research. My own field site of Arembepe, Brazil, for example, first entered the world of anthropology as a field-team village in the 1960s (see the box at the end of this chapter). It was one of four sites for the now defunct Columbia-Cornell-Harvard-Illinois Summer Field Studies Program in Anthropology. For at least three years, that program sent a total of about twenty undergraduates annually, the author included, to do brief summer research abroad. We were stationed in rural communities in four countries: Brazil, Ecuador, Mexico, and Peru. Since my wife, Isabel Wagley Kottak, and I began studying it in 1962, Arembepe has become a longitudinal field site. Three generations of researchers have monitored various aspects of change and development. The community has changed from a village into a town and illustrates the process of globalization at the local level. Its economy, religion, and social life have been transformed (Kottak 2006).

Brazilian and American researchers worked with us on team research projects during the 1980s (on television's impact) and the 1990s (on ecological awareness and environmental risk perception). Graduate students from the University of Michigan have drawn on our baseline information from the 1960s as they have studied various topics in Arembepe. In 1990 Doug Jones, a Michigan student doing biocultural research, used Arembepe as a field site to investigate standards of physical attractiveness. In

Janet Dunn, one of many anthropologists who have worked in Arembepe. Where is Arembepe, and what kinds of research have been done there?

1996–1997, Janet Dunn studied family planning and changing female reproductive strategies. Chris O'Leary, who first visited Arembepe in summer 1997, investigated a striking aspect of religious change there—the arrival of Protestantism; his dissertation research then examined changing food habits and nutrition in relation to globalization (O'Leary 2002). Arembepe is thus a site where various field workers have worked as members of a longitudinal team. The more recent researchers have built on prior contacts and findings to increase knowledge about how local people meet and manage new circumstances.

Culture, Space, and Scale

The previous sections on longitudinal and team research illustrate an important shift in cultural anthropology. Traditional ethnographic research focused on a single community or "culture," treated as more or less isolated and unique in time and space. The shift has been toward recognition of ongoing and inescapable flows of people, technology, images, and information. The study of such flows and linkages is now part of the anthropological analysis. In reflecting today's world—in which people, images, and information move about as never before—fieldwork must be more flexible and on a larger scale. Ethnography increasingly is multitimed and multisited. Malinowski could focus on Trobriand culture and spend most of his field time in a particular community. Nowadays we cannot afford to ignore, as Malinowski did, the "outsiders" who increasingly impinge on the places we study (e.g., migrants, refugees, terrorists, warriors, tourists, developers). Integral to our analyses now are the external organizations and forces (e.g., governments, businesses, nongovernmental organizations) now laying claim to land, people, and resources throughout the world. Also important is increased recognition of power differentials and how they affect cultures, and of the importance of diversity within cultures and societies.

In two volumes of essays edited by Akhil Gupta and James Ferguson (1997*a* and 1997*b*), several anthropologists describe problems in trying to locate cultures in bounded spaces. John Durham Peters (1997), for example, notes that, particularly because of the mass media, contemporary people simultaneously experience the local and the global. He describes them as culturally "bifocal"—both "nearsighted" (seeing local events) and "farsighted" (seeing images from far away). Given their bifocality, their interpretations of the local always are influenced by information from outside. Thus, their attitude about a clear blue sky at home is tinged by their knowledge, through weather reports, that a hurricane may be approaching.

The mass media, which anthropologists increasingly study, are oddities in terms of culture and space. Whose image and opinions are these? What culture or community do they represent? They certainly aren't local. Media images and messages flow electronically. TV brings them right to you. The Internet lets you discover new cultural possibilities at the click of a mouse. The Internet takes us to virtual places, but in truth the electronic mass media are placeless phenomena, which are transnational in scope and play a role in forming and maintaining cultural identities.

Anthropologists increasingly study people in motion. Examples include people living on or near national borders, nomads, seasonal migrants, homeless and displaced people, immigrants, and refugees. Anthropological research today may take us traveling along with the people we study, as they move from village to city, cross the border, or travel internationally on business. As we'll see in Chapter 13, ethnographers increasingly follow the people and images they study. As fieldwork changes, with less and less of a spatially set field, what can we take from traditional ethnography? Gupta and Ferguson correctly cite the "characteristically anthropological emphasis on daily routine and lived experience" (1997*a*, p. 5). The treatment of communities as discrete entities may be a thing of the past. However, "anthropology's traditional attention to the close observation of particular lives in particular places" has an enduring importance (Gupta and Ferguson 1997*b*, p. 25). The method of close observation helps distinguish cultural anthropology from sociology and survey research, to which we now turn.

Survey Research

As anthropologists work increasingly in large-scale societies, they have developed innovative ways of blending ethnography and survey research (Fricke 1994). Before examining such combinations of field methods, let's consider survey research, and the main differences between survey research and ethnography. Working mainly in large, populous nations, sociologists, political scientists, and economists have developed and refined the **survey research** design, which involves sampling, impersonal data collection, and statistical analysis. Survey research usually draws a **sample** (a manageable study group) from a much larger population. By studying a properly selected and representative sample, social scientists can make accurate inferences about the larger population.

In smaller-scale societies and communities, ethnographers get to know most of the people. Given the greater size and complexity of nations, survey research cannot help being more impersonal. Survey researchers call the people they study *respondents*. These are people who respond to questions during a survey. Sometimes survey researchers personally interview them. Sometimes, after an initial meeting, they ask respondents to fill out a questionnaire. In other cases researchers mail or e-mail printed questionnaires to randomly selected sample members or have paid assistants interview or telephone them. In a **random sample,** all members of the population have an equal statistical chance of being chosen for inclusion. A random sample is selected by randomizing procedures, such as tables of random numbers, which are found in many statistics textbooks.

Probably the most familiar example of sampling is the polling used to predict political races. The media hire agencies to estimate outcomes and do exit polls to find out what kinds of people voted for which candidates. During sampling, researchers gather information about age, gender, religion, occupation, income, and political party preference. These characteristics (**variables**—attributes that vary among members of a sample or population) are known to influence political decisions.

Many more variables affect social identities, experiences, and activities in a modern nation than in the small communities where ethnography grew up. In contemporary North America hundreds of factors influence our behavior and attitudes. These social predictors include our religion; the region of the country we grew up in; whether we come from a town, suburb, or city; and our parents' professions, ethnic origins, and income levels.

Ethnography can be used to supplement and fine-tune survey research. Anthropologists can transfer the personal, firsthand techniques of ethnography to virtually any setting that includes human beings. A combination of survey research and ethnography can provide new perspectives on life in **complex societies** (large and populous societies with social stratification and central governments). Preliminary ethnography also can help develop culturally appropriate questions for inclusion in surveys.

In any complex society, many predictor variables (*social indicators*) influence behavior and opinions. Because we must be able to detect, measure, and compare the influence of social indicators, many contemporary anthropological studies have a statistical foundation. Even in rural fieldwork, more anthropologists now draw samples, gather quantitative data, and use statistics to interpret them (see Bernard, ed. 1998; Bernard 2006). Quantifiable information may permit a more precise assessment of similarities and differences among communities. Statistical analysis can support and round out an ethnographic account of local social life.

However, in the best studies, the hallmark of ethnography remains: Anthropologists enter the community and get to know the people. They participate in local activities, networks, and associations in the city, town, or countryside. They observe and experience social conditions and problems. They watch the effects of national and international policies and programs on local life. The ethnographic method and the emphasis on personal relationships in social research are valuable gifts that cultural anthropology brings to the study of any society.

ANTHROPOLOGY TODAY

Even Anthropologists Get Culture Shock

I first lived in Arembepe (Brazil) during the (North American) summer of 1962. That was between my junior and senior years at New York City's Columbia College, where I was majoring in anthropology. I went to Arembepe as a participant in a now defunct program designed to provide undergraduates with experience doing ethnography— firsthand study of an alien society's culture and social life.

Brought up in one culture but intensely curious about others, anthropologists nevertheless experience culture shock, particularly on their first field trip. Culture shock refers to the whole set of feelings about being in an alien setting, and the ensuing reactions. It is a chilly, creepy feeling of alienation, of being without some of the most ordinary, trivial (and therefore basic) cues of one's culture of origin.

As I planned my first departure for Brazil, I could not know just how naked I would feel without the cloak of my own language and culture. My sojourn in Arembepe would be my first trip outside the United States. I was an urban boy who had grown up in Atlanta, Georgia, and New York City. I had little experience with rural life in my own country, none with Latin America, and I had received only minimal training in the Portuguese language.

We flew from New York City direct to Salvador, Bahia, Brazil with just a brief stopover in Rio de Janeiro; a longer visit would be a reward at the end of fieldwork. As our prop jet approached tropical Salvador, I couldn't believe the whiteness of the sand. "That's not snow, is it?" I remarked to a fellow field-team member. . . .

Conrad Kottak and his Brazilian nephew, Guilherme Roxo, revisit Arembepe in 2004 as part of a longitudinal study.

Continued

My first impressions of Bahia were of smells—alien odors of ripe and decaying mangoes, bananas, and passion fruit—and of swatting the ubiquitous fruit flies I had never seen before, although I had read extensively about their reproductive behavior in genetics classes. There were strange concoctions of rice, black beans, and gelatinous gobs of unidentifiable meats and floating pieces of skin. Coffee was strong and sugar crude, and every tabletop had containers for toothpicks and for manioc (cassava) flour to sprinkle, like Parmesan cheese, on anything one might eat. I remember oatmeal soup and a slimy stew of beef tongue in tomatoes. At one meal a disintegrating fish head, eyes still attached, but barely, stared up at me as the rest of its body floated in a bowl of bright orange palm oil. . . .

I only vaguely remember my first day in Arembepe. Unlike ethnographers who have studied remote tribes in the tropical forests of interior South America or the highlands of Papua New Guinea, I did not have to hike or ride a canoe for days to arrive at my field site. Arembepe was not isolated relative to such places, only relative to every other place I had ever been. . . .

I do recall what happened when we arrived. There was no formal road into the village. Entering through southern Arembepe, vehicles simply threaded their way around coconut trees, following tracks left by automobiles that had passed previously. A crowd of children had heard us coming, and they pursued our car through the village streets until we parked in front of our house, near the central square. Our first few days in Arembepe were spent with children following us everywhere. For weeks we had few moments of privacy. Children watched our every move through our living room window. Occasionally one made an incomprehensible remark. Usually they just stood there. . . .

The sounds, sensations, sights, smells, and tastes of life in northeastern Brazil, and in Arembepe, slowly grew familiar. . . . I grew accustomed to this world without Kleenex, in which globs of mucus habitually drooped from the noses of village children whenever a cold passed through Arembepe. A world where, seemingly without effort, women . . . carried 18-liter kerosene cans of water on their heads, where boys sailed kites and sported at catching houseflies in their bare hands, where old women smoked pipes, storekeepers offered *cachaça* (common rum) at nine in the morning, and men played dominoes on lazy afternoons when there was no fishing. I was visiting a world where human life was oriented toward water— the sea, where men fished, and the lagoon, where women communally washed clothing, dishes, and their own bodies.

Source: This description is adapted from my ethnographic study *Assault on Paradise: The Globalization of a Little Community in Brazil,* 4th ed. (New York: McGraw-Hill, 2006). Reprinted by permission of The McGraw-Hill Companies.

Summary

1. A code of ethics guides anthropologists' research and other professional activities. Anthropologists need to establish and maintain appropriate, collaborative, and nonexploitative relationships with colleagues and communities in the host country. Researchers must gain the informed consent of all affected parties—from the authorities who control access to the field site to the members of the community being studied.

2. Ethnographic methods include firsthand and participant observation, rapport building, interviews, genealogies, work with key consultants, or informants, collection of life histories, discovery of local beliefs and perceptions, problem-oriented and longitudinal research, and team research. Ethnographers work in actual communities and form personal relationships with local people as they study their lives.

3. An interview schedule is a form an ethnographer completes as he or she visits a series of households. Key cultural consultants, or informants, teach about particular areas of local life. Life histories dramatize the fact that culture bearers are individuals. Such case studies document personal experiences with culture and culture change. Genealogical information is particularly useful in societies in which principles of kinship and marriage organize social and political life. Emic approaches focus on native perceptions and explanations. Etic approaches give priority to the ethnographer's own observations and conclusions. Longitudinal research is the systematic study of an area or site over time. Forces of change are often too pervasive and complex to be understood by a lone ethnographer. Anthropological research may be done by teams and at multiple sites. Outsiders, flows, linkages, and people in motion are now included in ethnographic analyses.

4. Traditionally, anthropologists worked in small-scale societies; sociologists, in modern nations. Different techniques have developed to study such different kinds of societies. Social scientists working in complex societies use survey research to sample variation. Anthropologists do their fieldwork in communities and study the totality of social life. Sociologists study samples to make inferences about a larger population. Sociologists often are interested in causal relations among a very small number of variables. Anthropologists more typically are concerned with the interconnectedness of all aspects of social life.

5. The diversity of social life in modern nations and cities requires social survey procedures. However, anthropologists add the intimacy and direct investigation characteristic of ethnography. Anthropologists may use ethnographic procedures to study urban life. But they also make greater use of survey techniques and analysis of the mass media in their research in contemporary nations.

Key Terms

complex societies (p. 60)
cultural consultant (p. 53)
emic (p. 53)
etic (p. 53)
genealogical method (p. 52)
informed consent (p. 47)
interview schedule (p. 51)
key cultural consultants (p. 52)

life history (p. 53)
longitudinal research (p. 57)
participant observation (p. 48)
random sample (p. 60)
sample (p. 59)
survey research (p. 59)
variables (p. 60)

 Go to our Online Learning Center website at **www.mhhe.com/kottak** for Internet resources directly related to the content of this chapter.

Language and Communication

North Americans have certain stereotypes about how people in other regions talk. Some stereotypes, spread by the mass media, are more generalized than others are. Most Americans think they can imitate a "Southern accent." We also stereotype speech in New York City (the pronunciation of *coffee,* for example), Boston ("I pahked the kah in Hahvahd Yahd"), and Canada ("oot" for "out").

Regional patterns influence the way all Americans speak. In whichever state, college students from out of state easily recognize that their in-state classmates speak differently. In-state students, however, have difficulty hearing their own speech peculiarities because they are accustomed to them and view them as normal.

It is sometimes thought that midwesterners don't have accents. This belief stems from the fact that midwestern dialects don't have many stigmatized linguistic variants—speech patterns that people in other regions recognize and look down on, such as *r*lessness and *dem, dese,* and *dere* (instead of *them, these,* and *there*).

Far from having no accents, midwesterners, even in the same high school, exhibit linguistic diversity (see Eckert 1989, 2000). Dialect differences are immediately obvious to people, like me, who come from other parts of the country. One of the best examples of variable midwestern speech, involving vowels, is pronunciation of the *e* sound (called the /e/ phoneme), in such words as *ten, rent, French, section, lecture, effect, best,* and *test.* In southeastern Michigan, where I live and teach, there are four different ways of pronouncing this *e* sound. Speakers of Black English and immigrants from Appalachia often pronounce *ten* as *tin,* just as Southerners habitually do. Some Michiganders say *ten,* the correct pronunciation in Standard English. However, two other pronunciations also are common. Instead of *ten,* many Michiganders say *tan,* or *tun* (as though they were using the word *ton,* a unit of weight).

My students often astound me with their pronunciation. One day I met one of my Michigan-raised teaching assistants in the hall. She was deliriously happy. When I asked why, she replied, "I've just had the best suction."

"What?" I said.

She finally spoke more precisely. "I've just had the best saction." She considered this a clearer pronunciation of the word *section.*

Another TA complimented me, "You luctured to great effuct today." After an exam a student lamented that she had not done her "bust on the tust" (i.e., best on the test).

The truth is, regional patterns affect the way we all speak.

Language

Linguistic anthropology illustrates anthropology's characteristic interests in diversity, comparison, and change—but here the focus is on language. Language, spoken (*speech*) and written (*writing*—which has existed for about 6,000 years), is our primary means of communication. Like culture in general, of which language is a part, language is transmitted through learning. Language is based on arbitrary, learned associations between words and the things they stand for. Unlike the communication systems of other animals, language allows us to discuss the past and future, share our experiences with others, and benefit from their experiences.

Anthropologists study language in its social and cultural context (see Bonvillain 2008; Salzmann 2007). Some linguistic anthropologists reconstruct ancient languages by comparing their contemporary descendants and in doing so make discoveries about history. Others study linguistic differences to discover the varied worldviews and patterns of thought in a multitude of cultures. Sociolinguists examine dialects and styles in a single language to show how speech reflects social differences, as in the above discussion of regional speech contrasts. Linguistic anthropologists also explore the role of language in colonization and globalization (Geis 1987; Thomas 1999).

Nonhuman Primate Communication

Call Systems

Only humans speak. No other animal has anything approaching the complexity of language. The natural communication systems of other primates (monkeys and apes) are **call systems.** These vocal systems consist of a limited number of sounds—*calls*—that are produced only when particular environmental stimuli are encountered. Such calls may be varied in intensity and duration, but they are much less flexible than language because they are automatic and can't be combined. When primates encounter food and danger simultaneously, they can make only one call. They can't combine the calls for food and danger into a single utterance, indicating that both are present. At some point in human evolution, however, our ancestors began to combine calls and to understand the combinations. The number of calls also expanded, eventually becoming too great to be transmitted even partly through the genes. Communication came to rely almost totally on learning.

Although wild primates use call systems, the vocal tract of apes is not suitable for speech. Until the 1960s, attempts to teach spoken language to apes suggested that they lack linguistic abilities. In the 1950s, a couple raised a chimpanzee, Viki, as a member of their family and systematically tried to teach her to speak. However, Viki learned only four words ("mama," "papa," "up," and "cup").

Sign Language

More recent experiments have shown that apes can learn to use, if not speak, true language (Fouts 1997; Miles 1983). Several apes have learned to converse with people through means other than speech. One such communication system is American Sign Language, or ASL, which is widely used by hearing-impaired Americans. ASL employs a limited number of basic gesture units that are analogous to sounds in spoken language. These units combine to form words and larger units of meaning.

The first chimpanzee to learn ASL was Washoe, a female, who died in 2007 at the age of 42. Captured in West Africa, Washoe was acquired by R. Allen Gardner and Beatrice Gardner, scientists at the University of Nevada in Reno, in 1966, when she was a year old. Four years later, she moved to Norman, Oklahoma, to a converted farm that had become the Institute for Primate Studies. Washoe revolutionized the discussion of the language-learning abilities of apes (Carey 2007). At first she lived in a trailer and heard no spoken language. The researchers always used ASL to communicate with each other in her presence. The chimp gradually acquired a vocabulary of more than 100 signs representing English words (Gardner, Gardner, and Van Cantfort, eds. 1989). At the age of two, Washoe began to combine as many as five signs into rudimentary sentences such as "you, me, go out, hurry."

The second chimp to learn ASL was Lucy, Washoe's junior by one year. Lucy died, or was murdered by poachers, in 1986, after having been introduced to "the wild" in Africa in 1979 (Carter 1988). From her second day of life until her move to Africa, Lucy lived with a family in Norman, Oklahoma. Roger Fouts, a researcher from the nearby Institute for Primate Studies, came two days a week to test and improve Lucy's knowledge of ASL. During the rest of the week, Lucy used ASL to converse with her foster parents. After acquiring language, Washoe and Lucy exhibited several human traits: swearing, joking, telling lies, and trying to teach language to others (Fouts 1997).

When irritated, Washoe called her monkey neighbors at the institute "dirty monkeys." Lucy insulted her "dirty cat." On arrival at Lucy's place, Fouts once found a pile of excrement on the floor. When he asked the chimp what it was, she replied, "dirty, dirty," her expression for feces. Asked whose "dirty, dirty" it was, Lucy named Fouts's coworker, Sue. When Fouts refused to believe her about Sue, the chimp blamed the excrement on Fouts himself.

Cultural transmission of a communication system through learning is a fundamental attribute of language. Washoe, Lucy, and other chimps have tried to teach ASL to other animals, including their own offspring. Washoe taught gestures to other institute chimps, including her son Sequoia, who died in infancy (Fouts, Fouts, and Van Cantfort 1989).

Because of their size and strength as adults, gorillas are less likely subjects than chimps for such experiments. Lean adult male gorillas in the wild weigh 400 pounds (180 kilograms), and full-grown females can easily reach 250 pounds (110 kilograms). Because of this, psychologist Penny Patterson's work with gorillas at Stanford University seems more daring than the chimp experiments. Patterson raised her now full-grown female gorilla, Koko, in a trailer next to a Stanford museum. Koko's vocabulary surpasses that of any chimp. She regularly employs 400 ASL signs and has used about 700 at least once.

Koko and the chimps also show that apes share still another linguistic ability with humans: **productivity.** Speakers routinely use the rules of their language to produce

Apes, such as these Congo chimpanzees, use call systems to communicate in the wild. Their vocal systems consist of a limited number of sounds—calls—that are produced only when particular environmental stimuli are encountered.

entirely new expressions that are comprehensible to other native speakers. I can, for example, create "baboonlet" to refer to a baboon infant. I do this by analogy with English words in which the suffix -*let* designates the young of a species. Anyone who speaks English immediately understands the meaning of my new word. Koko, Washoe, Lucy, and others have shown that apes also are able to use language productively. Lucy used gestures she already knew to create "drinkfruit" for watermelon. Washoe, seeing a swan for the first time, coined "waterbird." Koko, who knew the gestures for "finger" and "bracelet," formed "finger bracelet" when she was given a ring.

Chimps and gorillas have a rudimentary capacity for language. They may never have invented a meaningful gesture system in the wild. However, given such a system, they show many humanlike abilities in learning and using it. Of course, language use by apes is a product of human intervention and teaching. The experiments mentioned here do not suggest that apes can invent language (nor are human children ever faced with that task). However, young apes have managed to learn the basics of gestural language. They can employ it productively and creatively, although not with the sophistication of human ASL users.

Apes also have demonstrated linguistic **displacement.** Absent in call systems, this is a key ingredient in language. Normally, each call is tied to an environmental stimulus such as food. Calls are uttered only when that stimulus is present. Displacement means that humans can talk about things that are not present. We don't have to see the objects before we say the words. Human conversations are not limited by place. We can discuss the past and future, share our experiences with others, and benefit from theirs.

Patterson has described several examples of Koko's capacity for displacement (Patterson 1978). The gorilla once expressed sorrow about having bitten Penny three days earlier. Koko has used the sign "later" to postpone doing things she doesn't want to do. Table 4.1 summarizes the contrasts between language, whether sign or spoken, and call systems.

TABLE 4.1

Language Contrasted with Call Systems

Human Language	Primate Call Systems
Has the capacity to speak of things and events that are not present (displacement).	Are stimuli-dependent; the food call will be made only in the presence of food; it cannot be faked.
Has the capacity to generate new expressions by combining other expressions (productivity).	Consist of a limited number of calls that cannot be combined to produce new calls.
Is group specific in that all humans have the capacity for language, but each linguistic community has its own language, which is culturally transmitted.	Tend to be species specific, with little variation among communities of the same species for each call.

Certain scholars doubt the linguistic abilities of chimps and gorillas (Sebeok and Umiker-Sebeok, eds. 1980; Terrace 1979). These people contend that Koko and the chimps are comparable to trained circus animals and don't really have linguistic ability. However, in defense of Patterson and the other researchers (Hill 1978; Van Cantfort and Rimpau 1982), only one of their critics has worked with an ape. This was Herbert Terrace, whose experience teaching a chimp sign language lacked the continuity and personal involvement that have contributed so much to Patterson's success with Koko.

No one denies the huge difference between human language and gorilla signs. There is a major gap between the ability to write a book or say a prayer and the few hundred gestures employed by a well-trained chimp. Apes aren't people, but they aren't just animals either. Let Koko express it: When asked by a reporter whether she was a person or an animal, Koko chose neither. Instead, she signed "fine animal gorilla" (Patterson 1978). For the latest on Koko, see http://koko.org.

The Origin of Language

Although the capacity to remember and combine linguistic symbols may be latent in the apes (Miles 1983), human evolution was needed for this seed to flower into language. A mutated gene known as FOXP2 helps explain why humans speak and chimps don't (Paulson 2005). The key role of FOXP2 in speech came to light in a study of a British family, identified only as KE, half of whose members had an inherited, severe deficit in speech (Trivedi 2001). The same variant form of FOXP2 that is found in chimpanzees causes this disorder. Those who have the nonspeech version of the gene cannot make the fine tongue and lip movements that are necessary for clear speech, and their speech is unintelligible—even to other members of the KE family (Trivedi 2001). Chimps have the same (genetic) sequence as the KE family members with the speech deficit. Comparing chimp and human genomes, it appears that the speech-friendly form of FOXP2 took hold in humans around 150,000 years ago. This mutation conferred selective advantages (linguistic and cultural abilities) that allowed those who had it to spread at the expense of those who did not (Paulson 2005).

Language offered a tremendous adaptive advantage to *Homo sapiens*. Language permits the information stored by a human society to exceed by far that of any non-human group. Language is a uniquely effective vehicle for learning. Because we can speak of things we have never experienced, we can anticipate responses before we encounter the stimuli. Adaptation can occur more rapidly in *Homo* than in the other primates because our adaptive means are more flexible.

Nonverbal Communication

Language is our principal means of communicating, but it isn't the only one we use. We *communicate* when we transmit information about ourselves to others and receive such information from them. Our expressions, stances, gestures, and movements, even if unconscious, convey information and are part of our communication styles. Deborah Tannen (1990) discusses differences in the communication styles of American men and women, and her comments go beyond language. She notes that American girls and women tend to look directly at each other when they talk, whereas American boys and men do not. Males are more likely to look straight ahead rather than turn and make eye contact with someone, especially another man, seated beside them. Also, in conversational groups, American men tend to relax and sprawl out. American women may adopt a similar relaxed posture in all-female groups, but when they are with men, they tend to draw in their limbs and adopt a tighter stance.

Kinesics is the study of communication through body movements, stances, gestures, and expressions. Linguists pay attention not only to what is said but to how it is said, and to features besides language itself that convey meaning. A speaker's enthusiasm is conveyed not only through words, but also through facial expressions, gestures, and other signs of animation. We use gestures, such as a jab of the hand, for emphasis. We vary our intonation and the pitch or loudness of our voices. We communicate through strategic pauses, and even by being silent. An effective communication strategy may be to alter pitch, voice level, and grammatical forms, such as declaratives ("I am . . ."), imperatives ("Go forth . . ."), and questions ("Are you . . . ?"). Culture teaches us that certain manners and styles should accompany certain kinds of speech. Our demeanor, verbal and nonverbal, when our favorite team is winning would be out of place at a funeral, or when a somber subject is being discussed.

Culture always plays a role in shaping the "natural." Cross-culturally, nodding does not always mean affirmative, nor does head shaking from side to side always mean negative. Brazilians wag a finger to mean no. Americans say "uh huh" to affirm, whereas in Madagascar a similar sound is made to deny. Americans point with their fingers; the people of Madagascar point with their lips.

Body movements communicate social differences. In Japan, bowing is a regular part of social interaction, but different bows are used depending on the social status of the people who are interacting. In Madagascar and Polynesia, people of lower status should not hold their heads above those of people of higher status. When one approaches someone older or of higher status, one bends one's knees and lowers one's head as a sign of respect. In Madagascar, one always does this, for politeness, when passing between two people. Although our gestures, facial expressions, and body stances have roots in our primate heritage, and can be seen in the monkeys and the apes, they have not escaped cultural shaping. Language, which is so highly dependent on the use of symbols, is the domain of communication in which culture plays the strongest role.

The Structure of Language

The scientific study of a spoken language (**descriptive linguistics**) involves several interrelated areas of analysis: phonology, morphology, lexicon, and syntax. **Phonology,** the study of speech sounds, considers which sounds are present and significant in a given language. **Morphology** studies the forms in which sounds combine to form *morphemes*—words and their meaningful parts. Thus, the word *cats* would be analyzed as containing two morphemes—*cat*, the name for a kind of animal, and *-s,* a morpheme indicating plurality. A language's **lexicon** is a dictionary containing all its morphemes and their meanings. **Syntax** refers to the arrangement and order of words

Syntax refers to the arrangement and order of words in phrases and sentences. A photo of Yoda from *Star Wars* (*The Empire Strikes Back*) this is. What's odd about Yoda's syntax?

in phrases and sentences. For example, do nouns usually come before or after verbs? Do adjectives normally precede or follow the nouns they modify?

Speech Sounds

From the movies and TV, and from meeting foreigners, we know something about foreign accents and mispronunciations. We know that someone with a marked French accent doesn't pronounce *r* like an American does. But at least someone from France can distinguish between "craw" and "claw," which someone from Japan may not be able to do. The difference between *r* and *l* makes a difference in English and in French, but it doesn't in Japanese. In linguistics we say that the difference between *r* and *l* is *phonemic* in English and French but not in Japanese. In English and French *r* and *l* are phonemes but not in Japanese. A **phoneme** is a sound contrast that makes a difference, that differentiates meaning.

We find the phonemes in a given language by comparing *minimal pairs,* words that resemble each other in all but one sound. The words have different meanings, but they differ in just one sound. The contrasting sounds are therefore phonemes in that language. An example in English is the minimal pair *pit/bit*. These two words are distinguished by a single sound contrast between /p/ and /b/ (we enclose phonemes in slashes). Thus /p/ and /b/ are phonemes in English. Another example is the different vowel sound of *bit* and *beat* (Figure 4.1). This contrast serves to distinguish these two words and the two vowel phonemes written /I/ and /i/ in English.

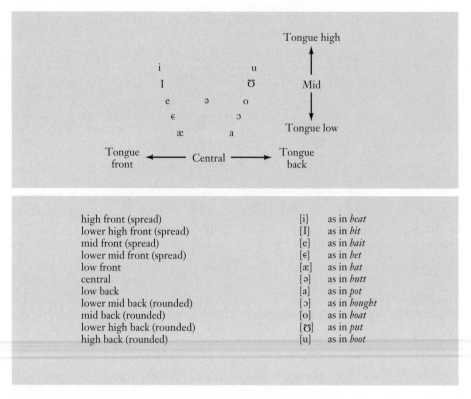

FIGURE 4.1 *Vowel phonemes in Standard American English* They are shown according to height of tongue and tongue position at front, center, or back of mouth. Phonetic symbols are identified by English words that include them; note that most are minimal pairs.

SOURCE: From *Aspects of Language*, 3rd ed. by Dwight Bolinger, Figure 2.1. Copyright © 1981 Heinle/Arts & Sciences, a part of Cengage Learning, Inc. Reproduced by permission. www.cengage.com/permissions.

Standard (American) English (SE), the "region-free" dialect of TV network newscasters, has about 35 phonemes—at least 11 vowels and 24 consonants. The number of phonemes varies from language to language—from 15 to 60, averaging between 30 and 40. The number of phonemes also varies between dialects of a given language. In North American English, for example, vowel phonemes vary noticeably from dialect to dialect. Readers should pronounce the words in Figure 4.1, paying attention to (or asking someone else) whether they distinguish each of the vowel sounds. Most North Americans don't pronounce them all.

Phonetics is the study of speech sounds in general, what people actually say in various languages, like the differences in vowel pronunciation described in the discussion of midwestern speech at the beginning of the chapter. **Phonemics** studies only the *significant* sound contrasts (phonemes) of a given language. In English, like /r/ and /l/ (remember *craw* and *claw*), /b/ and /v/ also are phonemes, occurring in minimal pairs like *bat* and *vat*. In Spanish, however, the contrast between [b] and [v] doesn't distinguish meaning, and they therefore are not phonemes (we enclose sounds that are not phonemic in brackets). Spanish speakers normally use the [b] sound to pronounce words spelled with either *b* or *v*.

In any language a given phoneme extends over a phonetic range. In English the phoneme /p/ ignores the phonetic contrast between the [p^h] in *pin* and the [p] in *spin*. Most English speakers don't even notice that there is a phonetic difference. The [p^h] is aspirated, so that a puff of air follows the [p]. The [p] in *spin* is not. (To see the difference, light a match, hold it in front of your mouth, and watch the flame as you pronounce the two words.) The contrast between [p^h] and [p] *is* phonemic in some languages, such as Hindi (spoken in India). That is, there are words whose meaning is distinguished only by the contrast between an aspirated and an unaspirated [p].

Native speakers vary in their pronunciation of certain phonemes, such as the /e/ phoneme in the midwestern United States. This variation is important in the evolution of language. Without shifts in pronunciation, there could be no linguistic change. The section on sociolinguistics below considers phonetic variation and its relationship to social divisions and the evolution of language.

Language, Thought, and Culture

The well-known linguist Noam Chomsky (1957) has argued that the human brain contains a limited set of rules for organizing language, so that all languages have a common structural basis. (Chomsky calls this set of rules *universal grammar.*) That people can learn foreign languages and that words and ideas translate from one language to another supports Chomsky's position that all humans have similar linguistic abilities and thought processes. Another line of support comes from creole languages. Such languages develop from pidgins, languages that form in situations of acculturation, when different societies come into contact and must devise a system of communication. Pidgins based on English and native languages developed through trade and colonialism in many world areas, including China, Papua New Guinea, and West Africa. Eventually, after generations of being spoken, pidgins may develop into *creole languages*. These are more mature languages, with developed grammatical rules and native speakers (people who learn the language as their primary one during enculturation).

Creoles are spoken in several Caribbean societies. Gullah, which is spoken by African Americans on coastal islands in South Carolina and Georgia, is a creole language. Supporting the idea that creoles are based on universal grammar is the fact that such languages all share certain features. Syntactically, all use particles (e.g., will, was) to form future and past tenses and multiple negation to deny or negate (e.g., he don't got none). Also, all form questions by changing inflection rather than by changing word order. For example, "You're going home for the holidays?" (with a rising tone at the end) rather than "Are you going home for the holidays?"

The Sapir-Whorf Hypothesis

Other linguists and anthropologists take a different approach to the relation between language and thought. Rather than seeking universal linguistic structures and processes, they believe that different languages produce different ways of thinking. This position sometimes is known as the **Sapir-Whorf hypothesis** after Edward Sapir (1931) and his student Benjamin Lee Whorf (1956), its prominent early advocates. Sapir and Whorf argued that the grammatical categories of particular languages lead their speakers to think about things in different ways. For example, English divides time into past, present, and future. Hopi, a language of the Pueblo region of the Native American Southwest, does not. Rather, Hopi distinguishes between events that exist or have existed (what we use present and past to discuss) and those that don't or don't yet (our future events, along with imaginary and hypothetical events). Whorf argued that this difference leads Hopi speakers to think about time and reality in different ways than English speakers do.

A similar example comes from Portuguese, which employs a future subjunctive verb form, introducing a degree of uncertainty into discussions of the future. In English we routinely use the future tense to talk about something we think will happen. We don't feel the need to qualify "The sun'll come out tomorrow," by adding "if it doesn't go supernova." We don't hesitate to proclaim "I'll see you next year," even when we can't be absolutely sure we will. The Portuguese future subjunctive qualifies the future event, recognizing that the future can't be certain. Our way of expressing the future as certain is so ingrained that we don't even think about it, just as the Hopi don't see the need to distinguish between present and past, both of which are real, while the future remains hypothetical. It seems, however, that language does not tightly restrict thought, because cultural changes can produce changes in thought and in language, as we'll see in the next section (see also Gumperz and Levinson, eds. 1996).

Shown here (in 1995) is Leigh Jenkins, who was or is director of Cultural Preservation for the Hopi tribal council. The Hopi language would not distinguish between *was* and *is* in the previous sentence. For the Hopi, present and past are real and are expressed grammatically in the same way while the future remains hypothetical and has a different grammatical expression.

Focal Vocabulary

A lexicon (or vocabulary) is a language's dictionary, its set of names for things, events, and ideas. Lexicon influences perception. Thus, Eskimos (or Inuit) have several distinct words for different types of snow that in English are all called *snow*. Most English speakers never notice the differences between these types of snow and might have trouble seeing them even if someone pointed them out. Eskimos recognize and think about differences in snow that English speakers don't see because our language gives us just one word.

Similarly, the Nuer of Sudan have an elaborate vocabulary to describe cattle. Eskimos have several words for snow and Nuer have dozens for cattle because of their particular histories, economies, and environments (Brown 1958; Eastman 1975). When the need arises, English speakers can also elaborate their snow and cattle vocabularies. For example, skiers name varieties of snow with words that are missing from the lexicons of Florida retirees. Similarly, the cattle vocabulary of a Texas rancher is much more ample than that of a salesperson in a New York City department store. Such specialized sets of terms and distinctions that are particularly important to certain groups (those with particular *foci* of experience or activity) are known as **focal vocabulary.**

Vocabulary is the area of language that changes most readily. New words and distinctions, when needed, appear and spread. For example, who would have "faxed" anything a generation ago? Names for items get simpler as they become common and important. A television has become a *TV,* an automobile a *car,* and a digital video disc a *DVD.*

Language, culture, and thought are interrelated. Opposing the Sapir-Whorf hypothesis, however, it might be more accurate to say that changes in culture produce changes in language and thought than to say the reverse. Consider differences between female and male Americans regarding the color terms they use (Lakoff 2004). Distinctions implied by such terms as *salmon, rust, peach, beige, teal, mauve, cranberry,* and *dusky orange* aren't in the vocabularies of most American men. However, many of them weren't even in American women's lexicons 50 years ago. These changes reflect changes in American economy, society, and culture. Color terms and distinctions have increased with the growth of the fashion and cosmetic industries. A similar contrast (and growth) in Americans' lexicons shows up in football, basketball, and hockey vocabularies. Sports fans, more often males than females, use more terms concerning, and make more elaborate distinctions between, the games they watch, such as hockey (see Table 4.2). Thus, cultural contrasts and changes affect lexical distinctions (for instance, *peach* versus *salmon*) within semantic domains (for instance, color terminology). **Semantics** refers to a language's meaning system.

The ways in which people divide up the world—the lexical contrasts they perceive as meaningful or significant—reflect their experiences (see Bicker, Sillitoe, and Pottier, eds. 2004). Anthropologists have discovered that certain sets of vocabulary items evolve in a determined order. For example, after studying more than 100 languages, Berlin and Kay (1969/1992) discovered 10 basic color terms: *white, black, red, yellow, blue, green,*

On May 26, 2008, in Detroit, Red Wings defenseman Brad Stuart (C) tries to keep Pittsburgh Penguins' Kris Letang (R) from getting a shot on Detroit Red Wings goalie Chris Osgood (L) in Detroit's 3-0 victory in game 2 of the Stanley Cup Finals. The Penguins would avenge that loss and claim the Stanley cup the following year. How might an avid hockey fan describe this photo?

TABLE 4.2

Focal Vocabulary for Hockey
Insiders have special terms for the major elements of the game

Elements of Hockey	Insiders' Term
puck	biscuit
goal/net	pipes
penalty box	sin bin
hockey stick	twig
helmet	bucket
space between a goalie's leg pads	five hole

brown, pink, orange, and *purple* (they evolved in more or less that order). The number of terms varied with cultural complexity. Representing one extreme were Papua New Guinea cultivators and Australian hunters and gatherers, who used only two basic terms, which translate as *black* and *white* or *dark* and *light.* At the other end of the continuum were European and Asian languages with all the color terms. Color terminology was most developed in areas with a history of using dyes and artificial coloring.

Sociolinguistics

No language is a uniform system in which everyone talks just like everyone else. The field of **sociolinguistics** investigates relationships between social and linguistic variation (Romaine 2000; Trudgill 2000). How do different speakers use a given language? How do linguistic features correlate with social diversity and stratification, including class, ethnic, and gender differences (Tannen 1990; Tannen, ed. 1993)? How is language used to express, reinforce, or resist power (Geis 1987; Lakoff 2000)?

Sociolinguists focus on features that vary systematically with social position and situation. To study variation, sociolinguists must observe, define, and measure variable use of language in real-world situations. To show that linguistic features correlate with social, economic, and political differences, the social attributes of speakers also must be measured and related to speech (Fasold 1990; Labov 1972*a*).

Variation within a language at a given time is historical change in progress. The same forces that, working gradually, have produced large-scale linguistic change over the centuries are still at work today. Linguistic change doesn't occur in a vacuum but in society. When new ways of speaking are associated with social factors, they are imitated, and they spread. In this way, a language changes.

Linguistic Diversity within Nations

As an illustration of the linguistic variation encountered in all nations, consider the contemporary United States. Ethnic diversity is revealed by the fact that millions of Americans learn first languages other than English. Spanish is the most common. Most of those people eventually become bilinguals, adding English as a second language. In many multilingual (including colonized) nations, people use two languages on different occasions—one in the home, for example, and the other on the job or in public (see this chapter's "Anthropology Today" section).

Whether bilingual or not, we all vary our speech in different contexts; we engage in **style shifts.** In certain parts of Europe, people regularly switch dialects. This phenomenon, known as **diglossia,** applies to "high" and "low" variants of the same language, for example, in German and Flemish (spoken in Belgium). People employ the high variant at universities and in writing, professions, and the mass media. They use the low variant for ordinary conversation with family members and friends.

Just as social situations influence our speech, so do geographical, cultural, and socioeconomic differences. Many dialects coexist in the United States with Standard (American) English (SE). SE itself is a dialect that differs, say, from "BBC English,"

Ethnic and linguistic diversity characterize many nations, especially in big cities, as is illustrated by this California sign written in seven languages: Chinese, Korean, Spanish, Vietnamese, Japanese, Tagalog, and English.

which is the preferred dialect in Great Britain. Different dialects are equally effective as systems of communication, which is language's main job. Our tendency to think of particular dialects as cruder or more sophisticated than others is a social rather than a linguistic judgment. We rank certain speech patterns as better or worse because we recognize that they are used by groups that we also rank. People who say *dese, dem,* and *dere* instead of *these, them,* and *there* communicate perfectly well with anyone who recognizes that the *d* sound systematically replaces the *th* sound in their speech. However, this form of speech has become an indicator of low social rank. We call it, like the use of *ain't,* "uneducated speech." The use of *dem, dese,* and *dere* is one of many phonological differences that Americans recognize and look down on.

Gender Speech Contrasts

Comparing men and women, there are differences in phonology, grammar, and vocabulary, and in the body stances and movements that accompany speech (Eckert and McConnell-Ginet 2003; Lakoff 2004; Tannen 1990). In phonology, American women tend to pronounce their vowels more peripherally ("rant," "rint" when saying the word "rent"), whereas men tend to pronounce theirs more centrally ("runt"). In public contexts, Japanese women tend to adopt an artificially high voice, for the sake of politeness, according to their traditional culture. Women tend to be more careful about uneducated speech. This trend shows up in both the United States and England. Men may adopt working-class speech because they associate it with masculinity. Perhaps women pay more attention to the media, in which standard dialects are employed.

According to Robin Lakoff (2004), the use of certain types of words and expressions has been associated with women's traditional lesser power in American society (see also Coates 1986; Romaine 1999; Tannen 1990; Tannen, ed. 1993). For example, *Oh dear, Oh fudge,* and *Goodness!* are less forceful than *Hell* and *Damn.* Watch the lips of a disgruntled athlete in a televised competition, such as a football game. What's the likelihood he's saying "Phooey on you"? Women, by contrast, are more likely to use such adjectives as *adorable, charming, sweet, cute, lovely,* and *divine* than men are.

Let's return to sports and color terminology for additional illustration of differences in lexical (vocabulary) distinctions that men and women make. Men typically know more terms related to sports, make more distinctions among them (e.g., runs versus points), and try to use the terms more precisely than women do. Correspondingly, influenced more by the fashion and cosmetics industries than men are, women use more color terms and attempt to use them more specifically than men do. Thus, when I lecture on sociolinguistics, and to make this point, I bring an off-purple shirt to class. Holding it up, I first ask women to say aloud what color the shirt is. The women rarely answer with a uniform voice, as they try to distinguish the actual shade (mauve, lavender, lilac, violet, or some other purplish hue). Then I ask the men, who consistently answer as one, "PURPLE." Rare is the man who on the spur of the moment can imagine the difference between *fuchsia* and *magenta.*

Differences in the linguistic strategies and behavior of men and women are examined in several books by the well-known sociolinguist Deborah Tannen (1990; ed. 1993). Tannen uses the terms "rapport" and "report" to contrast women's and men's overall linguistic styles. Women, says Tannen, typically use language and the body movements that accompany it to build rapport, social connections with others. Men, on the other hand, tend to make reports, reciting information that serves to establish a place for themselves in a hierarchy, as they also attempt to determine the relative ranks of their conversation mates.

Stratification and Symbolic Domination

We use and evaluate speech in the context of *extralinguistic* forces—social, political, and economic. Mainstream Americans evaluate the speech of low-status groups negatively, calling it "uneducated." This is not because these ways of speaking are bad in themselves but because they have come to symbolize low status. Consider variation in the pronunciation of *r*. In some parts of the United States *r* is regularly pronounced, and in other (*r*less) areas it is not. Originally, American *r*less speech was modeled on the fashionable speech of England. Because of its prestige, *r*lessness was adopted in many areas and continues as the norm around Boston and in the South.

New Yorkers sought prestige by dropping their *r*'s in the 19th century, after having pronounced them in the 18th. However, contemporary New Yorkers are going back to the 18th-century pattern of pronouncing *r*'s. What matters, and what governs linguistic change, is not the reverberation of a strong midwestern *r* but *social* evaluation, whether *r*'s happen to be "in" or "out."

Studies of *r* pronunciation in New York City have clarified the mechanisms of phonological change. William Labov (1972*b*) focused on whether *r* was pronounced after vowels in such words as *car, floor, card,* and *fourth.* To get data on how this linguistic variation correlated with social class, he used a series of rapid encounters with employees in three New York City department stores, each of whose prices and locations attracted a different socioeconomic group. Saks Fifth Avenue (68 encounters) catered to the upper middle class, Macy's (125) attracted middle-class shoppers, and S. Klein's (71) had predominantly lower-middle-class and working-class customers. The class origins of store personnel reflected those of their customers.

Having already determined that a certain department was on the fourth floor, Labov approached ground-floor salespeople and asked where that department was. After the salesperson had answered, "Fourth floor," Labov repeated his "Where?" in order to get a second response. The second reply was more formal and emphatic, the salesperson presumably thinking that Labov hadn't heard or understood the first answer. For each salesperson, therefore, Labov had two samples of /r/ pronunciation in two words.

Labov calculated the percentages of workers who pronounced /r/ at least once during the interview. These were 62 percent at Saks, 51 percent at Macy's, but only 20 percent at S. Klein's. He also found that personnel on upper floors, where he asked "What floor is this?" (and where more expensive items were sold), pronounced *r* more often than ground-floor salespeople did.

In Labov's study, *r* pronunciation was clearly associated with prestige. Certainly the job interviewers who had hired the salespeople never counted *r*'s before offering employment. However, they did use speech evaluations to make judgments about how effective certain people would be in selling particular kinds of merchandise. In other words, they practiced sociolinguistic discrimination, using linguistic features in deciding who got certain jobs.

Our speech habits help determine our access to employment and other material resources. Because of this, "proper language" itself becomes a strategic resource—and a path to wealth, prestige, and power (Gal 1989; Thomas and Wareing, eds. 2004). Illustrating this, many ethnographers have described the importance of verbal skill and oratory in politics (Beeman 1986; Bloch, ed. 1975; Brenneis 1988; Geis 1987; Lakoff 2000). Ronald Reagan, known as a "great communicator," dominated American society in the

1980s as a two-term president. Another twice-elected president, Bill Clinton, despite his southern accent, was known for his verbal skills in certain contexts (e.g., televised debates and town-hall meetings). Communications flaws may have helped doom the presidencies of Gerald Ford, Jimmy Carter, and George Bush the elder. Does his use of language affect your perception of the current president of the United States?

The French anthropologist Pierre Bourdieu views linguistic practices as *symbolic capital* that properly trained people may convert into economic and social capital. The value of a dialect—its standing in a "linguistic market"—depends on the extent to which it provides access to desired positions in the labor market. In turn, this reflects its legitimation by formal institutions—educational institutions, state, church, and prestige media. Even people who don't use the prestige dialect accept its authority and correctness, its "symbolic domination" (Bourdieu 1982, 1984). Thus, linguistic forms, which lack power in themselves, take on the power of the groups they symbolize. The education system, however (defending its own worth), denies

My dream was to became a shool teacher.
Mrs. Stone is rich.
I have talents but not opportunity.
I am used to standing behind
Mrs. Stone.
I have been a servant for 40 years.
Vickie Figueroa.

Proper language is a strategic resource, correlated with wealth, prestige, and power. How is linguistic (and social) stratification illustrated in this photo, including the handwritten comments below it?

linguistic relativity. It misrepresents prestige speech as being inherently better. The linguistic insecurity often felt by lower-class and minority speakers is a result of this symbolic domination.

Black English Vernacular (BEV)

The sociolinguist William Labov and several associates, both white and black, have conducted detailed studies of what they call **Black English Vernacular (BEV).** (*Vernacular* means ordinary, casual speech.) BEV is the "relatively uniform dialect spoken by the majority of black youth in most parts of the United States today, especially in the inner city areas of New York, Boston, Detroit, Philadelphia, Washington, Cleveland, . . . and other urban centers. It is also spoken in most rural areas and used in the casual, intimate speech of many adults" (Labov 1972*a*, p. xiii). This does not imply that all, or even most, African Americans speak BEV.

BEV is a complex linguistic system with its own rules, which linguists have described. Consider some of the phonological and grammatical differences between BEV and SE. One phonological difference is that BEV speakers are less likely to pronounce *r* than SE speakers are. Actually, many SE speakers don't pronounce *r*'s that come right before a consonant (ca*r*d) or at the end of a word (car). But SE speakers usually do pronounce an *r* that comes right before a vowel, either at the end of a word (fou*r* o'clock) or within a word (Ca*r*ol). BEV speakers, by contrast, are much more likely to omit such intervocalic (between vowels) *r*'s. The result is that speakers of the two dialects have different *homonyms* (words that sound the same but have different meanings). BEV speakers who don't pronounce intervocalic *r*'s have the following homonyms: Carol/Cal; Paris/pass.

Although never a native speaker of BEV, President Barack Obama speaking here in 2009 to the National Academy of Sciences, exemplifies an upwardly mobile person with an unusually effective mastery of SE.

Observing different phonological rules, BEV speakers pronounce certain words differently than SE speakers do. Particularly in the elementary school context, the homonyms of BEV-speaking students typically differ from those of their SE-speaking teachers. To evaluate reading accuracy, teachers should determine whether students are recognizing the different meanings of such BEV homonyms as *passed, past,* and *pass.* Teachers need to make sure students understand what they are reading, which is probably more important than whether they are pronouncing words correctly according to the SE norm.

Phonological rules may lead BEV speakers to omit *-ed* as a past-tense marker and *-s* as a marker of plurality. However, other speech contexts demonstrate that BEV speakers do understand the difference between past and present verbs, and between singular and plural nouns. Confirming this are irregular verbs (e.g., *tell, told*) and irregular plurals (e.g., *child, children*), in which BEV works the same as SE.

SE is not superior to BEV as a linguistic system, but it does happen to be the prestige dialect—the one used in the mass media, in writing, and in most public and professional contexts. SE is the dialect that has the most "symbolic capital." In areas of Germany where there is diglossia, speakers of Plattdeusch (Low German) learn the High German dialect to communicate appropriately in the national context. Similarly, upwardly mobile BEV-speaking students learn SE.

Historical Linguistics

Sociolinguists study contemporary variation in speech, which is language change in progress. **Historical linguistics** deals with longer-term change. Historical linguists can reconstruct many features of past languages by studying contemporary **daughter languages.** These are languages that descend from the same parent language and that have been changing separately for hundreds or even thousands of years. We call the original language from which they diverge the **protolanguage.** Romance languages such as French and Spanish, for example, are daughter languages of Latin, their common protolanguage. German, English, Dutch, and the Scandinavian languages are daughter languages of proto-Germanic. The Romance languages and the Germanic languages all belong to the Indo-European language family. Their common protolanguage is called Proto-Indo-European, PIE. Historical linguists classify languages according to their degree of relationship (see Figure 4.2—PIE family tree).

Language changes over time. It evolves—varies, spreads, divides into **subgroups** (languages within a taxonomy of related languages that are most closely related). Dialects of a single parent language become distinct daughter languages, especially if they are isolated from one another. Some of them split, and new "granddaughter" languages develop. If people remain in the ancestral homeland, their speech patterns also change. The evolving speech in the ancestral homeland should be considered a daughter language like the others.

A close relationship between languages doesn't necessarily mean that their speakers are closely related biologically or culturally, because people can adopt new languages. In the equatorial forests of Africa, "pygmy" hunters have discarded their ancestral languages and now speak those of the cultivators who have migrated to the area. Immigrants to the United States spoke many different languages on arrival, but their descendants now speak fluent English.

Knowledge of linguistic relationships often is valuable to anthropologists interested in history, particularly events during the past 5,000 years. Cultural features may (or may not) correlate with the distribution of language families. Groups that speak related languages may (or may not) be more culturally similar to each other than they are to groups whose speech derives from different linguistic ancestors. Of course, cultural similarities aren't limited to speakers of related languages. Even

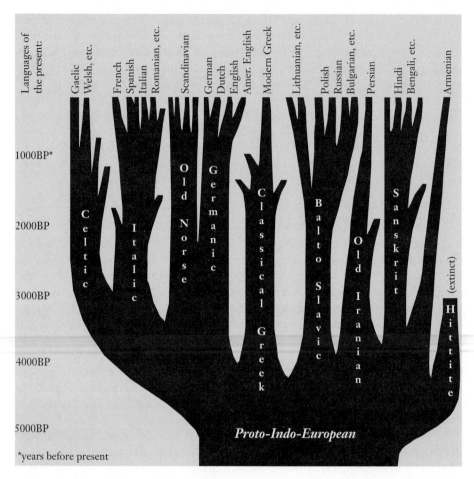

FIGURE 4.2   *PIE Family Tree*   Main languages and subgroups of the Indo-European language stock, showing approximate time to their divergence.

groups whose members speak unrelated languages have contact through trade, intermarriage, and warfare. Ideas and inventions diffuse widely among human groups. Many items of vocabulary in contemporary English, particularly food items such as "beef" and "pork," come from French. Even without written documentation of France's influence after the Norman Conquest of England in 1066, linguistic evidence in contemporary English would reveal a long period of important firsthand contact with France. Similarly, linguistic evidence may confirm cultural contact and borrowing when written history is lacking. By considering which words have been borrowed, we also can make inferences about the nature of the contact.

Language Loss

One aspect of linguistic history is language loss. When languages disappear, cultural diversity is reduced as well. According to linguist K. David Harrison, "When we lose a language, we lose centuries of thinking about time, seasons, sea creatures, reindeer, edible flowers, mathematics, landscapes, myths, music, the unknown and the every-day" (quoted in Maugh 2007). Harrison's recent book, *When Languages Die* (2007), notes that an indigenous language goes extinct every two weeks, as its last speakers die. The world's linguistic diversity has been cut in half (measured by number of distinct languages) in the past 500 years, and half of the remaining languages are predicted to disappear during this century. Colonial languages (e.g., English, Spanish, Portuguese, French, Dutch, Russian) have expanded at the expense of indigenous ones. Of approximately 7,000 remaining languages, about 20 percent are endangered, compared with 18 percent of mammals, 8 percent of plants, and 5 percent of birds (Maugh 2007).

Harrison, who teaches at Swarthmore College, is director of research for the Living Tongues Institute for Endangered Languages (http://www.livingtongues.org), which works to maintain, preserve, and revitalize endangered languages through mul-timedia documentation projects. Researchers from the institute use digital audio and video equipment to record the last speakers of the most endangered languages. *National Geographic*'s Enduring Voices Project (http://www.nationalgeographic.com/mission/enduringvoices/) strives to preserve endangered languages by identifying the geographic areas with unique, poorly understood, or threatened languages and by documenting those languages and cultures.

The website shows various language hot spots where the endangerment rate ranges from low to severe. The rate is high in an area encompassing Oklahoma, Texas, and New Mexico, where 40 Native American languages are at risk. The top hot spot is northern Australia, where 153 Aboriginal languages are endangered (Maugh 2007). Other hot spots are in central South America, the Pacific Northwest of North America, and eastern Siberia. In all these areas indigenous tongues have yielded, either volun-tarily or through coercion, to a colonial language.

ANTHROPOLOGY TODAY

Linguistic Diversity and the Internet

Despite language loss, linguistic diversity is alive and well in many countries, in-cluding India, as described below. Despite that nation's colonial history, only about a tenth of the Indian population speaks English. However, even many of those English speakers prefer to read, and to seek out Internet content, in their own re-gional languages. In this story we see how *local entrepreneurs and international companies such as Google, Yahoo, and Microsoft are rushing to meet the demand for Web content in local languages. This example illustrates one of the main les-sons of applied anthropology, that exter-nal inputs fit in best when they are tailored properly to local settings. We see also how Indians shift their linguistic styles—even languages—as they interact with friends, family, coworkers, and Internet sources in their daily lives.*

Continued

ANTHROPOLOGY TODAY   *Continued*

Asia already has twice as many Internet users as North America, and by 2012 it will have three times as many. Already, more than half of the search queries on Google come from outside the United States.

The globalization of the Web has inspired entrepreneurs like Ram Prakash Hanumanthappa, an engineer from outside Bangalore, India. Mr. Ram Prakash learned English as a teenager, but he still prefers to express himself to friends and family members in his native Kannada. But using Kannada on the Web involves computer keyboard maps that even Mr. Ram Prakash finds challenging to learn.

So in 2006 he developed Quillpad, an online service for typing in 10 South Asian languages. Users spell out words of local languages phonetically in Roman letters, and Quillpad's predictive engine converts them into local-language script. Bloggers and authors rave about the service, which has attracted interest from the cellphone maker Nokia and the attention of Google Inc., which has since introduced its own transliteration tool.

Mr. Ram Prakash said Western technology companies have misunderstood the linguistic landscape of India, where English is spoken proficiently by only about a tenth of the population and even many college-educated Indians prefer the contours of their native tongues for everyday speech. "You've

got to give them an opportunity to express themselves correctly, rather than make a fool out of themselves and forcing them to use English," he said.

Only there is a shortage of non-English content and applications. So, American technology giants are spending hundreds of millions of dollars each year to build and develop foreign-language Web sites and services—before local companies like Quillpad beat them to the punch and the profits. . . .

Nowhere are the obstacles, or the potential rewards, more apparent than in India, whose online population . . . is poised to become the third-largest in the world after China and the United States by 2012. Indians may speak one language to their boss, another to their spouse and a third to a parent. In casual speech, words can be drawn from a grab bag of tongues.

In the last two years, Yahoo and Google have introduced more than a dozen services to encourage India's Web users to search, blog, chat and learn in their mother tongues. Microsoft has built its Windows Live bundle of online consumer services in seven Indian languages. Facebook has enlisted hundreds of volunteers to translate its social networking site into Hindi and other regional languages, and Wikipedia now has more entries in Indian local languages than in Korean. Google's search service has lagged behind the local competition in China, and that has

Summary

1. Wild primates use call systems to communicate. Environmental stimuli trigger calls, which cannot be combined when multiple stimuli are present. Contrasts between language and call systems include displacement, productivity, and cultural transmission. Over time, our ancestral call systems grew too complex for genetic transmission, and hominid communication began to rely on learning. Humans still use nonverbal communication, such as facial expressions, gestures, and body stances and movements. But language is the main system humans use

made providing locally flavored services a priority for the company in India. Google's initiatives in India are aimed at opening the country's historically slow-growing personal computer market, and at developing expertise that Google will be able to apply to building services for emerging markets worldwide.

"India is a microcosm of the world," said Dr. Prasad Bhaarat Ram, Google India's head of research and development. "Having 22 languages creates a new level of complexity in which you can't take the same approach that you would if you had one predominant language and applied it 22 times."

Global businesses are spending hundreds of millions of dollars a year working their way down a list of languages into which to translate their Web sites, said Donald A. DePalma, the chief research officer of Common Sense Advisory, a consulting business in Lowell, Mass., that specializes in localizing Web sites. India—with relatively undeveloped e-commerce and online advertising markets—is actually lower on the list than Russia, Brazil and South Korea, Mr. DePalma said. . . .

English simply will not suffice for connecting with India's growing online market, a lesson already learned by Western television producers and consumer products makers. . . .

Even among the largely English-speaking base of around 50 million Web users in India today, nearly three-quarters prefer to read in a local language, according to a survey by JuxtConsult, an Indian market research company. Many cannot find the content they are seeking. "There is a huge shortage of local language content," said Sanjay Tiwari, the chief executive of JuxtConsult. A Microsoft initiative, Project Bhasha, coordinates the efforts of Indian academics, local businesses and solo software developers to expand computing in regional languages. The project's Web site, which counts thousands of registered members, refers to language as "one of the main contributors to the digital divide" in India.

The company is also seeing growing demand from Indian government agencies and companies creating online public services in local languages.

"As many of these companies want to push their services into rural India or tier-two towns or smaller towns, then it becomes essential they communicate with their customers in the local language," said Pradeep Parappil, a Microsoft program manager.

"Localization is the key to success in countries like India," said Gopal Krishna, who oversees consumer services at Yahoo India.

Source: Daniel Sorid, "Writing the Web's Future in Numerous Languages," *New York Times,* December 31, 2008. Copyright © 2008 The New York Times. Reprinted by permission.

to communicate. Chimps and gorillas can understand and manipulate nonverbal symbols based on language.

2. No language uses all the sounds the human vocal tract can make. Phonology—the study of speech sounds—focuses on sound contrasts (phonemes) that distinguish meaning. The grammars and lexicons of particular languages can lead their speakers to perceive and think in certain ways.

3. Linguistic anthropologists share anthropology's general interest in diversity in time and space. Sociolinguistics investigates relationships between social and linguistic variation by focusing on the actual use of language. Only when features

of speech acquire social meaning are they imitated. If they are valued, they will spread. People vary their speech, shifting styles, dialects, and languages.

4. As linguistic systems, all languages and dialects are equally complex, rule-governed, and effective for communication. However, speech is used, is evaluated, and changes in the context of political, economic, and social forces. Often the linguistic traits of a low-status group are negatively evaluated. This devaluation is not because of linguistic features per se. Rather, it reflects the association of such features with low social status. One dialect, supported by the dominant institutions of the state, exercises symbolic domination over the others.

5. Historical linguistics is useful for anthropologists interested in historical relationships among populations. Cultural similarities and differences often correlate with linguistic ones. Linguistic clues can suggest past contacts between cultures. Related languages—members of the same language family—descend from an original protolanguage. Relationships between languages don't necessarily mean there are biological ties between their speakers because people can learn new languages.

6. One aspect of linguistic history is language loss. The world's linguistic diversity has been cut in half in the past 500 years, and half of the remaining 7,000 languages are predicted to disappear during this century.

Key Terms

Black English Vernacular (BEV) (p. 82)
call systems (p. 65)
cultural transmission (p. 67)
daughter languages (p. 83)
descriptive linguistics (p. 70)
diglossia (p. 77)
displacement (p. 68)
focal vocabulary (p. 75)
historical linguistics (p. 83)
kinesics (p. 70)
lexicon (p. 70)
morphology (p. 70)

phoneme (p. 71)
phonemics (p. 72)
phonetics (p. 72)
phonology (p. 70)
productivity (p. 67)
protolanguage (p. 83)
Sapir-Whorf hypothesis (p. 74)
semantics (p. 75)
sociolinguistics (p. 77)
style shifts (p. 77)
subgroups (p. 83)
syntax (p. 70)

 Go to our Online Learning Center website at **www.mhhe.com/kottak** for Internet resources directly related to the content of this chapter.

Making a Living

❖ **Adaptive Strategies**
  Foraging
  Correlates of Foraging
❖ **Cultivation**
  Horticulture
  Agriculture
  Agricultural Intensification: People
    and the Environment
❖ **Pastoralism**
❖ **Economic Systems**
  Production in Nonindustrial
    Societies

Means of Production
Alienation in Industrial Economies
❖ **Economizing and Maximization**
  Alternative Ends
❖ **Distribution, Exchange**
  The Market Principle
  Redistribution
  Reciprocity
  Coexistence of Exchange Principles
  Potlatching
*Anthropology Today: Scarcity and the
  Betsileo*

I n today's globalizing world, communities and societies are being incorporated, at an accelerating rate, into larger systems. The origin (around 10,000 years ago) and spread of food production (plant cultivation and animal domestication) led to the formation of larger and more powerful social and political systems. Food production led to major changes in human life. The pace of cultural transformation increased enormously. This chapter provides a framework for understanding a variety of human adaptive strategies and economic systems.

Adaptive Strategies

The anthropologist Yehudi Cohen (1974) used the term *adaptive strategy* to describe a society's system of economic production. Cohen argued that the most important reason for similarities between two (or more) unrelated societies is their possession of a similar adaptive strategy. In other words, similar economic causes have similar socio-cultural effects. For example, there are clear similarities among societies that have a foraging (hunting and gathering) strategy. Cohen developed a typology of societies based on correlations between their economies and their social features. His typology includes these five adaptive strategies: foraging, horticulture, agriculture, pastoralism, and industrialism. Industrialism is discussed in the chapter, "The World System and Colonialism." The present chapter focuses on the first four adaptive strategies.

Foraging

Until 10,000 years ago all humans were foragers. However, environmental differences did create substantial contrasts among the world's foragers. Some, like the people who lived in Europe during the ice ages, were big-game hunters. Today, hunters in the Arctic still focus on large animals and herd animals; they have much less vegetation and variety in their diets than do tropical foragers. Moving from colder to hotter areas, the number of species increases. The tropics contain tremendous biodiversity, and tropical foragers typically hunt and gather a wide range of plant and animal species. The same may be true in temperate areas. For example, on the North Pacific Coast of North America, foragers could draw on varied sea, river, and land species, such as salmon and other fish, sea mammals, berries, and mountain goats. Despite differences caused by such environmental variation, all foraging economies have shared one essential feature: People rely on nature to make their living.

Animal domestication (initially of sheep and goats) and plant cultivation (of wheat and barley) began 10,000 to 12,000 years ago in the Middle East. Cultivation based on different crops, such as corn (maize), manioc (cassava), and potatoes, arose independently in the Americas. In both hemispheres most foragers eventually turned to food production. Today most foragers have at least some dependence on food production or on food producers (Kent 1992).

The foraging way of life survived into modern times in certain forests, deserts, islands, and very cold areas—places where food production was not practicable with simple technology (see Lee and Daly 1999). In many areas, foragers were exposed to the "idea" of food production but never adopted it because their own economies provided a perfectly adequate and nutritious diet—with a lot less work. In some places, people reverted to foraging after trying food production and abandoning it. In most areas where hunter-gatherers did survive, foraging should be described as "recent" rather than "contemporary." *All modern foragers live in nation-states and depend to some extent on government assistance.* They are in contact with food-producing neighbors as well as with missionaries and other outsiders. We should not view contemporary foragers as isolated or pristine survivors of the Stone Age. Modern foragers are influenced by national and international policies and political and economic events in the world system.

Although foraging is disappearing rapidly as a way of life, we can trace the outlines of Africa's two broad belts of recent foraging. One is the Kalahari Desert of southern Africa. This is the home of the San ("Bushmen"), who include the Ju/'hoansi (see Kent 1996; Lee 2003). The other main African foraging area is the equatorial forest of central and eastern Africa, home of the Mbuti, Efe, and other "pygmies" (Bailey et al. 1989; Turnbull 1965).

People still do, or until recently did, subsistence foraging in certain remote forests in Madagascar, Southeast Asia, Malaysia, the Philippines, and on certain islands off the Indian coast. Some of the best-known recent foragers are the aborigines of Australia. Those Native Australians lived on their island continent for more than 60,000 years without developing food production.

The Western Hemisphere also had recent foragers. The Eskimos, or Inuit, of Alaska and Canada are well-known hunters. These (and other) northern foragers now use modern technology, including rifles and snowmobiles, in their subsistence activities (Pelto 1973). The native populations of California, Oregon, Washington, and British Columbia all were foragers, as were those of inland subarctic Canada and the Great Lakes. For many Native Americans, fishing, hunting, and gathering remain important subsistence (and sometimes commercial) activities.

Coastal foragers also lived near the southern tip of South America, in Patagonia. On the grassy plains of Argentina, southern Brazil, Uruguay, and Paraguay, there were other hunter-gatherers. The contemporary Aché of Paraguay usually are called "hunter-gatherers" although they now get just a third of their livelihood from foraging. The Aché also grow crops, have domesticated animals, and live in or near mission posts, where they receive food from missionaries (Hawkes, O'Connell, and Hill 1982; Hill et al. 1987).

Throughout the world, foraging survived in environments that posed major obstacles to food production. (Some foragers took refuge in such areas after the rise of food production, the state, colonialism, or the modern world system.) The difficulties of cultivating at the North Pole are obvious. In southern Africa the Dobe Ju/'hoansi San area studied by Richard Lee and others is surrounded by a waterless belt 43 to 124 miles (70 to 200 kilometers) in breadth (Solway and Lee 1990).

Environmental obstacles to food production aren't the only reason foragers survived. See Figure 5.1 for the distribution of recent hunter-gatherers. Their niches had one thing in common—their marginality. Their environments were not of immediate interest to

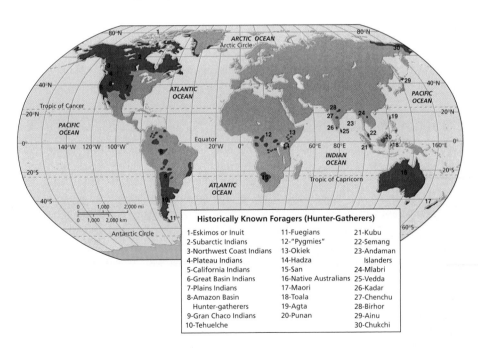

FIGURE 5.1 *Worldwide Distribution of Recent Hunter-Gatherers*

farmers, herders, or colonialists. The foraging way of life did persist in a few areas that could be cultivated, even after contact with farmers. Those tenacious foragers, like the indigenous peoples of what is now California and the Pacific Northwest, did not adopt food production, because they were supporting themselves adequately by hunting and gathering. As the modern world system spreads, the number of foragers continues to decline.

Most of the estimated 100,000 San who survive today live in poverty on society's fringes. Each year more and more foragers come under the control of nation-states and are influenced by forces of globalization. As described by Motseta (2006), between 1997 and 2002, the government of Botswana in southern Africa relocated about 3,000 Basarwa San Bushmen outside their ancestral territory, which was converted into a reserve for wildlife protection. The Basarwa received some compensation for their land, along with access to schools, medical facilities, and job training in resettlement centers. However, critics claim this resettlement turned a society of free hunter-gatherers into communities dependent on food aid and government handouts (Motseta 2006).

In 2006 Botswana's High Court ruled that the Basarwa had been wrongly evicted from the "Central Kalahari Game Reserve." In the context of global political action for cultural rights, this verdict was hailed as a victory for indigenous peoples around the world (Motseta 2006). In December 2006 Botswana's attorney general recognized the court order to allow the Basarwa to return to their ancestral lands, while imposing conditions likely to prevent most of them from doing so. Only the 189 people who actually filed the lawsuit would have automatic right of return with their children, compared with some 2,000 Basarwa wishing to return. The others would have to apply for special permits. Returning Basarwa would be allowed to build only temporary structures and to use enough water for subsistence needs. Water would be a major obstacle since the government shut the main well in 2002, and water is scarce in the Kalahari. Furthermore, anyone wishing to hunt would have to apply for a permit. So goes the foraging way of life in the world today.

Correlates of Foraging

Typologies, such as Cohen's adaptive strategies, are useful because they suggest **correlations**—that is, association or covariation between two or more variables. (Correlated variables are factors that are linked and interrelated, such as food intake and body weight, such that when one increases or decreases, the other changes too.) Ethnographic studies in hundreds of societies have revealed many correlations between the economy and social life. Associated (correlated) with each adaptive strategy is a bundle of particular sociocultural features. Correlations, however, rarely are perfect. Some foragers lack cultural features usually associated with foraging, and some of those features are found in groups with other adaptive strategies.

What, then, are some correlates of foraging? People who subsisted by hunting and gathering often, but not always (see the section on potlatching), lived in band-organized societies. Their basic social unit, the **band,** was a small group of fewer than a hundred people, all related by kinship or marriage. Among some foragers, band size stayed about the same year-round. In others, the band split up for part of the year. Families left to gather resources that were better exploited by just a few people. Later, they regrouped for cooperative work and ceremonies.

One typical characteristic of the foraging life was mobility. In many San groups, as among the Mbuti of Congo, people shifted band membership several times in a lifetime. One might be born, for example, in a band in which one's mother had kin. Later, one's family might move to a band in which the father had relatives. Because bands were exogamous (people married outside their own band) one's parents came from two different bands, and one's grandparents might have come from four. People could join any band to which they had kin or marital links. A couple could live in, or shift between, the husband's and the wife's band.

All human societies have some kind of division of labor based on gender. (See the chapter on gender for more on this.) Among foragers, men typically hunt and fish while women gather and collect, but the specific nature of the work varies among cultures. Sometimes women's work contributes most to the diet. Sometimes male hunting and fishing predominate. Among foragers in tropical and semitropical areas, gathering tends to contribute more to the diet than hunting and fishing do.

All foragers make social distinctions based on age. Often old people receive great respect as guardians of myths, legends, stories, and traditions. Younger people value the elders' special knowledge of ritual and practical matters. Most foraging societies are *egalitarian*. This means that contrasts in prestige are minor and are based on age and gender.

When considering issues of "human nature," we should remember that the egalitarian band was a basic form of human social life for most of our history. Food production has existed less than 1 percent of the time *Homo* has spent on earth. However, it has produced huge social differences. We now consider the main economic features of food-producing strategies.

Cultivation

In Cohen's typology, the three adaptive strategies based on food production in non-industrial societies are horticulture, agriculture, and pastoralism. Just as they do in the United States and Canada, people in nonindustrial societies carry out a variety of economic activities. Each adaptive strategy refers to the main economic activity. Pastoralists (herders), for example, consume milk, butter, blood, and meat from their animals as mainstays of their diet. However, they also add grain to their diet by doing some cultivating or by trading with neighbors.

Horticulture

Horticulture and agriculture are two types of cultivation found in nonindustrial societies. Both differ from the farming systems of industrial nations such as the United States and Canada, which use large land areas, machinery, and petrochemicals. According to Cohen, **horticulture** is cultivation that makes intensive use of *none* of the factors of production: land, labor, capital, and machinery. Horticulturalists use simple tools such as hoes and digging sticks to grow their crops. Their fields lie fallow for varying lengths of time. Horticulture often involves *slash-and-burn* techniques. Here, horticulturalists clear land by cutting down (slashing) and burning forest or bush or by setting fire to the grass covering the plot. The vegetation is broken down, pests are killed, and the ashes remain to fertilize the soil. Crops then are sown, tended, and harvested. Use of the plot is not continuous. Often it is cultivated only for a year or two.

When horticulturalists abandon a plot because of soil exhaustion or a thick weed cover, they clear another piece of land, and the original plot reverts to forest. After several years of fallowing, the cultivator returns to farm the original plot again. Because the relationship between people and land is not permanent, horticulture also is called *shifting cultivation*. Shifting cultivation does not mean that whole villages must move when plots are abandoned. Among the Kuikuru of the South American tropical forest, one village of 150 people remained in the same place for 90 years (Carneiro 1956). Kuikuru houses were large and well made. Because the work involved in building them

In slash-and-burn horticulture, the land is cleared by cutting down (slashing) and burning trees and bush, using simple technology. After such clearing, this woman uses a digging stick to plant mountain rice in Madagascar. What might be the environmental effects of slash-and-burn cultivation?

was substantial, the Kuikuru preferred to walk farther to their fields than to construct a new village. They shifted their plots rather than their settlements. On the other hand, horticulturalists in the montaña (Andean foothills) of Peru lived in small villages of about 30 people (Carneiro 1961/1968). Their houses were small and simple. After a few years in one place, these people built new villages near virgin land. Because their houses were so simple, they preferred rebuilding to walking even a half mile to their fields.

Agriculture

Agriculture requires more labor than horticulture does because it uses land intensively and continuously. The greater labor demands associated with agriculture reflect its use of domesticated animals, irrigation, or terracing.

Domesticated Animals

Many agriculturists use animals as means of production—for transport, as cultivating machines, and for their manure. Asian farmers typically incorporate cattle and/or water buffalo into their agricultural economies. Those rice farmers may use cattle to trample pre-tilled flooded fields, thus mixing soil and water, before transplanting. Many agriculturists attach animals to plows and harrows for field preparation before planting or transplanting. Also, agriculturists typically collect manure from their animals, using it to fertilize their plots, thus increasing yields. Animals are attached to carts for transport and also to implements of cultivation.

Irrigation

While horticulturalists must await the rainy season, agriculturists can schedule their planting in advance because they control water. Like other irrigation experts in the Philippines, the Ifugao water their fields with canals from rivers, streams, springs, and ponds. Irrigation makes it possible to cultivate a plot year after year. Irrigation enriches the soil because the irrigated field is a unique ecosystem with several species of plants and animals, many of them minute organisms, whose wastes fertilize the land.

An irrigated field is a capital investment that usually increases in value. It takes time for a field to start yielding; it reaches full productivity only after several years of cultivation. The Ifugao, like other irrigators, have farmed the same fields for generations. In some agricultural areas, including the Middle East, however, salts carried in the irrigation water can make fields unusable after 50 or 60 years.

Terracing

Terracing is another agricultural technique the Ifugao have mastered. Their homeland has small valleys separated by steep hillsides. Because the population is dense, people need to farm the hills. However, if they simply planted on the steep hillsides, fertile soil and crops would be washed away during the rainy season. To prevent this, the Ifugao cut into the hillside and build stage after stage of terraced fields rising above the valley floor. Springs located above the terraces supply their irrigation water. The labor necessary to build and maintain a system of terraces is great. Terrace walls

Agriculture requires more labor than horticulture does and uses land intensively and continuously. Labor demands associated with agriculture reflect its use of domesticated animals, irrigation, and terracing. Shown here, rice farmers in Saramsa, Sikkim, India, work in flooded terraces.

crumble each year and must be partially rebuilt. The canals that bring water down through the terraces also demand attention.

Costs and Benefits of Agriculture

Agriculture requires human labor to build and maintain irrigation systems, terraces, and other works. People must feed, water, and care for their animals. But agricultural land can yield one or two crops annually for years, or even generations. An agricultural field does not necessarily produce a higher single-year yield than does a horticultural plot. The first crop grown by horticulturalists on long-idle land may be larger than that from an agricultural plot of the same size. Furthermore, because agriculturists work harder than horticulturalists do, agriculture's yield relative to the labor invested also is lower. Agriculture's main advantage is that the long-term yield per area is far greater and more dependable. Because a single field sustains its owners year after year, there is no need to maintain a reserve of uncultivated land as horticulturalists do. This is why agricultural societies tend to be more densely populated than horticultural ones are.

Agricultural Intensification: People and the Environment

The range of environments available for food production has widened as people have increased their control over nature. For example, in arid areas of California, where

Native Americans once foraged, modern irrigation technology now sustains rich agricultural estates. Agriculturists live in many areas that are too arid for nonirrigators or too hilly for nonterracers. Increasing labor intensity and permanent land use have major demographic, social, political, and environmental consequences.

Thus, because of their permanent fields, agriculturists are sedentary. People live in larger and more permanent communities located closer to other settlements. Growth in population size and density increases contact between individuals and groups. There is more need to regulate interpersonal relations, including conflicts of interest. Economies that support more people usually require more coordination in the use of land, labor, and other resources (see the next chapter).

Intensive agriculture has significant environmental effects. Irrigation ditches and paddies (fields with irrigated rice) become repositories for organic wastes, chemicals (such as salts), and disease microorganisms. Intensive agriculture typically spreads at the expense of trees and forests, which are cut down to be replaced by fields. Accompanying such deforestation is loss of environmental diversity (see Srivastava, Smith, and Forno 1999). Agricultural economies grow increasingly specialized. They focus on one or a few caloric staples, such as rice, and on the animals that aid the agricultural economy. Because tropical horticulturalists typically cultivate dozens of plant species simultaneously, a horticultural plot mirrors the botanical diversity that is found in a tropical forest. Agricultural plots, by contrast, reduce ecological diversity by cutting down trees and concentrating on just a few staple foods. Such crop specialization is true of agriculturists both in the tropics (e.g., Indonesian paddy farmers) and outside the tropics (e.g., Middle Eastern irrigation farmers).

Agriculturists attempt to reduce risk in production by favoring stability in the form of a reliable annual harvest and long-term production. Tropical foragers and horticulturalists, by contrast, attempt to reduce risk by relying on multiple species and benefiting from ecological diversity. The agricultural strategy is to put all one's eggs in one big and very dependable basket. The strategy of tropical foragers and horticulturalists is to have several smaller baskets, a few of which may fail without endangering subsistence. The agricultural strategy makes sense when there are lots of children to raise and adults to be fed. Foraging and horticulture, of course, are associated with smaller, sparser, and more mobile populations.

Agricultural economies also pose a series of regulatory problems. How is water to be managed? How are disputes about access to and distribution of water to be resolved? With more people living closer together on more valuable land, agriculturists are more likely to come into conflict than foragers and horticulturalists are. The social and political implications of food production and intensification are examined more fully in the chapter "Political Systems."

Pastoralism

Pastoralists live in North Africa, the Middle East, Europe, Asia, and sub-Saharan Africa. These herders are people whose activities focus on such domesticated animals as cattle, sheep, goats, camels, yak, and reindeer. East African pastoralists, like many others, live in symbiosis with their herds. (*Symbiosis* is an obligatory interaction between groups—here humans and animals—that is beneficial to each.) Herders attempt to protect their animals and to ensure their reproduction in return for food and other products, such as leather. Herds provide dairy products and meat.

People use livestock in various ways. Natives of North America's Great Plains, for example, didn't eat, but only rode, their horses. (Europeans reintroduced horses to the Western Hemisphere; the native American horse had become extinct thousands of years earlier.) For Plains Indians, horses served as "tools of the trade," means of production used to *hunt* buffalo, a main target of their economies. So the Plains Indians were not true pastoralists but hunters who used horses—as many agriculturists use animals—as means of production.

Pastoralists, by contrast, typically use their herds for food. They consume their meat, blood, and milk, from which they make yogurt, butter, and cheese. Although some pastoralists rely on their herds more completely than others do, it is impossible to base subsistence solely on animals. Most pastoralists therefore supplement their diet by hunting, gathering, fishing, cultivating, or trading.

The Samis (also known as Lapps or Laplanders) of Norway, Sweden, and Finland domesticated the reindeer, which their ancestors used to hunt, in the 16th century. Like other herders, they follow their animals as they make an annual trek, in this case from coast to interior. Today's Samis use modern technology, such as snowmobiles and four-wheel-drive vehicles, to accompany their herds on their annual nomadic trek. Although their environment is harsher, the Samis, like other herders, live in nation-states and must deal with outsiders, including government officials, as they follow their herds and make their living through animal husbandry, trade, and sales (Hoge 2001).

Unlike foraging and cultivation, which existed throughout the world before the Industrial Revolution, pastoralism was confined almost totally to the Old World. Before European conquest, the only pastoralists in the Americas lived in the Andean region of South America. They used their llamas and alpacas for food and wool and in agriculture and transport. Much more recently, Navajo of the southwestern United States developed a pastoral economy based on sheep, which were brought to North America by Europeans. The populous Navajo became the major pastoral population in the Western Hemisphere.

Two patterns of movement occur with pastoralism: *nomadism* and *transhumance*. Both are based on the fact that herds must move to use pasture available in particular places in different seasons. In pastoral **nomadism,** the entire group—women, men, and children—moves with the animals throughout the year. The Middle East and North Africa provide numerous examples of pastoral nomads. In Iran, for example, the Basseri and the Qashqai ethnic groups traditionally followed a nomadic route more than 300 miles (480 kilometers) long (see Salzman 2004).

With **transhumance,** part of the group moves with the herds, but most people stay in the home village. There are examples from Europe and Africa. In Europe's Alps it is just the shepherds and goatherds—not the whole village—who accompany the flocks to highland meadows in summer. Among the Turkana of Uganda, men and boys accompany the herds to distant pastures, while much of the village stays put and does some horticultural farming. During their annual trek, pastoral nomads trade for crops and other products with more sedentary people. Transhumants don't have to trade for crops. Because only part of the population accompanies the herds, transhumants can maintain year-round villages and grow their own crops.

Economic Systems

An **economy** is a system of production, distribution, and consumption of resources; *economics* is the study of such systems. Economists focus on modern nations and capitalist systems. Anthropologists have broadened understanding of economic principles by gathering data on nonindustrial economies. Economic anthropology studies economics in a comparative perspective (see Gudeman, ed. 1999; Plattner, ed. 1989; Sahlins 2004; Wilk 1996).

A **mode of production** is a way of organizing production—"a set of social relations through which labor is deployed to wrest energy from nature by means of tools, skills, organization, and knowledge" (Wolf 1982, p. 75). In the capitalist mode of production, money buys labor power, and there is a social gap between the people (bosses and workers) involved in the production process. By contrast, in nonindustrial societies, labor usually is not bought but is given as a social obligation. In such a *kin-based* mode of production, mutual aid in production is one among many expressions of a larger web of social relations.

Societies representing each of the adaptive strategies just discussed (e.g., foraging) tend to have similar modes of production. Differences in the mode of production within a given strategy may reflect differences in environments, target resources, or cultural traditions (Kelly 1995). Thus a foraging mode of production may be based on individual hunters or teams, depending on whether the game is a solitary or a herd animal. Gathering usually is more individualistic than hunting, although collecting teams may assemble when abundant resources ripen and must be harvested quickly. Fishing may be done alone (as in ice or spear fishing) or in crews (as with open-sea fishing and hunting of sea mammals).

Production in Nonindustrial Societies

Although some kind of division of economic labor related to age and gender is a cultural universal, the specific tasks assigned to each sex and to people of different ages vary (see the chapter "Gender"). Many horticultural societies assign a major productive role to women, but some make men's work primary. Similarly, among pastoralists men generally tend large animals, but in some societies women do the milking. Jobs accomplished through teamwork in some cultivating societies are done in other societies by smaller groups or by individuals working over a longer period.

The Betsileo of Madagascar have two stages of teamwork in rice cultivation: transplanting and harvesting. Both feature a traditional division of labor by age and gender which is well known and repeated across the generations. The first job in transplanting is the trampling of a flooded, previously tilled, field by young men driving cattle, in order to mix earth and water. They bring cattle to the fields just before transplanting. The young men yell at and beat the cattle, striving to drive them into a frenzy so that they will trample the fields properly. Trampling breaks up clumps of earth and mixes irrigation water with soil to form a smooth mud into which women transplant seedlings. Once the tramplers leave the field, older men arrive. With their spades they break up the clumps the cattle missed. Meanwhile, the owner and other adults uproot rice seedlings and bring them to the field. Women plant the seedlings.

At harvest time, four or five months later, young men cut the rice off the stalks. Young women carry it to the clearing above the field. Older women arrange and stack it. The oldest men and women then stand on the stack, stomping and compacting it. Three days later, young men thresh the rice, beating the stalks against a rock to remove the grain. Older men then beat the stalks with sticks to make sure all the grains have fallen off.

Means of Production

In nonindustrial societies there is a more intimate relationship between the worker and the means of production than there is in industrial nations. **Means, or factors, of production** include land (territory), labor, and technology.

Land

Among foragers, ties between people and land were less permanent than among food producers. Although many bands had territories, the boundaries usually were not marked, and there was no way they could be enforced. The hunter's stake in an animal was more important than where the animal finally died. A person acquired the rights to use a band's territory by being born in the band or by joining it through a tie of kinship, marriage, or fictive kinship. In Botswana in southern Africa, Ju/'hoansi San women habitually used specific tracts of berry-bearing trees. When a woman changed bands, she immediately acquired a new gathering area.

Among food producers, rights to the means of production also come through kinship and marriage. Descent groups (groups whose members claim common ancestry) are common among nonindustrial food producers. Those who descend from the founder share the group's territory and resources. If the adaptive strategy is horticulture, the estate includes gardens and fallow land for shifting cultivation. As members of a descent group, pastoralists have access to animals to start their own herds, to grazing land, to garden land, and to other means of production.

Labor, Tools, and Specialization

Like land, labor is a means of production. In nonindustrial societies, access to both land and labor comes through social links such as kinship, marriage, and descent. Mutual aid in production is merely one aspect of ongoing social relations that are expressed on many other occasions.

Nonindustrial societies contrast with industrial nations regarding another means of production—technology. Manufacturing often is linked to age and gender. Women may weave and men may make pottery, or vice versa. Most people of a particular age and gender share the technical knowledge associated with that age and gender. If married women customarily make baskets, most married women know how to make baskets. Neither technology nor technical knowledge is very specialized.

Some tribal societies, however, do promote specialization. Among the Yanomami of Venezuela and Brazil, for instance, certain villages manufacture clay pots and others make hammocks. They don't specialize, as one might suppose, because certain raw materials happen to be available near particular villages. Clay suitable for pots is widely available. Everyone knows how to make pots, but not everybody does so. Craft specialization reflects the social and political environment rather than the natural environment. Such specialization promotes trade, which is the first step in creating an alliance with enemy villages (Chagnon 1997).

Alienation in Industrial Economies

There are significant contrasts between industrial and nonindustrial economies. When factory workers produce for their employer's profit, they may be *alienated* from the items they make: They don't feel strong pride in or personal identification with their products. They see their product as belonging to someone other than the man or woman whose labor actually produced it. In nonindustrial societies, by contrast, people usually see their work through from start to finish and feel a sense of accomplishment.

In nonindustrial societies the economic relation between coworkers is just one aspect of a more general social relation. They aren't just coworkers but kin or in-laws. In industrial nations, people usually don't work with relatives and neighbors. If coworkers are friends, the personal relationship often develops out of their common employment rather than being based on a previous association.

Thus, industrial workers have impersonal relations with their products, coworkers, and employers. People sell their labor for cash, and work stands apart from family life. In nonindustrial societies, however, the relations of production, distribution, and consumption are *social relations with economic aspects*. Economy is not a separate entity but is *embedded* in the society.

A Case of Industrial Alienation

For decades, the government of Malaysia has promoted export-oriented industry, allowing transnational companies to install manufacturing operations in rural Malaysia. In search of cheaper labor, corporations headquartered in Japan, Western Europe, and the United States have moved labor-intensive factories to developing countries. Malaysia has hundreds of Japanese and American subsidiaries, which produce garments, foodstuffs, and electronics components. Thousands of young Malaysian women from peasant families now assemble microchips and microcomponents for transistors and capacitors. Aihwa Ong (1987) did a study of electronics assembly workers in an area where 85 percent of the workers were young unmarried females from nearby villages.

Ong found that, unlike village women, female factory workers had to cope with a rigid work routine and constant supervision by men. The discipline that factories value was being taught in local schools, where uniforms helped prepare girls for the factory dress code. Village women wear loose, flowing tunics, sarongs, and sandals, but factory workers had to don tight overalls and heavy rubber gloves, in which they felt constrained. Assembling electronics components requires precise, concentrated labor. Labor in these factories illustrates the separation of intellectual and manual activity—the alienation that Karl Marx considered the defining feature of industrial work. One woman said about her bosses, "They exhaust us very much, as if they do not think that we too are human beings" (Ong 1987, p. 202). Nor does factory work bring women a substantial financial reward, given low wages, job uncertainty, and family claims on wages. Although young women typically work just a few years, production quotas, three daily shifts, overtime, and surveillance take their toll in mental and physical exhaustion.

One response to factory relations of production has been spirit possession (factory women are possessed by spirits). Ong interprets this phenomenon as the women's unconscious protest against labor discipline and male control of the industrial setting. Sometimes possession takes the form of mass hysteria. Spirits have simultaneously invaded as many as 120 factory workers. Weretigers (the Malay equivalent of the werewolf) arrive to avenge the construction of a factory on aboriginal burial grounds. Disturbed earth and grave spirits swarm on the shop floor. First the women see the spirits; then their bodies are invaded. The weretigers send the women into sobbing, laughing, and shrieking fits. To deal with possession, factories employ local medicine men, who sacrifice chickens and goats to fend off the spirits. This solution works only some of the time; possession still goes on. Ong argues that spirit possession expresses anguish at, and resistance to, capitalist relations of production. By engaging in this form of rebellion, however, factory women avoid a direct confrontation with the

Large numbers of young Asian women from peasant families now routinely assemble electronic components. Unlike village women, factory workers often face a rigid work schedule and constant supervision by men. This photo (taken October 14, 2003) shows female workers on the assembly line at the Chint Group low-voltage electrical appliance factory in Taizhou, China.

source of their distress. Ong concludes that spirit possession, while expressing repressed resentment, doesn't do much to modify factory conditions. (Other tactics, such as unionization, would do more.) Spirit possession may even help maintain the current system by operating as a safety valve for accumulated tensions.

Economizing and Maximization

Economic anthropologists have been concerned with two main questions:

1. How are production, distribution, and consumption organized in different societies? This question focuses on *systems* of human behavior and their organization.
2. What motivates people in different societies to produce, distribute or exchange, and consume? Here the focus is not on systems of behavior but on the *individuals* who participate in those systems.

Anthropologists view economic systems and motivations in a cross-cultural perspective. Motivation is a concern of psychologists, but it also has been a concern of economists and anthropologists. American economists assume that producers and distributors make decisions rationally, using the *profit motive,* as do consumers when they shop around for the best value. Although anthropologists know that the profit motive is not universal, the assumption that individuals try to maximize profits is basic to capitalism and to Western economic theory. In fact, the subject matter of economics often is defined as economizing, or the rational allocation of scarce means (or resources) to alternative ends (or uses).

What does that mean? Classical economic theory assumes that our wants are infinite while our means are limited. People must make choices about how to use their scarce resources—their time, labor, money, and capital. (The "Anthropology Today" box at the end of this chapter disputes the idea that people always make economic choices based on scarcity.) Western economists assume that when confronted with choices and decisions, people tend to make the one that maximizes profit. This is assumed to be the most rational choice.

The idea that individuals choose to maximize profits was a basic assumption of the classical economists of the 19th century and one held by many contemporary economists. However, certain economists now recognize that individuals may be motivated by many other goals. Depending on the society and the situation, people may try to maximize profit, wealth, prestige, pleasure, comfort, or social harmony. Individuals may want to realize their personal or family ambitions or those of another group to which they belong (see Sahlins 2004).

Alternative Ends

To what uses do people put their scarce resources? Throughout the world, people devote some of their time and energy to building up a *subsistence fund* (Wolf 1966). In other words, they have to work to eat, to replace the calories they use in daily activity. People also must invest in a *replacement fund.* They must maintain their technology and other items essential to production. If a hoe or plow breaks, they must repair or replace it. They also must obtain and replace items that are essential not to production but to everyday life, such as clothing and shelter.

People everywhere also have to invest in a *social fund*. They must help their friends, relatives, in-laws, and neighbors. It is useful to distinguish between a social fund and a *ceremonial fund*. The latter term refers to expenditures on ceremonies or rituals. To prepare a festival honoring one's ancestors, for example, requires time and the outlay of wealth.

Citizens of nonindustrial states also must allocate scarce resources to a *rent fund*. We think of rent as payment for the use of property. Rent fund, however, has a wider meaning. It refers to resources that people must render to an individual or agency that is superior politically or economically. Tenant farmers and sharecroppers, for example, either pay rent or give some of their produce to their landlords, as peasants did under feudalism.

Peasants are small-scale agriculturists who live in nonindustrial states and have rent fund obligations (see Kearney 1996). They produce to feed themselves, to sell their produce, and to pay rent. All peasants have two things in common:

1. They live in state-organized societies.
2. They produce food without the elaborate technology—chemical fertilizers, tractors, airplanes to spray crops, and so on—of modern farming or agribusiness.

Besides paying rent to landlords, peasants must satisfy government obligations, paying taxes in the form of money, produce, or labor. The rent fund is not simply an *additional* obligation for peasants. Often it becomes their foremost and unavoidable duty. Sometimes their own diets suffer as a result. The demands of social superiors may divert resources from subsistence, replacement, social, and ceremonial funds.

Motivations vary from society to society, and people often lack freedom of choice in allocating their resources. Because of obligations to pay rent, peasants may allocate their scarce means toward ends that are not their own but those of government officials. Thus, even in societies in which there is a profit motive, people often are prevented from rationally maximizing self-interest by factors beyond their control.

Distribution, Exchange

The economist Karl Polanyi (1968) stimulated the comparative study of exchange, and several anthropologists followed his lead. Polanyi defined three principles that guide exchanges: the market principle, redistribution, and reciprocity. These principles all can be present in the same society, but in that case they govern different kinds of transactions. In any society, one of them usually dominates. The principle of exchange that dominates in a given society is the one that allocates the means of production.

The Market Principle

In today's world capitalist economy, the **market principle** dominates. It governs the distribution of the means of production—land, labor, natural resources, technology, and capital. With market exchange, items are bought and sold, using money, with an eye to maximizing profit, and value is determined by the *law of supply and demand* (things cost more the scarcer they are and the more people want them). Bargaining is characteristic of market-principle exchanges. The buyer and seller strive to maximize— to get their "money's worth." Bargaining doesn't require that the buyer and seller meet. Consumers bargain whenever they shop around or use advertisements or the Internet in their decision making (see Madra 2004).

Redistribution

Redistribution operates when goods, services, or their equivalent move from the local level to a center. The center may be a capital, a regional collection point, or a store-house near a chief's residence. Products often move through a hierarchy of officials for storage at the center. Along the way officials and their dependents may consume some of them, but the exchange principle here is *re*distribution. The flow of goods eventually reverses direction—out from the center, down through the hierarchy, and back to the common people.

One example of a redistributive system comes from the Cherokee, the original owners of the Tennessee Valley. Productive farmers who subsisted on maize, beans, and squash, supplemented by hunting and fishing, the Cherokee had chiefs. Each of their main villages had a central plaza, where meetings of the chief's council took place and where redistributive feasts were held. According to Cherokee custom, each family farm had an area where the family could set aside part of their annual harvest for the chief. This supply of corn was used to feed the needy, as well as travelers and warriors journeying through friendly territory. This store of food was available to all who needed it, with the understanding that it "belonged" to the chief and was available through his generosity. The chief also hosted the redistributive feasts held in the main settlements (Harris 1978).

Reciprocity

Reciprocity is exchange between social equals, who normally are related by kinship, marriage, or another close personal tie. Because it occurs between social equals, it is dominant in the more egalitarian societies—among foragers, cultivators, and pastoralists. There are three degrees of reciprocity: *generalized, balanced,* and *negative* (Sahlins 1968, 2004; Service 1966). These may be imagined as areas of a continuum defined by these questions:

1. How closely related are the parties to the exchange?
2. How quickly and unselfishly are gifts reciprocated?

Generalized reciprocity, the purest form of reciprocity, is characteristic of exchanges between closely related people. In balanced reciprocity, social distance increases, as does the need to reciprocate. In negative reciprocity, social distance is greatest and reciprocation is most calculated. This range, from generalized to negative, is called the **reciprocity continuum.**

With **generalized reciprocity,** someone gives to another person and expects nothing immediate in return. Such exchanges are not primarily economic transactions but expressions of personal relationships. Most parents don't keep accounts of every penny they spend on their children. They merely hope their children will respect their culture's customs involving obligations to parents.

Among foragers, generalized reciprocity usually has governed exchanges. People routinely have shared with other band members (Bird-David 1992; Kent 1992). So strong is the ethic of sharing that most foragers have lacked an expression for "thank you." To offer thanks would be impolite because it would imply that a particular act of sharing, which is the keystone of egalitarian society, was unusual. Among the Semai, foragers of central Malaysia (Dentan 1979), to express gratitude would suggest surprise at the hunter's success (Harris 1974).

Balanced reciprocity applies to exchanges between people who are more distantly related than are members of the same band or household. In a horticultural society, for example, a man presents a gift to someone in another village. The recipient may be a cousin, a trading partner, or a brother's fictive kinsman. The giver expects something in return. This may not come immediately, but the social relationship will be strained if there is no reciprocation.

Exchanges in nonindustrial societies also may illustrate **negative reciprocity,** mainly in dealing with people on the fringes of or outside their social systems. To people who live in a world of close personal relations, exchanges with outsiders are full of ambiguity and distrust. Exchange is one way of establishing friendly relations, but when trade begins, the relationship is still tentative. Often the initial exchange is close to being purely economic; people want to get something back immediately. Just as in market economies, but without using money, they try to get the best possible immediate return for their investment.

Generalized reciprocity and balanced reciprocity are based on trust and a social tie. Negative reciprocity involves the attempt to get something for as little as possible, even if it means being cagey or deceitful or cheating. Among the most extreme and "negative" examples of negative reciprocity was 19th-century horse thievery by North American Plains Indians. Men would sneak into camps and villages of neighboring tribes to steal horses. A similar pattern of livestock (cattle) raiding continues today in East Africa, among tribes such as the Kuria (Fleisher 2000). In these cases, the party that starts the raiding can expect reciprocity—a raid on their own village—or worse. The Kuria hunt down cattle thieves and kill them. It's still reciprocity, governed by "Do unto others as they have done unto you."

One way of reducing the tension in situations of potential negative reciprocity is to engage in "silent trade." One example was the silent trade of the Mbuti pygmy foragers of the African equatorial forest and their neighboring horticultural villagers. There was no personal contact during their exchanges. A Mbuti hunter left game, honey, or another forest product at a customary site. Villagers collected it and left crops in exchange. Often the parties bargained silently. If one felt the return was insufficient, he or she simply left it at the trading site. If the other party wanted to continue trade, it was increased.

Coexistence of Exchange Principles

In today's North America, the market principle governs most exchanges, from the sale of the means of production to the sale of consumer goods. We also have redistribution. Some of our tax money goes to support the government, but some of it also comes back to us in the form of social services, education, health care, and road building. We also have reciprocal exchanges. Generalized reciprocity characterizes the relationship between parents and children. However, even here the dominant market mentality surfaces in comments about the high cost of raising children and in the stereotypical statement of the disappointed parent: "We gave you everything money could buy."

Exchanges of gifts, cards, and invitations exemplify reciprocity, usually balanced. Everyone has heard remarks like "They invited us to their daughter's wedding, so when ours gets married, we'll have to invite them" and "They've been here for dinner three times and haven't invited us yet. I don't think we should ask them back until they do." Such precise balancing of reciprocity would be out of place in a foraging band, where resources are communal (common to all) and daily sharing based on generalized reciprocity is an essential ingredient of social life and survival.

Potlatching

One of the most famous cultural practices studied by ethnographers is the **potlatch.** This is a festive event within a regional exchange system among tribes of the North Pacific Coast of North America, including the Salish and Kwakiutl of Washington and British Columbia. Some tribes still practice the potlatch, sometimes as a memorial to the dead (Kan 1986, 1989). At each such event, assisted by members of their communities, potlatch sponsors traditionally gave away food, blankets, pieces of copper, or other items. In return for this, they got prestige. To give a potlatch enhanced one's reputation. Prestige increased with the lavishness of the potlatch, the value of the goods given away in it.

The potlatching tribes were foragers, but atypical ones for relatively recent times. They were sedentary and had chiefs. They had access to a wide variety of land and sea resources. Among their most important foods were salmon, herring, candlefish, berries, mountain goats, seals, and porpoises (Piddocke 1969).

According to classical economic theory, the profit motive is universal, with the goal of maximizing material benefits. How then does one explain the potlatch, in which substantial wealth is given away (and even destroyed—see below)? Christian missionaries considered potlatching to be wasteful and antithetical to the Protestant work ethic. By 1885, under pressure from Indian agents, missionaries, and Indian converts to Christianity, both Canada and the United States had outlawed potlatching. Between 1885 and 1951 the custom went underground. By 1951 both countries had discreetly dropped the antipotlatching laws from the books (Miller n.d.).

Some scholars seized on this view of the potlatch as a classic case of economically wasteful behavior. The economist and social commentator Thorstein Veblen cited potlatching as an example of conspicuous consumption in his influential book *Theory of the Leisure Class* (1899/1992), claiming that potlatching was based on an economically irrational drive for prestige. This interpretation stressed the lavishness

This historic photo shows Tlingit clan members attending a potlatch at Sitka, Alaska, in 1904. Such ancestral headdresses have been repatriated recently from museums back to Tlingit clans. Have you ever partaken in anything like a potlatch?

and supposed wastefulness, especially of the Kwakiutl displays, to support the contention that in some societies people strive to maximize prestige at the expense of their material well-being. This interpretation has been challenged.

Ecological anthropology, also known as *cultural ecology,* is a theoretical school that attempts to interpret cultural practices, such as the potlatch, in terms of their long-term role in helping humans adapt to their environments. Wayne Suttles (1960) and Andrew Vayda (1961/1968) saw potlatching not in terms of its immediate wastefulness, but in terms of its long-term role as a cultural adaptive mechanism. This view also helps us understand similar patterns of lavish feasting throughout the world. Here is the ecological interpretation: *Customs such as the potlatch are cultural adaptations to alternating periods of local abundance and shortage.*

How does this work? Although the natural environment of the North Pacific Coast is favorable, resources do fluctuate from year to year and place to place. Salmon and herring aren't equally abundant every year in a given locality. One village can have a good year while another is experiencing a bad one. Later their fortunes reverse. In this context, the potlatch cycle had adaptive value, and the potlatch was not a competitive display that brought no material benefit.

A village enjoying an especially good year had a surplus of subsistence items, which it could trade for more durable wealth items, such as blankets, canoes, or pieces of copper. Wealth, in turn, by being distributed, could be converted into prestige. Members of several villages were invited to any potlatch and got to take home the resources that were given away. In this way, potlatching linked villages together in a regional economy—an exchange system that distributed food and wealth from wealthy to needy communities. In return, the potlatch sponsors and their villages got prestige. The decision to potlatch was determined by the health of the local economy. If there had been subsistence surpluses, and thus a buildup of wealth over several good years, a village could afford a potlatch to convert its surplus food and wealth into prestige.

The long-term adaptive value of intercommunity feasting becomes clear when a formerly prosperous village had a run of bad luck. Its people started accepting invitations to potlatches in villages that were doing better. The tables were turned as the temporarily rich became temporarily poor and vice versa. The newly needy accepted food and wealth items. They were willing to receive rather than bestow gifts and thus to relinquish some of their stored-up prestige. They hoped their luck would eventually improve so that resources could be recouped and prestige regained.

The potlatch linked local groups along the North Pacific Coast into a regional alliance and exchange network. Potlatching and intervillage exchange had adaptive functions, regardless of the motivations of the individual participants. The anthropologists who stressed rivalry for prestige were not wrong. They were merely emphasizing *motivations* at the expense of an analysis of economic and ecological *systems*.

The use of feasts to enhance individual and community reputations and to redistribute wealth is not peculiar to populations of the North Pacific Coast. Competitive feasting is widely characteristic of nonindustrial food producers. But among most surviving foragers, who live in marginal areas, resources are too meager to support feasting on such a level. In such societies, sharing rather than competition prevails.

ANTHROPOLOGY TODAY

Scarcity and the Betsileo

In the late 1960s my wife and I lived among the Betsileo people of Madagascar, studying their economy and social life (Kottak 1980). Soon after our arrival we met two well-educated schoolteachers (first cousins) who were interested in our research. The woman's father was a congressional representative who became a cabinet minister during our stay. Their family came from a historically important and typical Betsileo village called Ivato, which they invited us to visit with them.

We had traveled to many other Betsileo villages, where often we were displeased with our reception. As we drove up, children would run away screaming. Women would hurry inside. Men would retreat to doorways, where they lurked bashfully. This behavior expressed the Betsileo's great fear of the *mpakafo*. Believed to cut out and devour his victim's heart and liver, the mpakafo is the Malagasy vampire. These cannibals are said to have fair skin and to be very tall. Because I have light skin and stand over six feet tall, I was a natural suspect. The fact that such creatures were not known to travel

Continued

with their wives helped convince the Betsileo that I wasn't really a mpakafo.

When we visited Ivato, its people were different—friendly and hospitable. Our very first day there we did a brief census and found out who lived in which households. We learned people's names and their relationships to our schoolteacher friends and to each other. We met an excellent informant who knew all about the local history. In a few afternoons I learned much more than I had in the other villages in several sessions.

Ivatans were so willing to talk because we had powerful sponsors, village natives who had made it in the outside world, people the Ivatans knew would protect them. The schoolteachers vouched for us, but even more significant was the cabinet minister, who was like a grandfather and benefactor to everyone in town. The Ivatans had no reason to fear us because their more influential native son had asked them to answer our questions.

Once we moved to Ivato, the elders established a pattern of visiting us every evening. They came to talk, attracted by the inquisitive foreigners but also by the wine, tobacco, and food we offered. I asked questions about their customs and beliefs. I eventually developed interview schedules about various subjects, including rice production. I used these forms in Ivato and in two other villages I was studying less intensively. Never have I interviewed as easily as I did in Ivato.

As our stay neared its end, our Ivatan friends lamented, saying, "We'll miss you. When you leave, there won't be any more cigarettes, any more wine, or any more questions." They wondered what it would be like for us back in the United States. They knew we had an automobile and that we regularly purchased things, including the wine, cigarettes, and food we shared with them. We could afford to buy products

they never would have. They commented, "When you go back to your country, you'll need a lot of money for things like cars, clothes, and food. We don't need to buy those things. We make almost everything we use. We don't need as much money as you, because we produce for ourselves."

The Betsileo weren't unusual for nonindustrial people. Strange as it may seem to an American consumer, those rice farmers actually believed *they had all they needed*. The lesson from the Betsileo of the 1960s is that scarcity, which economists view as universal, is variable. Although shortages do arise in nonindustrial societies, the concept of scarcity (insufficient means) is much less developed in stable subsistence-oriented societies than in the societies characterized by industrialism, particularly as the reliance on consumer goods increases.

But, with globalization over the past few decades, significant changes have affected the Betsileo—and most nonindustrial peoples. On my last visit to Ivato, in 2006, the effects of cash and of rapid population increase were evident there—and throughout Madagascar—where the national growth rate has been about 3 percent per year. Madagascar's population doubled between 1966 and 1991—from 6 to 12 million people. Today it stands near 18 million (Kottak 2004). One result of population pressure has been agricultural intensification. In Ivato, farmers who formerly had grown only rice in their rice fields now were using the same land for commercial crops, such as carrots, after the annual rice harvest. Another change affecting Ivato in recent years has been the breakdown of social and political order, fueled by increasing demand for cash.

Cattle rustling has become a growing threat. Cattle thieves (sometimes from neighboring villages) have terrorized peasants who previously felt secure in their

Women hull rice in a Betsileo village. In the village of Ivato, farmers who traditionally grew only rice in their fields now use the same land for commercial crops, such as carrots, after the annual rice harvest.

villages. Some of the rustled cattle are driven to the coasts for commercial export to nearby islands. Prominent among the rustlers are relatively well-educated young men who have studied long enough to be comfortable negotiating with outsiders, but who have been unable to find formal work, and who are unwilling to work the rice fields like their peasant ancestors. The formal education system has familiarized them with external institutions and norms, including the need for cash. The concepts of scarcity, commerce, and negative reciprocity now thrive among the Betsileo.

I have witnessed other striking evidence of the new addiction to cash during my most recent visits to Betsileo country. Near Ivato's county seat, people now sell precious stones—tourmalines, which were found by chance in local rice fields. We saw an amazing sight: dozens of villagers

destroying an ancestral resource, digging up a large rice field, seeking tourmalines—clear evidence of the encroachment of cash on the local subsistence economy.

Throughout the Betsileo homeland, population growth and density are propelling emigration. Locally, land, jobs, and money are all scarce. One woman with ancestors from Ivato, herself now a resident of the national capital (Antananarivo), remarked that half the children of Ivato now lived in that city. Although she was exaggerating, a census of all the descendants of Ivato reveals a substantial emigrant and urban population.

Ivato's recent history is one of increasing participation in a cash economy. That history, combined with the pressure of a growing population on local resources, has made scarcity not just a concept but a reality for Ivatans and their neighbors.

Summary

1. Cohen's adaptive strategies include foraging (hunting and gathering), horticulture, agriculture, pastoralism, and industrialism. Foraging was the only human adaptive strategy until the advent of food production (farming and herding) 10,000 years ago. Food production eventually replaced foraging in most places. Almost all modern foragers have some dependence on food production or food producers.
2. Horticulture doesn't use land or labor intensively. Horticulturalists cultivate a plot for one or two years (sometimes longer) and then abandon it. There is always a fallow period. Agriculturists farm the same plot of land continuously and use labor intensively. They use one or more of the following: irrigation, terracing, domesticated animals as means of production, and manuring.
3. The pastoral strategy is mixed. Nomadic pastoralists trade with cultivators. Part of a transhumant pastoral population cultivates while another part takes the herds to pasture. Except for some Peruvians and the Navajo, who are recent herders, the New World lacks native pastoralists.
4. Economic anthropology is the cross-cultural study of systems of production, distribution, and consumption. In nonindustrial societies, a kin-based mode of production prevails. One acquires rights to resources and labor through membership in social groups, not impersonally through purchase and sale. Work is just one aspect of social relations expressed in varied contexts.
5. Economics has been defined as the science of allocating scarce means to alternative ends. Western economists assume the notion of scarcity is universal—which it isn't—and that in making choices, people strive to maximize personal profit. In nonindustrial societies, indeed as in our own, people often maximize values other than individual profit.
6. In nonindustrial societies, people invest in subsistence, replacement, social, and ceremonial funds. States add a rent fund: People must share their output with their social superiors. In states, the obligation to pay rent often becomes primary.
7. Besides studying production, economic anthropologists study and compare exchange systems. The three principles of exchange are the market principle, redistribution, and reciprocity, which may coexist in a given society. The primary exchange mode is the one that allocates the means of production.
8. Patterns of feasting and exchanges of wealth among villages are common among nonindustrial food producers, as among the potlatching societies of North America's North Pacific Coast. Such systems help even out the availability of resources over time.

Key Terms

agriculture (p. 95)

balanced reciprocity (p. 106)

band (p. 92)

correlation (p. 92)

economy (p. 99)

generalized reciprocity (p. 106)

horticulture (p. 93)

market principle (p. 104)

means (or factors) of
    production (p. 100)

mode of production (p. 99)

negative reciprocity (p. 106)

nomadism, pastoral (p. 98)

pastoralists (p. 97)

peasants (p. 104)

potlatch (p. 107)

reciprocity (p. 105)

reciprocity continuum (p. 105)

redistribution (p. 105)

transhumance (p. 98)

 Go to our Online Learning Center website at **www.mhhe.com/kottak** for Internet resources directly related to the content of this chapter.

Political Systems

Anthropologists and political scientists share an interest in political systems and organization, but the anthropological approach is global and comparative and includes nonstates as well as the states and nation-states usually studied by political scientists. Anthropological studies have revealed substantial variation in power, authority, and legal systems in different societies. (*Power* is the ability to exercise one's will over others; *authority* is the socially approved use of power.) (See Gledhill 2000; Kurtz 2001; Lewellen 2003; Nugent and Vincent, eds. 2004; Wolf with Silverman 2001.)

What Is "The Political"?

Morton Fried offered this definition of political organization:

> Political organization comprises those portions of social organization that
> specifically relate to the individuals or groups that manage the affairs of public
> policy or seek to control the appointment or activities of those individuals or
> groups. (Fried 1967, pp. 20–21)

This definition certainly fits contemporary North America. Under "individuals or groups that manage the affairs of public policy" come federal, state (provincial), and local (municipal) governments. Those who seek to influence public policy include such interest groups as political parties, unions, corporations, consumers, activists, action committees, religious groups, and nongovernmental organizations (NGOs).

Citizens routinely use collective action to influence public policy. Shown here, in Boston on April 14, 2008, hundreds of senior activists rally at the Massachusetts State House to urge representatives to pass legislation to maintain affordable housing and other senior benefits. Have any of your actions influenced public policy?

Fried's definition is much less applicable to nonstates, where it often was difficult to detect any "public policy." For this reason, I prefer to speak of *socio*political organization in discussing the regulation or management of relations among groups and their representatives. Political regulation includes such processes as decision making, social control, and conflict resolution. The study of political regulation draws our attention to those who make decisions and resolve conflicts (are there formal leaders?).

Ethnographic and archaeological studies in hundreds of places have revealed many correlations between economy and social and political organization.

Types and Trends

Decades ago, the anthropologist Elman Service (1962) listed four types, or levels, of political organization: band, tribe, chiefdom, and state. Today, none of the first three types can be studied as a self-contained form of political organization, since all exist within the context of nation-states and are subject to state control (see Ferguson 2002). There is archaeological evidence for early bands, tribes, and chiefdoms that existed before the first states appeared. However, since anthropology came into being long after the origin of the state, anthropologists never have been able to observe "in the flesh" a band, tribe, or chiefdom outside the influence of some state. There still may be local political leaders (e.g., village heads) and regional figures (e.g., chiefs) of the sort discussed in this chapter, but all now exist and function within the context of state organization (see "Anthropology Today" at the end of this chapter).

A **band** refers to a small *kin-based* group (all its members are related by kinship or marriage) found among foragers. **Tribes** had economies based on nonintensive food production (horticulture and pastoralism). Living in villages and organized into kin groups based on common descent (clans and lineages—see the next chapter), tribes lacked a formal government and had no reliable means of enforcing political decisions. **Chiefdom** refers to a form of sociopolitical organization intermediate between the tribe and the state. In chiefdoms, social relations were based mainly on kinship, marriage, descent, age, generation, and gender—just as they were in bands and tribes. Although chiefdoms were kin-based, they featured differential access to resources (some people had more wealth, prestige, and power than others did) and a permanent political structure. The **state** is a form of sociopolitical organization based on a formal government structure and socioeconomic stratification.

The four labels in Service's typology are much too simple to account for the full range of political diversity and complexity known to archaeology and ethnography. We'll see, for instance, that tribes have varied widely in their political systems and institutions. Nevertheless, Service's typology does highlight some significant contrasts in political organization, especially those between states and nonstates. For example, in bands and tribes—unlike states, which have clearly visible governments—political organization did not stand out as separate and distinct from the total social order. In bands and tribes, it was difficult to characterize an act or event as political rather than merely social.

Service's labels "band," "tribe," "chiefdom," and "state" are categories or types within a **sociopolitical typology.** These types are correlated with the adaptive strategies (economic typology) discussed in the chapter "Making a Living." Thus, foragers (an economic type) tended to have band organization (a sociopolitical type). Similarly, many horticulturalists and pastoralists lived in tribes. Although most chiefdoms had farming economies, herding was important in some Middle Eastern chiefdoms. Nonindustrial states usually had an agricultural base.

With food production came larger, denser populations and more complex economies than was the case among foragers. These features posed new regulatory problems, which gave rise to more complex relations and linkages. Many sociopolitical trends reflect the increased regulatory demands associated with food production. Archaeologists have studied these trends through time, and cultural anthropologists have observed them among more contemporary groups.

Bands and Tribes

This chapter examines a series of societies with different political systems. A common set of questions will be addressed for each one. What kinds of social groups does the society have? How do the groups link up with larger ones? How do the groups represent themselves to each other? How are their internal and external relations regulated? To answer these questions, we begin with bands and tribes and then consider chiefdoms and states.

Foraging Bands

Modern hunter-gatherers represent today's remnants of foraging band societies. The strong ties they maintain with sociopolitical groups outside the band make them markedly different from Stone Age hunter-gatherers. Modern foragers live in nation-states and an interlinked world. The pygmies of Congo, for example, have for generations shared a social world and economic exchanges with their neighbors who are cultivators. All foragers now trade with food producers. In addition, most contemporary hunter-gatherers rely on governments and on missionaries for at least part of what they consume.

The San

The Basarwa San are an example of foraging bands whose lives have been impacted significantly by outside groups. In the chapter "Making a Living," we saw how the Basarwa San are affected by policies of the government of Botswana, which relocated them after converting their ancestral lands into a wildlife reserve (Motseta 2006). The government of Botswana is not the first to implement policies and systems that affect the Basarwa San. San speakers ("Bushmen") of southern Africa have been influenced by Bantu speakers (farmers and herders) for 2,000 years and by Europeans for centuries. Edwin Wilmsen (1989) argues that many San descend from herders who were pushed into the desert by poverty or oppression. He sees the San today as a rural underclass in a larger political and economic system dominated by Europeans and Bantu food producers. As a result of this system, many San now tend cattle for wealthier Bantu rather than foraging independently. They also have domesticated animals, indicating their movement away from their foraging lifestyle.

Among tropical foragers, women make an important economic contribution through gathering, as is true among the San shown here in Namibia. What evidence do you see in this photo that contemporary foragers participate in the modern world system?

Susan Kent (1992, 1996) notes a tendency to stereotype foragers, to treat them all as alike. They used to be stereotyped as isolated, primitive survivors of the Stone Age. A new stereotype sees them as culturally deprived people forced by states, colonialism, or world events into marginal environments. Although this view often is exaggerated, it probably is more accurate than the former one.

Kent (1996) stresses variation among foragers, focusing on diversity in time and space among the San. The nature of San life has changed considerably since the 1950s and 1960s, when a series of anthropologists from Harvard University, including Richard Lee, embarked on a systematic study of life in the Kalahari. Lee and others have documented many of the changes in various publications (Lee 1979, 1984, 2003; Silberbauer 1981; Tanaka 1980). Such longitudinal research monitors variation in time, while field work in many San areas has revealed variation in space. One of the most important contrasts was found to be that between settled (sedentary) and nomadic groups (Kent and Vierich 1989). Although sedentism has increased substantially in recent years, some San groups (along rivers) have been sedentary for generations. Others, including the Dobe Ju/'hoansi San studied by Lee (1984, 2003) and the Kutse San that Kent studied, have retained more of the hunter-gatherer lifestyle.

To the extent that foraging has been the basis of subsistence for bands, however, contemporary and recent hunter-gatherers like the San can illustrate links between a foraging economy and other aspects of band society and culture. For example, San groups that still are mobile, or that were so until recently, emphasize social, political, and gender equality, which are traditional band characteristics. A social system based on kinship, reciprocity, and sharing is appropriate for an economy with few people and limited resources. The nomadic pursuit of wild plants and animals tends to discourage permanent settlement, wealth accumulation, and status distinctions. In this context, families and bands have been adaptive social units. People have to share meat when they get it; otherwise it rots.

In the past, foraging bands—small, nomadic or seminomadic social units— formed seasonally when component nuclear families got together. The particular families in a band varied from year to year. Marriage and kinship created ties between members of different bands. Trade and visiting also linked them. Band leaders were leaders in name only. In such an egalitarian society, they were first among equals. Sometimes they gave advice or made decisions, but they had no way to enforce their decisions. Given the spread of states and the modern world system, it is increasingly difficult for ethnographers to find and observe such patterns of band organization.

The Inuit

The aboriginal Inuit (Hoebel 1954, 1954/1968), another group of foragers, provide a good example of methods of settling disputes—**conflict resolution**—in stateless societies. All societies have ways of settling disputes (of variable effectiveness) along with cultural rules or norms about proper and improper behavior. *Norms* are cultural standards or guidelines that enable individuals to distinguish between appropriate and inappropriate behavior in a given society (N. Kottak 2002). While rules and norms are cultural universals, only state societies, those with established governments, have formal laws that are formulated, proclaimed, and enforced.

Foragers lacked formal **law** in the sense of a legal code with trial and enforcement, but they did have methods of social control and dispute settlement. The absence of law did not mean total anarchy. As described by E. A. Hoebel (1954) in a classic ethnographic study of conflict resolution, a sparse population of some 20,000 Inuit spanned 6,000 miles (9,500 kilometers) of the Arctic region. The most significant social groups were the nuclear family and the band. Personal relationships linked the families and bands. Some bands had headmen. There were also shamans (part-time religious specialists). However, these positions conferred little power on those who occupied them.

Hunting and fishing by men were the primary Inuit subsistence activities. The diverse and abundant plant foods available in warmer areas, where female labor in gathering is important, were absent in the Arctic. Traveling on land and sea in a bitter environment, Inuit men faced more dangers than women did. The traditional male role took its toll in lives, so that adult women outnumbered men. This permitted some men to have two or three wives. The ability to support more than one wife conferred a certain amount of prestige, but it also encouraged envy. (*Prestige* is esteem, respect, or approval for culturally valued acts or qualities.) If a man seemed to be taking additional wives just to enhance his reputation, a rival was likely to steal one of them. Most disputes were between men and originated over women, caused by wife stealing or adultery.

A jilted husband had several options. He could try to kill the wife stealer. However, if he succeeded, one of his rival's kinsmen surely would try to kill him in retaliation. One dispute could escalate into several deaths as relatives avenged a succession of murders. No government existed to intervene and stop such a *blood feud* (a murderous feud between families). However, one also could challenge a rival to a song battle. In a public setting, contestants made up insulting songs about each other. At the end of the match, the audience proclaimed the winner. However, if a man whose wife had been stolen won, there was no guarantee she would return. Often she stayed with her abductor.

Thefts are common in societies with marked property differentials, like our own, but thefts are uncommon among foragers. Each Inuit had access to the resources needed to sustain life. Every man could hunt, fish, and make the tools necessary for subsistence. Every woman could obtain the materials needed to make clothing, prepare food, and do domestic work. Inuit men could even hunt and fish in the territories of other local groups. There was no notion of private ownership of territory or animals.

Tribal Cultivators

As is true of foraging bands, there are no totally autonomous tribes in today's world. Still, there are societies, for example, in Papua New Guinea and in South America's tropical forests, in which tribal principles continue to operate. Tribes typically have a horticultural or pastoral economy and are organized by village life or membership in *descent groups* (kin groups whose members trace descent from a common ancestor). Tribes lack socioeconomic stratification (i.e., a class structure) and a formal government of their own. A few tribes still conduct small-scale warfare, in the form of intervillage raiding. Tribes have more effective regulatory mechanisms than foragers do, but tribal societies have no sure means of enforcing political decisions. The main

regulatory officials are village heads, "big men," descent-group leaders, village coun-
cils, and leaders of pantribal associations (see below). All these figures and groups
have limited authority.

Like foragers, horticulturalists tend to be egalitarian, although some have marked
gender stratification: an unequal distribution of resources, power, prestige, and personal
freedom between men and women (see the chapter "Gender"). Horticultural villages
usually are small, with low population density and open access to strategic resources.
Age, gender, and personal traits determine how much respect people receive and how
much support they get from others. Egalitarianism diminishes, however, as village size
and population density increase. Horticultural villages usually have headmen—rarely,
if ever, headwomen.

The Village Head

The Yanomami (Chagnon 1997) are Native Americans who live in southern Venezuela
and the adjacent part of Brazil. Their tribal society has about 26,000 people living in
200 to 250 widely scattered villages, each with a population between 40 and 250. The
Yanomami are horticulturalists who also hunt and gather. Their staple crops are
bananas and plantains (a bananalike crop). There are more significant social groups
among the Yanomami than exist in a foraging society. The Yanomami have families,
villages, and descent groups. Their descent groups, which span more than one village,
are patrilineal (ancestry is traced back through males only) and exogamous (people
must marry outside their own descent group). However, local branches of two different descent groups may live in the same village and intermarry.

As has been true in many village-based tribal societies, traditionally among the
Yanomami the only leadership position has been that of **village head** (always a man).
His authority, like that of a foraging band's leader, is severely limited. If a headman
wants something done, he must lead by example and persuasion. The headman lacks
the right to issue orders. He can only persuade, harangue, and try to influence public
opinion. For example, if he wants people to clean up the central plaza in preparation
for a feast, he must start sweeping it himself, hoping his covillagers will take the hint
and relieve him.

When conflict erupts within the village, the headman may be called on as a
mediator who listens to both sides. He will give an opinion and advice. If a disputant
is unsatisfied, the headman has no power to back his decisions and no way to impose
punishments. Like the band leader, he is first among equals.

A Yanomami village headman also must lead in generosity. Because he must be
more generous than any other villager, he cultivates more land. His garden provides
much of the food consumed when his village holds a feast for another village. The
headman represents the village in its dealings with outsiders, including the Venezuelan
government agents described in "Anthropology Today" at the end of this chapter.

The way a person acts as headman depends on his personal traits and the number of supporters he can muster. One village headman, Kaobawa, intervened in a
dispute between a husband and a wife and kept him from killing her (Chagnon
1983/1992). He also guaranteed safety to a delegation from a village with which a

covillager of his wanted to start a war. Kaobawa was a particularly effective headman. He had demonstrated his fierceness in battle, but he also knew how to use diplomacy to avoid offending other villagers. No one in the village had a better personality for the headmanship. Nor (because Kaobawa had many brothers) did anyone have more supporters. Among the Yanomami, when a group is dissatisfied with a village headman, its members can leave and found a new village; this is done from time to time.

Yanomami society, with its many villages and descent groups, is more complex than a band-organized society. The Yanomami also face more regulatory problems. A headman sometimes can prevent a specific violent act, but intervillage raiding has been a feature of some areas of Yanomami territory, particularly those studied by Chagnon (1997).

We also must stress that the Yanomami are not isolated from outside events, including missionization. They live in two nation-states, Venezuela and Brazil, and external warfare waged by Brazilian ranchers and miners increasingly has threatened them (Chagnon 1997; Cultural Survival Quarterly 1989; Ferguson 1995). During a Brazilian gold rush between 1987 and 1991, one Yanomami died each day, on average, from external attacks. By 1991, there were some 40,000 Brazilian miners in the Brazilian Yanomami homeland. Some Indians were killed outright. The miners introduced new diseases, and the swollen population ensured that old diseases became epidemic. In 1991, a commission of the American Anthropological Association reported on the plight of the Yanomami (*Anthropology Newsletter,* September 1991). Brazilian Yanomami were dying at a rate of 10 percent annually, and their fertility rate had dropped to zero. Since then, both the Brazilian and the Venezuelan governments have intervened to protect the Yanomami. One Brazilian president declared a huge Yanomami territory off-limits to outsiders. Unfortunately, local politicians, miners, and ranchers have increasingly evaded the ban. The future of the Yanomami remains uncertain.

The "Big Man"

Many societies of the South Pacific, particularly in the Melanesian Islands and Papua New Guinea, had a kind of political leader that we call the big man. The **big man** (almost always a male) was an elaborate version of the village head, but with one significant difference. The village head's leadership is within one village; the big man had supporters in several villages. The big man therefore was a regulator of *regional* political organization.

The Kapauku Papuans live in Irian Jaya, Indonesia (which is on the island of New Guinea). Anthropologist Leopold Pospisil (1963) studied the Kapauku (then 45,000 people), who grow crops (with the sweet potato as their staple) and raise pigs. Their economy is too complex to be described as simple horticulture. Kapauku cultivation has used varied techniques for specific kinds of land. Labor-intensive cultivation in valleys involves mutual aid in turning the soil before planting. The digging of long drainage ditches, which a big man often helped organize, is even more complex. Kapauku plant cultivation supports a larger and denser population than does the simpler horticulture of the Yanomami. Kapauku society could not survive in its current form without collective cultivation and political regulation of the more complex economic tasks.

The key political figure among the Kapauku was the big man, known as a *tonowi*. A tonowi achieved his status through hard work, amassing wealth in the form of pigs and other native riches.

The term *status* often is used as a synonym for prestige. In that context, "She's got a lot of status" means she's got a lot of prestige; people look up to her. Among social scientists, that's not the primary meaning of "status." Social scientists use *status* more neutrally—for any social position, no matter what the prestige. In this sense, **status** encompasses the various positions that people occupy in society, such as spouse, parent, trading partner, teacher, student, salesperson, big man, and many others. People always occupy multiple statuses (e.g., son, brother, father, big man). Among the statuses we occupy, particular ones dominate in particular settings, such as son or daughter at home and student in the classroom.

Some statuses are **ascribed:** People have little or no choice about occupying them. Age is an ascribed status; we can't choose not to age. One's status as a member of the nobility, or as a male or a female, usually is ascribed; people are born members of a certain social category and remain so all their lives. **Achieved statuses,** by contrast, aren't automatic; they come through choices, actions, efforts, talents, or accomplishments, and may be positive or negative. Examples of achieved statuses include big man, healer, senator, convicted felon, terrorist, salesperson, union member, father, and college student.

The achieved status of big man rested on certain characteristics that distinguished the big man from his fellows: wealth, generosity, eloquence, physical fitness, bravery, and supernatural powers. Men became big men because they had certain personalities. They amassed resources during their own lifetime; they did not inherit their wealth or position. A man who was determined enough could become a big man, creating wealth through hard work and good judgment. Wealth resulted from successful pig breeding and trading. As a man's pig herd and prestige grew, he attracted supporters. He sponsored ceremonial pig feasts in which pigs were slaughtered and their meat distributed to guests.

Unlike the Yanomami village head, a big man's wealth exceeded that of his fellows. His supporters, recognizing his past favors and anticipating future rewards, recognized him as a leader and accepted his decisions as binding. The big man was an important regulator of regional events in Kapauku life. He helped determine the dates for feasts and markets. He persuaded people to sponsor feasts, which distributed pork and wealth. He initiated economic projects requiring the cooperation of a regional community.

The Kapauku big man again exemplifies a generalization about leadership in tribal societies: If someone achieves wealth and widespread respect and support, he or she must be generous. The big man worked hard not to hoard wealth but to be able to give away the fruits of his labor, to convert wealth into prestige and gratitude. A stingy big man would lose his support, his reputation plummeting. Selfish and greedy big men sometimes were murdered by their fellows (Zimmer-Tamakoshi 1997).

Are contemporary North American politicians like Melanesian big men? Politically valuable attributes of a Melanesian big man included wealth, generosity, eloquence, physical fitness, bravery, and supernatural powers. Americans routinely use their own wealth to finance campaigns. Big men get their loyalists to produce and deliver wealth in the form of pigs, just as modern politicians persuade their supporters to make campaign contributions. And, like big men, successful American politicians try to be generous with their supporters. Payback may take the form of a night in the Lincoln bedroom, a strategic dinner invitation, an ambassadorship, or largesse to a place that was particularly supportive.

Big men amass wealth and then give away pigs. Successful American politicians give away "pork." As with the big man, eloquence and communication skills contribute to political success (e.g., Ronald Reagan, Bill Clinton, Barack Obama), although lack of such skills isn't necessarily fatal. What about physical fitness? Hair, height, and health are still political advantages. Bravery, for instance, demonstrated through distinguished military service, also helps political careers (e.g., Wesley Clark and John McCain), but it certainly isn't required. Supernatural powers? Candidates who proclaim themselves atheists are as rare as self-identified witches. Almost all political candidates claim to belong to a mainstream religion. Some even present their candidacies as

The big man persuades people to organize feasts, which distribute pork and wealth. Shown here is such a regional event, drawing on several villages, in Papua New Guinea. Big men owe their status to their individual personalities rather than to inherited wealth or position. Does our society have equivalents of big men?

promoting divine wishes. On the other hand, contemporary politics isn't just about personality, as it is in big man systems. We live in a state-organized, stratified society with inherited wealth, power, and privilege, all of which have political implications. As is typical of states, inheritance and kin connections play a role in political success. Just think of Kennedys, Bushes, Gores, Clintons, and Gandhis.

Pantribal Sodalities and Age Grades

Big men could forge regional political organization, albeit temporarily, by mobilizing people from several villages. Other social and political mechanisms in tribal societies—such as a belief in common ancestry, kinship, or descent—could be used to link local groups within a region. The same descent group, for example, might span several villages, and its dispersed members might follow a descent group leader.

Principles other than kinship also can link local groups. In a modern nation, a labor union, national sorority or fraternity, political party, or religious denomination may provide such a nonkin-based link. In tribes, nonkin groups called associations or sodalities may serve the same linking function. Often, sodalities are based on common age or gender, with all-male sodalities more common than all-female ones.

Pantribal sodalities (those that extend across the whole tribe, spanning several villages) sometimes arose in areas where two or more different cultures came into regular contact. Such sodalities were especially likely to develop in the presence of warfare between tribes. Drawing their membership from different villages of the same tribe, pantribal sodalities could mobilize men in many local groups for attack or retaliation against another tribe.

In the cross-cultural study of nonkin groups, we must distinguish between those that are confined to a single village and those that span several local groups. Only the latter, the pantribal groups, are important in general military mobilization and regional political organization. Localized men's houses and clubs, limited to particular villages, are found in many horticultural societies in tropical South America, Melanesia, and Papua New Guinea. These groups may organize village activities and even intervillage raiding. However, their leaders are similar to village heads and their political scope is mainly local. The following discussion concerns pantribal groups.

The best examples of pantribal sodalities come from the Central Plains of North America and from tropical Africa. During the 18th and 19th centuries, Native American societies of the Great Plains of the United States and Canada experienced a rapid growth of pantribal sodalities. This development reflected an economic change that followed the spread of horses, which had been reintroduced to the Americas by the Spanish, to the states between the Rocky Mountains and the Mississippi River. Many Plains Indian societies changed their adaptive strategies because of the horse. At first they had been foragers who hunted bison (buffalo) on foot. Later they adopted a mixed economy based on hunting, gathering, and horticulture. Finally they changed to a much more specialized economy based on horseback hunting of bison (eventually with rifles).

As the Plains tribes were undergoing these changes, other Indians also adopted horseback hunting and moved into the Plains. Attempting to occupy the same area, groups came into conflict. A pattern of warfare developed in which the members of one tribe raided another, usually for horses. The new economy demanded that people follow the movement of the bison herds. During the winter, when the bison dispersed, a tribe fragmented into small bands and families. In the summer, as huge herds assembled on the Plains, members of the tribe reunited. They camped together for social, political, and religious activities, but mainly for communal bison hunting.

Only two activities in the new adaptive strategy demanded strong leadership: organizing and carrying out raids on enemy camps (to capture horses) and managing the summer bison hunt. All the Plains societies developed pantribal sodalities, and leadership roles within them, to police the summer hunt. Leaders coordinated hunting efforts, making sure that people did not cause a stampede with an early shot or an ill-advised action. Leaders imposed severe penalties, including seizure of a culprit's wealth, for disobedience.

Some Plains sodalities were **age sets** of increasing rank. Each set included all the men—from that tribe's component bands–born during a certain time span. Each set had its distinctive dances, songs, possessions, and privileges. Members of each set

Among the Masai of Kenya and Tanzania, men born during the same four-year period were circumcised together. They belonged to the same named group, an age set, throughout their lives. The sets moved through grades, of which the most important was the warrior grade. Here we see the warrior (*ilmurran*) age grade dancing with a group of girls of a lower age grade (*intoyie*). Do we have any equivalents of age sets or grades in our own society?

had to pool their wealth to buy admission to the next higher level as they moved up the age hierarchy. Most Plains societies had pantribal warrior associations whose rituals celebrated militarism. As noted previously, the leaders of these associations organized bison hunting and raiding. They also arbitrated disputes during the summer, when many people came together.

Many tribes that adopted this Plains strategy of adaptation had once been foragers for whom hunting and gathering had been individual or small-group affairs. They never had come together previously as a single social unit. Age and gender were available as social principles that could quickly and efficiently forge unrelated people into pantribal groups.

Raiding of one tribe by another, this time for cattle rather than horses, also was common in eastern and southeastern Africa, where pantribal sodalities, including age sets, also developed. Among the pastoral Masai of Kenya, men born during the same four-year period were circumcised together and belonged to the same named group, an age set, throughout their lives. The sets moved through age grades, the most important of which was the warrior grade. Members of a set felt a strong allegiance to one another. Masai women lacked comparable set organization, but they also passed through culturally recognized age grades: the initiate, the married woman, and the postmenopausal woman.

To understand the difference between an age set and an age grade, think of a college class, the Class of 2014, for example, and its progress through the university. The age set would be the group of people constituting the Class of 2014, while the first ("freshman"), sophomore, junior, and senior years would represent the age grades.

Not all societies with age grades also have age sets. When there are no sets, men can enter or leave a particular grade individually or collectively, often by going through a predetermined ritual. The grades most commonly recognized in Africa are these:

1. Recently initiated youths
2. Warriors
3. One or more grades of mature men who play important roles in pantribal government
4. Elders, who may have special ritual responsibilities

In certain parts of West Africa and Central Africa, the pantribal sodalities are *secret societies,* made up exclusively of men or women. Like our college fraternities and sororities, these associations have secret initiation ceremonies. Among the Mende of Sierra Leone, men's and women's secret societies were very influential. The men's group, the Poro, trained boys in social conduct, ethics, and religion and supervised political and economic activities. Leadership roles in the Poro often overshadowed village headship and played an important part in social control, dispute management, and tribal political regulation. Age, gender, and ritual can link members of different local groups into a single social collectivity in a tribe and thus create a sense of ethnic identity, of belonging to the same cultural tradition.

Nomadic Politics

Although many pastoralists, such as the Masai, live in tribes, a range of demographic and sociopolitical diversity occurs with pastoralism. A comparison of pastoralists shows that as regulatory problems increase, political hierarchies are more complex. Political organization is less personal, more formal, and less kinship-oriented. The pastoral strategy of adaptation does not dictate any particular political organization. Unlike the Masai and other tribal herders, some pastoralists have chiefs and live in nation-states.

The scope of political authority among pastoralists expands considerably as regulatory problems increase in densely populated regions. Consider two Iranian pastoral nomadic tribes—the Basseri and the Qashqai (Salzman 1974). Starting each year from a plateau near the coast, these groups took their animals to grazing land 17,000 feet (5,400 meters) above sea level. The Basseri and the Qashqai shared this route with one another and with several other ethnic groups.

Use of the same pasture land at different times was carefully scheduled. Ethnic-group movements were tightly coordinated. Expressing this schedule is *il-rah,* a concept common to all Iranian nomads. A group's il-rah is its customary path in time and space. It is the schedule, different for each group, of when specific areas can be used in the annual trek.

Each tribe had its own leader, known as the *khan* or *il-khan.* The Basseri khan, because he dealt with a smaller population, faced fewer problems in coordinating its movements than did the leaders of the Qashqai. Correspondingly, his rights, privileges, duties, and authority were weaker. Nevertheless, his authority exceeded that of any political figure discussed so far. The khan's authority still came from his personal traits rather than from his office. That is, the Basseri followed a particular khan not because of a political position he happened to fill but because of their personal allegiance and loyalty to him as a man. The khan relied on the support of the heads of the descent groups into which Basseri society was divided.

In Qashqai society, however, allegiance shifted from the person to the office. The Qashqai had multiple levels of authority and more powerful chiefs or khans. Managing 400,000 people required a complex hierarchy. Heading it was the il-khan, helped by a deputy, under whom were the heads of constituent tribes, under each of whom were descent-group heads.

A case illustrates just how developed the Qashqai authority structure was. A hailstorm prevented some nomads from joining the annual migration at the appointed time. Although everyone recognized that they were not responsible for their delay, the il-khan assigned them less favorable grazing land, for that year only, in place of their usual pasture. The tardy herders and other Qashqai considered the judgment fair and didn't question it. Thus, Qashqai authorities regulated the annual migration. They also adjudicated disputes between people, tribes, and descent groups.

These Iranian cases illustrate the fact that pastoralism often is just one among many specialized economic activities within complex nation-states and regional systems. As part of a larger whole, pastoral tribes are constantly pitted against other ethnic groups. In these nations, the state becomes a final authority, a higher-level regulator that attempts to limit conflict between ethnic groups. State organization arose not just to manage agricultural economies but also to regulate the activities of ethnic groups within expanding social and economic systems (see Das and Poole, eds. 2004).

Chiefdoms

Having looked at bands and tribes, we turn to more complex forms of sociopolitical organization—chiefdoms and states. The first states emerged in the Old World about 5,500 years ago. The first chiefdoms developed perhaps a thousand years earlier, but few survive today. In many parts of the world, the chiefdom was a transitional form of organization that emerged during the evolution of tribes into states. State formation began in Mesopotamia (currently Iran and Iraq). It next occurred in Egypt, the Indus Valley of Pakistan and India, and northern China. A few thousand years later states arose in two parts of the Western Hemisphere—Mesoamerica (Mexico, Guatemala, Belize) and the central Andes (Peru and Bolivia). Early states are known as *archaic states,* or nonindustrial states, in contrast to modern industrial nation-states. Robert Carneiro defines the state as "an autonomous political unit encompassing many communities within its territory, having a centralized government with the power to collect taxes, draft men for work or war, and decree and enforce laws" (Carneiro 1970, p. 733).

The chiefdom and the state, like many categories used by social scientists, are *ideal types*. That is, they are labels that make social contrasts seem sharper than they really are. In reality there is a continuum from tribe to chiefdom to state. Some societies had many attributes of chiefdoms but retained tribal features. Some advanced chiefdoms had many attributes of archaic states and thus are difficult to assign to either category. Recognizing this "continuous change" (Johnson and Earle 2000), some anthropologists speak of "complex chiefdoms" (Earle 1987, 1997), which are almost states.

Political and Economic Systems in Chiefdoms

Areas with chiefdoms included the circum-Caribbean (e.g., Caribbean islands, Panama, Colombia), lowland Amazonia, what is now the southeastern United States, and Polynesia. Between the emergence and spread of food production and the expansion of the Roman empire, much of Europe was organized at the chiefdom level. Europe reverted to this level for centuries after the fall of Rome in the fifth century C.E. Chiefdoms created the megalithic cultures of Europe, such as the one that built Stonehenge. Bear in mind that chiefdoms and states can fall (disintegrate) as well as rise.

Much of our ethnographic knowledge about chiefdoms comes from Polynesia, where they were common at the time of European exploration. In chiefdoms, social relations are based mainly on kinship, marriage, descent, age, generation, and gender— just as they are in bands and tribes. This is a fundamental difference between chiefdoms and states. States bring nonrelatives together and oblige them all to pledge allegiance to a government.

Unlike bands and tribes, however, chiefdoms are characterized by *permanent political regulation* of the territory they administer. They have a clear-cut and enduring regional political system. Chiefdoms may include thousands of people living in many villages or hamlets. Regulation is carried out by the chief and his or her assistants, who occupy political offices. An **office** is a permanent position, which must be refilled when it is vacated by death or retirement. Because offices are refilled systematically, the structure of a chiefdom endures across the generations, ensuring permanent political regulation.

In the Polynesian chiefdoms, the chiefs were full-time political specialists in charge of regulating the economy—production, distribution, and consumption. Polynesian chiefs relied on religion to buttress their authority. They regulated production by commanding or prohibiting (using religious taboos) the cultivation of certain lands and crops. Chiefs also regulated distribution and consumption. At certain seasons— often on a ritual occasion such as a first-fruit ceremony—people would offer part of their harvest to the chief through his or her representatives. Products moved up the hierarchy, eventually reaching the chief. Conversely, illustrating obligatory sharing with kin, chiefs sponsored feasts at which they gave back much of what they had received.

Such a flow of resources to and then from a central office is known as *chiefly redistribution*. Redistribution offers economic advantages. If the different areas specialized in particular crops, goods, or services, chiefly redistribution made those products available to the entire society. Chiefly redistribution also played a role in risk management. It stimulated production beyond the immediate subsistence level and provided a central storehouse for goods that might become scarce at times of famine (Earle 1987, 1997).

Stonehenge, England, and an educational display designed for tourists and
visitors. Chiefdoms created the megalithic cultures of Europe, such as the one
that built Stonehenge over 5,000 years ago. Between the emergence and spread
of food production and the expansion of the Roman empire, much of Europe
was organized at the chiefdom level, to which it reverted after the fall of Rome.

Social Status in Chiefdoms

Social status in chiefdoms was based on seniority of descent. Because rank, power,
prestige, and resources came through kinship and descent, Polynesian chiefs kept
extremely long genealogies. Some chiefs (without writing) managed to trace their
ancestry back 50 generations. All the people in the chiefdom were thought to be related
to each other. Presumably, all were descended from a group of founding ancestors.

The status of chief was ascribed, based on seniority of descent. The chief would be the oldest child (usually son) of the oldest child of the oldest child, and so on. Degrees of seniority were calculated so intricately on some islands that there were as many ranks as people. For example, the third son would rank below the second, who in turn would rank below the first. The children of an eldest brother, however, would all rank above the children of the next brother, whose children would in turn outrank those of younger brothers. However, even the lowest-ranking person in a chiefdom was still the chief's relative. In such a kin-based context, everyone, even a chief, had to share with his or her relatives.

Because everyone had a slightly different status, it was difficult to draw a line between elites and common people. Other chiefdoms calculated seniority differently and had shorter genealogies than did those in Polynesia. Still, the concern for seniority and the lack of sharp gaps between elites and commoners are features of all chiefdoms.

Status Systems in Chiefdoms and States

The status systems of chiefdoms and states are similar in that both are based on **differential access** to resources. This means that some men and women had privileged access to power, prestige, and wealth. They controlled strategic resources such as land and water. Earle characterizes chiefs as "an incipient aristocracy with advantages in wealth and lifestyle" (1987, p. 290). Nevertheless, differential access in chiefdoms was tied very much to kinship. The people with privileged access were generally chiefs and their nearest relatives and assistants.

Compared with chiefdoms, archaic states drew a much firmer line between elites and masses, distinguishing at least between nobles and commoners. Kinship ties did not extend from the nobles to the commoners because of *stratum endogamy*—marriage within one's own group. Commoners married commoners; elites married elites.

Such a division of society into socioeconomic strata contrasts strongly with bands and tribes, whose status systems are based on prestige, rather than on differential access to resources. The prestige differentials that do exist in bands reflect special qualities and abilities. Good hunters get respect from their fellows if they are generous. So does a skilled curer, dancer, storyteller—or anyone else with a talent or skill that others appreciate.

In tribes, some prestige goes to descent-group leaders, to village heads, and especially to the big man. All these figures must be generous, however. If they accumulate more resources—such as property or food—than others in the village, they must share them with the others. Since strategic resources are available to everyone, social classes based on the possession of unequal amounts of resources can never exist.

In many tribes, particularly those with patrilineal descent (descent traced through males only), men have much greater prestige and power than women do. The gender contrast in rights may diminish in chiefdoms, where prestige and access to resources are based on seniority of descent, so that some women are senior to some men. Unlike big men, chiefs are exempt from ordinary work and have rights and privileges that are unavailable to the masses. Like big men, however, they still return much of the wealth they take in.

The Emergence of Stratification

The status system in chiefdoms, although based on differential access, differed from the status system in states because the privileged few were always relatives and assistants of the chief. However, this type of status system didn't last very long. Chiefs would start acting like kings and try to erode the kinship basis of the chiefdom. In Madagascar they would do this by demoting their more distant relatives to commoner status and banning marriage between nobles and commoners (Kottak 1980). Such moves, if accepted by the society, created separate social strata—*unrelated* groups that differ in their access to wealth, prestige, and power. (A *stratum* is one of two or more groups that contrast in social status and access to strategic resources. Each stratum includes people of both sexes and all ages.) The creation of separate social strata is called **stratification,** and its emergence signified the transition from chiefdom to state. *The presence of stratification* is one of the key distinguishing features of a *state*.

The influential sociologist Max Weber (1922/1968) defined three related dimensions of social stratification: (1) Economic status, or **wealth,** encompasses all a person's material assets, including income, land, and other types of property. (2) **Power,** the ability to exercise one's will over others—to do what one wants—is the basis of political status. (3) **Prestige**—the basis of social status—refers to esteem, respect, or approval for acts, deeds, or qualities considered exemplary. Prestige, or "cultural capital" (Bourdieu 1984), gives people a sense of worth and respect, which they may often convert into economic advantage (Table 6.1).

In archaic states—for the first time in human evolution—there were contrasts in wealth, power, and prestige between entire groups (social strata) of men and women.

Wealth and prestige aren't always correlated. Shown here, on March 18, 2008, eight county tax office employees claim the $276 million Powerball prize at the West Virginia Lottery Offices in Charleston, West Virginia. Do you think these women's prestige will rise as a result of winning the lottery?

TABLE 6.1

Max Weber's Three Dimensions of Stratification

wealth	$\longrightarrow$	economic status
power	$\longrightarrow$	political status
prestige	$\longrightarrow$	social status

Each stratum included people of both sexes and all ages. The **superordinate** (the higher or elite) stratum had privileged access to wealth, power, and other valued resources. Access to resources by members of the **subordinate** (lower or underprivileged) stratum was limited by the privileged group.

Open- and Closed-Class Systems

Inequalities, which are built into the structure of state-organized societies, tend to persist across the generations. The extent to which they do or don't is a measure of the openness of the stratification system, the ease of social mobility it permits. **Vertical mobility** is an upward or downward change in a person's social status. A truly **open-class system** would facilitate mobility. Individual achievement and personal merit would determine social rank. Hierarchical social statuses would be achieved on the basis of people's efforts. Ascribed statuses (family background, ethnicity, gender, religion) would be less important.

Stratification has taken many forms, including caste, slavery, and class systems. **Caste systems** are closed, hereditary systems of stratification that often are dictated by religion. Hierarchical social status is ascribed at birth, so that people are locked into their parents' social position. Caste lines are clearly defined, and legal and religious sanctions are applied against those who seek to cross them.

In **slavery,** the most inhumane, coercive, and degrading form of legal stratification, people who are conquered or stolen from their homelands become someone's property. In the Atlantic slave trade millions of human beings were treated as commodities. The plantation systems of the Caribbean, the southeastern United States, and Brazil were based on forced slave labor. Lacking control over the means of production as well as their own destinies, slaves were forced to live and work at their master's whim. Defined as lesser—or less than—human beings, slaves lacked legal rights. They could be sold and resold; their families were split apart. Unlike the poorest nonslaves, enslaved people had nothing to sell—not even their own labor (Mintz 1985).

Modern class structures, featuring forms of stratification more open than slavery, caste systems, or the status systems of ancient states have developed in recent times. Still, socioeconomic stratification continues as a defining feature of all states, archaic or industrial. The elites control a significant part of the means of production, for example, land, herds, water, capital, farms, or factories. Those born at the bottom of the hierarchy have reduced chances of social mobility. Because of elite ownership rights, ordinary people lack free access to resources. Only in states do the elites get to keep their differential wealth. Unlike big men and chiefs, they don't have to give it back to the people whose labor has built and increased it.

States

Table 6.2 summarizes the information presented so far on bands, tribes, chiefdoms, and states. States, remember, are autonomous political units with social classes and a formal government, based on law. States tend to be large and populous, as compared to bands, tribes, and chiefdoms. Certain statuses, systems, and subsystems with specialized functions are found in all states (see Sharma and Gupta 2006). They include the following:

1. *Population control:* fixing of boundaries, establishment of citizenship categories, and the taking of a census.
2. *Judiciary:* laws, legal procedure, and judges.
3. *Enforcement:* permanent military and police forces.
4. *Fiscal:* taxation.

In archaic states, these subsystems were integrated by a ruling system or government composed of civil, military, and religious officials (Fried 1960).

Population Control

To know whom they govern, states typically conduct censuses. States demarcate boundaries that separate them from other societies. Customs agents, immigration officers, navies, and coast guards patrol frontiers. Even nonindustrial states have boundary-maintenance forces. In Buganda, an archaic state on the shores of Lake Victoria in Uganda, the king rewarded military officers with estates in outlying provinces. They became his guardians against foreign intrusion.

TABLE 6.2

Economic Basis of and Political Regulation in Bands, Tribes, Chiefdoms, and States

Sociopolitical Type	Economic Type	Examples	Type of Regulation
Band	Foraging	Inuit, San	Local
Tribe	Horticulture, pastoralism	Yanomami, Masai, Kapauku	Local, temporary, regional
Chiefdom	Intensive horti-culture, pastoral nomadism, agriculture	Qashqai, Polynesia, Cherokee	Permanent, regional
State	Agriculture, industrialism	Ancient Mesopotamia, contemporary U.S., and Canada	Permanent, regional

States also control population through administrative subdivision: provinces, districts, "states," counties, subcounties, and parishes. Lower-level officials manage the populations and territories of the subdivisions.

In nonstates, people work and relax with their relatives, in-laws, and agemates—people with whom they have a personal relationship. Such a personal social life existed throughout most of human history, but food production spelled its eventual decline. After millions of years of human evolution, it took only a few thousand years for the population increase and regulatory problems spawned by food production to lead from tribe to chiefdom to state. With state organization, kinship's pervasive role diminished. Descent groups may continue as kin groups within archaic states, but their importance in political organization declines.

States foster geographic mobility and resettlement, severing longstanding ties among people, land, and kin (Smith 2003). Population displacements have increased in the modern world and with globalization. War, famine, and job seeking across national boundaries churn up migratory currents. People in states come to identify themselves by new statuses, both ascribed and achieved—including ethnicity, residence, occupation, party, religion, and team or club affiliation—rather than only as members of a descent group or extended family.

States also manage their populations by granting different rights and obligations to citizens and noncitizens. Status distinctions among citizens are also common. Many archaic states granted different rights to nobles, commoners, and slaves. Unequal rights within state-organized societies persist in today's world. In recent American history, before the Emancipation Proclamation, there were different laws for enslaved and free people. In European colonies, separate courts judged cases involving only natives and cases involving Europeans. In contemporary America, a military code of justice and court system continue to coexist alongside the civil judiciary.

Judiciary

States have *laws* based on precedent and legislative proclamations. Without writing, laws may be preserved in oral tradition, with justices, elders, and other specialists responsible for remembering them. Oral traditions as repositories of legal wisdom have continued in some nations with writing, such as Great Britain. Laws regulate relations between individuals and groups.

Crimes are violations of the legal code, with specified types of punishment. However, a given act, such as killing someone, may be legally defined in different ways (e.g., as manslaughter, justifiable homicide, or first-degree murder). Furthermore, even in contemporary North America, where justice is supposed to be "blind" to social distinctions, the poor are prosecuted more often and more severely than are the rich.

To handle disputes and crimes, all states have courts and judges. Precolonial African states had subcounty, county, and district courts, plus a high court formed by the king or queen and his or her advisers. Most states allow appeals to higher courts, although people are encouraged to solve problems locally.

A striking contrast between states and nonstates is intervention in family affairs. In states, aspects of parenting and marriage enter the domain of public law. Governments step in to halt blood feuds and regulate previously private disputes. States attempt to curb *internal* conflict, but they aren't always successful. About 85 percent of the world's armed conflicts since 1945 have begun within states—in efforts to overthrow a ruling regime or as disputes over tribal, religious, and ethnic minority issues (see Chatterjee 2004). Only 15 percent have been fights across national borders (Barnaby, ed. 1984). Rebellion, resistance, repression, terrorism, and warfare continue (see Nordstrom 2004; Tishkov 2004). Indeed, recent states have perpetrated some of history's bloodiest deeds.

Enforcement

All states have agents to enforce judicial decisions. Confinement requires jailers. If there is a death penalty, it requires executioners. Agents of the state have the power to collect fines and confiscate property.

As a relatively new form of sociopolitical organization, states have competed successfully with nonstates throughout the world. A government suppresses internal disorder (with police) and guards the nation against external threats (with the military). Military organization helps states subdue neighboring nonstates, but this is not the only reason for the spread of state organization. Although states impose hardships, they also offer advantages. They provide protection from outsiders and preserve internal order. By promoting internal peace, states enhance production. Their economies support massive, dense populations, which supply armies and colonists to promote expansion. A major concern of government is to defend hierarchy, property, and the power of the law.

Fiscal Systems

A financial or **fiscal** system is needed in states to support rulers, nobles, officials, judges, military personnel, and thousands of other specialists. As in the chiefdom, the state intervenes in production, distribution, and consumption. The state may decree that a certain area will produce certain things or forbid certain activities in particular places. Although, like chiefdoms, states also have redistribution (through taxation), generosity and sharing are played down. Less of what comes in flows back to the people.

In nonstates, people customarily share with relatives, but residents of states face added obligations to bureaucrats and officials. Citizens must turn over a substantial portion of what they produce to the state. Of the resources that the state collects, it reallocates part for the general good and uses another part (often larger) for the elite.

The state does not bring more freedom or leisure to the common people, who usually work harder than do people in nonstates. They may be called on to build monumental public works. Some of these projects, such as dams and irrigation systems, may be economically necessary. People also build temples, palaces, and tombs for the elites.

Markets and trade usually are under at least some state control, with officials overseeing distribution and exchange, standardizing weights and measures, and collecting taxes on goods passing into or through the state. Taxes support government and the ruling class, which is clearly separated from the common people in regard to activities, privileges, rights, and obligations. Taxes also support the many specialists—administrators, tax collectors, judges, lawmakers, generals, scholars, and priests. As the state matures, the segment of the population freed from direct concern with subsistence grows.

ANTHROPOLOGY TODAY

Yanomami Update: Venezuela Takes Charge, Problems Arise

Never have people lived in isolation from other human beings. People have been linked through cultural practices including marriage, religion (e.g., the missionization described here), trade, travel, exploration, warfare, and conquest. As is described below, local people today must heed not only their own customs but also laws, policies, and decisions made by outsiders. As you read this account, pay attention to the various interest groups involved and how their goals and wishes might clash. Also consider the levels of political regulation (local, regional, national, and international) that determine how contemporary people such as the Yanomami live their lives and maintain their health, autonomy, and cultural traditions. Consider as well the effectiveness of Yanomami leaders in dealing with agents of the Venezuelan state.

PUERTO AYACUCHO, Venezuela—Three years after President Hugo Chávez expelled American missionaries from the Venezuelan Amazon, accusing them of using proselytism of remote tribes as a cover for espionage, resentment is festering here over what some tribal leaders say was official negligence. . . .

Some leaders of the Yanomami, one of South America's largest forest-dwelling tribes, say that 50 people in their communities in the southern rain forest have died since the expulsion of the missionaries in 2005 because of recurring shortages of medicine and fuel, and unreliable transportation out of the jungle to medical facilities.

Mr. Chávez's government disputes the claims and points to more spending than ever on social welfare programs for the Yanomami. The spending is part of a broader plan to assert greater military and social control over expanses of rain forest that are viewed as essential for Venezuela's sovereignty. . . .

In recent interviews here, government officials contended that the Yanomami could be exaggerating their claims to win more resources from the government and undercut its authority in the Amazon. . . .

The Yanomami claims come amid growing concern in Venezuela over indigenous health care after a scandal erupted in August over a tepid official response to a mystery disease that killed 38 Warao Indians in the country's northeast.

"This government makes a big show of helping the Yanomami, but rhetoric is one thing and reality another," said Ramón González, 49, a Yanomami leader from the village of Yajanamateli who traveled recently to Puerto Ayacucho, the capital of Amazonas State, to ask military officials and civilian doctors for improved health care.

"The truth is that Yanomami lives are still considered worthless," said Mr. González. "The boats, the planes, the money, it's all for the criollos, not for us," he said, using a term for nonindigenous Venezuelans. . . .

There are about 26,000 Yanomami in the Amazon rain forest, in Venezuela and Brazil, where they subsist as seminomadic hunters and cultivators of crops like manioc and bananas.

The elites of archaic states reveled in the consumption of *sumptuary goods*—jewelry, exotic food and drink, and stylish clothing reserved for, or affordable only by, the rich. Peasants' diets suffered as they struggled to meet government demands. Commoners perished in territorial wars that had little relevance to their own needs. Are any of these observations true of contemporary states?

They remain susceptible to ailments for which they have weak defenses, including respiratory diseases and drug-resistant strains of malaria. In Puerto Ayacucho, they can be seen wandering through the traffic-clogged streets, clad in the modern uniform of T-shirts and baggy pants, toting cellphones. . . .

Mr. González and other Yanomami leaders provided the names of 50 people, including 22 children, who they said died from ailments like malaria and pneumonia after the military limited civilian and missionary flights to their villages in 2005. The military replaced the missionaries' operations with its own fleet of small planes and helicopters, but critics say the missions were infrequent or unresponsive.

The Yanomami leaders said they made the list public after showing it to health and military officials and receiving a cold response. "They told us we should be grateful for the help we're already being given," said Eduardo Mejía, 24, a Yanomami leader from the village of El Cejal.

"The missionaries were in Amazonas for 50 years, creating dependent indigenous populations in some places, so their withdrawal was bound to have positive and negative effects," said Carlos Botto, a senior official with Caicet, a government research institute that focuses on tropical diseases.

"But one cannot forget that the Yanomami and other indigenous groups have learned how to exert pressure on the government in order to receive food or other benefits," he said. "This does not mean there aren't challenges in providing them with health care, but caution is necessary with claims like these."

The dispute has also focused attention on an innovative government project created in late 2005, the Yanomami Health Plan. With a staff of 46, it trains some Yanomami to be health workers in their villages while sending doctors into the jungle to provide health care to remote communities.

"We have 14 doctors in our team, with 11 trained in Cuba for work in jungle areas," said Meydell Simancas, 32, a tropical disease specialist who directs the project from a compound here once owned by New Tribes Mission.

Dr. Simancas said that more than 20 Yanomami had been trained as paramedics, and that statistics showed that doctors had increased immunizations and programs to control malaria and river blindness across Amazonas.

The Yanomami leaders complaining of negligence acknowledged Dr. Simancas's good intentions. But they said serious problems persisted in coordinating access to doctors and medicine with the military, which the Yanomami and government doctors both rely on for travel in and out of the rain forest. . . .

Yanomami leaders point to what they consider to be a broad pattern of neglect and condescension from public officials. . . .

Summary

1. Although no ethnographer has been able to observe a polity uninfluenced by some state, many anthropologists use a sociopolitical typology that classifies societies as bands, tribes, chiefdoms, or states. Foragers tended to live in egalitarian, band-organized, societies. Personal networks linked individuals, families, and bands. Band leaders were first among equals, with no sure way to enforce decisions. Disputes rarely arose over strategic resources, which were open to all.

2. Political authority and power increased with the growth in population size and density and in the scale of regulatory problems. More people mean more relations among individuals and groups to regulate. Increasingly complex economies pose further regulatory problems.

3. Heads of horticultural villages are local leaders with limited authority. They lead by example and persuasion. Big men have support and authority beyond a single village. They are regional regulators, but temporary ones. In organizing a feast, they mobilize labor from several villages. Sponsoring such events leaves them with little wealth but with prestige and a reputation for generosity.

4. Age and gender also can be used for regional political integration. Among North America's Plains Indians, men's associations (pantribal sodalities) organized raiding and buffalo hunting. Such men's associations tend to emphasize the warrior grade. They serve for offense and defense when there is intertribal raiding for animals. Among pastoralists, the degree of authority and political organization reflects population size and density, interethnic relations, and pressure on resources.

5. The state is an autonomous political unit that encompasses many communities. Its government collects taxes, drafts people for work and war, and decrees and enforces laws. The state is a form of sociopolitical organization based on central government and social stratification—a division of society into classes. Early states are known as archaic, or nonindustrial, states, in contrast to modern industrial nation-states.

6. Unlike tribes, but like states, chiefdoms had permanent regional regulation and differential access to resources. But chiefdoms lacked stratification. Unlike states, but like bands and tribes, chiefdoms were organized by kinship, descent, and marriage. Chiefdoms emerged in several areas, including the circum-Caribbean, lowland Amazonia, the southeastern United States, and Polynesia.

7. Weber's three dimensions of stratification are wealth, power, and prestige. In early states—for the first time in human history—contrasts in wealth, power, and prestige between entire groups of men and women came into being. A socioeconomic stratum includes people of both sexes and all ages. The superordinate—higher or elite—stratum enjoys privileged access to resources.

8. Certain systems are found in all states: population control, judiciary, enforcement, and fiscal. These are integrated by a ruling system or government composed of civil, military, and religious officials. States conduct censuses and demarcate boundaries. Laws are based on precedent and legislative proclamations. Courts

and judges handle disputes and crimes. A police force maintains internal order, as a military defends against external threats. A financial or fiscal system supports rulers, officials, judges, and other specialists.

Key Terms

achieved status (p. 122)

age set (p. 125)

ascribed status (p. 122)

band (p. 116)

big man (p. 121)

caste systems (p. 132)

chiefdom (p. 116)

conflict resolution (p. 118)

differential access (p. 130)

fiscal (p. 135)

law (p. 119)

office (p. 128)

open-class system (p. 132)

pantribal sodality (p. 124)

power (p. 131)

prestige (p. 131)

slavery (p. 132)

sociopolitical typology (p. 116)

state (p. 116)

status (p. 122)

stratification (p. 131)

subordinate (p. 132)

superordinate (p. 132)

tribe (p. 116)

vertical mobility (p. 132)

village head (p. 120)

wealth (p. 131)

 Go to our Online Learning Center website at **www.mhhe.com/kottak** for Internet resources directly related to the content of this chapter.

Families, Kinship, and Marriage

The societies anthropologists traditionally have studied have stimulated a strong interest in families, along with larger systems of kinship and marriage. The wide web of kinship—as vitally important in daily life in nonindustrial societies as work outside the home is in our own—has become an essential part of anthropology because of its importance to the people we study. We are ready to take a closer look at the systems of kinship and marriage that have organized human life for much of our history.

Ethnographers quickly recognize social divisions, or groups, within any society they study. They learn about significant groups by observing their activities and membership. Often people live in the same village or neighborhood or work, socialize, or celebrate together because they are related in some way. A significant kin group might consist of descendants of the same grandfather. These people live in neighboring houses, farm adjoining fields, and help each other in daily tasks. Groups based on other kin links get together less often in that society.

The nuclear family (parents and children) is one kind of kin group that is widespread in human societies. Other kin groups include extended families (families consisting of three or more generations) and descent groups—lineages and clans.

Much of kinship is *culturally constructed,* that is, based on learning and variable from culture to culture (Schneider 1967; McKinnon 2005). Different societies have different kinds of families, households, kin groups, marriage customs, and living arrangements. Consider the term *family,* which is basic, familiar (so much so it even shares its root with *familiar*), and difficult to define in a way that applies to all cultures. A **family** is a group of people (e.g., parents, children, siblings, grandparents, grand-children, uncles, aunts, nephews, nieces, cousins, spouses, siblings-in-law, parents-in-law, children-in-law) who are considered to be related in some way, for example, by "blood" (common ancestry or descent) or marriage. Some families, such as the nuclear family, are residentially based; its members live together. Others are not; they live apart but come together for family reunions of various sorts from time to time.

Consider a striking contrast between the United States and Brazil, the two most populous countries of the Western Hemisphere, in the meaning and role of family. American adults usually define their family as consisting of their spouse and children. However, when middle-class Brazilians talk about their family (*família*), they mean their parents, siblings, aunts, uncles, grandparents, and cousins. Later they add their children, but rarely the husband or wife, who has his or her own family. The children are shared by the two families. Because middle-class Americans typically lack an extended family support system, marriage assumes more importance. The husband–wife relationship is supposed to take precedence over either spouse's relationship with his or her own parents. This places a significant strain on North American marriages.

Living in a less mobile society, Brazilians stay in closer face-to-face contact with their relatives, including members of the extended family, than North Americans do. Residents of Rio de Janeiro and São Paulo, two of South America's largest cities, are reluctant to leave those urban centers to live away from family and friends. Brazilians find it hard to imagine, and unpleasant to live in, social worlds without relatives. Contrast this with a characteristic American theme: learning to live with strangers.

Families

Nuclear and Extended Families

A nuclear family is *impermanent;* it lasts only as long as the parents and children remain together. Most people belong to at least two nuclear families at different times in their lives. They are born into a family consisting of their parents and siblings. When they reach adulthood, they may marry and establish a nuclear family that includes the spouse and eventually children. Since most societies permit divorce, some people establish more than one family through marriage.

Anthropologists distinguish between the **family of orientation** (the family in which one is born and grows up) and the **family of procreation** (formed when one marries and has children). From the individual's point of view, the critical relation-ships are with parents and siblings in the family of orientation and with spouse and children in the family of procreation. In Brazil, as we just saw, the family of orienta-tion predominates, whereas in the United States it is the family of procreation.

In most societies, relations with nuclear family members (parents, siblings, and children) take precedence over relations with other kin. Nuclear family organi-zation is very widespread but not universal, and its significance in society differs greatly from one place to another. In a few societies, such as the classic Nayar case described below, nuclear families are rare or nonexistent. In others, the nuclear family plays no special role in social life. Other social units—most notably descent groups and extended families—can assume many of the functions otherwise associated with the nuclear family.

Consider an example from the former Yugoslavia. Traditionally, among the Muslims of western Bosnia (Lockwood 1975), nuclear families lacked autonomy. Several such families lived in an extended family household called a *zadruga*. The zadruga was headed by a male household head and his wife, the senior woman. It included married sons and their wives and children, and unmarried sons and daughters. Each nuclear family had a sleeping room, decorated and partly furnished from the bride's trousseau. However, possessions—even clothing and trousseau items—were shared by zadruga members. Such a residential unit is known as a *patrilocal* extended family because each couple resides in the husband's father's household after marriage.

The zadruga took precedence over its component units. There were three successive meal settings—for men, women, and children, respectively. Traditionally, all children over the age of 12 slept together in boys' or girls' rooms. When a woman wished to visit another village, she sought the permission of the male zadruga head. Although men usually felt closer to their own children than to those of their brothers, they were obliged to treat them equally. Children were disciplined by any adult in the household. When a nuclear family broke up, children under age 7 went with the mother. Older children could choose between their parents. Children were considered part of the household where they were born even if their mother left. One widow who remarried had to leave her five children, all over the age of 7, in their father's zadruga, now headed by his brother.

Another example of an alternative to the nuclear family is provided by the Nayars (or Nair), a large and powerful caste on the Malabar Coast of southern India (Gough 1959; Shivaram 1996). Their traditional kinship system was matrilineal (descent traced only through females). Nayar lived in matrilineal extended family compounds called *tarawads*. The tarawad was a residential complex with several buildings, its own temple, granary, water well, orchards, gardens, and land holdings. Headed by a senior woman, assisted by her brother, the tarawad housed her siblings, sisters' children, and other matrikin—matrilineal relatives.

Traditional Nayar marriage seems to have been hardly more than a formality: a kind of coming-of-age ritual. A young woman would go through a marriage ceremony with a man, after which they might spend a few days together at her tarawad. Then the man would return to his own tarawad, where he lived with his sisters, aunts, and other matrikin. Nayar men belonged to a warrior class, who left home regularly for military expeditions, returning permanently to their tarawad on retirement. Nayar women could have multiple sexual partners. Children became members of the mother's tarawad; they were not considered to be relatives of their biological father. Indeed, many Nayar children didn't even know who their biological father (genitor) was. Child care was the responsibility of the tarawad. Nayar society therefore reproduced itself biologically without the nuclear family.

Unable to survive economically as nuclear family units, relatives may band together in an expanded family household and pool their resources. This photo, taken in 2002 in Munich, Germany, shows German Roma, or Gypsies. Together with her children and grandchildren, this grandmother resides in an expanded family household.

Industrialism and Family Organization

For many Americans and Canadians, the nuclear family is the only well-defined kin group. Family isolation arises from geographic mobility, which is associated with industrialism, so that a nuclear family focus is characteristic of many modern nations. Born into a family of orientation, North Americans leave home for college or work, and the break with parents is under way. Selling our labor on the market, we often move to places where jobs are available. Eventually most North Americans marry and start a family of procreation.

Many married couples live hundreds of miles from their parents. Their jobs have determined where they live. Such a postmarital residence pattern is **neolocality:** Married couples are expected to establish a new place of residence—a "home of their own." Among middle-class North Americans, neolocal residence is both a cultural preference and a statistical norm. Most middle-class Americans eventually establish households and nuclear families of their own.

There are significant differences between middle-class and poorer North Americans. For example, in the lower class the incidence of *expanded family households* (those that include nonnuclear relatives) is greater than it is in the middle class. When an expanded family household includes three or more generations, it is an **extended family household,** such as the zadruga. Another type of expanded family is the *collateral household,* which includes siblings and their spouses and children.

In contemporary North America, single-parent families have increased at a rapid rate. In 1960, 88 percent of American children lived with both parents, compared with 68 percent today. This divorced mom, Valerie Jones, enjoys a candlelight dinner with her kids. What do you see as the main differences between nuclear families and single-parent families?

The higher proportion of expanded family households among poorer Americans has been explained as an adaptation to poverty (Stack 1975). Unable to survive economically as nuclear family units, relatives band together in an expanded household and pool their resources. Adaptation to poverty causes kinship values and attitudes to diverge from middle-class norms. Thus, when North Americans raised in poverty achieve financial success, they often feel obligated to provide financial help to a wide circle of less fortunate relatives (see Willie 2003).

Changes in North American Kinship

Although the nuclear family remains a cultural ideal for many Americans, Table 7.1 and Figure 7.1 show that nuclear families accounted for just 22.5 percent of American households in 2007. Other domestic arrangements now outnumber the "traditional" American household more than four to one. There are several reasons for this changing household composition. Women increasingly are joining men in the cash workforce. This often removes them from their family of orientation while making it economically feasible to delay marriage. Furthermore, job demands compete with romantic attachments. The median age at first marriage for American women rose from 21 years in 1970 to 26 in 2008. For men the comparable ages were 23 and 27 (U.S. Census Bureau 2009).

Also, the U.S. divorce rate has risen, making divorced Americans much more common today than they were in 1970. U.S. Census Bureau figures show that between

TABLE 7.1

Changes in Family and Household Organization in the United States, 1970 versus 2007

	1970	2007
Numbers:		
Total number of households	63 million	116 million
Number of people per household	3.1	2.6
Percentages:		
Married couples living with children	40%	23%
Family households	81%	68%
Households with five or more people	21%	10%
People living alone	17%	27%
Percentage of single-mother families	5%	12%
Percentage of single-father families	0%	4%
Households with own children under 18	45%	32%

SOURCES: From U.S. Census data in J. M. Fields, "America's Families and Living Arrangements: 2003," *Current Population Reports*, P20-553, November 2004, http://www.census.gov/prod/2004pubs/p20-553.pdf, p. 4; J. M. Fields and L. M. Casper, "America's Families and Living Arrangements: Population Characteristics, 2000," *Current Population Reports*, P20-537, June 2001, http://www.census.gov/prod/2001pubs/p20-537.pdf; U.S. Census Bureau, *Statistical Abstract of the United States 2009*, Tables 58, 60, 63, http://www.census.gov/compendia/statab/2009edition.html.

1970 and 2007 the number of divorced Americans quintupled—some 23 million in 2007 versus 4.3 million in 1970. (Note, however, that each divorce creates two divorced people.) Table 7.2 shows the ratio of divorces to marriages in the United States for selected years between 1950 and 2006. The major jump in the American divorce rate took place between 1960 and 1980. During that period the ratio of divorces to marriage doubled. Since 1980 the ratio has stayed the same, slightly below 50 percent. That is, each year there are about half as many new divorces as there are new marriages.

The rate of growth in single-parent families also has outstripped population growth, quintupling from fewer than 4 million in 1970 to 19 million in 2007. (The overall American population in 2007 was 1.5 times its size in 1970.) The percentage (22.6 percent) of children living in fatherless (mother-headed, no resident dad) households in 2007 was more than twice the 1970 rate, while the percentage (3.2 percent) in motherless (father-headed, no resident mom) homes increased fourfold. About 57 percent of American women and 60 percent of American men were currently married in 2006, versus 60 and 65 percent, respectively, in 1970 (Fields 2004; Fields and Casper 2001; *Statistical Abstract of the United States 2009*). Recent census data also reveal that more American women are now living without a husband than with one. In 2005, 51 percent of women said they were living without a spouse, compared with 35 percent in 1950 and 49 percent in 2000 (Roberts et al. 2007). To be sure, contemporary Americans maintain social lives through work, friendship, sports, clubs, religion, and organized social activities. However, the growing isolation from kin that these figures suggest may well be unprecedented in human history.

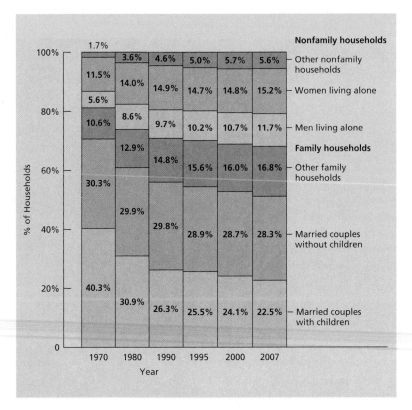

FIGURE 7.1   *Households by Type: Selected Years, 1970 to 2007 (percent distribution).*

SOURCES: J. M. Fields, "America's Families and Living Arrangements: 2003," *Current Population Reports,* P20-553, November 2004, http://www.census.gov/prod/2004pubs/p20-553.pdf, p. 4; *Statistical Abstract of the United States* 2009, Table 58, p. 52, and Table 60, p. 53, http://www.census.gov/compendia/statab/2009edition.html.

TABLE 7.2

Ratio of Divorces to Marriages per 1,000 U.S. Population, Selected Years, 1950–2006

1950	1960	1970	1980	1990	2000	2006
23%	26%	33%	50%	48%	49%	48%

SOURCE: *Statistical Abstract of the United States 2009,* Table 77, p. 63, http://www.census.gov/compendia/statab/2009edition.html.

TABLE 7.3

Household and Family Size in the United States and Canada, 1980 versus 2007

	1980	2007
Average family size:		
United States	3.3	3.1
Canada	3.4	3.0
Average household size:		
United States	2.9	2.6
Canada	2.9	2.6

SOURCES: J. M. Fields, "America's Families and Living Arrangements: 2003," *Current Population Reports,* P20-553, November 2004, http://www.census.gov/prod/2004pubs/p20-553.pdf, pp. 3–4; U.S. Census Bureau, *Statistical Abstract of the United States,* 2009, Table 58, p. 52; *Statistics Canada,* 2006 Census, http://www12.statcan.ca/english/census06/data/topics/, http://www40.statcan.ca/101/cst01/famil532.

Table 7.3 documents similar changes in family and household size in the United States and Canada between 1980 and 2007. Those figures confirm a general trend toward smaller families and living units in North America. This trend is also detectable in Western Europe and other industrial nations.

Immigrants often are shocked by what they perceive as weak kinship bonds and lack of proper respect for family in contemporary North America. In fact, most of the people whom middle-class North Americans see every day are either nonrelatives or members of the nuclear family. On the other hand, Stack's (1975) study of welfare-dependent families in a ghetto area of a midwestern city shows that regular sharing with nonnuclear relatives is an important strategy that the urban poor use to adapt to poverty.

The Family among Foragers

Foraging societies are far removed from industrial nations in terms of social complexity, but they do feature geographic mobility, which is associated with nomadic or seminomadic hunting and gathering. Here again, the nuclear family often is the most significant kin group, although in no foraging society is it the only group based on kinship. The two basic social units of traditional foraging societies are the nuclear family and the band.

Unlike middle-class couples in industrial nations, foragers don't usually reside neolocally. Instead, they join a band in which either the husband or the wife has relatives. However, couples and families may move from one band to another several times. Although nuclear families are ultimately as impermanent among foragers as they are in any other society, they usually are more stable than bands are.

Many foraging societies lacked year-round band organization. The Native American Shoshone of Utah and Nevada provide an example. The resources available to the Shoshone were so meager that for most of the year families traveled alone through the countryside hunting and gathering. In certain seasons families assembled to hunt cooperatively as a band, but after just a few months together they dispersed.

In neither industrial nor foraging economies are people permanently tied to the land. The mobility and the emphasis on small, economically self-sufficient family units promote the nuclear family as a basic kin group in both types of societies.

Descent

We've seen that the nuclear family is important in industrial nations and among foragers. The analogous group among nonindustrial food producers is the descent group. A **descent group** is a *permanent* social unit whose members claim common ancestry. Descent group members believe they all descend from those common ancestors. The group endures even though its membership changes, as members are born and die, move in and move out. Often, descent-group membership is determined at birth and is life-long. In this case, it is an ascribed status.

Descent Groups

Descent groups frequently are exogamous (members seek their mates from other descent groups). Two common rules serve to admit certain people as descent-group members while excluding others. With a rule of **patrilineal descent,** people automatically have lifetime membership in their father's group. The children of the group's men join the group, but the children of the group's women are excluded. With **matrilineal descent,** people join the mother's group automatically at birth and stay members throughout life. Matrilineal descent groups therefore include only the children of the group's women. (In Figures 7.2 and 7.3, which show patrilineal and matrilineal

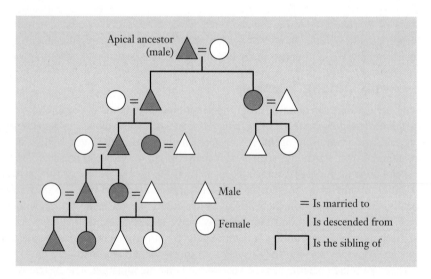

FIGURE 7.2   *A Patrilineage Five Generations Deep* Lineages are based on demonstrated descent from an apical ancestor. With patrilineal descent, children of the group's men (shaded) are included as descent-group members. Children of the group's women are excluded; they belong to *their* father's patrilineage.

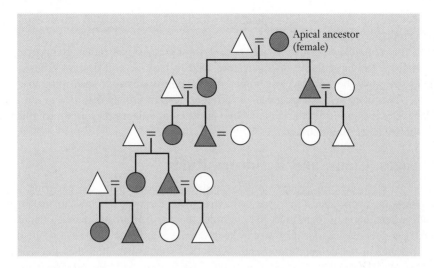

FIGURE 7.3   *A Matrilineage Five Generations Deep* Matrilineages are based on
demonstrated descent from a female ancestor. Only the children of the group's women
(shaded) belong to the matrilineage. The children of the group's men are excluded;
they belong to *their* mother's matrilineage.

descent groups, respectively, the triangles stand for males and the circles for females.)
Matrilineal and patrilineal descent are types of **unilineal descent.** This means the
descent rule uses one line only, either the male or the female line. Patrilineal descent
is much more common than matrilineal descent is. In a sample of 564 societies (Murdock
1957), about three times as many were found to be patrilineal (247 to 84).

How do lineages and clans differ? A lineage uses *demonstrated descent.* Members descend from the same *apical ancestor,* the person who stands at the apex,
or top, of the common genealogy. For example, Adam and Eve are the apical ances-
tors of the biblical Jews, and, according to the Bible, of all humanity. Since Eve is
said to have come from Adam's rib, Adam stands as the original apical ancestor for
the patrilineal genealogy laid out in the Bible.

How do lineages and clans differ? A lineage uses *demonstrated descent.* Members recite the names of their forebears from the apical ancestor through the present.
(This doesn't mean their recitations are accurate, only that lineage members think they
are.) In the Bible the litany of men who "begat" other men is a demonstration of
genealogical descent for a large patrilineage that ultimately includes Jews and Arabs
(who share Abraham as their last common apical ancestor).

Unlike lineages, clans use *stipulated descent.* Clan members merely say they
descend from the apical ancestor, without trying to trace the actual genealogical links.
The Betsileo of Madagascar have both clans and lineages. Descent may be demonstrated for the most recent 8–10 generations, then stipulated for the more remote past—
sometimes with mermaids and vaguely defined foreign royalty mentioned among the
founders (Kottak 1980). Like the Betsileo, many societies have both lineages and clans.
In such a case, clans have more members and cover a larger geographical area than

lineages do. Sometimes a clan's apical ancestor is not a human at all but an animal or plant (called a *totem*).

The economic types that usually have descent group organization are horticulture, pastoralism, and agriculture. Such societies tend to have several descent groups. Any one of them may be confined to a single village, but usually they span more than one village. Two or more local branches of different descent groups may live in the same village. Descent groups in the same village or different villages may establish alliances through frequent intermarriage.

Lineages, Clans, and Residence Rules

As we've seen, descent groups, unlike families, are permanent and enduring units, with new members added in every generation. Members have access to the lineage estate, where some of them must live, in order to benefit from and manage that estate across the generations. An easy way to keep members at home is to have a rule about who belongs to the descent group and where they should live after they get married. Patrilineal and matrilineal descent, and the postmarital residence rules that usually accompany them, ensure that about half the people born in each generation will spend their lives on the ancestral estate.

Patrilocality is the rule that when a couple marries, it moves to the husband's community, so that their children will grow up in their father's village. Patrilocality is associated with patrilineal descent. This makes sense. If the group's male members are expected to exercise their rights in the ancestral estate, it's a good idea to raise them on that estate and to keep them there after they marry. This can be done by having wives move to the husband's village, rather than vice versa.

A less common postmarital residence rule, often associated with matrilineal descent, is **matrilocality:** Married couples live in the wife's community, and their children grow up in their mother's village. This rule keeps related women together. Together, patrilocality and matrilocality are known as *unilocal* rules of postmarital residence.

Marriage

"Love and marriage," "marriage and the family": These familiar phrases show how we link the romantic love of two individuals to marriage, and how we link marriage to reproduction and family creation. But marriage is an institution with significant roles and functions in addition to reproduction. What is marriage, anyway?

No definition of marriage is broad enough to apply easily to all societies and situations. A commonly quoted definition comes from *Notes and Queries on Anthropology:*

> Marriage is a union between a man and a woman such that the children born
> to the woman are recognized as legitimate offspring of both partners. (Royal
> Anthropological Institute 1951, p. 111)

This definition isn't valid universally for several reasons. In many societies, marriages unite more than two spouses. Here we speak of *plural marriages,* as when a man weds two (or more) women, or a woman weds a group of brothers—an arrangement called *fraternal polyandry* that is characteristic of certain Himalayan cultures. In the Brazilian community of Arembepe, people can choose among various forms of marital union. Most people live in long-term "common-law" domestic partnerships that are not legally sanctioned. Some have civil marriages, which are licensed and legalized by a justice of the peace. Still others go through religious ceremonies, so they are united in "holy matrimony," although not legally. And some have both civil and religious ties. The different forms of union permit someone to have multiple spouses (e.g., one common-law, one civil, one religious) without ever getting divorced.

Some societies recognize various kinds of same-sex marriages. In Sudan, a Nuer woman could marry a woman if her father had only daughters but no male heirs, who are necessary if his patrilineage is to survive. He might ask his daughter to stand as a son in order to take a bride. This daughter would become the socially recognized husband of another woman (the wife). This was a symbolic and social relationship rather than a sexual one. The "wife" had sex with a man or men (whom her female "husband" had to approve) until she got pregnant. The children born to the wife were accepted as the offspring of both the female husband and the wife. Although the female husband was not the actual *genitor,* the biological father, of the children, she was their *pater,* or socially recognized father. What's important in this Nuer case is *social* rather than *biological paternity.* We see again how kinship is socially constructed. The bride's children were considered the legitimate offspring of her female husband, who was biologically a woman but socially a man, and the descent line continued.

Incest and Exogamy

In nonindustrial societies, a person's social world includes two main categories—friends and strangers. Strangers are potential or actual enemies. Marriage is one of the primary ways of converting strangers into friends, of creating and maintaining personal and political alliances, relationships of affinity. **Exogamy,** the practice of seeking a mate outside one's own group, has adaptive value because it links people into a wider social network that nurtures, helps, and protects them in times of need.

Incest refers to sexual relations with a relative. All cultures have taboos against it. However, although the taboo is a cultural universal, cultures define their kin, and thus incest, differently. When unilineal descent is very strongly developed, the parent who belongs to a different descent group than your own isn't considered a relative. Thus, with strict patrilineality, the mother is not a relative but a kind of in-law who has married a member of your own group—your father. With strict matrilineality, the father isn't a relative because he belongs to a different descent group.

The Lakher of Southeast Asia are strictly patrilineal (Leach 1961). Using the male ego (the reference point, the person in question) in Figure 7.4, let's suppose that ego's father and mother get divorced. Each remarries and has a daughter by a second marriage. A Lakher always belongs to his or her father's group, all the members of which (one's *agnates,* or patrikin) are considered too closely related to marry because they are members of the same patrilineal descent group. Therefore, ego can't marry his father's daughter by the second marriage, just as in contemporary North America it's illegal for half-siblings to marry.

However, in contrast to our society, where all half-siblings are tabooed in marriage, the Lakher would permit ego to marry his mother's daughter by a different

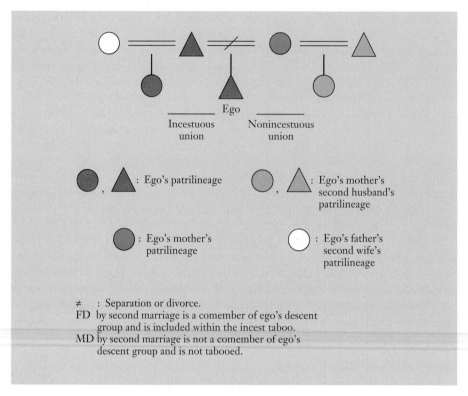

FIGURE 7.4   *Patrilineal Descent-Group Identity and Incest among the Lakher*

father. She is not ego's relative because she belongs to her own father's descent group rather than ego's. The Lakher illustrate very well that definitions of relatives, and therefore of incest, vary from culture to culture.

Although Tabooed, Incest Does Happen

There is no simple or universally accepted explanation for the fact that all cultures ban incest. Do primate studies offer any clues? Research with primates does show that adolescent males (among monkeys) or females (among apes) often move away from the group in which they were born (Rodseth et al. 1991). This emigration reduces the frequency of incestuous unions, but it doesn't eliminate them. DNA testing of wild chimps has confirmed incestuous unions between adult sons and their mothers, who reside in the same group. Human behavior with respect to mating with close relatives may express a generalized primate tendency, in which we see both urges and avoidance.

A cross-cultural study of 87 societies (Meigs and Barlow 2002) revealed that incest did occur in several of them. For example, among the Yanomami, Chagnon reported that "incest, far from being feared, is widely practiced" (1967, p.66). Meyer Fortes observed about the Ashanti: "In the old days it [incest] was punished by death. Nowadays the culprits are heavily fined" (Fortes 1950, p.257). Among 24 Ojibwa individuals from whom he obtained information about incest, A. Irving Hallowell found eight cases of parent–child incest and ten cases of brother–sister incest (Hallowell 1955, pp. 294–95).

In ancient Egypt, sibling marriage apparently was allowed not just for royalty but for commoners as well, in at least some districts. Based on official census records from Roman Egypt (first to third centuries C.E.) preserved on papyrus, 24 percent of all documented marriages in the Arsinoites district were between brothers and sisters. In the second century C.E., the rates were 37 percent for the city of Arsinoe and 19 percent for the surrounding villages. These figures are much higher than any other documented levels of inbreeding among humans (Scheidel 1997).

According to Anna Meigs and Kathleen Barlow (2002), for Western societies with nuclear family organization, father–daughter incest is most common with step-fathers, but it also happens with biological fathers, especially those who were absent or did little caretaking of their daughters in childhood (Williams and Finkelhor 1995). In a carefully designed study, Linda M. Williams and David Finkelhor (1995) found father–daughter incest to be least likely when there was substantial paternal parenting of daughters who were four to five years old. This experience enhanced the father's parenting skills and his feelings of nurturance, protectiveness, and identification with his daughter, thus reducing the risk of incest.

It has been argued (Hobhouse 1915; Lowie 1920/1961) that the incest taboo is universal because incest horror is instinctive: Humans have a genetically programmed disgust toward incest. Because of this feeling, early humans banned it. However, cultural universality doesn't necessarily entail an instinctual basis. Fire making, for example, is a cultural universal, but it certainly isn't an ability transmitted by the genes. Furthermore, if people really did have an instinctive horror of mating with blood relatives, a formal incest taboo would be unnecessary. No one would do it. However, as we have just seen, and as social workers, judges, psychiatrists, and psychologists know, incest is more common than we might suppose.

Endogamy

The practice of exogamy pushes social organization outward, establishing and preserving alliances among groups. In contrast, rules of **endogamy** dictate mating or marriage within a group to which one belongs. Endogamic rules are less common but are still familiar to anthropologists. Indeed, most cultures *are* endogamous units, although they usually do not need a formal rule requiring people to marry someone from their own society. In our own society, classes and ethnic groups are quasi-endogamous groups. Members of an ethnic or religious group often want their children to marry within that group, although many of them do not do so. The outmarriage rate varies among such groups, with some more committed to endogamy than others.

Caste

An extreme example of endogamy is India's caste system, which was formally abolished in 1949, although its structure and effects linger. Castes are stratified groups in which membership is ascribed at birth and is lifelong. Indian castes are grouped into five major categories, or *varna*. Each is ranked relative to the other four, and these categories extend throughout India. Each varna includes a large number of castes (*jati*), each of which includes people within a region who may intermarry. All the jati in a single varna in a given region are ranked, just as the varna themselves are ranked.

Occupational specialization often sets off one caste from another. A community may include castes of agricultural workers, merchants, artisans, priests, and sweepers. The untouchable varna, found throughout India, includes castes whose ancestry, ritual status, and occupations are considered so impure that higher-caste people consider even casual contact with untouchables to be defiling.

The belief that intercaste sexual unions lead to ritual impurity for the higher-caste partner has been important in maintaining endogamy. A man who has sex with a lower-caste woman can restore his purity with a bath and a prayer. However, a woman who has intercourse with a man of a lower caste has no such recourse. Her defilement cannot be undone. Because the women have the babies, these differences protect the purity of the caste line, ensuring the pure ancestry of high-caste children. Although Indian castes are endogamous groups, many of them are internally subdivided into exogamous lineages. Traditionally this meant that Indians had to marry a member of another descent group from the same caste. This shows that rules of exogamy and endogamy can coexist in the same society.

Marital Rights and Same-Sex Marriage

The British anthropologist Edmund Leach (1955) observed that, depending on the society, several kinds of rights are allocated by marriage. According to Leach, marriage can, but doesn't always, accomplish the following:

1. Establish the legal father of a woman's children and the legal mother of a man's.
2. Give either or both spouses a monopoly in the sexuality of the other.
3. Give either or both spouses rights to the labor of the other.
4. Give either or both spouses rights over the other's property.
5. Establish a joint fund of property—a partnership—for the benefit of the children.
6. Establish a socially significant "relationship of affinity" between spouses and their relatives.

The discussion of same-sex marriage that follows will serve to illustrate the six rights just listed by seeing what happens in their absence (see also Stone 2004). What if same-sex marriages, which by and large remain illegal in the United States, were legal? Could a same-sex marriage establish legal parentage of children born to one or both partners after the partnership is formed? In the case of a different-sex marriage, children born to the wife after the marriage takes place usually are defined legally as her husband's regardless of whether he is the genitor.

Nowadays, of course, DNA testing makes it possible to establish paternity, just as modern reproductive technology makes it possible for a lesbian couple to have one or both partners artificially inseminated (see Levine 2008). When same-sex marriage

In Cambridge, Massachusetts, on November 9, 2008, about 75 people protested California's passage of Proposition 8 banning same-sex marriages. The rally was organized through a Facebook listing inviting people to show support for gay marriages in California and to draw national attention to the issue of gay and lesbian civil rights. As of this writing, same-sex marriage is legal in six of the United States and formally banned in three times that number of states.

is legal, the social construction of kinship easily can make both partners parents. If a Nuer woman married to a woman can be the pater of a child she did not father, why can't two lesbians be the *maters* (socially recognized mothers) of a child one of them did not father? And if a married different-sex couple can adopt a child and have it be theirs through the social and legal construction of kinship, the same logic could be applied to a gay male or lesbian couple.

Continuing with Leach's list of the rights transmitted by marriage, same-sex marriage certainly could give each spouse rights to the sexuality of the other. Same-sex marriages, as forms of monogamous commitment, have been endorsed by representatives of many religions, including Unitarians, Quakers (the Society of Friends), and reform Jewish synagogues (Eskridge 1996). In June 2003 a court ruling established same-sex marriages as legal in the province of Ontario, Canada. On June 28, 2005, Canada's House of Commons voted to guarantee full marriage rights to same-sex couples throughout that nation. In the United States six states—Massachusetts, Connecticut, Iowa, Vermont, Maine, and New Hampshire—allowed same-sex marriage as of 2009. Civil unions for same-sex couples are legal in New Jersey. In reaction to same-sex marriage, voters in at least 18 U.S. states have approved measures in their state constitutions defining marriage as an exclusively heterosexual union. On November 4, 2008, Californians voted 52 percent to 48 percent to override the right to same-sex marriage, which the courts had approved earlier that year.

Legal same-sex marriages can easily give each spouse rights to the other spouse's labor and its products. Some societies do allow marriage between members of the same biological sex. Several Native American groups had figures known as *berdaches*. These were biological men who assumed many of the mannerisms, behavior patterns, and tasks of women. Sometimes berdaches married men, who shared the products of their labor from hunting and traditional male roles, as the berdache fulfilled the traditional wifely role. Also, in some Native American cultures, a marriage of a "manly-hearted woman" to another woman brought the traditional male–female division of labor to their household. The manly woman hunted and did other male tasks, while the wife played the traditional female role.

There's no logical reason why same-sex marriage cannot give spouses rights over the other's property. But in the United States, the same inheritance rights that apply to male–female couples usually do not apply to same-sex couples. For instance, even in the absence of a will, property can pass to a widow or a widower without going through probate. The wife or husband pays no inheritance tax. This benefit is not available to gay men and lesbians. When a same-sex partner is in a nursing home, prison, or hospital, the other partner may not have the same visiting rights as would a husband, wife, or biological relative (Weston 1991).

What about Leach's fifth right—to establish a joint fund of property—to benefit the children? Here again, gay and lesbian couples are at a disadvantage. If there are children, property is separately, rather than jointly, transmitted. Some organizations do make staff benefits, such as health and dental insurance, available to same-sex domestic partners.

Finally, there is the matter of establishing a socially significant "relationship of affinity" between spouses and their relatives. In many societies, one of the main roles of marriage is to establish an alliance between groups, in addition to the individual bond. Affinals are relatives through marriage, such as a brother-in-law or mother-in-law. For same-sex couples in contemporary North America, affinal relations are problematic. In an unofficial union, terms like "daughter-in-law" and "mother-in-law" may sound strange. Many parents are suspicious of their children's sexuality and lifestyle choices and may not recognize a relationship of affinity with a child's partner of the same sex.

This discussion of same-sex marriage has been intended to illustrate the different kinds of rights that typically accompany marriage, by seeing what may happen when there is a permanent pair bond without legal sanction. In just six of the United States are such unions fully legal. As we have seen, same-sex unions have been recognized in different historical and cultural settings. In certain African cultures, including the Igbo of Nigeria and the Lovedu of South Africa, women could marry other women. In situations in which women, such as prominent market women in West Africa, are able to amass property and other forms of wealth, they may take a wife. Such marriage allows the prominent woman to strengthen her social status and the economic importance of her household (Amadiume 1987).

Marriage across Cultures

Outside industrial societies, marriage often is more a relationship between groups than one between individuals. We think of marriage as an individual matter. Although the bride and groom usually seek their parents' approval, the final choice (to live together, to marry, to divorce) lies with the couple. The idea of romantic love symbolizes this individual relationship.

In nonindustrial societies, although there can be romantic love (Goleman 1992), marriage is a group concern. People don't just take a spouse; they assume obligations to a group of in-laws. When residence is patrilocal, for example, a woman must leave the community where she was born. She faces the prospect of spending the rest of her life in her husband's village, with his relatives. She may even have to transfer her major allegiance from her own group to her husband's.

Bridewealth and Dowry

In societies with descent groups, people enter marriage not alone but with the help of the descent group. Descent-group members often contribute to the **bridewealth,** a customary gift before, at, or after the marriage from the husband and his kin to the wife and her kin. Another word for bridewealth is *brideprice,* but this term is inaccurate because people with the custom don't usually think of marriage as a commercial relationship between a man and an object that to be bought and sold.

Bridewealth compensates the bride's group for the loss of her companionship and labor. More important, it makes the children born to the woman full members of her husband's descent group. For this reason, the institution also is called **progeny price.** Rather than the woman herself, it is her children who are permanently transferred to the husband's group. Whatever we call it, such a transfer of wealth at marriage is common in patrilineal groups. In matrilineal societies, children are members of the mother's group, and there is no reason to pay a progeny price.

Dowry is a marital exchange in which the wife's group provides substantial gifts to the husband's family. Dowry, best known from India but also practiced in Europe, correlates with low female status. Women are perceived as burdens. When husbands and their families take a wife, they expect to be compensated for the added responsibility.

Bridewealth exists in many more cultures than dowry does, but the nature and quantity of transferred items differ. In many African societies, cattle constitute bridewealth, but the number of cattle given varies from society to society. As the value of bridewealth increases, marriages become more stable. Bridewealth is insurance against divorce.

Imagine a patrilineal society in which a marriage requires the transfer of about 25 cattle from the groom's descent group to the bride's. Michael, a member of descent group A, marries Sarah from group B. His relatives help him assemble the bridewealth. He gets the most help from his close agnates—his older brother, father, father's brother, and closest patrilineal cousins.

The distribution of the cattle once they reach Sarah's group mirrors the manner in which they were assembled. Sarah's father, or her oldest brother if the father is dead, receives her bridewealth. He keeps most of the cattle to use as bridewealth for his sons' marriages. However, a share also goes to everyone who will be expected to help when Sarah's brothers marry.

When Sarah's brother David gets married, many of the cattle go to a third group—C, which is David's wife's group. Thereafter, they may serve as bridewealth to still other groups. Men constantly use their sisters' bridewealth cattle to acquire their own wives. In a decade, the cattle given when Michael married Sarah will have been exchanged widely.

In such societies marriage entails an agreement between descent groups. If Sarah and Michael try to make their marriage succeed but fail to do so, both groups may conclude that the marriage can't last. Here it becomes especially obvious that marriages are relationships between groups as well as between individuals. If Sarah has a younger sister or niece (her older brother's daughter, for example), the concerned parties may agree to Sarah's replacement by a kinswoman.

However, incompatibility isn't the main problem that threatens marriage in societies with bridewealth. Infertility is a more important concern. If Sarah has no children, she and her group have not fulfilled their part of the marriage agreement. If the relationship is to endure, Sarah's group must furnish another woman, perhaps her younger sister, who can have children. If this happens, Sarah may choose to stay in her husband's village. Perhaps she will someday have a child. If she does stay on, her husband will have established a plural marriage.

Most nonindustrial food-producing societies, unlike most industrial nations, allow **plural marriages,** or *polygamy*. There are two varieties; one is common and the other is very rare. The more common variant is **polygyny,** in which a man has more than one wife. The rare variant is **polyandry,** in which a woman has more than one husband. If the infertile wife remains married to her husband after he has taken a substitute wife provided by her descent group, this is polygyny.

Durable Alliances

It is possible to exemplify the group-alliance nature of marriage by examining still another common practice—continuation of marital alliances when one spouse dies.

Sororate

What happens if Sarah dies young? Michael's group will ask Sarah's group for a substitute, often her sister. This custom is known as the **sororate** (Figure 7.5). If Sarah has no sister, or if all her sisters already are married, another woman from her group may be available. Michael marries her, there is no need to return the bridewealth, and the alliance continues.

The sororate exists in both matrilineal and patrilineal societies. In a matrilineal society with matrilocal postmarital residence, a widower may remain with his wife's group by marrying her sister or another female member of her matrilineage (Figure 7.5).

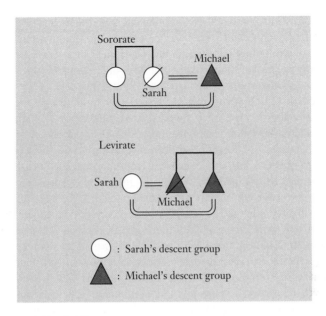

FIGURE 7.5   *Sororate and Levirate*

Levirate

What happens if the husband dies? In many societies, the widow may marry his brother. This custom is known as the **levirate** (Figure 7.5). Like the sororate, it is a continuation marriage that maintains the alliance between descent groups, in this case by replacing the husband with another member of his group. The implications of the levirate vary with age. One study found that in African societies the levirate, although widely permitted, rarely involves cohabitation of the widow and her new husband. Furthermore, widows don't automatically marry the husband's brother just because they are allowed to. Often they prefer to make other arrangements (Potash 1986).

Divorce

In some societies marriages may seem to go on forever, but in our own they are fairly brittle. Ease of divorce varies across cultures. What factors work for and against divorce? As we've seen, marriages that are political alliances between groups are more difficult to dissolve than are marriages that are more individual affairs, of concern mainly to the married couple and their children. Substantial bridewealth may decrease the divorce rate for individuals; replacement marriages (levirate and sororate) also work to preserve group alliances. Divorce tends to be more common in matrilineal than in patrilineal societies. When residence is matrilocal (in the wife's home village), the wife may simply send off a man with whom she's incompatible.

Among the Hopi of the American Southwest, houses were owned by matrilineal clans, with matrilocal postmarital residence. The household head was the senior woman of that household, which also included her daughters and their husbands and children. A son-in-law had no important role there; he returned to his own mother's home for his clan's social and religious activities. In this matrilineal society, women were socially and economically secure and the divorce rate was high. Consider the Hopi of Oraibi (Orayvi) pueblo, northeastern Arizona (Levy 1992; Titiev 1992). In a study of the marital histories of 423 Oraibi women, Mischa Titiev found 35 percent to have been divorced at least once. Jerome Levy found that 31 percent of 147 adult women had been divorced and remarried at least once. For comparison, of all ever-married women in the United States, only 4 percent had been divorced in 1960, 10.7 percent in 1980, and 11.5 percent in 2004. Titiev characterizes Hopi marriages as unstable. Part of this brittleness was due to conflicting loyalties to matrikin versus spouse. Most Hopi divorces appear to have been matters of personal choice. Levy generalizes that, cross-culturally, high divorce rates are correlated with a secure female economic position. In Hopi society women were secure in their home and land ownership and in the custody of their children. In addition, there were no formal barriers to divorce.

Divorce is harder in a patrilineal society, especially when substantial bridewealth would have to be reassembled and repaid if the marriage failed. A woman residing patrilocally (in her husband's household and community) might be reluctant to leave him. Unlike the Hopi, where the kids stay with the mother, in patrilineal, patrilocal societies the children of divorce would be expected to remain with their father, as members of his patrilineage. From the women's perspective this is a strong impediment to divorce.

Among foragers, different factors favor or oppose divorce. What factors work against durable marriages? Since foragers tend to lack descent groups, the political alliance functions of marriage are less important to them than they are to food producers. Foragers also tend to have minimal material possessions. The process of dissolving a joint fund of property is less complicated when spouses do not hold substantial resources in common. What factors work in opposition to divorce among foragers? In societies in which the family is an important year-round unit with a gender-based division of labor, ties between spouses tend to be durable. Also, sparse populations mean few alternative spouses if a marriage doesn't work out.

In contemporary Western societies, we have the idea that romantic love is necessary for a good marriage (see Ingraham 2008). When romance fails, so may the marriage. Or it may not fail, if the other rights associated with marriage, as discussed previously in this chapter, are compelling. Economic ties and obligations to children, along with other factors, such as concern about public opinion, or simple inertia, may keep marriages intact after sex, romance, or companionship fade.

Plural Marriages

In contemporary North America, where divorce is fairly easy and common, **polygamy** (marriage to more than one spouse at the same time) is against the law. Marriage in industrial nations joins individuals, and relationships between individuals can be severed more easily than can those between groups. North Americans are allowed to practice *serial monogamy:* Individuals may have more than one spouse but never, legally, more than one at the same time. As stated earlier, the two forms of polygamy are polygyny and polyandry. Polyandry is practiced in only a few societies, notably among certain groups in Tibet, Nepal, and India. Polygyny is much more common.

Polygyny

We must distinguish between the social approval of plural marriage and its actual frequency in a particular society. Many cultures approve of a man's having more than one wife. However, even when polygyny is encouraged, most people are monogamous, and polygyny characterizes only a fraction of the marriages. Why?

One reason is equal sex ratios. In the United States, about 105 males are born for every 100 females. In adulthood the ratio of men to women equalizes, and eventually it reverses. The average North American woman outlives the average man. In many nonindustrial societies as well, the male-biased sex ratio among children reverses in adulthood.

The custom of men marrying later than women also promotes polygyny. Among Nigeria's Kanuri people (Cohen 1967), men got married between the ages of 18 and 30; women, between 12 and 14. The age difference between spouses meant there were more widows than widowers. Most of the widows remarried, some in polygynous unions. Among the Kanuri and in other polygynous societies, such as the Tiwi of northern Australia, widows made up a large number of the women involved in plural marriages (Hart, Pilling, and Goodale 1988).

In certain societies, the first wife requests a second wife to help with household chores. The second wife's status is lower than that of the first; they are senior and junior wives. The senior wife sometimes chooses the junior one from among her close kinswomen. Among the Betsileo of Madagascar, the different wives always lived in different villages. A man's first and senior wife, called "Big Wife," lived in the village where he cultivated his best rice field and spent most of his time. High-status men with several rice fields and multiple wives had households near each field. They spent most of their time with the senior wife but visited the others throughout the year.

Plural wives can play important political roles in nonindustrial states. The king of the Merina, a populous society in the highlands of Madagascar, had palaces for each of his 12 wives in different provinces. He stayed with them when he traveled through the kingdom. They were his local agents, overseeing and reporting on provincial matters. The king of Buganda, the major precolonial state of Uganda, took hundreds of wives, representing all the clans in his nation. Everyone in the kingdom became the king's in-law, and all the clans had a chance to provide the next ruler. This was a way of giving the common people a stake in the government.

These examples show there is no single explanation for polygyny. Its context and function vary from society to society and even within the same society. Some men are polygynous because they have inherited a widow from a brother. Others have plural wives because they seek prestige or want to increase household productivity. Men and women with political and economic ambitions cultivate marital alliances that serve their aims. In many societies, including the Betsileo of Madagascar and the Igbo of Nigeria, women arrange the marriages.

Shown here in Mali is an Islamic marabout (religious teacher) with his two wives and children. Would you expect most marriages to be polygynous in a society that allows polygyny?

Polyandry

Polyandry is rare and is practiced under very specific conditions. Most of the world's polyandrous peoples live in South Asia—Tibet, Nepal, India, and Sri Lanka. In some of these areas, polyandry seems to be a cultural adaptation to mobility associated with customary male travel for trade, commerce, and military operations. Polyandry ensures there will be at least one man at home to accomplish male activities within a gender-based division of labor. Fraternal polyandry is also an effective strategy when resources are scarce. Brothers with limited resources (in land) pool their resources in expanded (polyandrous) households. They take just one wife. Polyandry restricts the number of wives and heirs. Less competition among heirs means that land can be transmitted with minimal fragmentation.

ANTHROPOLOGY TODAY

Five Wives and 55 Children

Many societies, including Turkey, as described here, that once permitted plural marriage have outlawed it. This news story reports on polygyny, the form of polygamy (plural marriage) in which a man has more than one wife. Anthropologists also have studied the rarer custom of polyandry, in which a woman has more than one husband. Marriage usually is a domestic partnership, but secondary wives may or may not reside near the first wife. In this Turkish case the five wives have their own homes. Polygamy, although formally outlawed, has survived in Turkey since the Ottoman period, when having several wives was viewed as a symbol of power, wealth, and sexual prowess. Unlike the past, when the practice was customary (for men who could afford it) and not illegal, polygamy can put contemporary women at risk. Because their marriages have no official status, secondary wives who are abused or mistreated have no legal recourse. Like all institutions studied by anthropologists, customs involving plural marriage are changing in the contemporary world and in the context of nation-states and globalization.

ISIKLAR, Turkey, July 6—With his 5 wives, 55 children and 80 grandchildren, 400 sheep, 1,200 acres of land and a small army of servants, Aga Mehmet Arslan would seem an unlikely defender of monogamy.

Though banned, polygamy is widespread in the Isiklar region. Yet if he were young again, said Mr. Arslan, a sprightly, potbellied, 64-year-old Kurdish village chieftain, he would happily trade in his five wives for one.

"Marrying five wives is not sinful, and I did so because to have many wives is a sign of power," he said, perched on a divan in a large cushion-filled room at his house, where a portrait of Turkey's first president, Mustafa Kemal Ataturk, who outlawed polygamy in 1926, is prominently displayed.

"But I wouldn't do it again," he added, listing the challenges of having so many kin—like the need to build each wife a house away from the others to prevent friction and his struggle to remember all of his children's names. "I was uneducated back then, and God commands us to be fruitful and multiply."

Though banned by Ataturk as part of an effort to modernize the Turkish republic and empower women, polygamy remains widespread in this deeply religious and rural Kurdish region of southeastern Anatolia, home to one-third of Turkey's 71 million people. The practice is generally accepted under the Koran.

Polygamy is creating cultural clashes in a country struggling to reconcile the secularism of the republic with its Muslim traditions. It also risks undermining Turkey's drive to gain entry into the European Union.

"The E.U. is looking for any excuse not to let Turkey in, and polygamy reinforces the stereotype of Turkey as a backward country," said Handan Coskun, director of a women's center.

Because polygamous marriages are not recognized by the state—imams who conduct them are subject to punishment—the wives have no legal status, making them vulnerable when marriages turn violent. Yet the local authorities here typically turn a blind eye because the practice is viewed as a tradition. . . .

In Turkey, polygamy experts explain the practice as a hangover from the Ottoman period, when harem culture abounded and having several wives was viewed as a symbol of influence, sexual prowess and wealth.

Continued

Remzi Otto, a sociology professor at Dicle University in Diyarbakir, who conducted a survey of 50 polygamous families, said some men took second wives if their first wives could not conceive sons. Some also take widowed women and orphan girls as second wives to give them a social safety net. Love, he added, can also play a role.

"Many men in this region are forced into marriages when they are as young as 13, so finding their own wife is a way to rebel and express their independence," he said.

Isiklar, the remote village where Mr. Arslan is the aga, or chief, can be found at the end of a long dirt road, surrounded by sweeping verdant fields. Most of the local residents share the surname Arslan, which means lion in Turkish and connotes virility.

Mr. Arslan said he regretted his multiple marriages and had forbidden his sons to take more than one wife. He is also educating his daughters. "I have done nothing shameful," he said. "I don't drink. I treat everyone with respect. But having so many wives can create problems."

His biggest headache, he said, stems from jealousy among the wives, the first of whom he married out of love. "My rule is to behave equally toward all of my wives," he said. "But the first wife was very, very jealous when the second wife came. When the third arrived, the first two created an alliance against her. So I have to be a good diplomat."

Summary

1. Kinship and marriage organize social and political life in nonindustrial societies. One widespread kin group is the nuclear family, consisting of a married couple and their children. Other groups, such as extended families and descent groups, may assume functions usually associated with the nuclear family. Nuclear families tend to be especially important in foraging and industrial societies.

2. In contemporary North America, the nuclear family is the characteristic kin group for the middle class. Expanded households and sharing with extended family kin occur more frequently among the poor, who may pool their resources in dealing with poverty. Today, however, even in the American middle class, nuclear family households are declining as single-person households and other domestic arrangements increase.

3. The descent group is a basic kin group among nonindustrial food producers (farmers and herders). Unlike families, descent groups have perpetuity, lasting for generations. Descent-group members share and manage an estate. Lineages are based on demonstrated descent; clans, on stipulated descent. Unilineal (patrilineal and matrilineal) descent is associated with unilocal (patrilocal and matrilocal, respectively) postmarital residence.

4. All societies have an incest taboo. Because kinship is socially constructed, the taboo applies to different relatives in different societies. Human behavior with respect to mating with close relatives may express a generalized primate tendency,

Mr. Arslan, who owns land, real estate and shops throughout the region, said the financial burden of so many offspring could be overwhelming. "When I go to the shoe shop, I buy 100 pairs of shoes at a time," he said. "The clerk at the store thinks I'm a shoe salesman and tells me to go visit a wholesaler."

He also has trouble keeping track of his children. He recently saw two boys fighting in the street and told them they would bring shame on their families. "Do you not recognize me?" one replied. "I am your son." . . .

Women's groups say polygamy is putting women at risk. "These women can be abused, raped, mistreated, and because their marriages are not legal, they have nowhere to turn," said Ms. Coskun, the director of the women's center, which has opened bread-making factories in poor rural areas where women can work and take classes on women's rights . . .

Back in Isiklar, Mr. Arslan acknowledged that polygamy was an outmoded practice. "God has been giving to me because I am giving to my family," he said. "But if you want to be happy, marry one wife."

Source: Dan Bilefsky, "Polygamy Fosters Culture Clashes (and Regrets) in Turkey." From *The New York Times,* July 10, 2006. Copyright © 2006 The New York Times. Reprinted by permission.

illustrating both urges and avoidance. But types, risks, and avoidance of incest also reflect specific kinship structures. Exogamy extends social and political ties outward; endogamy does the reverse. Endogamic rules are common in stratified societies. One extreme example is India, where castes are the endogamous units.

5. The discussion of same-sex marriage, which, by and large, is illegal in the United States, illustrates the various rights that go along with marriage. Marriage establishes the legal parents of children. It gives spouses rights to the sexuality, labor, and property of the other. And it establishes a socially significant "relationship of affinity" between spouses and each other's relatives.

6. In societies with descent groups, marriages are relationships between groups as well as between spouses. With bridewealth, the groom and his relatives transfer wealth to the bride and her relatives. As the bridewealth's value increases, the divorce rate declines. Bridewealth customs show that marriages among nonindustrial food producers create and maintain group alliances. So do the sororate, by which a man marries the sister of his deceased wife, and the levirate, by which a woman marries the brother of her deceased husband.

7. The ease and frequency of divorce vary across cultures. When marriage is a matter of intergroup alliance, as is typically true in societies with descent groups, divorce is less common. A large fund of joint property also complicates divorce.

8. Many societies permit plural marriages. The two kinds of polygamy are polygyny and polyandry. The former involves multiple wives; the latter, multiple husbands. Polygyny is much more common than polyandry.

Key Terms

bridewealth (p. 157)	matrilineal descent (p. 148)
clan (p. 149)	matrilocality (p. 150)
descent group (p. 148)	neolocality (p. 143)
dowry (p. 157)	patrilineal descent (p. 148)
endogamy (p. 153)	patrilocality (p. 150)
exogamy (p. 151)	plural marriages (p. 158)
extended family household (p. 143)	polyandry (p. 158)
family (p. 141)	polygamy (p. 160)
family of orientation (p. 141)	polygyny (p. 158)
family of procreation (p. 141)	progeny price (p. 157)
incest (p. 151)	sororate (p. 158)
levirate (p. 159)	unilineal descent (p. 149)
lineage (p. 149)	

 Go to our Online Learning Center website at **www.mhhe.com/kottak** for Internet resources directly related to the content of this chapter.

C H A P T E R   **8**

Gender

Because anthropologists study biology, society, and culture, they are in a unique position to comment on nature (biological predispositions) and nurture (environment) as determinants of human behavior. Human attitudes, values, and behavior are limited not only by our genetic predispositions—which often are difficult to identify—but also by our experiences during enculturation. Our attributes as adults are determined both by our genes and by our environment during growth and development.

Questions about nature and nurture emerge in the discussion of human sex–gender roles and sexuality. Men and women differ genetically. Women have two X chromosomes, and men have an X and a Y. The father determines a baby's sex because only he has the Y chromosome to transmit. The mother always provides an X chromosome.

The chromosomal difference is expressed in hormonal and physiological contrasts. Humans are sexually dimorphic, more so than some primates, such as gibbons (small tree-living Asiatic apes) and less so than others, such as gorillas and orangutans. **Sexual dimorphism** refers to differences in male and female biology besides the contrasts in breasts and genitals. Women and men differ not just in primary (genitalia and reproductive organs) and secondary (breasts, voice, hair distribution) sexual characteristics, but in average weight, height, strength, and longevity. Women tend to live longer than men and have excellent endurance capabilities. In a given population, men tend to be taller and to weigh more than women do. Of course, there is a considerable overlap between the sexes in terms of height, weight, and physical strength, and there has been a pronounced reduction in sexual dimorphism during human biological evolution.

Just how far, however, do such genetically and physiologically determined differences go? What effects do they have on the way men and women act and are treated

167

in different societies? Anthropologists have discovered both similarities and differences in the roles of men and women in different cultures. The predominant anthropological position on sex–gender roles and biology may be stated as follows:

> The biological nature of men and women [should be seen] not as a narrow
> enclosure limiting the human organism, but rather as a broad base upon which a
> variety of structures can be built. (Friedl 1975, p. 6)

Although in most societies men tend to be somewhat more aggressive than
women are, many of the behavioral and attitudinal differences between the sexes
emerge from culture rather than biology. Sex differences are biological, but gender
encompasses all the traits that a culture assigns to and inculcates in males and females.
"Gender," in other words, refers to the cultural construction of whether one is female,
male, or something else.

Given the "rich and various constructions of gender" within the realm of
cultural diversity, Susan Bourque and Kay Warren (1987) note that the same images
of masculinity and femininity do not always apply. Anthropologists have gathered
systematic ethnographic data about similarities and differences involving gender in
many cultural settings (Bonvillain 2008; Brettell and Sargent 2005; Gilmore 2001;
Kimmel 2007; Mascia-Lees and Black 2000; Nanda 2000; Ward and Edelstein
2008). Anthropologists can detect recurrent themes and patterns involving gender
differences. They also can observe that gender roles vary with environment, economy,

The realm of cultural diversity contains richly different social constructions and expressions of gender
roles, as is illustrated by these Wodaabe male celebrants in Niger. (Look closely for suggestions of
diffusion.) For what reasons do men decorate their bodies in our society?

adaptive strategy, and type of political system. Before we examine the cross-cultural data, some definitions are in order.

Gender roles are the tasks and activities a culture assigns to the sexes. Related to gender roles are **gender stereotypes,** which are oversimplified but strongly held ideas about the characteristics of males and females. **Gender stratification** describes an unequal distribution of rewards (socially valued resources, power, prestige, human rights, and personal freedom) between men and women, reflecting their different positions in a social hierarchy. According to Ann Stoler (1977), the economic determinants of gender status include freedom or autonomy (in disposing of one's labor and its fruits) and social power (control over the lives, labor, and produce of others).

In stateless societies, gender stratification often is more obvious in regard to prestige than it is in regard to wealth. In her study of the Ilongots of northern Luzon in the Philippines, Michelle Rosaldo (1980*a*) described gender differences related to the positive cultural value placed on adventure, travel, and knowledge of the external world. More often than women, Ilongot men, as headhunters, visited distant places. They acquired knowledge of the external world, amassed experiences there, and returned to express their knowledge, adventures, and feelings in public oratory. They received acclaim as a result. Ilongot women had inferior prestige because they lacked external experiences on which to base knowledge and dramatic expression. On the basis of Rosaldo's study and findings in other stateless societies, Ong (1989) argues that we must distinguish between prestige systems and actual power in a given society. High male prestige may not entail economic or political power held by men over their families.

Recurrent Gender Patterns

Ethnologists compare ethnographic data from several cultures (i.e., cross-cultural data) to discover and explain differences and similarities. Data relevant to the cross-cultural study of gender can be drawn from the domains of economics, politics, domestic activity, kinship, and marriage. Table 8.1 shows cross-cultural data from 185 randomly selected societies on the division of labor by gender.

Remembering the discussion in the chapter "Culture" of universals, generalities, and particularities, the findings in Table 8.1 about the division of labor by gender illustrate generalities rather than universals. That is, among the societies known to ethnography, there is a very strong tendency for men to build boats, but there are exceptions. One was the Hidatsa, a Native American group in which the women made the boats used to cross the Missouri River. (Traditionally, the Hidatsa were village farmers and bison hunters on the North American Plains; they now live in North Dakota.) Another exception: Pawnee women worked wood; this is the only Native American group that assigned this activity to women. (The Pawnee, also traditionally Plains farmers and bison hunters, originally lived in what is now central Nebraska and central Kansas; they now live on a reservation in north central Oklahoma.)

Exceptions to cross-cultural generalizations may involve societies or individuals. That is, a society like the Hidatsa can contradict the cross-cultural generalization that

TABLE 8.1

Generalities in the Division of Labor by Gender, Based on Data from 185 Societies

Generally Male Activities	Swing (Male or Female) Activities	Generally Female Activities
Hunting of large aquatic animals (e.g., whales, walrus)	Making fire	Gathering fuel (e.g., firewood)
Smelting of ores	Body mutilation	Making drinks
Metalworking	Preparing skins	Gathering wild vegetal foods
Lumbering	Gathering small land animals	Dairy production (e.g., churning)
Hunting large land animals	Planting crops	Spinning
Working wood	Making leather products	Doing the laundry
Hunting fowl	Harvesting	Fetching water
Making musical instruments	Tending crops	Cooking
Trapping	Milking	Preparing vegetal food (e.g., processing cereal grains)
Building boats	Making baskets	
Working stone	Carrying burdens	
Working bone, horn, and shell	Making mats	
Mining and quarrying	Caring for small animals	
Setting bones	Preserving meat and fish	
Butchering*	Loom weaving	
Collecting wild honey	Gathering small aquatic animals	
Clearing land	Clothing manufacture	
Fishing	Making pottery	
Tending large herd animals		
Building houses		
Preparing the soil		
Making nets		
Making rope		

*All the activities above "butchering" are almost always done by men; those from "butchering" through "making rope" usually are done by men.

SOURCE: Murdock and Provost 1973.

men build boats by assigning that task to women. Or, in a society where the cultural expectation is that only men build boats, a particular woman or women can contradict that expectation by doing the male activity. Table 8.1 shows that in a sample of 185 societies, certain activities ("swing activities") are assigned to either or both men and women. Among the most important of such activities are planting, tending, and harvesting crops.

We'll see below that some societies customarily assign more farming chores to women, whereas others call on men to be the main farm laborers. Among the tasks almost always assigned to men (Table 8.1), some (e.g., hunting large animals on land and sea) seem clearly related to the greater average size and strength of males. Others, such as working wood and making musical instruments, seem more culturally arbitrary. And women, of course, are not exempt from arduous and time-consuming physical labor, such as gathering firewood and fetching water. In Arembepe, Bahia, Brazil, women routinely transported water in five-gallon tins, balanced on their heads, from wells and lagoons located long distances from their homes.

Both women and men have to fit their activities into 24-hour days. Based on cross-cultural data, Table 8.2 shows that the time and effort spent in subsistence activities by men and women tend to be about equal. If anything, men do slightly less subsistence work than women do. Think about how female domestic activities could have been specified in greater detail in Table 8.1. The original coding of the data in Table 8.1 probably illustrates a male bias in that extradomestic activities received much more prominence than domestic activities did. For example, is collecting wild honey (listed in Table 8.1) more necessary or time-consuming than cleaning a baby's bottom (absent from Table 8.1)? Also, notice that Table 8.1 does not mention trade and market activity, in which either or both men and women are active.

Cross-culturally the subsistence contributions of men and women are roughly equal (Table 8.2). But in domestic activities and child care, female labor predominates, as we see in Tables 8.3 and 8.4. Table 8.3 shows that in about half the societies studied, men did virtually no domestic work. Even in societies where men did some

TABLE 8.2

Time and Effort Expended on Subsistence Activities by Men and Women*

More by men	16
Roughly equal	61
More by women	23

*Percentage of 88 randomly selected societies for which information was available on this variable.
SOURCE: Whyte 1978.

TABLE 8.3

Who Does the Domestic Work?*

Males do virtually none	51
Males do some, but mostly done by females	49

*Percentage of 92 randomly selected societies for which information was available on this variable.
SOURCE: Whyte 1978.

domestic chores, the bulk of such work was done by women. Adding together their subsistence activities and their domestic work, women tend to work more hours than men do. Has this changed in the contemporary world?

What about child care? Women tend to be the main caregivers in most societies, but men often play a role. Table 8.4 uses cross-cultural data to answer the question, "Who—men or women—has final authority over the care, handling, and discipline of children younger than four years?" Women have primary authority over infants in two-thirds of the societies. Given the critical role of breast-feeding in ensuring infant survival, it makes sense, for infants especially, for the mother to be the primary caregiver.

There are differences in male and female reproductive strategies. Women work to ensure their progeny will survive by establishing a close bond with each baby. It's also advantageous for a woman to have a reliable mate to ease the child-rearing process and ensure the survival of her children. (Again, there are exceptions, for example, the matrilineal Nayars discussed in the previous chapter). Women can have only so many babies during their reproductive years, which begin after menarche (the advent of first menstruation) and end with menopause (cessation of menstruation.) Men, in contrast, have a longer reproductive period, which can last into the elder years. If they choose to do so, men can enhance their reproductive success by impregnating several women over a longer time period. Although men do not always have multiple mates, they do have a greater tendency to do so than women do (see Tables 8.5, 8.6, and 8.7). Among the societies known to ethnography, polygyny is much more common than polyandry (see Table 8.5).

TABLE 8.4

Who Has Final Authority over the Care, Handling, and Discipline of Infant Children (under Four Years Old)?*

Males have more say	18
Roughly equal	16
Females have more say	66

*Percentage of 67 randomly selected societies for which information was available on this variable.
SOURCE: Whyte 1978.

TABLE 8.5

Does the Society Allow Multiple Spouses?*

Only for males	77
For both, but more commonly for males	4
For neither	16
For both, but more commonly for females	2

*Percentage of 92 randomly selected societies.
SOURCE: Whyte 1978.

TABLE 8.6

Is There a Double Standard with Respect to PREMARITAL Sex*

Yes—females are more restricted	44
No—equal restrictions on males and females	56

*Percentage of 73 randomly selected societies for which information was available on this variable.
SOURCE: Whyte 1978.

TABLE 8.7

Is There a Double Standard with Respect to EXTRAMARITAL Sex*

Yes—females are more restricted	43
Equal restrictions on males and females	55
Males punished more severely for transgression	3

*Percentage of 75 randomly selected societies for which information was available on this variable.
SOURCE: Whyte 1978.

Men mate, within and outside marriage, more than women do. Table 8.6 shows cross-cultural data on premarital sex, and Table 8.7 summarizes the data on extramarital sex. In both cases men are less restricted than women are, although the restrictions are equal in about half the societies studied.

Double standards that restrict women more than men illustrate gender stratification. Several studies have shown that economic roles affect gender stratification. In one cross-cultural study, Sanday (1974) found that gender stratification decreased when men and women made roughly equal contributions to subsistence. She found that gender stratification was greatest when the women contributed either much more or much less than the men did.

Gender among Foragers

In foraging societies gender stratification was most marked when men contributed much *more* to the diet than women did. This was true among the Inuit and other northern hunters and fishers. Among tropical and semitropical foragers, by contrast, gathering usually supplies more food than hunting and fishing do. Gathering generally is women's work. Men usually hunt and fish, but women also do some fishing and may hunt small animals. When gathering is prominent, gender status tends to be more equal than it is when hunting and fishing are the main subsistence activities.

Gender status also is more equal when the domestic and public spheres aren't sharply separated. (*Domestic* means within or pertaining to the home.) Strong differentiation between the home and the outside world is called the **domestic–public dichotomy** or the *private–public contrast*. The outside world can include politics, trade, warfare, or work. Often when domestic and public spheres are clearly separated, public activities have greater prestige than domestic ones do. This can promote gender stratification, because men are more likely to be active in the public domain than women are. Cross-culturally, women's activities tend to be closer to home than men's are. Thus, another reason hunter-gatherers have less gender stratification than food producers do is that the domestic–public dichotomy is less developed among foragers.

Certain roles tend to be more sex-linked than others. Men are the usual hunters and warriors. Given such weapons as spears, knives, and bows, men make better fighters because they are bigger and stronger on average than are women in the same population (Divale and Harris 1976). The male hunter–fighter role also reflects a tendency toward greater male mobility. In foraging societies, women are either pregnant or lactating during much of their childbearing period. Late in pregnancy and after childbirth, carrying a baby limits a woman's movements. However, among the Agta of the Philippines (Griffin and Estioko-Griffin, eds. 1985), women not only gather, but they also hunt with dogs while carrying their babies with them. Still, considering cross-cultural data, women rarely are the primary hunters (Friedl 1975). Warfare, which also requires mobility, is not found in most foraging societies, nor is interregional trade well developed. Warfare and trade are two public arenas that contribute to status inequality of males and females among food producers.

The Ju/'hoansi San illustrate the extent to which the activities and spheres of influence of men and women may overlap among foragers (Draper 1975). Traditional Ju/'hoansi gender roles were interdependent. During gathering, women discovered information about game animals, which they passed on to the men. Men and women spent about the same amount of time away from the camp, but neither worked more than three days a week. The Ju/'hoansi saw nothing wrong in doing the work of the other gender. Men often gathered food and collected water. A general sharing ethos dictated that men distribute meat and that women share the fruits of gathering.

It is among foragers that the public and private spheres are least separate, hierarchy is least marked, aggression and competition are most discouraged, and the rights, activities, and spheres of influence of men and women overlap the most. Our ancestors lived entirely by foraging until 10,000 years ago. Despite the popular stereotype of the club-wielding caveman dragging his mate by the hair, relative gender equality is a much more likely ancestral pattern.

Gender among Horticulturalists

Gender roles and stratification among cultivators vary widely, depending on specific features of the economy and social structure. Demonstrating this, Martin and Voorhies (1975) studied a sample of 515 horticultural societies, representing all parts of the world. They looked at several factors, including descent and postmarital residence, the percentage of the diet derived from cultivation, and the relative productivity of men and women.

TABLE 8.8

Male and Female Contributions to Production in Cultivating Societies

	Horticulture (percentage of 104 societies)	Agriculture (percentage of 93 societies)
Women are primary cultivators	50%	15%
Men are primary cultivators	17	81
Equal contributions to cultivation	33	3

SOURCE: Martin and Voorhies 1975, p. 283.

Women turned out to be the main producers in horticultural societies. In 50 percent of those societies, women did most of the cultivating. In 33 percent, contributions to cultivation by men and women were equal (see Table 8.8). In only 17 percent did men do most of the work. Women tended to do a bit more cultivating in matrilineal compared with patrilineal societies. They dominated horticulture in 64 percent of the matrilineal societies versus 50 percent of the patrilineal ones.

Reduced Gender Stratification—Matrilineal–Matrilocal Societies

Cross-cultural variation in gender status is related to rules of descent and postmarital residence (Friedl 1975; Martin and Voorhies 1975). Among horticulturalists with matrilineal descent and *matrilocality* (residence after marriage with the wife's relatives), female status tends to be high. Matriliny and matrilocality disperse related males, rather than consolidating them. By contrast, patriliny and *patrilocality* (residence after marriage with the husband's kin) keep male relatives together—an advantage given warfare. Matrilineal–matrilocal systems tend to occur in societies where population pressure on strategic resources is minimal and warfare is infrequent.

Women tend to have high status in matrilineal, matrilocal societies for several reasons. Descent-group membership, succession to political positions, allocation of land, and overall social identity all come through female links. Among the matrilineal Malays of Negeri Sembilan, Malaysia (Peletz 1988), matriliny gave women sole inheritance of ancestral rice fields. Matrilocality created solidary clusters of female kin. These Malay women had considerable influence beyond the household (Swift 1963). In such matrilineal contexts, women are the basis of the entire social structure. Although public authority nominally may be assigned to the men, much of the power and decision making actually may belong to the senior women.

Matriarchy

Cross-culturally, anthropologists have described tremendous variation in the roles of men and women, and the power differentials between them. If a patriarchy is a political system ruled by men, what would a matriarchy be? Would a matriarchy be a political

A Minangkabau bride and groom in West Sumatra, Indonesia, where anthropologist Peggy Reeves Sanday has conducted several years of ethnographic field work.

system ruled by women, or a political system in which women play a much more prominent role than men do in social and political organization? Anthropologist Peggy Sanday (2002) has concluded that matriarchies exist, but not as mirror images of patriarchies. The superior power that men typically have in a patriarchy isn't matched by women's equally disproportionate power in a matriarchy. Many societies, including the Minangkabau of West Sumatra, Indonesia, whom Sanday has studied for decades, lack the substantial power differentials that typify patriarchal systems. Minangkabau women play a central role in social, economic, and ceremonial life and as key symbols. The primacy of matriliny and matriarchy is evident at the village level, as well as regionally, where seniority of matrilineal descent serves as a way to rank villages.

The four million Minangkabau constitute one of Indonesia's largest ethnic groups. Located in the highlands of West Sumatra, their culture is based on the coexistence of matrilineal custom and a nature-based philosophy called adat, complemented by Islam, a more recent (16th-century) arrival. The Minangkabau view men and women as cooperative partners for the common good rather than competitors ruled by self-interest. People gain prestige when they promote social harmony rather than by vying for power.

Sanday considers the Minangkabau a matriarchy because women are the center, origin, and foundation of the social order. Senior women are associated with the central pillar of the traditional house, the oldest one in the village. The oldest village in a cluster is called the "mother village." In ceremonies, women are addressed by the term used for their mythical Queen Mother. Women control land inheritance, and couples reside matrilocally. In the wedding ceremony, the wife collects her husband from his household and, with her female kin, escorts him to hers. If there is a divorce, the husband simply takes his things and leaves. Yet despite the special position of women, the Minangkabau matriarchy is not the equivalent of female rule, given the Minangkabau belief that all decision making should be by consensus.

Increased Gender Stratification—
Patrilineal–Patrilocal Societies

Martin and Voorhies (1975) link the decline of matriliny and the spread of the
patrilineal–patrilocal complex (consisting of patrilineality, patrilocality, warfare, and
male supremacy) to pressure on resources. Faced with scarce resources, patrilineal–
patrilocal cultivators such as the Yanomami often wage warfare against other villages.
This favors patrilocality and patriliny, customs that keep related men together in the
same village, where they make strong allies in battle. Such societies tend to have a
sharp domestic–public dichotomy, and men tend to dominate the prestige hierarchy.

In some parts of Papua New Guinea, the patrilineal–patrilocal complex
has extreme social repercussions. Regarding females as dangerous and
polluting, men may segregate themselves in men's houses (such as this
one, located near the Sepik River), where they hide their precious ritual
objects from women. Are there places like this in your society?

Men may use their public roles in warfare and trade and their greater prestige to symbolize and reinforce the devaluation or oppression of women.

The patrilineal–patrilocal complex characterizes many societies in highland Papua New Guinea. Women work hard growing and processing subsistence crops, raising and tending pigs (the main domesticated animal and a favorite food), and doing domestic cooking, but they are isolated from the public domain, which men control. Men grow and distribute prestige crops, prepare food for feasts, and arrange marriages. The men even get to trade the pigs and control their use in ritual.

In densely populated areas of the Papua New Guinea highlands, male–female avoidance is associated with strong pressure on resources (Lindenbaum 1972). Men fear all female contacts, including sex. They think that sexual contact with women will weaken them. Indeed, men see everything female as dangerous and polluting. They segregate themselves in men's houses and hide their precious ritual objects from women. They delay marriage, and some never marry.

By contrast, the sparsely populated areas of Papua New Guinea, such as recently settled areas, lack taboos on male–female contacts. The image of woman as polluter fades, heterosexual intercourse is valued, men and women live together, and reproductive rates are high.

Gender among Agriculturists

When the economy is based on agriculture, women typically lose their role as primary cultivators. Certain agricultural techniques, particularly plowing, have been assigned to men because of their greater average size and strength (Martin and Voorhies 1975). Except when irrigation is used, plowing eliminates the need for constant weeding, an activity usually done by women.

Cross-cultural data illustrate these contrasts in productive roles between agricultural and horticultural economies. Women were the main workers in 50 percent of the horticultural societies surveyed but in only 15 percent of the agricultural groups. Male subsistence labor dominated 81 percent of the agricultural societies but only 17 percent of the horticultural ones (Martin and Voorhies 1975) (see Table 8.8).

With the advent of agriculture, women were cut off from production for the first time in human history. Belief systems started contrasting men's valuable extradomestic labor with women's domestic role, now viewed as inferior. (**Extradomestic** means outside the home; within or pertaining to the public domain.) Changes in kinship and postmarital residence patterns also hurt women. Descent groups and polygyny declined with agriculture, and the nuclear family became more common. Living with her husband and children, a woman was isolated from her kinswomen and cowives. Female sexuality is carefully supervised in agricultural economies; men have easier access to divorce and extramarital sex, reflecting a "double standard."

Still, female status in agricultural societies is not inevitably bleak. Gender stratification is associated with plow agriculture rather than with intensive cultivation per se. Studies of peasant gender roles and stratification in France and Spain (Harding 1975; Reiter 1975), which have plow agriculture, show that people think of the house as the female sphere and the fields as the male domain. However, such a dichotomy is not inevitable, as my own research among Betsileo agriculturists in Madagascar shows.

Betsileo women play a prominent role in agriculture, contributing a third of the hours invested in rice production. They have their customary tasks in the division of labor, but their work is more seasonal than men's is. No one has much to do during the ceremonial season, between mid-June and mid-September. Men work in the rice fields almost daily the rest of the year. Women's cooperative work occurs during transplanting (mid-September through November) and harvesting (mid-March through early May). Along with other members of the household, women do daily weeding in December and January. After the harvest, all family members work together winnowing the rice and then transporting it to the granary.

If we consider the strenuous daily task of husking rice by pounding (a part of food preparation rather than production per se), women actually contribute slightly more than 50 percent of the labor devoted to producing and preparing rice before cooking.

Not just women's prominent economic role but traditional social organization enhances female status among the Betsileo. Although postmarital residence is mainly patrilocal, descent rules permit married women to keep membership in and a strong allegiance to their own descent groups. Kinship is broadly and bilaterally (on both sides—as in contemporary North America) calculated. The Betsileo exemplify Aihwa Ong's (1989) generalization that bilateral (and matrilineal) kinship systems, combined with subsistence economies in which the sexes have complementary roles in food production and distribution, are characterized by reduced gender stratification. Such societies are common among South Asian peasants (Ong 1989).

Traditionally, Betsileo men participate more in politics, but the women also hold political office. Women sell their produce and products in markets, invest in cattle, sponsor ceremonies, and are mentioned during offerings to ancestors. Arranging marriages, an important extradomestic activity, is more women's concern than men's. Sometimes Betsileo women seek their own kinswomen as wives for their sons, reinforcing their own prominence in village life and continuing kin-based female solidarity in the village.

The Betsileo illustrate the idea that intensive cultivation does not necessarily entail sharp gender stratification. We can see that gender roles and stratification reflect not just the type of adaptive strategy but also specific cultural attributes. Betsileo women continue to play a significant role in their society's major economic activity, rice production.

Patriarchy and Violence

Patriarchy describes a political system ruled by men in which women have inferior social and political status, including basic human rights. Barbara Miller (1997), in a study of systematic neglect of females, describes women in rural northern India as "the endangered sex." Societies that feature a full-fledged patrilineal–patrilocal complex, replete with warfare and intervillage raiding, also typify patriarchy. Such practices as dowry murders, female infanticide, and clitoridectomy exemplify patriarchy, which extends from tribal societies such as the Yanomami to state societies such as India and Pakistan.

Although more prevalent in certain social settings than in others, family violence and domestic abuse of women are worldwide problems. Domestic violence certainly occurs in nuclear family settings, such as Canada and the United States. Cities, with their impersonality and isolation from extended kin networks, are breeding groups for domestic violence.

We've seen that gender stratification typically is reduced in matrilineal, matrifocal, and bilateral societies in which women have prominent roles in the economy and social life. When a woman lives in her own village, she has kin nearby to look after and protect her interests. Even in patrilocal polygynous settings, women often count on the support of their cowives and sons in disputes with potentially abusive husbands. Such settings, which tend to provide a safe haven for women, are retracting rather than expanding in today's world, however. Isolated families and patrilineal social forms have spread at the expense of matrilineality. Many nations have declared polygyny illegal. More and more women, and men, find themselves cut off from extended kin and families of orientation.

With the spread of the women's rights movement and the human rights movement, attention to domestic violence and abuse of women has increased. Laws have been passed and mediating institutions established. Brazil's female-run police stations for battered women provide an example, as do shelters for victims of domestic abuse in the United States and Canada. But patriarchal institutions do persist in what should be a more enlightened world.

Gender and Industrialism

The domestic–public dichotomy, which is developed most fully among patrilineal–patrilocal food producers and plow agriculturists, also has affected gender stratification in industrial societies, including the United States and Canada. Gender roles have been changing rapidly in North America. The "traditional" idea that "a woman's place is in the home" actually emerged in the United States as industrialism spread after 1900. Earlier, pioneer women in the Midwest and West had been recognized as fully productive workers in farming and home industry. Under industrialism, attitudes about gendered work came to vary with class and region. In early industrial Europe, men, women, and children had flocked to factories as wage laborers. Enslaved Americans of both sexes had done grueling work in cotton fields. With abolition, southern African American women continued working as field hands and domestics. Poor white women labored in the South's early cotton mills. In the 1890s more than 1 million American women held menial and repetitive unskilled factory positions (Margolis 1984; Martin and Voorhies 1975).

After 1900, European immigration produced a male labor force willing to work for wages lower than those of American-born men. Those immigrant men moved into factory jobs that previously had gone to women. As machine tools and mass production further reduced the need for female labor, the notion that women were biologically unfit for factory work began to gain ground (Martin and Voorhies 1975).

Maxine Margolis (1984, 2000) has shown how gendered work, attitudes, and beliefs have varied in response to American economic needs. For example, wartime shortages of men have promoted the idea that work outside the home is women's patriotic duty. During the world wars the notion that women are unfit for hard physical labor faded. Inflation and the culture of consumption also have spurred female employment. When prices or demand rise, multiple paychecks help maintain family living standards.

During the world wars the notion that women were biologically unfit for hard physical labor faded. Shown here is World War II's famous Rosie the Riveter. Is there a comparable poster woman today? What does her image say about modern gender roles?

The steady increase in female paid employment since World War II also reflects the baby boom and industrial expansion. American culture traditionally has defined clerical work, teaching, and nursing as female occupations. With rapid population growth and business expansion after World War II, the demand for women to fill such jobs grew steadily. Employers also found they could increase their profits by paying women lower wages than they would have to pay returning male war veterans.

Margolis (1984, 2000) contends that changes in the economy lead to changes in attitudes toward and about women. Economic changes paved the way for the contemporary women's movement, which also was spurred by the publication of Betty

TABLE 8.9

Cash Employment of American Mothers, Wives, and Husbands, 1960–2007*

Year	Percentage of Married Women, Husband Present with Children under six	Percentage of All Married Women†	Percentage of All Married Men‡
1960	19	32	89
1970	30	40	86
1980	45	50	81
1990	59	58	79
2007	62	62	77

*Civilian population 16 years of age and older.

†Husband present.

‡Wife present.

SOURCE: *Statistical Abstract of the United States 2009*, Table 576, p. 375; Table 579, p. 376. http://www.census.gov/compendia/statab/2009edition.html.

Friedan's book *The Feminine Mystique* in 1963 and the founding of NOW, the National Organization of Women, in 1966. The movement in turn promoted expanded work opportunities for women, including the goal of equal pay for equal work. Between 1970 and 2007, the female percentage of the American workforce rose from 38 to 46 percent. In other words, almost half of all Americans who work outside the home are women. Over 71 million women now have paid jobs, compared with 82 million men. Women fill more than half (56 percent) of all professional jobs (*Statistical Abstract of the United States 2009*, p. 384). And it's not mainly single women working, as once was the case. Table 8.9 presents figures on the ever-increasing cash employment of American wives and mothers, including those with children under 6 years old.

Note in Table 8.9 that the cash employment of American married men has been falling while that of American married women has been rising. There has been a dramatic change in behavior and attitudes since 1960, when 89 percent of all married men worked, compared with just 32 percent of married women. The comparable figures in 2007 were 77 percent and 62 percent. Ideas about the gender roles of males and females have changed. Compare your grandparents and your parents. Chances are you have a working mother, but your grandmother was more likely a stay-at-home mom. Your grandfather is more likely than your father to have worked in manufacturing and to have belonged to a union. Your father is more likely than your grandfather to have shared child care and domestic responsibilities. Age at marriage has been delayed for both men and women. College educations and professional degrees have increased. What other changes do you associate with the increase in female employment outside the home?

The Feminization of Poverty

Alongside the economic gains of many American women stands an opposite extreme: the feminization of poverty, or the increasing representation of women (and their children) among America's poorest people. Women head over half of U.S. households with incomes below the poverty line. In 1959 female-headed households accounted for just one-fourth of the American poor. Since then that figure has more than doubled.

Married couples are much more secure economically than single mothers are. The average income for married-couple families is more than twice that of families maintained by a single woman. The median one-earner family maintained by a single woman had an annual income of $28,829 in 2006. This was less than one-half the median income ($69,404) of a married-couple household. (*Statistical Abstract of the United States, 2009,* p. 446).

The feminization of poverty isn't just a North American trend. The percentage of female-headed households has been increasing worldwide. In Western Europe, for example, female-headed households rose from 24 percent in 1980 to 31 percent in 1990. The figure ranges from below 20 percent in certain South Asian and Southeast Asian countries to almost 50 percent in certain African countries and the Caribbean (Buvinic 1995).

Why must so many women be solo household heads? Where are the men going, and why are they leaving? Among the causes are male migration, civil strife (men off fighting), divorce, abandonment, widowhood, unwed adolescent parenthood, and, more generally, the idea that children are women's responsibility. Globally, households headed by women tend to be poorer than those headed by men. In one study, the percentage of single-parent families considered poor was 18 percent in Britain, 20 percent in Italy, 25 percent in Switzerland, 40 percent in Ireland, 52 percent in Canada, and 63 percent in the United States.

It is widely believed that one way to improve the situation of poor women is to encourage them to organize. New women's groups can in some cases revive or replace traditional forms of social organization that have been disrupted. Membership in a group can help women to mobilize resources, to rationalize production, and to reduce the risks and costs associated with credit. Organization also allows women to develop self-confidence and to decrease dependence on others. Through such organization, poor women throughout the world are working to determine their own needs and priorities and to change things so as to improve their social and economic situation (Buvinic 1995).

What Determines Gender Variation?

We see that gender roles and stratification have varied widely across cultures and through history. Among many foragers and matrilineal cultivators, there is little gender stratification. Competition for resources leads to warfare and the intensification of production. These conditions favor patriliny and patrilocality. To the extent that women lose their productive roles in agricultural societies, the domestic–public dichotomy is accentuated and gender stratification is sharpened. With industrialism, attitudes about gender vary in the context of female extradomestic employment. Gender is flexible and varies with cultural, social, political, and economic factors. The variability of gender in time and space suggests that it will continue to change. The biology of the sexes is not a narrow enclosure limiting humans but a broad base upon which a variety of structures can be built (Friedl 1975).

Sexual Orientation

Sexual orientation refers to a person's habitual sexual attraction to, and sexual activities with, persons of the opposite sex (*heterosexuality*), the same sex (*homosexuality*), or both sexes (*bisexuality*). *Asexuality*, indifference toward, or lack of attraction to either sex, also is a sexual orientation. All four of these forms are found in contemporary North America, and throughout the world. But each type of desire and experience holds different meanings for individuals and groups. For example, an asexual disposition may be acceptable in some places but may be perceived as a character flaw in others. Male–male sexual activity may be a private affair in Mexico, rather than public, socially sanctioned, and encouraged as among the Etoro (see below) of Papua New Guinea (see also Blackwood and Wieringa, eds. 1999; Boellstorff 2007; Kimmel and Plante 2004; Kottak and Kozaitis 2008; Nanda 2000).

Recently in the United States there has been a tendency to see sexual orientation as fixed and biologically based. There is not enough information at this time to determine the exact extent to which sexual orientation is based on biology. What we can say is that all human activities and preferences, including erotic expression, are at least partially culturally constructed.

In any society, individuals will differ in the nature, range, and intensity of their sexual interests and urges. No one knows for sure why such individual sexual differences exist. Part of the answer probably is biological, reflecting genes or hormones (Wade 2005). Another part may have to do with experiences during growth and development. But whatever the reasons for individual variation, culture always plays a role in molding individual sexual urges toward a collective norm. And such sexual norms vary from culture to culture.

What do we know about variation in sexual norms from society to society, and over time? A classic cross-cultural study (Ford and Beach 1951) found wide variation in attitudes about masturbation, bestiality (sex with animals), and homosexuality. In a single society, such as the United States, attitudes about sex differ over time and with socioeconomic status, region, and rural versus urban residence. However, even in the 1950s, prior to the "age of sexual permissiveness" (the pre-HIV period from the mid-1960s through the 1970s), research showed that almost all American men (92 percent) and more than half of American women (54 percent) admitted to masturbation. In the famous Kinsey report (Kinsey, Pomeroy, and Martin 1948), 37 percent of the men surveyed admitted having had at least one sexual experience leading to orgasm with another male. In a later study of 1,200 unmarried women, 26 percent reported same-sex sexual activities. (Because Kinsey's research relied on nonrandom samples, it should be considered merely illustrative, rather than a statistically accurate representation, of sexual behavior at the time.)

Sex acts with people of the same sex were absent, rare, or secret in only 37 percent of 76 societies for which data were available in the Ford and Beach study (1951). In the others, various forms of same-sex sexual activity were acceptable. Sometimes sexual relations between people of the same sex involved transvestism on the part of one of the partners (see Kulick 1998). Transvestism did not characterize male–male sex among the Sudanese Azande, who valued the warrior role (Evans-Pritchard 1970). Prospective warriors—young men aged 12 to 20—left their families

Neither man nor woman, hijras constitute India's third gender. Many hijras get their income from performing at ceremonies, begging, or prostitution. The beauty contest shown here was organized by an AIDS prevention and relief organization that works with the local hijra community.

and shared quarters with adult fighting men, who paid bridewealth for, and had sex with, them. During this apprenticeship, the young men did the domestic duties of women. Upon reaching warrior status, these young men took their own younger male brides. Later, retiring from the warrior role, Azande men married women. Flexible in their sexual expression, Azande males had no difficulty shifting from sex with older men (as male brides), to sex with younger men (as warriors), to sex with women (as husbands) (see Murray and Roscoe, eds. 1998).

Consider also the Etoro (Kelly 1976), a group of 400 people who subsist by hunting and horticulture in the Trans-Fly region of Papua New Guinea. The Etoro illustrate the power of culture in molding human sexuality. The following account, based on ethnographic field work by Raymond C. Kelly in the late 1960s, applies only to Etoro males and their beliefs. Etoro cultural norms prevented the male anthropologist who studied them from gathering comparable information about female attitudes. Note, also, that the activities described have been discouraged by missionaries. Since there has been no restudy of the Etoro specifically focusing on these activities, the extent to which these practices continue today is unknown. For this reason, I'll use the past tense in describing them.

Etoro opinions about sexuality were linked to their beliefs about the cycle of birth, physical growth, maturity, old age, and death. Etoro men believed that semen was necessary to give life force to a fetus, which was, they believed, implanted in a woman by an ancestral spirit. Sexual intercourse during pregnancy nourished the growing fetus. The Etoro believed that men had a limited lifetime supply of semen. Any sex act leading to ejaculation was seen as draining that supply, and as sapping a man's virility and vitality. The birth of children, nurtured by semen, symbolized a necessary sacrifice that would lead to the husband's eventual death. Heterosexual intercourse, required only for reproduction, was discouraged. Women who wanted too much sex were viewed as witches, hazardous to their husbands' health. Etoro culture allowed heterosexual intercourse only about 100 days a year. The rest of the time it was tabooed. Seasonal birth clustering shows the taboo was respected.

So objectionable was male–female sex that it was removed from community life. It could occur neither in sleeping quarters nor in the fields. Coitus could happen only in the woods, where it was risky because poisonous snakes, the Etoro claimed, were attracted by the sounds and smells of male–female sex.

Although coitus was discouraged, sex acts between men were viewed as essential. Etoro believed that boys could not produce semen on their own. To grow into men and eventually give life force to their children, boys had to acquire semen orally from older men. From the age of 10 until adulthood, boys were inseminated by older men. No taboos were attached to this. Such oral insemination could proceed in the sleeping area or garden. Every three years, a group of boys around the age of 20 was formally initiated into manhood. They went to a secluded mountain lodge, where they were visited and inseminated by several older men.

Male–male sex among the Etoro was governed by a code of propriety. Although sexual relations between older and younger males were considered culturally essential, those between boys of the same age were discouraged. A boy who took semen from other youths was believed to be sapping their life force and stunting their growth. A boy's rapid physical development might suggest he was getting semen from other boys. Like a sex-hungry wife, he might be shunned as a witch.

These sexual practices among the Etoro rested not on hormones or genes but on cultural beliefs and traditions. The Etoro shared a cultural pattern, which Gilbert Herdt (1984) calls "ritualized homosexuality," with some 50 other tribes in Papua New Guinea, especially in that country's Trans-Fly region. These societies illustrate one extreme of a male–female avoidance pattern that is widespread in Papua New Guinea and indeed in many patrilineal–patrilocal societies.

Flexibility in sexual expression seems to be an aspect of our primate heritage. Both masturbation and same-sex sexual activity exist among chimpanzees and other primates. Male bonobos (pygmy chimps) regularly engage in a form of mutual masturbation known as "penis fencing." Females get sexual pleasure from rubbing their genitals against those of other females (de Waal 1997). Our primate sexual potential is molded by culture, the environment, and reproductive necessity. Heterosexual coitus is practiced in all human societies—which, after all, must reproduce themselves—but alternatives also are widespread (Rathus, Nevid, and Fichner-Rathus 2008). Like gender roles and attitudes more generally, the sexual component of human personality and identity—just how we express our "natural" sexual urges—is a matter that culture and environment determine and limit.

ANTHROPOLOGY TODAY

Careers Give Indian Women New Independence

This story describes changes in work patterns, gender roles, and marriage choices in contemporary India. Like women in the United States, although still to a lesser degree, Indian women are entering the workforce after college and deferring marriage. Although young Indian women are changing their behavior, they still adhere to traditional norms that value virginity until eventual marriage, often arranged. Again as in the contemporary United States, many of the jobs these women occupy are part of a new global economy based on services and information.

BANGALORE, India—Not long ago, an Indian woman, even a working Indian woman, would almost always have moved from her parents' house to her husband's. Perhaps her only freedom would be during college, when she might live on campus or take a room for a year or two at what is known-here as the working women's hostel.

That trajectory has begun to loosen, as a surging economy creates new jobs, prompts young professionals to leave home and live on their own and slowly, perhaps unwittingly, nudges a traditional society to accept new freedoms for women. . . .

The changes are sharpest in the lives of women who have found a footing in the new economy and who are for the most part middle-class, college-educated professionals exploring jobs that simply did not exist a generation ago.

High-technology workers and fashion designers, aerobics instructors and radio D.J.'s, these women in their 20s are living independently for the first time, far from their families. Many are deferring marriage for a year or two, maybe more, while they make money and live lives that most of their mothers could not have dreamed of.

Bangalore, also known as Bengaluru, the capital of India's technology and back-office business, is the epicenter of these changes. Once a quiet, leafy city favored by retirees, it now crawls with young people, with more than half of its 4.3 million residents under the age of 30, according to the 2001 census. . . .

When Shubha Khaddar, 23, trudges home from work and stops to pick up something for dinner, she rarely finds herself alone. "You'll find 10 other girls like you coming back with sabji," Ms. Khaddar said, sabji being Hindi for vegetables.

As she left one recent morning for the public relations firm where she works, her parting words to Pallavi Maddala, 23, her roommate and a software engineer, were to bring back some idlis, or steamed rice cakes, for dinner. She would be home late. Besides, idlis would be a low-fat option.

Ms. Khaddar had been on a diet, partly egged on by her mother, who is trying to improve her marriage prospects from across the country, in Delhi. On the refrigerator, she had pasted a snarky yellow note to herself: "Lose Weight, You Fat Pig.". . .

Both women were trying to stave off their mothers' intervention in the marriage department, though not entirely. Ms. Khaddar had been seeing someone but had yet to tell her parents, nor completely closed the door on her mother's plans.

Ms. Maddala, for her part, welcomed the prospect of having a husband chosen for her but not now, and not the overseas Indians for whom her mother has an affinity.

Not long ago, Ms. Maddala showed Ms. Khaddar a photograph of one such prospect, a young man living in the United States. "The picture just freaked me out," Ms. Khaddar recalled this morning, while

Continued

ANTHROPOLOGY TODAY *Continued*

getting herself ready for work. "I said, 'Dude, you're not getting married to that.'". . .

More than anything, Ms. Maddala said, she wanted to savor her independence a bit longer. . . .

In this deeply traditional society, accustomed to absorbing influences of all kinds over the centuries, change comes slowly, if at all. And so the new economy, and the new lifestyle it has engendered, has hardly wiped away the old values, particularly with respect to marriage.

Public opinion polls in recent years routinely have revealed that young people, men and women both, still cling to ideas of virginity before marriage, and fairly large numbers say they prefer to marry within their own caste and community. The great big Indian wedding is bigger than ever. Dowry—and deaths at the hands of women's in-laws who consider their dowries to be inadequate—prevails. . . .

Indian women are marrying later, though still relatively young compared with the West. The mean age of marriage inched to 18.3 in 2001 from 17.7 years in 1991, according to the census, and as late as 22.6 years for the college-educated.

Nearly a third of the work force is female, with rural women employed mostly in agriculture and urban women in services. Although their ranks are minuscule at the top rungs of corporate India, it is common to see women in jobs that either did not

exist a generation ago, or in jobs that would rarely be filled by women, whether gas station attendants or cafe baristas, magazine editors or software programmers. . . .

"I think it's a very significant shift," said Urvashi Butalia, publisher of Zubaan Books, based in New Delhi, which promotes women's writing. "It signals a kind of change and acceptability. It testifies to women's desire and wish to be economically independent, to be able to interact in public space and be in the same world as men."

Equally important, she said, is the attitude adjustment among elders. "For families to accept that women will remain single, that they will live on their own, that they will work and defer marriage, is a very, very significant shift," she said. "Even if it's very small, it's beginning to happen in a society where before, if you wanted to do that you'd be out on a limb."

Ms. Butalia, 55, went out on that limb herself. Thirty years ago, she joined a New Delhi publishing house where she recalls being told that women were not welcome in executive positions because they inevitably married and quit. As it happened, she remained single, becoming one of the best known figures in Indian publishing. . . .

Source: Somini Sengupta, "Careers Give India's Women New Independence," from *The New York Times,* November 23, 2007. Copyright © 2007 The New York Times. Reprinted by permission.

Summary

1. Gender roles are the tasks and activities that a culture assigns to each sex. Gender stereotypes are oversimplified ideas about attributes of males and females. Gender stratification describes an unequal distribution of rewards by gender, reflecting different positions in a social hierarchy. Cross-cultural comparison reveals some recurrent patterns involving the division of labor by

gender and gender-based differences in reproductive strategies. Gender roles and gender stratification also vary with environment, economy, adaptive strategy, level of social complexity, and degree of participation in the world economy.

2. When gathering is prominent, gender status is more equal than when hunting or fishing dominates a foraging economy. Gender status also is more equal when the domestic and public spheres aren't sharply separated. Foragers lack two public arenas that contribute to higher male status among food producers: warfare and organized interregional trade.

3. Gender stratification also is linked to descent and residence. Women's status in matrilineal societies tends to be high because overall social identity comes through female links. Women in many societies, especially matrilineal ones, wield power and make decisions. Scarcity of resources promotes intervillage warfare, patriliny, and patrilocality. The localization of related males is adaptive for military solidarity. Men may use their warrior role to symbolize and reinforce the social devaluation and oppression of women.

4. With the advent of plow agriculture, women were removed from production. The distinction between women's domestic work and men's "productive" labor reinforced the contrast between men as public and valuable and women as homebound and inferior. Patriarchy describes a political system ruled by men in which women have inferior social and political status, including basic human rights.

5. Americans' attitudes toward gender roles vary with class and region. When the need for female labor declines, the idea that women are unfit for many jobs increases, and vice versa. Factors such as war, falling wages, and inflation help explain female cash employment and Americans' attitudes toward it. Countering the economic gains of many American women is the feminization of poverty. This has become a global phenomenon, as impoverished female-headed households have increased worldwide.

6. There has been a recent tendency to see sexual orientation as fixed and biologically based. But, to some extent at least, all human activities and preferences, including erotic expression, are influenced by culture. Sexual orientation stands for a person's habitual sexual attraction to, and activities with, persons of the opposite sex (heterosexuality), the same sex (homosexuality), or both sexes (bisexuality). Sexual norms vary widely from culture to culture.

Key Terms

domestic–public dichotomy (p. 173)
extradomestic (p. 178)
gender roles (p. 169)
gender stereotypes (p. 169)
gender stratification (p. 169)

patriarchy (p. 179)
patrilineal–patrilocal complex (p. 177)
sexual dimorphism (p. 167)
sexual orientation (p. 184)

 Go to our Online Learning Center website at **www.mhhe.com/kottak** for Internet resources directly related to the content of this chapter.

Religion

The anthropologist Anthony F. C. Wallace defined **religion** as "belief and ritual concerned with supernatural beings, powers, and forces" (1966, p. 5). The supernatural is the extraordinary realm outside (but believed to impinge on) the observable world. It is nonempirical and inexplicable in ordinary terms. It must be accepted "on faith." Supernatural beings—gods and goddesses, ghosts, and souls—are not of the material world. Nor are supernatural forces, some of which may be wielded by beings. Other sacred forces are impersonal; they simply exist. In many societies, however, people believe they can benefit from, become imbued with, or manipulate supernatural forces (see Bowie 2006; Bowen 2008; Crapo 2006; Lambek 2008; Stein and Stein 2008; Warms, Garber, and McGee 2009).

Another definition of religion (Reese 1999) focuses on bodies of people who gather together regularly for worship. These congregants or adherents subscribe to and internalize a common system of meaning. They accept (adhere to or believe in) a set of doctrines involving the relationship between the individual and divinity, the supernatural, or whatever is taken to be the ultimate nature of reality. Anthropologists have stressed the collective, shared, and enacted nature of religion, the emotions it generates, and the meanings it embodies. Emile Durkheim (1912/2001), an early scholar of religion, stressed religious *effervescence,* the bubbling up of collective emotional intensity generated by worship. Victor Turner (1969/1995) updated Durkheim's notion, using the term *communitas,* an intense community spirit, a feeling of great social solidarity, equality, and togetherness. The word *religion* derives from the Latin *religare*— "to tie, to bind," but it is not necessary for all members of a given religion to meet together as a common body. Subgroups meet regularly at local congregation sites.

They may attend occasional meetings with adherents representing a wider region. And they may form an imagined community with people of similar faith throughout the world.

Like ethnicity and language, religion also is associated with social divisions within and between societies and nations. Religion both unites and divides. Participation in common rites may affirm, and thus maintain, the social solidarity of a religion's adherents. However, as we know from daily headlines, religious difference also may be associated with bitter enmity.

In studying religion cross-culturally, anthropologists pay attention to the social nature and roles of religion as well as to the nature, content, and meaning to people of religious doctrines, acts, events, settings, practitioners, and organizations. We also consider such verbal manifestations of religious beliefs as prayers, chants, myths, texts, and statements about ethics and morality (see Cunningham 1999; Klass 2003; Lehmann, Meyers, and Moro 2005; Stein and Stein 2005). Religion, by either definition offered here, exists in all human societies. It is a cultural universal. However, we'll see that it isn't always easy to distinguish the supernatural from the natural and that different societies conceptualize divinity, supernatural entities, and ultimate realities very differently.

Expressions of Religion

When did religion begin? No one knows for sure. There are suggestions of religion in Neandertal burials and on European cave walls, where painted stick figures may represent shamans, early religious specialists. Nevertheless, any statement about when, where, why, and how religion arose, or any description of its original nature, can be only speculative. Although such speculations are inconclusive, however, many have revealed important functions and effects of religious behavior. Several theories will be examined now.

Spiritual Beings

The founder of the anthropology of religion was the Englishman Sir Edward Burnett Tylor (1871/1958). Religion was born, Tylor thought, as people tried to understand conditions and events they could not explain by reference to daily experience. Tylor believed that our ancestors—and contemporary nonindustrial peoples—were particularly intrigued with death, dreaming, and trance. People see images they may remember when they wake up or come out of the trance state. Tylor concluded that attempts to explain dreams and trances led early humans to believe that two entities inhabit the body, one active during the day and the other—a double or soul—active during sleep and trance states. Although they never meet, they are vital to each other. When the double permanently leaves the body, the person dies. Death is departure of the soul. From the Latin for soul, *anima,* Tylor named this belief animism. The soul was one sort of spiritual entity; people remembered various images from their dreams and trances—other spirits. For Tylor, **animism,** the earliest form of religion, was a belief in spiritual beings.

Tylor proposed that religion evolved through stages, beginning with animism. *Polytheism* (the belief in multiple gods) and then *monotheism* (the belief in a single, all-powerful deity) developed later. Because religion originated to explain things people didn't understand, Tylor thought it would decline as science offered better explanations. To an extent, he was right. We now have scientific explanations for many things that religion once elucidated. Nevertheless, because religion persists, it must do something more than explain the mysterious. It must, and does, have other functions and meanings.

Powers and Forces

Besides animism—and sometimes coexisting with it in the same society—is a view of the supernatural as a domain of impersonal power, or *force,* which people can control under certain conditions. (You'd be right to think of *Star Wars*.) Such a conception of the supernatural is particularly prominent in Melanesia, the area of the South Pacific that includes Papua New Guinea and adjacent islands. Melanesians believed in **mana,** a sacred impersonal force existing in the universe. Mana can reside in people, animals, plants, and objects.

Melanesian mana was similar to our notion of efficacy or luck. Melanesians attributed success to mana, which people could acquire or manipulate in different ways, such as through magic. Objects with mana could change someone's luck. For example, a charm or amulet belonging to a successful hunter might transmit the hunter's mana to the next person who held or wore it. A woman might put a rock in her garden, see her yields improve dramatically, and attribute the change to the force contained in the rock.

Beliefs in manalike forces are widespread, although the specifics of the religious doctrines vary. Consider the contrast between mana in Melanesia and Polynesia (the islands included in a triangular area marked by Hawaii to the north, Easter Island to the east, and New Zealand to the southwest). In Melanesia, one could acquire mana by chance, or by working hard to get it. In Polynesia, however, mana wasn't potentially available to everyone but was attached to political offices. Chiefs and nobles had more mana than ordinary people did.

So charged with mana were the highest chiefs that contact with them was dangerous to the commoners. The mana of chiefs flowed out of their bodies wherever they went. It could infect the ground, making it dangerous for others to walk in the chief's footsteps. It could permeate the containers and utensils chiefs used in eating. Contact between chief and commoners was dangerous because mana could have an effect like an electric shock. Because high chiefs had so much mana, their bodies and possessions were **taboo** (set apart as sacred and off-limits to ordinary people). Contact between a high chief and commoners was forbidden. Because ordinary people couldn't bear as much sacred current as royalty could, when commoners were accidentally exposed, purification rites were necessary.

One function of religion is to explain. A belief in souls explains what happens in sleep, trance, and death. Melanesian mana explains differential success that people can't understand in ordinary, natural terms. People fail at hunting, war, or gardening not because they are lazy, stupid, or inept but because success comes—or doesn't come—from the supernatural world.

The beliefs in spiritual beings (e.g., animism) and supernatural forces (e.g., mana) fit within the definition of religion given at the beginning of this chapter. Most religions include both spirits and impersonal forces. Likewise the supernatural beliefs of contemporary North Americans include beings (gods, saints, souls, demons) and forces (charms, talismans, crystals, and sacred objects).

Magic and Religion

Magic refers to supernatural techniques intended to accomplish specific aims. These techniques include spells, formulas, and incantations used with deities or with impersonal forces. Magicians use *imitative magic* to produce a desired effect by imitating it. If magicians wish to injure or kill someone, they may imitate that effect on an image of the victim. Sticking pins in "voodoo dolls" is an example. With *contagious magic,* whatever is done to an object is believed to affect a person who once had contact with it. Sometimes practitioners of contagious magic use body products from prospective victims—their nails or hair, for example. The spell performed on the body product is believed to reach the person eventually and work the desired result (see Stein and Stein 2008).

We find magic in societies with diverse religious beliefs. It can be associated with animism, mana, polytheism, or monotheism. Magic is neither simpler nor more primitive than animism or the belief in mana.

Uncertainty, Anxiety, Solace

Religion and magic don't just explain things. They serve emotional needs as well as cognitive (e.g., explanatory) ones. For example, supernatural beliefs and practices can help reduce anxiety. Religion helps people face death and endure life crises. Magical techniques can dispel doubts that arise when outcomes are beyond human control.

Although all societies have techniques to deal with everyday matters, there are certain aspects of people's lives over which they lack control. When people face uncertainty and danger, according to Malinowski, they turn to magic. Malinowski found that the Trobriand Islanders used magic when sailing, a hazardous activity. He proposed that because people can't control matters such as wind, weather, and the fish supply, they turn to magic (Malinowski 1931/1978).

Malinowski noted that it was only when confronted by situations they could not control that Trobrianders, out of psychological stress, turned from technology to magic. Despite our improving technical skills, we can't still control every outcome, and magic persists in contemporary societies. Magic is particularly evident in baseball, where George Gmelch (1978, 2001) describes a series of rituals, taboos, and sacred objects. Like Trobriand sailing magic, these behaviors serve to reduce psychological stress, creating an illusion of magical control when real control is

Illustrating baseball magic, Minnesota Twins outfielder Carlos Gomez kisses his bat, which he likes to talk to, smell, threaten—and reward when he gets a hit. Baseball magic is most common in batting and pitching. Why is that?

lacking. Even the best pitchers have off days and bad luck. Examples of pitchers' magic include tugging one's cap between pitches, touching the resin bag after each bad pitch, and talking to the ball. Gmelch's conclusions confirm Malinowski's that magic is most prevalent in situations of chance and uncertainty. All sorts of magical behavior surround pitching and batting, where uncertainty is rampant, but few rituals involve fielding, where players have much more control. (Batting averages of .350 or higher are very rare after a full season, but a fielding percentage below .900 is a disgrace.)

Rituals

Several features distinguish **rituals** from other kinds of behavior (Rappaport 1974, 1999). Rituals are formal—stylized, repetitive, and stereotyped. People perform them in special (sacred) places and at set times. Rituals include *liturgical orders*—sequences of words and actions invented prior to the current performance of the ritual in which they occur.

These features link rituals to plays, but there are important differences. Plays have audiences rather than participants. Actors merely *portray* something, but ritual performers—who make up congregations—are *in earnest*. Rituals convey information about the participants and their traditions. Repeated year after year, generation after generation, rituals translate enduring messages, values, and sentiments into action.

Rituals are *social* acts. Inevitably, some participants are more committed than others to the beliefs that lie behind the rites. However, just by taking part in a joint public act, the performers signal that they accept a common social and moral order, one that transcends their status as individuals.

Rites of Passage

Magic and religion, as Malinowski noted, can reduce anxiety and allay fears. Ironically, beliefs and rituals also can *create* anxiety and a sense of insecurity and danger (Radcliffe-Brown 1962/1965). Anxiety may arise *because* a rite exists. Indeed, participation in a collective ritual may build up stress, whose common reduction, through the completion of the ritual, enhances the solidarity of the participants.

Rites of passage, such as the collective circumcision of teenagers, can be very stressful. The traditional vision quests of Native Americans, particularly the Plains Indians, illustrate **rites of passage** (customs associated with the transition from one place or stage of life to another), which are found throughout the world. Among the Plains Indians, to move from boyhood to manhood, a youth temporarily separated from his community. After a period of isolation in the wilderness, often featuring fasting and drug consumption, the young man would see a vision, which would become his guardian spirit. He would return then to his community as an adult.

The rites of passage of contemporary societies include confirmations, baptisms, bar and bat mitzvahs, and fraternity hazing. Passage rites involve changes in social status, such as from boyhood to manhood and from nonmember to sorority sister. More generally, a rite of passage may mark any change in place, condition, social position, or age.

All rites of passage have three phases: separation, liminality, and incorporation. In the first phase, people withdraw from the group and begin moving from one place or status to another. In the third phase, they reenter society, having completed the rite. The *liminal* phase is the most interesting. It is the period between states, the limbo during which people have left one place or state but haven't yet entered or joined the next (Turner 1967/1974).

Liminality always has certain characteristics. Liminal people occupy ambiguous social positions. They exist apart from ordinary distinctions and expectations, living in a time out of time. They are cut off from normal social contacts. A variety of contrasts may demarcate liminality from regular social life. For example, among the Ndembu of Zambia, a chief underwent a rite of passage before taking office. During the liminal period, his past and future positions in society were ignored, even reversed. He was subjected to a variety of insults, orders, and humiliations.

Passage rites often are collective. Several individuals—boys being circumcised, fraternity or sorority initiates, men at military boot camps, football players in summer training camps, women becoming nuns—pass through the rites together as a group.

Passage rites are often collective. A group—such as these initiates in Togo or these Navy trainees in San Diego—passes through the rites as a unit. Such liminal people experience the same treatment and conditions and must act alike. They share communitas, an intense community spirit, a feeling of great social solidarity or togetherness.

TABLE 9.1

Oppositions between Liminality and Normal Social Life

Liminality	Normal Social Structure
transition	state
homogeneity	heterogeneity
communitas	structure
equality	inequality
anonymity	names
absence of property	property
absence of status	status
nakedness or uniform dress	dress distinctions
sexual continence or excess	sexuality
minimization of sex distinctions	maximization of sex distinctions
absence of rank	rank
humility	pride
disregard of personal appearance	care for personal appearance
unselfishness	selfishness
total obedience	obedience only to superior rank
sacredness	secularity
sacred instruction	technical knowledge
silence	speech
simplicity	complexity
acceptance of pain and suffering	avoidance of pain and suffering

SOURCE: From *The Ritual Process* by Victor Turner. Copyright © 1969 by Aldine Publishers. Reprinted by permission of Aldine Transaction, a division of Transaction Publishers.

Table 9.1 summarizes the contrasts or oppositions between liminality and normal social life. Most notable is a social aspect of *collective liminality* called **communitas** (Turner 1967/1974), an intense community spirit, a feeling of great social solidarity, equality, and togetherness. People experiencing liminality together form a community of equals. The social distinctions that have existed before or will exist afterward are forgotten temporarily. Liminal people experience the same treatment and conditions and must act alike. Liminality may be marked ritually and symbolically by *reversals* of ordinary behavior. For example, sexual taboos may be intensified, or conversely, sexual excess may be encouraged. Liminal symbols mark entities and circumstances as extraordinary—outside and beyond ordinary social space and routine social events.

Liminality is basic to every passage rite. Furthermore, in certain societies, including our own, liminal symbols may be used to set off one (religious) group from another, and from society as a whole. Such "permanent liminal groups" (e.g., sects, brotherhoods, and cults) are found most characteristically in nation-states. Such liminal features as humility, poverty, equality, obedience, sexual abstinence, and silence may be required for all sect or cult members. Those who join such a group agree to its rules. As if they were undergoing a passage rite—but in this case a never-ending one—they may rid themselves of their previous possessions and cut themselves off from former social links, including those with family members.

Identity as a group member is expected to transcend individuality. Cult members often wear uniform clothing. They may try to reduce distinctions based on age and gender by using a common hair style (shaved head, short hair, or long hair). With such cults, the individual, so important in American culture, is submerged in the collective. This is one reason Americans are so fearful and suspicious of "cults."

Not all collective rites are rites of passage. Most societies observe occasions on which people come together to worship and, in doing so, affirm and reinforce their solidarity. Rituals such as the totemic ceremonies described below are *rites of intensification:* They demand collective adherence to the rules of ritual behavior and create emotions (the collective spiritual effervescence described by Durkheim 1912/2001) that enhance and intensify social solidarity.

Totemism

Totemism was important in the religions of the Native Australians. *Totems* could be animals, plants, or geographical features. In each tribe, groups of people had particular totems. Members of each totemic group believed themselves to be descendants of their totem. They customarily neither killed nor ate it, but this taboo was lifted once a year, when people assembled for ceremonies dedicated to the totem. These annual rites were believed to be necessary for the totem's survival and reproduction.

Totemism uses nature as a model for society. The totems are usually animals and plants, which are part of nature. People relate to nature through their totemic association with natural species. Because each group has a different totem, social differences mirror natural contrasts. Diversity in the natural order becomes a model for diversity in the social order. However, although totemic plants and animals occupy different niches in nature, on another level they are united because they all are part of nature. The unity of the human social order is enhanced by symbolic association with and imitation of the natural order (Durkheim 1912/2001; Lévi-Strauss 1963; Radcliffe-Brown 1962/1965).

In contemporary nations, too, totems continue to mark groups, such as states and universities (e.g., Badgers, Buckeyes, and Wolverines), professional teams (Lions, and Tigers, and Bears), and political parties (donkeys and elephants). Although the modern context is more secular, one can still witness, in intense college football rivalries, some of the effervescence Durkheim noted in Australian totemic religion and other rites of intensification.

Totems are sacred emblems symbolizing common identity. This is true not just among Native Australians, but also among Native American groups of the North Pacific Coast of North America, whose totem poles are well known. Their totemic carvings, which commemorated, and told visual stories about, ancestors, animals, and spirits, were also associated with ceremonies. In totemic rites, people gather together to honor their totem. In so doing, they use ritual to maintain the social oneness that the totem symbolizes.

Social Control

Religion has meaning for people. It helps them cope with adversity and tragedy. It offers hope that things will get better. Lives can be transformed through spiritual healing. Sinners can repent and be saved—or they can go on sinning and be damned. If the faithful truly internalize a system of religious rewards and punishments, their religion becomes a powerful influence on their beliefs, behavior, and what they teach their children.

Many people engage in religious activity because it seems to work. Prayers get answered. Faith healers heal. Sometimes it doesn't take much to convince the faithful that religious actions are efficacious. Many American Indian people in southwestern Oklahoma use faith healers at high monetary costs, not just because it makes them feel better about the uncertain, but because it works (Lassiter 1998). Each year legions of Brazilians visit a church, Nosso Senhor do Bomfim, in the city of Salvador, Bahia. They vow to repay "Our Lord" (Nosso Senhor) if healing happens. Showing that the vows work, and are repaid, are the thousands of *ex votos,* plastic impressions of every conceivable body part, that adorn the church, along with photos of people who have been cured.

Religion can work by getting inside people and mobilizing their emotions—their joy, their wrath, their righteousness. People feel a deep sense of shared joy, meaning, experience, communion, belonging, and commitment to their religion. The power of religion affects action. When religions meet, they can coexist peacefully, or their differences can be a basis for enmity and disharmony, even battle. Religious fervor has inspired Christians on crusades against the infidel and has led Muslims to wage holy wars against non-Islamic peoples. Throughout history, political leaders have used religion to promote and justify their views and policies.

By late September 1996, the Taliban Movement had firmly imposed an extreme form of social control through religious repression on Afghanistan and its people. Led by Muslim clerics, the Taliban aimed to create their version of an Islamic society modeled on the teachings of the Koran (Burns 1997). Various repressive measures were instituted. The Taliban barred women from work and girls from school. Females past puberty were prohibited from talking to unrelated men. Women needed an approved reason, such as shopping for food, to leave their homes. Men, who were required to grow bushy beards, also faced an array of bans—against playing cards, listening to music, keeping pigeons, and flying kites.

To enforce their decrees, the Taliban sent armed enforcers throughout the country. These agents took charge of "beard checks" and other forms of scrutiny on behalf of a religious police force known as the General Department for the Preservation of Virtue and the Elimination of Vice (Burns 1997). By late fall 2001 the Taliban had been overthrown, with a new interim government established in Kabul, the Afghan capital, on December 22. The collapse of the Taliban followed American bombing of Afghanistan in response to the September 11, 2001, attacks on New York's World Trade Center and Washington's Pentagon. As the Taliban yielded Kabul to victorious northern alliance forces, local men flocked to barbershops to have their beards trimmed or shaved. They were using a key Taliban symbol to celebrate the end of religious repression.

Note that in the case of the Taliban, forms of social control were used to support a strict religious orthodoxy. This wasn't repression in religion's name, but repressive religion. In other countries, secular leaders seeking power may use religious rhetoric to get it.

How may leaders mobilize communities and, in so doing, gain support for their own policies? One way is by persuasion; another is by instilling hatred or fear. Consider witchcraft accusations. Witch hunts can be powerful means of social control by creating a climate of danger and insecurity that affects everyone, not just the people who are likely targets. No one wants to seem deviant, to be accused of being a witch. Witch hunts often take aim at people who can be accused and punished with least chance of retaliation. During the great European witch craze, during the 15th, 16th, and 17th centuries (Harris 1974), most accusations and convictions were against poor women with little social support.

Witchcraft accusations often are directed at socially marginal or anomalous individuals. Among the Betsileo of Madagascar, for example, who prefer patrilocal post-marital residence, men living in their wife's or their mother's village violate a cultural norm. Linked to their anomalous social position, just a bit of unusual behavior (e.g., staying up late at night) on their part is sufficient for them to be called witches and avoided as a result. In tribes and peasant communities, people who stand out economically, especially if they seem to be benefiting at the expense of others, often face witchcraft accusations, leading to social ostracism or punishment. In this case witchcraft accusation becomes a **leveling mechanism,** a custom or social action that operates to reduce status differences and thus to bring standouts in line with community norms—another form of social control.

To ensure proper behavior, religions offer rewards (e.g., the fellowship of the religious community) and punishments (e.g., the threat of being cast out or excommunicated). Religions, especially the formal organized ones typically found in state societies, often prescribe a code of ethics and morality to guide behavior. The Judaic Ten Commandments laid down a set of prohibitions against killing, stealing, adultery, and other misdeeds. Crimes are breaches of secular laws, as sins are breaches of religious strictures. Some rules (e.g., the Ten Commandments) proscribe or prohibit behavior; others prescribe behavior. The Golden Rule, for instance, is a religious guide to do unto others as you would have them do unto you. Moral codes are ways of maintaining order and stability. Codes of morality and ethics are constantly repeated in religious sermons, catechisms, and the like. They become internalized psychologically. They guide behavior and produce regret, guilt, shame, and the need for forgiveness, expiation, and absolution when they are not followed.

Kinds of Religion

Religion is a cultural universal. But religions exist in particular societies, and cultural differences show up systematically in religious beliefs and practices. For example, the religions of stratified, state societies differ from those of societies with less marked social contrasts and power differentials.

Considering several societies, Wallace (1966) identified four types of religion: shamanic, communal, Olympian, and monotheistic (Table 9.2). The simplest type is shamanic religion. Unlike priests, **shamans** aren't full-time religious officials but part-time religious

TABLE 9.2

Wallace's Typology of Religions

Type of Religion	Type of Practitioner	Conception of Supernatural	Type of Society
Monotheistic	Priests, ministers, etc.	Supreme being	States
Olympian	Priesthood	Hierarchical pantheon with powerful deities	Chiefdoms and archaic states
Communal	Part-time specialists; occasional community-sponsored events, including collective rites	Several deities with some control over nature	Food-producing tribes
Shamanic	Shaman (part-time practitioner)	Zoomorphic (plants and animals)	Foraging bands

figures who mediate between people and supernatural beings and forces. All societies have medico-magico-religious specialists. *Shaman* is the general term encompassing curers ("witch doctors"), mediums, spiritualists, astrologers, palm readers, and other diviners. Wallace found shamanic religions to be most characteristic of foraging societies.

Shamans sometimes set themselves off symbolically from ordinary people by assuming a different or ambiguous sex or gender role. (In nation-states, priests, nuns, and vestal virgins do something similar by taking vows of celibacy and chastity.) Among the Chukchee of Siberia (Bogoras 1904) male shamans copied the dress, speech, hair arrangements, and lifestyles of women. These shamans took other men as husbands and sex partners and received respect for their supernatural and curative expertise. Female shamans could join a fourth gender, copying men and taking wives.

Communal religions have, in addition to shamans, community rituals such as harvest ceremonies and collective rites of passage. Although communal religions lack *full-time* religious specialists, they believe in several deities (**polytheism**) who control aspects of nature. Although some hunter-gatherers, including Australian totemites, have communal religions, these religions are more typical of farming societies.

Olympian religions, which arose with state organization and marked social stratification, add full-time religious specialists—professional *priesthoods*. Like the state itself, the priesthood is hierarchically and bureaucratically organized. The term *Olympian* comes from Mount Olympus, home of the classical Greek gods. Olympian religions are polytheistic. They include powerful anthropomorphic gods with specialized functions, for example, gods of love, war, the sea, and death. Olympian *pantheons* (collections of supernatural beings) were prominent in the religions of many nonindustrial nation-states, including the Aztecs of Mexico, several African and Asian kingdoms, and classical Greece and Rome. Wallace's fourth type—**monotheism**—also has priesthoods and notions of divine power, but it views the supernatural differently. In monotheism, all supernatural phenomena are manifestations of, or are under the control of, a single eternal, omniscient, omnipotent, and omnipresent supreme being.

Robert Bellah (1978) coined the term "world-rejecting religion" to describe most forms of Christianity. The first world-rejecting religions arose in ancient civilizations, along with literacy and a specialized priesthood. These religions are so-named because of their tendency to reject the natural (mundane, ordinary, material, secular) world and to focus instead on a higher (sacred, transcendent) realm of reality. The divine is a domain of exalted morality to which humans can only aspire. Salvation through fusion with the supernatural is the main goal of such religions.

World Religions

Information on the world's major religions today is provided in Table 9.3 (number of adherents) and Figure 9.1 (percentage of world population). Based on people's claimed religions, Christianity is the world's largest, with some 2.1 billion adherents. Islam, with

TABLE 9.3

Religions of the World, by Estimated Number of Adherents, 2005

Christianity	2.1 billion
Islam	1.5 billion
Secular/Nonreligious/Agnostic/Atheist	1.1 billion
Hinduism	900 million
Chinese traditional religion	394 million
Buddhism	376 million
Primal-indigenous	300 million
African traditional and diasporic	100 million
Sikhism	23 million
Juche	19 million
Spiritism	15 million
Judaism	14 million
Baha'i	7 million
Jainism	4.2 million
Shinto	4 million
Cao Dai	4 million
Zoroastrianism	2.6 million
Tenrikyo	2 million
Neo-Paganism	1 million
Unitarian-Universalism	800 thousand
Rastafarianism	600 thousand
Scientology	500 thousand

SOURCE: Reprinted by permission of Ontario Consultants on Religious Tolerance, www.religioustolerance.org.

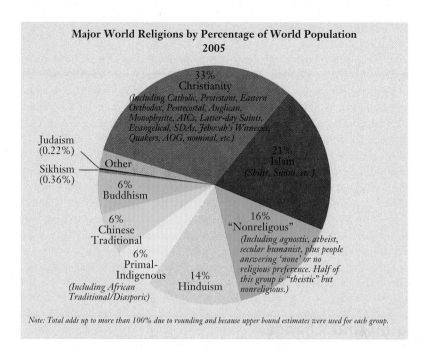

FIGURE 9.1 *Major World Religions by Percentage of World Population, 2005*

SOURCE: www.adherents.com. Reprinted by permission.

Colonialism and missionization have abetted the spread of Christianity, the world's largest religion. Shown here, devout Catholics, including a Portuguese nun and several Mozambican women, celebrate the Pope's visit to Mozambique, a former Portuguese colony, in September 1988.

some 1.5 billion practitioners, is next, followed by Hinduism, then Chinese traditional religion (also known as Chinese folk religion or Confucianism), and Buddhism. More than a billion people claim no official religion, but only about a fifth of them are self-proclaimed atheists. Worldwide, Islam is growing at a rate of about 2.9 percent annually, versus 2.3 percent for Christianity, whose overall growth rate is the same as the rate of world population increase (Ontario Consultants 2001; Adherents.com 2002).

Within Christianity, there is variation in the growth rate. There were an estimated 680 million "born-again" Christians (e.g., Pentecostals and Evangelicals) in the world in 2001, with an annual worldwide growth rate of 7 percent, versus just 2.3 percent for Christianity overall. (This would translate into 1.2 billion Pentecostals/Evangelicals by 2010.) The global growth rate of Roman Catholics has been estimated at only 1.3 percent, compared with a Protestant growth rate of 3.3 percent per year (Winter 2001). Much of this explosive growth, especially in Africa, is of a type of Protestantism that would be scarcely recognizable to most Americans, given its incorporation of many animistic elements.

Religion and Change

Religious fundamentalists seek order based on strict adherence to purportedly traditional standards, beliefs, rules, and customs. Christian and Islamic fundamentalists recognize, decry, and attempt to redress change, yet they also contribute to change (Antoun 2008). In a worldwide process, new religions challenge established churches. In the United States, for example, conservative Christian TV hosts have become influential broadcasters and opinion shapers. In Latin America evangelical Protestantism is winning millions of converts from Roman Catholicism.

Like political organization, religion helps maintain social order. And like political mobilization, religious energy can be harnessed not just for change but also for revolution. Reacting to conquest or to actual or perceived foreign domination, for instance, religious leaders may seek to alter or revitalize their society. In an "Islamic Revolution," for example, Iranian ayatollahs marshaled religious fervor to create national solidarity and radical change. We call such movements nativistic movements (Linton 1943) or revitalization movements (Wallace 1956).

Revitalization Movements

Revitalization movements are social movements that occur in times of change, in which religious leaders emerge and undertake to alter or revitalize a society. Christianity originated as a revitalization movement. Jesus was one of several prophets who preached new religious doctrines while the Middle East was under Roman rule. It was a time of social unrest, when a foreign power ruled the land. Jesus inspired a new, enduring, and major religion. His contemporaries were not so successful.

The Handsome Lake religion arose around 1800 among the Iroquois of New York State (Wallace 1969). Handsome Lake, the founder of this revitalization movement, was a leader of one of the Iroquois tribes. The Iroquois had suffered because of their support of the British against the American colonials. After the colonial victory and a wave of immigration to their homeland, the Iroquois were dispersed on small reservations. Unable to pursue traditional horticulture and hunting in their homeland, the Iroquois became heavy drinkers and quarreled among themselves.

Handsome Lake was a heavy drinker who started having visions from heavenly messengers. The spirits warned him that unless the Iroquois changed their ways, they would be destroyed. His visions offered a plan for coping with the new order. Witchcraft, quarreling, and drinking would end. The Iroquois would copy European farming techniques, which, unlike traditional Iroquois horticulture, stressed male rather than female labor. Handsome Lake preached that the Iroquois should also abandon their communal long houses and matrilineal descent groups for more permanent marriages and individual family households. The teachings of Handsome Lake produced a new church and religion, one that still has members in New York and Ontario. This revitalization movement helped the Iroquois adapt to and survive in a modified environment. They eventually gained a reputation among their non-Indian neighbors as sober family farmers.

Cargo Cults

Like the Handsome Lake religion just discussed, cargo cults are revitalization movements. Such movements may emerge when natives have regular contact with industrial societies but lack their wealth, technology, and living standards. Some such movements attempt to *explain* European domination and wealth and to achieve similar success magically by mimicking European behavior and manipulating symbols of the desired life style. The **cargo cults** of Melanesia and Papua New Guinea weave Christian doctrine with aboriginal beliefs. They take their name from their focus on cargo—European goods of the sort natives have seen unloaded from the cargo holds of ships and airplanes.

In one early cult, members believed that the spirits of the dead would arrive in a ship. These ghosts would bring manufactured goods for the natives and would kill all the whites. More recent cults replaced ships with airplanes (Worsley 1959/1985). Many cults have used elements of European culture as sacred objects. The rationale is that Europeans use these objects, have wealth, and therefore must know the "secret of cargo." By mimicking how Europeans use or treat objects, natives hope also to come upon the secret knowledge needed to gain cargo.

For example, having seen Europeans' reverent treatment of flags and flagpoles, the members of one cult began to worship flagpoles. They believed the flagpoles were sacred towers that could transmit messages between the living and the dead. Other natives built airstrips to entice planes bearing canned goods, portable radios, clothing, wristwatches, and motorcycles. Near the airstrips they made effigies of towers, airplanes, and radios. They talked into the cans in a magical attempt to establish radio contact with the gods. Can you think of anything in your own society (including the media) that features similar behavior?

Some cargo cult prophets proclaimed that success would come through a reversal of European domination and native subjugation. The day was near, they preached, when natives, aided by God, Jesus, or native ancestors, would turn the tables. Native skins would turn white, and those of Europeans would turn brown; Europeans would die or be killed.

Cargo cults blend aboriginal and Christian beliefs. Melanesian myths told of ancestors shedding their skins and changing into powerful beings and of dead people returning to life. Christian missionaries, who had been in Melanesia since the late 19th century, also spoke of resurrection. The cults' preoccupation with cargo is related to traditional Melanesian big-man systems. In the chapter "Political Systems," we saw that a Melanesian big man had to be generous. People worked for the big man, helping him amass wealth, but eventually he had to give a feast and give away all that wealth.

Because of their experience with big-man systems, Melanesians believed that all wealthy people eventually had to give their wealth away. For decades they had attended Christian missions and worked on plantations. All the while they expected Europeans to return the fruits of their labor as their own big men did. When the Europeans refused to distribute the wealth or even to let natives know the secret of its production and distribution, cargo cults developed.

Like arrogant big men, Europeans would be leveled, by death if necessary. However, natives lacked the physical means of doing what their traditions said they should do. Thwarted by well-armed colonial forces, natives resorted to magical leveling. They called on supernatural beings to intercede, to kill or otherwise deflate the European big men and redistribute their wealth.

Cargo cults are religious responses to the expansion of the world capitalist economy. However, this religious mobilization had political and economic results. Cult participation gave Melanesians a basis for common interests and activities and thus

A cargo cult in Vanuatu, a country in Melanesia. Boys and men march with spears, imitating British colonial soldiers. Does anything in your own society remind you of a cargo cult?

helped pave the way for political parties and economic interest organizations. Previously separated by geography, language, and customs, Melanesians started forming larger groups as members of the same cults and followers of the same prophets. The cargo cults paved the way for political action through which the indigenous peoples eventually regained their autonomy.

Secular Rituals

In concluding this discussion of religion, we may recognize some problems with the definition of religion given at the beginning of this chapter. The first problem: If we define religion with reference to supernatural beings, powers, and forces, how do we classify ritual-like behaviors that occur in secular contexts? Some anthropologists believe there are both sacred and secular rituals. Secular rituals include formal, invariant, stereotyped, earnest, repetitive behavior and rites of passage that take place in nonreligious settings.

A second problem: If the distinction between the supernatural and the natural is not consistently made in a society, how can we tell what is religion and what isn't? The Betsileo of Madagascar, for example, view witches and dead ancestors as real people who play roles in ordinary life. However, their occult powers are not empirically demonstrable.

A third problem: The behavior considered appropriate for religious occasions varies tremendously from culture to culture. One society may consider drunken frenzy the surest sign of faith, whereas another may inculcate quiet reverence. Who is to say which is "more religious"?

ANTHROPOLOGY TODAY

France Celebrates Foremost Anthropologist of Religion

During the last week of November 2008, France (along with several other countries) celebrated the 100th birthday of Claude Lévi-Strauss. Father of a school known as structural anthropology and a key figure in the anthropology of religion (especially myth and folklore), Lévi-Strauss is known for his many theoretical books and his studies of Native Americans in lowland South America. Described here, too, is the Musée du Quai Branly, site of events honoring the French master, which he inspired and helped establish, and to which he donated items from his own ethnographic collection.

That museum, which has become one of Paris's key tourist destinations, is a tribute to the arts, beliefs, and cosmology of non-Western peoples. This account suggests a more prominent public role for anthropology in France than in the United States. Undoubtedly this prominence reflects France's colonial history, to be examined in the next chapter.

PARIS—Claude Lévi-Strauss, who altered the way Westerners look at other civilizations, turned 100 on Friday [November 28, 2008]. France celebrated with films, lectures and free admission to the museum he inspired, the Musée du Quai Branly. Mr. Lévi-Strauss is cherished in France. . . .

Continued

ANTHROPOLOGY TODAY   *Continued*

At the Quai Branly, 100 scholars and writers read from or lectured on the work of Mr. Lévi-Strauss, while documentaries about him were screened, and guided visits were provided to the collections, which include some of his own favorite artifacts.

Stéphane Martin, the president of the museum, . . . along with the French culture minister, Christine Albanel, and the minister of higher education and research, Valérie Pécresse, presided over the unveiling of a plaque outside the museum's theater, which is already named for Mr. Lévi-Strauss, who did not attend the festivities. Ms. Pécresse announced a new annual 100,000 euro prize (about $127,000) in his name for a researcher in "human sciences" working in France. President Nicolas Sarkozy visited Mr. Lévi-Strauss on Friday evening at his home. . . .

The museum was the grand project of former president Jacques Chirac, who loved anthropology and embraced the idea of a colloquy of civilizations, as opposed to the academic quality of the old Musée de l'Homme, which Philippe Descola, the chairman of the anthropology department at the Collège de France, described as "an empty shell—full of artifacts but dead to themselves."

The new museum, which has 1.3 million visitors a year, was a sort of homage to Mr. Lévi-Strauss, who "blessed it from the beginning," Mr. Descola said. . . .

In 1996, when asked his opinion of the project, Mr. Lévi-Strauss said in a handwritten letter to Mr. Chirac: "It takes into account the evolution of the world since the Musée de l'Homme was created. An ethnographic museum can no longer, as at that time, offer an authentic vision of life in these societies so different from ours. With perhaps a few exceptions that will not last, these societies are progressively integrated into world politics and economy. When I see the objects that I collected in the field between 1935 and 1938 again—and it's also true of others—I know that their relevance has become either documentary or, mostly, aesthetic."

The building is striking and controversial, imposing the ideas of the star architect Jean Nouvel on the organization of the spaces. But Mr. Martin says it is working well for the museum, whose marvelous objects—"fragile flowers of difference," as Mr. Lévi-Strauss once called them—can be seen on varying levels of aesthetics and serious study. They are presented as artifacts of great beauty but also with defining

Summary

1. Religion, a cultural universal, consists of belief and behavior concerned with supernatural beings, powers, and forces. Religion also encompasses the feelings, meanings, and congregations associated with such beliefs and behavior. Anthropological studies have revealed many expressions and functions of religion.

2. Tylor considered animism—the belief in spirits or souls—to be religion's earliest and most basic form. He focused on religion's explanatory role, arguing that religion would eventually disappear as science provided better explanations. Besides animism, yet another view of the supernatural also occurs in nonindustrial societies, seeing the supernatural as a domain of raw, impersonal power or force

context, telling visitors not only what they are, but also what they were meant to be when they were created. . . .

On Tuesday there was a day-long colloquium at the Collège de France, where Mr. Lévi-Strauss once taught. Mr. Descola said that centenary celebrations were being held in at least 25 countries.

"People realize he is one of the great intellectual heroes of the 20th century," he said in an interview. "His thought is among the most complex of the 20th century, and it's hard to convey his prose and his thinking in English. But he gave a proper object to anthropology: not simply as a study of human nature, but a systematic study of how cultural practices vary, how cultural differences are systematically organized."

Mr. Levi-Strauss took difference as the basis for his study, not the search for commonality, which defined 19th-century anthropology, Mr. Descola said. In other words, he took cultures on their own terms rather than try to relate everything to the West. . . .

One of the most remarkable aspects of the Quai Branly is its landscaping, designed by Gilles Clément to reflect the questing spirit of Mr. Lévi-Strauss. Mr. Clément tried to create a "non-Western garden," he said in an interview, "with more the spirit of the savannah," where most of the animist civilizations live whose artifacts fill the museum itself.

He tried to think through the symbols of the cosmology of these civilizations, their systems of gods and beliefs, which also animate their agriculture and their gardens. The garden here uses the symbol of the tortoise, not reflected literally, "but in an oval form that recurs," Mr. Clément said.

"We find the tortoise everywhere," he continued. "It's an animal that lives a long time, so it represents a sort of reassurance, or the eternal, perhaps."

Mr. Lévi-Strauss "is very important to me," Mr. Clément said, adding: "He represents an extremely subversive vision with his interest in populations that were disdained. He paid careful attention, not touristically but profoundly, to the human beings on the earth who think differently from us. It's a respect for others, which is very strong and very moving. He knew that cultural diversity is necessary for cultural creativity, for the future."

Source: Steven Erlanger, "100th Birthday Tributes Pour in for Lévi-Strauss," from The New York Times, November 19, 2008. Copyright © 2008 The New York Times. Reprinted by permission.

(called mana in Polynesia and Melanesia). People can manipulate and control mana under certain conditions.

3. When ordinary technical and rational means of doing things fail, people may turn to magic. Often they use magic when they lack control over outcomes. Religion offers comfort and psychological security at times of crisis. On the other hand, rites can also create anxiety. Rituals are formal, invariant, stylized, earnest acts in which people subordinate their particular beliefs to a social collectivity. Rites of passage have three stages: separation, liminality, and incorporation. Such rites can mark any change in social status, age, place, or social condition. Collective rites are often cemented by communitas, a feeling of intense solidarity.

4. Religion establishes and maintains social control through a series of moral and ethical beliefs and real and imagined rewards and punishments, internalized in

individuals. Religion also achieves social control by mobilizing its members for collective action.

5. Wallace defines four types of religion: shamanic, communal, Olympian, and monotheistic. Each has its characteristic ceremonies and practitioners. The world's major religions vary in their growth rates, with Islam expanding more rapidly than Christianity. Religion helps maintain social order, but it also can promote change. Revitalization movements blend old and new beliefs and have helped people adapt to changing conditions. There are secular as well as religious rituals.

Key Terms

animism (p. 191)

cargo cults (p. 205)

communal religions (p. 201)

communitas (p. 197)

leveling mechanism (p. 200)

liminality (p. 195)

magic (p. 193)

mana (p. 192)

monotheism (p. 201)

Olympian religions (p. 201)

polytheism (p. 201)

religion (p. 190)

revitalization movements (p. 204)

rites of passage (p. 195)

rituals (p. 194)

shaman (p. 200)

taboo (p. 192)

 Go to our Online Learning Center website at **www.mhhe.com/kottak** for Internet resources directly related to the content of this chapter.

The World System and Colonialism

Although fieldwork in small communities has been anthropology's hallmark, isolated groups are impossible to find today. Truly isolated societies probably never have existed. For thousands of years, human groups have been in contact with one another. Local societies always have participated in a larger system, which today has global dimensions—we call it the *modern world system,* by which we mean a world in which nations are economically and politically interdependent.

The World System

The world system and the relations among the countries within it are shaped by the capitalist world economy. A huge increase in international trade during and after the 15th century led to the **capitalist world economy** (Wallerstein 1982, 2004*b*), a single world system committed to production for sale or exchange, with the object of maximizing profits, rather than supplying domestic needs. **Capital** refers to wealth or resources invested in business, with the intent of using the means of production to make a profit.

World-system theory can be traced to the French social historian Fernand Braudel. In his three-volume work *Civilization and Capitalism, 15th–18th Century* (1981, 1982, 1992), Braudel argued that society consists of interrelated parts assembled into a system. Societies are subsystems of larger systems, with the world system the largest. The key claim of **world-system theory** is that an identifiable social system, based on wealth and power differentials, extends beyond individual countries. That system is formed by a set of economic and political relations that has characterized much of the globe since the 16th century, when the Old World established regular contact with the New World (see Bodley 2008).

According to Wallerstein (1982, 2004b), countries within the world system occupy three different positions of economic and political power: core, periphery, and semiperiphery. The geographic center, or **core,** the dominant position in the world system, includes the strongest and most powerful nations. In core nations, "the complexity of economic activities and the level of capital accumulation is the greatest" (Thompson 1983, p. 12). With its sophisticated technologies and mechanized production, the core churns out products that flow mainly to other core countries. Some also go to the periphery and semiperiphery. According to Arrighi (1994), the core monopolizes the most profitable activities, especially the control of world finance.

Semiperiphery and periphery countries have less power, wealth, and influence than the core does. The **semiperiphery** is intermediate between the core and the periphery. Contemporary nations of the semiperiphery are industrialized. Like core nations, they export both industrial goods and commodities, but they lack the power and economic dominance of core nations. Thus Brazil, a semiperiphery nation, exports

Illustrating the contemporary global spread of capitalism, this photo, taken in October 2007, shows cell phone use and modern fashion advertising in Beijing's SunDong'An mall.

automobiles to Nigeria (a periphery nation) and auto engines, orange juice extract, coffee, and shrimp to the United States (a core nation). The **periphery** includes the world's least privileged and powerful countries. Economic activities there are less mechanized than are those in the semiperiphery, although some degree of industrialization has reached even peripheral nations. The periphery produces raw materials, agricultural commodities, and, increasingly, human labor for export to the core and the semiperiphery (Shannon 1996).

In the United States and Western Europe today, immigration—legal and illegal—from the periphery and semiperiphery supplies cheap labor for agriculture in core countries. U.S. states as distant as California, Michigan, and South Carolina make significant use of farm labor from Mexico. The availability of relatively cheap workers from noncore nations such as Mexico (in the United States) and Turkey (in Germany) benefits farmers and business owners in core countries, while also supplying remittances to families in the semiperiphery and periphery. As a result of 21st-century telecommunications technology, cheap labor doesn't even need to migrate to the United States. Thousands of families in India are being supported as American companies "outsource" jobs—from telephone assistance to software engineering—to nations outside the core.

The Emergence of the World System

As Europeans took to ships, developing a transoceanic trade-oriented economy, people throughout the world entered Europe's sphere of influence. In the 15th century Europe established regular contact with Asia, Africa, and eventually the New World (the Caribbean and the Americas). Christopher Columbus's first voyage from Spain to the Bahamas and the Caribbean in 1492 was soon followed by additional voyages. These journeys opened the way for a major exchange of people, resources, products, ideas, and diseases, as the Old and New Worlds were forever linked (Crosby 2003; Diamond 1997; Fagan 1998; Viola and Margolis 1991). Led by Spain and Portugal, Europeans extracted silver and gold, conquered the natives (taking some as slaves), and colonized their lands.

Previously in Europe as throughout the world, rural people had produced mainly for their own needs, growing their own food and making clothing, furniture, and tools from local products. Production beyond immediate needs was undertaken to pay taxes and to purchase trade items such as salt and iron. As late as 1650 the English diet was based on locally grown starches (Mintz 1985). In the 200 years that followed, however, the English became extraordinary consumers of imported goods. One of the earliest and most popular of those goods was sugar (Mintz 1985).

Sugarcane originally was domesticated in Papua New Guinea, and sugar was first processed in India. Reaching Europe via the Middle East and the eastern Mediterranean, it was carried to the New World by Columbus (Mintz 1985). The climate of Brazil and the Caribbean proved ideal for growing sugarcane, and Europeans built plantations there to supply the growing demand for sugar. This led to the development in the 17th century of a plantation economy based on a single cash crop—a system known as *monocrop* production.

The demand for sugar in a growing international market spurred the development of the transatlantic slave trade and New World plantation economies based on slave labor. By the 18th century, an increased English demand for raw cotton led to rapid settlement of what is now the southeastern United States and the emergence there of another slave-based monocrop production system. Like sugar, cotton was a key trade item that fueled the growth of the world system.

Industrialization

By the 18th century the stage had been set for the **Industrial Revolution**—the historical transformation (in Europe, after 1750) of "traditional" into "modern" societies through industrialization of the economy. Industrialization required capital for investment. The established system of transoceanic trade and commerce supplied this capital from the enormous profits it generated. Wealthy people sought investment opportunities and eventually found them in machines and engines to drive machines. Capital and scientific innovation fueled invention. Industrialization increased production in both farming and manufacturing.

European industrialization developed from (and eventually replaced) the *domestic system* of manufacture (or home-handicraft system). In this system, an organizer-entrepreneur supplied the raw materials to workers in their homes and collected the finished products from them. The entrepreneur, whose sphere of operations might span several villages, owned the materials, paid for the work, and arranged the marketing.

Causes of the Industrial Revolution

The Industrial Revolution began with cotton products, iron, and pottery. These were widely used goods whose manufacture could be broken down into simple routine motions that machines could perform. When manufacturing moved from homes to factories, where machinery replaced handwork, agrarian societies evolved into industrial ones. As factories produced cheap staple goods, the Industrial Revolution led to a dramatic increase in production. Industrialization fueled urban growth and created a new kind of city, with factories crowded together in places where coal and labor were cheap.

The Industrial Revolution began in England rather than in France. Why? Unlike the English, the French didn't have to transform their domestic manufacturing system by industrializing. Faced with an increased need for products, with a late 18th-century population at least twice that of Great Britain, France could simply augment its domestic system of production by drawing in new homes. Thus, the French were able to increase production *without innovating*—they could enlarge the existing system rather than adopt a new one. To meet mounting demand for staples—at home and in the colonies—England had to industrialize.

As its industrialization proceeded, Britain's population began to increase dramatically. It doubled during the 18th century (especially after 1750) and did so again between 1800 and 1850. This demographic explosion fueled consumption, but British

The Art of STOCKING-FRAME-WORK-KNITTING.

Engrav'd for the Universal Magazine 1750 for J. Hinton at the Kings Arms in St Pauls Church Yard LONDON.

In the home-handicraft, or domestic, system of production, an organizer supplied raw materials to workers in their homes and collected their products. Family life and work were intertwined, as in this English scene. Is there a modern equivalent to the domestic system of production?

entrepreneurs couldn't meet the increased demand with the traditional production methods. This spurred further experimentation, innovation, and rapid technological change.

English industrialization drew on national advantages in natural resources. Britain was rich in coal and iron ore, and had navigable waterways and easily negotiated coasts. It was a seafaring island-nation located at the crossroads of international trade. These features gave Britain a favored position for importing raw materials and exporting manufactured goods. Another factor in England's industrial growth was the fact that much of its 18th-century colonial empire was occupied by English settler families who looked to the mother country as they tried to replicate European civilization in the New World. These colonies bought large quantities of English staples.

It also has been argued that particular cultural values and religion contributed to industrialization. Many members of the emerging English middle class were Protestant nonconformists. Their beliefs and values encouraged industry, thrift, the dissemination of new knowledge, inventiveness, and willingness to accept change (Weber 1904/1958).

Socioeconomic Effects of Industrialization

The socioeconomic effects of industrialization were mixed. English national income tripled between 1700 and 1815 and increased 30 times more by 1939. Standards of comfort rose, but prosperity was uneven. At first, factory workers got wages higher than those available in the domestic system. Later, owners started recruiting labor in places where living standards were low and labor (including that of women and children) was cheap.

Social ills worsened with the growth of factory towns and industrial cities, amid conditions like those Charles Dickens described in *Hard Times*. Filth and smoke polluted the 19th-century cities. Housing was crowded and unsanitary, with insufficient water and sewage disposal facilities. People experienced rampant disease and rising death rates. This was the world of Ebenezer Scrooge, Bob Cratchit, Tiny Tim—and Karl Marx.

Industrial Stratification

The social theorists Karl Marx and Max Weber focused on the stratification systems associated with industrialization. From his observations in England and his analysis of 19th-century industrial capitalism, Marx (Marx and Engels 1848/1976) saw socioeconomic stratification as a sharp and simple division between two opposed classes: the bourgeoisie (capitalists) and the proletariat (propertyless workers). The bourgeoisie traced its origins to overseas ventures and the world capitalist economy, which had created a wealthy commercial class.

Industrialization shifted production from farms and cottages to mills and factories, where mechanical power was available and where workers could be assembled to operate heavy machinery. The **bourgeoisie** were the owners of the factories, mines, large farms, and other means of production. The **working class,** or **proletariat,** was made up of people who had to sell their labor to survive. With the decline of subsistence production and with the rise of urban migration and the possibility of unemployment, the bourgeoisie came to stand between workers and the means of production.

Industrialization hastened the process of *proletarianization*—the separation of workers from the means of production. The bourgeoisie also came to dominate the means of communication, the schools, and other key institutions. *Class consciousness* (recognition of collective interests and personal identification with one's economic group) was a vital part of Marx's view of class. He saw bourgeoisie and proletariat as socioeconomic divisions with radically opposed interests. Marx viewed classes as powerful collective forces that could mobilize human energies to influence the course of history. On the basis of their common experience, workers would develop class consciousness, which could lead to revolutionary change. Although no proletarian revolution was to occur in England, workers did develop organizations to protect their interests and increase their share of industrial profits. During the 19th century, trade unions and socialist parties emerged to express a rising anticapitalist spirit. The concerns of the English labor movement were to remove young children from factories and limit the hours during which women and children could work. The profile of stratification in industrial core nations gradually took shape. Capitalists controlled production, but labor was organizing for better wages and working conditions. By 1900 many governments had factory legislation and social-welfare programs. Mass living standards in core nations rose as population grew.

In today's capitalist world system the class division between owners and workers is now worldwide. However, publicly traded companies complicate the division between capitalists and workers in industrial nations. Through pension plans and personal investments, some American workers now have a proprietary interest in the means of production. They are part-owners rather than propertyless workers. The key difference is that the wealthy have *control* over these means. The key capitalist now is not the factory owner, who may have been replaced by thousands of stockholders, but the CEO or the chair of the board of directors, neither of whom may actually own the corporation.

Modern stratification systems aren't simple and dichotomous. They include (particularly in core and semiperiphery nations) a middle class of skilled and professional workers. Gerhard Lenski (1966) argues that social equality tends to increase in advanced industrial societies. The masses improve their access to economic benefits and political power. In Lenski's scheme, the shift of political power to the masses reflects the growth of the middle class, which reduces the polarization between owning and working classes. The proliferation of middle-class occupations creates opportunities for social mobility. The stratification system grows more complex (Giddens 1973).

In the United States this complex stratification system has gone largely unnoticed by many Americans. Most contemporary Americans, for example, think they belong to, and claim identity with, the middle class, which they tend to perceive as a vast undifferentiated group. However, there are substantial differences in income and wealth between the richest and the poorest Americans, and the gap is widening. According to U.S. Census data from 1967 to 2000, the top (richest) fifth, or quintile, of American households increased their share of national income by 13.5 percent, while all other quintiles fell. The percentage share of the lowest fifth fell most dramatically—17.6 percent. The divergence continues: In 2006 the highest quintile of households got 50.5 percent (versus 49.7 percent in 2000) of all national income, while the lowest fifth got only 3.4 percent (versus 3.6 in 2000). Comparable figures in 1967 were 43.8 percent and 4.0 percent. The 2006 ratio was 15:1, versus 14:1 in 2000 and 11:1 in 1967. In other words, the richest fifth of American households, with a mean annual income of $168,170, is now 15 times wealthier than the poorest fifth, with a mean annual income of $11,352 (DeNavas-Walt, Proctor, and Lee; U. S. Census Bureau—2006http://www.census.gov/hhes/www/income/histinc/h03ar. html). When we consider wealth (investments, property, possessions, etc.) rather than income, the contrast is even more striking: 1 percent of American families hold just over one-third of the nation's wealth (Council on International and Public Affairs 2006).

Weber faulted Marx for an overly simple and exclusively economic view of stratification. As we saw in the chapter "Political Systems," Weber (1922/1968) defined three dimensions of social stratification: wealth, power, and prestige. Although, as Weber showed, wealth, power, and prestige are separate components of social ranking, they tend to be correlated. Weber also believed that social identities based on ethnicity, religion, race, nationality, and other attributes could take priority over class (social identity based on economic status). In addition to class contrasts, the modern world system *is* cross-cut by collective identities based on ethnicity, religion, and nationality (Shannon 1996). Class conflicts tend to occur within nations, and nationalism has prevented global class solidarity, particularly of proletarians.

Although the capitalist class dominates politically in most countries, growing wealth has made it easier for core nations to grant higher wages (Hopkins and Wallerstein 1982). However, the improvement in core workers' living standards wouldn't have occurred without the world system. Without the periphery, core capitalists would have trouble maintaining their profits and also satisfying the demands of core workers. In the periphery, wages and living standards are much lower. The current *world stratification system* features a substantial contrast between both capitalists and workers in the core nations and workers on the periphery (see Kerbo 2006).

Colonialism

World-system theory stresses the existence of a global culture and economy. It emphasizes historical contacts, linkages, and power differentials between local people and international forces. The major forces influencing cultural interaction during the past 500 years have been commercial expansion, industrial capitalism, and the dominance of colonial and core nations (Wallerstein 1982, 2004b; Wolf 1982). As state formation had done previously, industrialization accelerated local participation in larger networks. According to Bodley (2007), perpetual expansion is a distinguishing feature of industrial economic systems. Bands and tribes were small, self-sufficient, subsistence-based systems. Industrial economies, by contrast, are large, highly specialized systems in which market exchanges occur with profit as the primary motive (Bodley 2007).

During the 19th century European business interests initiated a concerted search for markets. This process led to European imperialism in Africa, Asia, and Oceania. **Imperialism** refers to a policy of extending the rule of a country or empire over foreign nations and of taking and holding foreign colonies. Imperialism goes back to early states, including Egypt in the Old World and the Incas in the New. A Greek empire was forged by Alexander the Great, and Julius Caesar and his successors spread the Roman empire. More recent examples include the British, French, and Soviet empires (Scheinman 1980).

After 1850, European imperial expansion was aided by improved transportation, which facilitated the colonization of vast areas of sparsely settled lands in the interior of North and South America and Australia. The new colonies purchased masses of goods from the industrial centers and shipped back wheat, cotton, wool, mutton, beef, and leather. The first phase of European colonialism had been the exploration and exploitation of the Americas and the Caribbean after Columbus. A new second phase began as European nations competed for colonies between 1875 and 1914, setting the stage for World War I.

Colonialism is the political, social, economic, and cultural domination of a territory and its people by a foreign power for an extended time (see Bremen and Shimizu, eds. 1999; Cooper and Stoler, eds. 1997). If imperialism is almost as old as the state, colonialism can be traced back to the Phoenicians, who established colonies along the eastern Mediterranean 3,000 years ago. The ancient Greeks and Romans were avid colonizers, as well as empire builders.

The first phase of modern colonialism began with the European "Age of Discovery"—of the Americas and of a sea route to the Far East. After 1492, the Spanish, the original conquerors of the Aztecs and the Incas, explored and colonized widely in the New World—the Caribbean, Mexico, the southern portions of what was to become the United States, and Central and South America. In South America, Portugal ruled over Brazil. Rebellions and wars aimed at independence ended the first phase of European colonialism by the early 19th century. Brazil declared independence from Portugal in 1822. By 1825 most of Spain's colonies were politically independent. Spain held onto Cuba and the Philippines until 1898, but otherwise withdrew from the colonial field. During the first phase of colonialism, Spain and Portugal, along with Britain and France, were major colonizing nations. The latter two (Britain and France) dominated the second phase.

British Colonialism

At its peak about 1914, the British empire covered a fifth of the world's land surface and ruled a fourth of its population (see Figure 10.1). Like several other European nations. Britain had two stages of colonialism. The first began with the Elizabethan voyages of the 16th century. During the 17th century, Britain acquired most of the eastern coast of North America, Canada's St. Lawrence basin, islands in the Caribbean, slave stations in Africa, and interests in India.

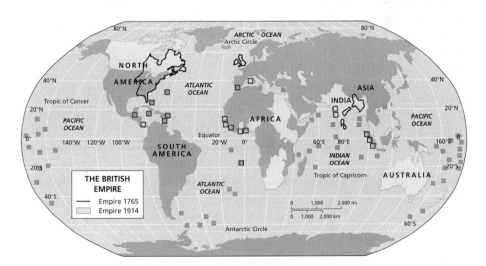

FIGURE 10.1   *Map of British Empire in 1765 and 1914*

The British shared the exploration of the New World with the Spanish, Portuguese, French, and Dutch. The British by and large left Mexico, along with Central and South America, to the Spanish and the Portuguese. The end of the Seven Years' War in 1763 forced a French retreat from most of Canada and India, where France previously had competed with Britain (Cody 1998; Farr 1980).

The American revolution ended the first stage of British colonialism. A second colonial empire, on which the "sun never set," rose from the ashes of the first. Beginning in 1788, but intensifying after 1815, the British settled Australia. Britain had acquired Dutch South Africa by 1815. The establishment of Singapore in 1819 provided a base for a British trade network that extended to much of South Asia and along the coast of China. By this time, the empires of Britain's traditional rivals, particularly Spain, had been severely diminished in scope. Britain's position as imperial power and the world's leading industrial nation was unchallenged (Cody 1998; Farr 1980).

During the Victorian Era (1837–1901), as Britain's acquisition of territory and of further trading concessions continued, Prime Minister Benjamin Disraeli implemented a foreign policy justified by a view of imperialism as shouldering "the white man's burden"—a phrase coined by the poet Rudyard Kipling. People in the empire were seen as unable to govern themselves, so that British guidance was needed to civilize and Christianize them. This paternalistic and racist doctrine served to legitimize Britain's acquisition and control of parts of central Africa and Asia (Cody 1998).

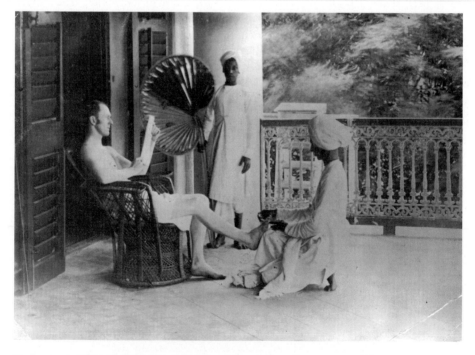

On January 1, 1900, a British officer in India receives a pedicure from a servant. What does this photo say to you about colonialism? Who gives pedicures in your society?

After World War II, the British empire began to fall apart, with nationalist movements for independence. India became independent in 1947, as did Ireland in 1949. Decolonization in Africa and Asia accelerated during the late 1950s. Today, the ties that remain between Britain and its former colonies are mainly linguistic or cultural rather than political (Cody 1998).

French Colonialism

French colonialism also had two phases. The first began with the explorations of the early 1600s. Prior to the French revolution in 1789, missionaries, explorers, and traders carved out niches for France in Canada, the Louisiana territory, several Caribbean islands, and parts of India, which were lost along with Canada to Great Britain in 1763 (Harvey 1980).

The foundations of the second French empire were established between 1830 and 1870. In Great Britain the sheer drive for profit led expansion, but French colonialism was spurred more by the state, church, and armed forces than by pure business interests. France acquired Algeria and part of what eventually became Indochina (Cambodia, Laos, and Vietnam). By 1914 the French empire covered 4 million square miles and included some 60 million people (see Figure 10.2). By 1893 French rule had been fully established in Indochina. Tunisia and Morocco became French protectorates in 1883 and 1912, respectively (Harvey 1980).

To be sure, the French, like the British, had substantial business interests in their colonies, but they also sought, again like the British, international glory and prestige. The French promulgated a *mission civilisatrice,* their equivalent of Britain's "white man's burden." The goal was to implant French culture, language, and religion, Roman Catholicism, throughout the colonies (Harvey 1980).

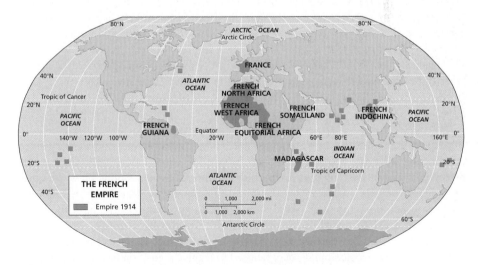

FIGURE 10.2   *Map of the French Empire at Its Height around 1914*

The French used two forms of colonial rule: *indirect rule,* governing through native leaders and established political structures, in areas with long histories of state organization, such as Morocco and Tunisia; and *direct rule* by French officials in many areas of Africa, where the French imposed new government structures to control diverse societies, many of them previously stateless. Like the British empire, the French empire began to disintegrate after World War II. France fought long—and ultimately futile—wars to keep its empire intact in Indochina and Algeria (Harvey 1980).

Colonialism and Identity

Many geopolitical labels in the news today had no equivalent meaning before colonialism. Whole countries, along with social groups and divisions within them, were colonial inventions. In West Africa, for example, by geographic logic, several adjacent countries could be one (Togo, Ghana, Ivory Coast, Guinea, Guinea-Bissau, Sierra Leone, Liberia). Instead, they are separated by linguistic, political, and economic contrasts promoted under colonialism.

Hundreds of ethnic groups and "tribes" are colonial constructions (see Ranger 1996). The Sukuma of Tanzania, for instance, were first registered as a single tribe by the colonial administration. Then missionaries standardized a series of dialects into a single Sukuma language into which they translated the Bible and other religious texts. Thereafter, those texts were taught in missionary schools and to European foreigners and other non-Sukuma speakers. Over time this standardized the Sukuma language and ethnicity (Finnstrom 1997).

As in most of East Africa, in Rwanda and Burundi farmers and herders live in the same areas and speak the same language. Historically they have shared the same social world, although their social organization is "extremely hierarchical," almost "castelike" (Malkki 1995, p. 24). There has been a tendency to see the pastoral Tutsis as superior to the agricultural Hutus. Tutsis have been presented as nobles, Hutus as commoners. Yet when distributing identity cards in Rwanda, the Belgian colonizers simply identified all people with more than 10 head of cattle as Tutsi. Owners of fewer cattle were registered as Hutu (Bjuremalm 1997). Years later, these arbitrary colonial registers were used systematically for "ethnic" identification during the mass killings (genocide) that took place in Rwanda in 1994 (as portrayed vividly in the film *Hotel Rwanda*).

Postcolonial Studies

In anthropology, history, and literature, the field of postcolonial studies has gained prominence since the 1970s (see Ashcroft, Griffiths, and Tiffin 1989; Cooper and Stoler, eds. 1997). **Postcolonial** refers to the study of the interactions between European nations and the societies they colonized (mainly after 1800). In 1914, European empires, which broke up after World War II, ruled more than 85 percent of the world (Petraglia-Bahri 1996). The term "postcolonial" also has been used to describe the second half of the 20th century in general, the period succeeding colonialism. Even more generically, "postcolonial" may be used to signify a position against imperialism and Eurocentrism (Petraglia-Bahri 1996).

The former colonies (*postcolonies*) can be divided into settler, nonsettler, and mixed (Petraglia-Bahri 1996). The settler countries, with large numbers of European colonists and sparser native populations, include Australia and Canada. Examples of nonsettler countries include India, Pakistan, Bangladash, Sri Lanka, Malaysia, Indonesia, Nigeria, Senegal, Madagascar, and Jamaica. All these had substantial native populations and relatively few European settlers. Mixed countries include South Africa, Zimbabwe, Kenya, and Algeria. Such countries had significant European settlement despite having sizable native populations.

Given the varied experiences of such countries, "postcolonial" has to be a loose term. The United States, for instance, was colonized by Europeans and fought a war for independence from Britain. Is the United States a postcolony? It usually isn't perceived as such, given its current world power position, its treatment of native Americans (sometimes called internal colonization), and its annexation of other parts of the world (Petraglia-Bahri 1996). Research in postcolonial studies is growing, permitting a wide-ranging investigation of power relations in varied contexts. Broad topics in the field include the formation of an empire, the impact of colonization, and the state of the postcolony today (Petraglia-Bahri 1996).

Development

During the Industrial Revolution, a strong current of thought viewed industrialization as a beneficial process of organic development and progress. Many economists still assume that industrialization increases production and income. They seek to create in Third World ("developing") countries a process like the one that first occurred spontaneously in 18th-century Great Britain.

We have seen that Britain used the notion of a white man's burden to justify its imperialist expansion and that France claimed to be engaged in a *mission civilisatrice,* a civilizing mission, in its colonies. Both these ideas illustrate an **intervention philosophy,** an ideological justification for outsiders to guide native peoples in specific directions. Economic development plans also have intervention philosophies. John Bodley (2008) argues that the basic belief behind interventions—whether by colonialists, missionaries, governments, or development planners—has been the same for more than 100 years. This belief is that industrialization, modernization, Westernization, and individualism are desirable evolutionary advances and that development schemes that promote them will bring long-term benefits to local people. In a more extreme form, intervention philosophy may pit the assumed wisdom of enlightened colonial or other First World planners against the purported conservatism, ignorance, or "obsolescence" of "inferior" or "backward" local people.

Neoliberalism

One currently influential intervention philosophy is neoliberalism. This term encompasses a set of assumptions that have become widespread during the last 30 years. Neoliberal policies are being implemented in developing nations, including postsocialist societies (e.g., those of the former Soviet Union). **Neoliberalism** is the current form of the classic economic liberalism laid out in Adam Smith's famous capitalist manifesto, *The Wealth of Nations,* published in 1776, soon after the Industrial Revolution. Smith advocated laissez-faire (hands-off) economics as the basis of capitalism: The government should stay out of its nation's economic affairs. Free trade, Smith thought, was the best way for a nation's economy to develop. There should be no restrictions on manufacturing, no barriers to commerce, and no tariffs. This philosophy is called "liberalism" because it aimed at liberating or freeing the economy from government controls. Economic liberalism encouraged "free" enterprise and competition, with the goal of generating profits. (Note the difference between this meaning of *liberal* and the one that has been popularized on American talk radio, in which "liberal" is used—usually as a derogatory term—as the opposite of "conservative." Ironically, Adam Smith's liberalism is today's capitalist "conservatism.")

Economic liberalism prevailed in the United States until President Franklin Roosevelt's New Deal during the 1930s. The Great Depression produced a turn to Keynesian economics, which challenged liberalism. John Maynard Keynes (1927, 1936) insisted that full employment was necessary for capitalism to grow, that governments and central banks should intervene to increase employment, and that government should promote the common good.

Especially since the fall of Communism (1989–1991), there has been a revival of economic liberalism, now known as neoliberalism, which has been spreading globally. Around the world, neoliberal policies have been imposed by powerful financial institutions such as the International Monetary Fund (IMF), the World Bank, and the Inter-American Development Bank (see Edelman and Haugerud 2004). Neoliberalism entails open (tariff- and barrier-free) international trade and investment. Profits are sought through lowering of costs, whether through improving productivity, laying off workers, or seeking workers who accept lower wages. In exchange for loans, the governments of postsocialist and developing nations have been required to accept the neoliberal premise that deregulation leads to economic growth, which will eventually benefit everyone through a process sometimes called "trickle down." Accompanying the belief in free markets and the idea of cutting costs is a tendency to impose austerity measures that cut government expenses. This can entail reduced public spending on education, health care, and other social services (Martinez and Garcia 2000).

The Second World

The labels "First World," "Second World," and "Third World" represent a common, although ethnocentric, way of categorizing nations. The *First World* refers to the "democratic West"—traditionally conceived in opposition to a "Second World" ruled by "Communism." The *Second World* refers to the former Soviet Union and the socialist and once-socialist countries of Eastern Europe and Asia. Proceeding with this classification, the "less-developed countries" or "developing nations" make up the *Third World.*

Communism

The two meanings of communism involve how it is written, whether with a lowercase (small) or an uppercase (large) *c*. Small-*c* **communism** describes a social system in which property is owned by the community and in which people work for the common good. Large-*C* **Communism** was a political movement and doctrine seeking to overthrow capitalism and to establish a form of communism such as that which prevailed in the Soviet Union (USSR) from 1917 to 1991. The heyday of Communism was a 40-year period from 1949 to 1989, when more Communist regimes existed than at any time before or after. Today only five Communist states remain—China, Cuba, Laos, North Korea, and Vietnam, compared with 23 in 1985.

Communism, which originated with Russia's Bolshevik Revolution in 1917, and took its inspiration from Karl Marx and Friedrich Engels, was not uniform over time or among countries. All Communist systems were *authoritarian* (promoting obedience to authority rather than individual freedom). Many were *totalitarian* (banning rival parties and demanding total submission of the individual to the state). Several features distinguished Communist societies from other authoritarian regimes (e.g., Spain under Franco) and from socialism of a social democratic type. First, the Communist Party monopolized power in every Communist state. Second, relations within the party were highly centralized and strictly disciplined. Third, Communist nations had state ownership, rather than private ownership, of the means of production. Finally, all Communist regimes, with the goal of advancing communism, cultivated a sense of belonging to an international movement (Brown 2001).

Social scientists have tended to refer to such societies as socialist rather than Communist. Today research by anthropologists is thriving in *postsocialist* societies—those that once emphasized bureaucratic redistribution of wealth according to a central plan (Verdery 2001). In the postsocialist period, states that once had planned economies have been following the neoliberal agenda, by divesting themselves of state-owned resources in favor of privatization. Some of them have moved toward formal liberal democracy, with political parties, elections, and a balance of powers (Grekova 2001).

Postsocialist Transitions

Neoliberal economists assumed that dismantling the Soviet Union's planned economy would raise gross domestic product (GDP) and living standards. The goal was to enhance production by substituting a decentralized market system and providing incentives through privatization. In October 1991, Boris Yeltsin, who had been elected president of Russia that June, announced a program of radical market-oriented reform, pursuing a changeover to capitalism. Yeltsin's program of "shock therapy" cut subsidies to farms and industries and ended price controls. Since then, postsocialist Russia has faced many problems. The anticipated gains in productivity did not materialize. After the fall of the Soviet Union, Russia's GDP fell by half. Poverty increased, with a quarter of the population now living below the poverty line. Life expectancy and the birth rate declined. Another problem to emerge in the postsocialist transition is corruption. In response, the World Bank and other international organizations have launched anticorruption programs worldwide. *Corruption* is defined as the abuse of public office for private gain.

The World Bank's approach to corruption assumes a clear and sharp distinction between the state (the public or official domain) and the private sphere, and that the two should be kept separate. The idea that the public sphere can be separated neatly from the private sphere is ethnocentric. According to Janine Wedel (2002), postsocialist states provide rich contexts in which to explore variability in relations between public and private domains. Alexei Yurchak (2002, 2005) describes two spheres that operate in Russia today; these spheres do not mesh neatly with the assumption of a public–private split. He calls them the official–public sphere and the personal–public sphere, referring to domains that coexist and sometimes overlap. State officials may respect the law (official–public), while also working with informal or even criminal groups (personal–public). Officials switch from official–public to personal–public behavior all the time, in order to accomplish specific tasks.

The World System Today

The process of industrialization continues today, although nations have shifted their positions within the world system (Table 10.1). By 1900, the United States had become a core nation within the world system and had overtaken Great Britain in iron, coal, and cotton production. In a few decades (1868–1900). Japan had changed from a medieval handicraft economy to an industrial one, joining the semiperiphery by 1900 and moving to the core between 1945 and 1970. Figure 10.3 is a map showing the modern world system.

Twentieth-century industrialization added hundreds of new industries and millions of new jobs. Production increased, often beyond immediate demand, spurring strategies, such as advertising, to sell everything industry could churn out. Mass production gave rise to a culture of consumption, which valued acquisitiveness and conspicuous consumption (Veblen 1934). Industrialization entailed a shift from reliance on renewable resources to the use of fossil fuels. Fossil fuel energy, stored over millions of years, is being depleted rapidly to support a previously unknown and probably unsustainable level of consumption. (See also the chapter "Global Issues Today.")

TABLE 10.1

Ascent and Decline of Nations within the World System

Periphery to Semiperiphery	Semiperiphery to Core	Core to Semiperiphery
United States (1800–1860)	United States (1860–1900)	Spain (1620–1700)
Japan (1868–1900)	Japan (1945–1970)	
Taiwan (1949–1980)	Germany (1870–1900)	
S. Korea (1953–1980)		

SOURCE: Reprinted by permission of Westview Press from *An Introduction to the World-System Perspective* by Thomas Richard Shannon. Copyright Westview Press 1989, Boulder, Colorado.

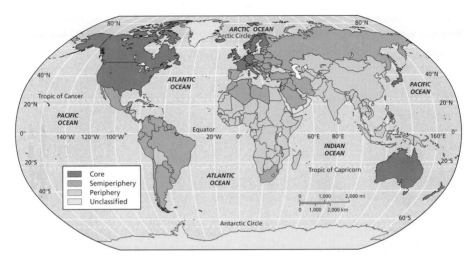

FIGURE 10.3   *The World System Today*

SOURCE: From *Anthropology: The Exploration of Human Diversity,* 10th ed., Figure 23.5, p. 660, by Conrad Kottak. Reprinted by permission of The McGraw-Hill Companies.

Table 10.2 compares energy consumption in various types of cultures. Americans are the world's foremost consumers of nonrenewable resources. In terms of energy consumption, the average American is about 35 times more expensive than the average forager or tribesperson. Since 1900, the United States has tripled its per capita energy use. It also has increased its total energy consumption thirtyfold.

Table 10.3 compares energy consumption, per capita and total, in the United States and selected other countries. The United States represents 21.8 percent of the world's annual energy consumption, compared with China's 14.5 percent, but the average American consumes 6.6 times the energy used by the average Chinese, and 23 times the energy used by the average inhabitant of India.

TABLE 10.2

Energy Consumption in Various Contexts

Type of Society	Daily Kilocalories per Person
Bands and tribes	4,000–12,000
Preindustrial states	26,000 (maximum)
Early industrial states	70,000
Americans in 1970	230,000
Americans in 1990	275,000

SOURCE: From *Anthropology and Contemporary Human Problems,* by John H. Bodley. Copyright © 1985. Reprinted by permission of The McGraw-Hill Companies.

TABLE 10.3

Energy Consumption in Selected Countries, 2005

	Total	Per Capita
World	462.8*	72[†]
United States	100.7	340
China	67.1	51
Russia	30.3	212
India	16.2	15
Germany	14.5	176
Canada	14.3	436
France	11.4	182
United Kingdom	10.0	166

*462.8 quadrillion (462,800,000,000,000,000) Btu.
[†]72 million Btu.
SOURCE: Based on data in *Statistical Abstract of the United States*, 2009 (Table 1356), p. 841.

Industrial Degradation

Industrialization and factory labor now characterize many societies in Latin America, Africa, the Pacific, and Asia. One effect of the spread of industrialization has been the destruction of indigenous economies, ecologies, and populations. Two centuries ago, as industrialization was developing, 50 million people still lived in politically independent bands, tribes, and chiefdoms. Occupying vast areas, those nonstate societies, although not totally isolated, were only marginally affected by nation-states and the world capitalist economy. In 1800 bands, tribes, and chiefdoms controlled half the globe and 20 percent of its population (Bodley 2008). Industrialization tipped the balance in favor of states (see Hornborg and Crumley 2007).

As industrial states have conquered, annexed, and "developed" nonstates, there has been genocide on a grand scale. *Genocide* refers to a deliberate policy of exterminating a group through warfare or murder. Examples include the Holocaust, Rwanda in 1994, and Bosnia in the early 1990s. Bodley (2008) estimates that an average of 250,000 indigenous people perished annually between 1800 and 1950. Besides warfare, the causes included foreign diseases (to which natives lacked resistance), slavery, land grabbing, and other forms of dispossession and impoverishment.

Many native groups have been incorporated within nation-states, in which they have become ethnic minorities. Some such groups have been able to recoup their population. Many indigenous peoples survive and maintain their ethnic identity despite having lost their ancestral cultures to varying degrees (partial ethnocide). And many descendants of tribespeople live on as culturally distinct and self-conscious colonized peoples, many of whom aspire to autonomy. As the original inhabitants of their territories, they are called **indigenous peoples** (see Maybury-Lewis 2002).

Industrial degradation today. In Cape Town, a South African
boy crosses a severely polluted river. In this impoverished
slum, 1,000 families share three toilets and two water taps.

Around the world many contemporary nations are repeating—at an accelerated rate—the process of resource depletion that started in Europe and the United States during the Industrial Revolution. Fortunately, however, today's world has some environmental watchdogs that did not exist during the first centuries of the Industrial Revolution. Given national and international cooperation and sanctions, the modern world may benefit from the lessons of the past (see Hornborg, McNeill, and Martinez-Alier, eds. 2007).

ANTHROPOLOGY TODAY

Mining Giant Compatible with Sustainability Institute?

The spread of industrialization, illustrated by the mining described here, has contributed to the destruction of indigenous economies, ecologies, and populations. Today, multinational conglomerates, along with nations such as Papua New Guinea as described here, are repeating—at an accelerated rate—the process of resource depletion that started in Europe and the United States during the Industrial Revolution. Fortunately, however, today's world has some environmental watchdogs, including anthropologists, that did not exist during the first centuries of the Industrial Revolution. Described here is a conundrum confronting a major university. Is a firm whose operations have destroyed the landscapes and livelihoods of indigenous peoples a proper advisor for an institute devoted to ecological sustainability?

Continued

ANTHROPOLOGY TODAY   *Continued*

In the 1990s, the giant mining company now known as BHP Billiton drew worldwide condemnation for the environmental damage caused by its copper and gold mine in Papua New Guinea. Its mining practices destroyed the way of life of thousands of farming and fishing families who lived along and subsisted on the rivers polluted by the mine, and it was only after being sued in a landmark class-action case that the company agreed to compensate them.

Today several activists and academics who work on behalf of indigenous people around the world say the company continues to dodge responsibility for the problems its mines create for communities in undeveloped parts of the world.

Yet at the University of Michigan at Ann Arbor, BHP Billiton enjoys a loftier reputation: It is one of 14 corporate members of an External Advisory Board for the university's new Graham Environmental Sustainability Institute.

Critics at and outside the university contend that Michigan's decision to enlist BHP Billiton as an adviser to an institute devoted to sustainability reflects badly on the institution and allows the company to claim a mantle of environmental and social responsibility that it does not deserve.

The institute's director says he is satisfied that the company is serious about operating in a more sustainable way. . . .

The arguments echo the discussions about corporate "greenwashing" that have arisen at Stanford University and the University of California at Berkeley over major research grants from ExxonMobil and BP, respectively, and more recently,

the debate at the Smithsonian Institution among its trustees over whether to accept a gift from the American Petroleum Institute for a museum exhibition about oceans. (The gift was withdrawn in November.)

For one BHP Billiton critic at Michigan, the issue is personal. Stuart Kirsch, an associate professor of anthropology, has spent most of his academic career documenting the damage caused by BHP Billiton's Ok Tedi mine in Papua New Guinea. . . .

Mr. Kirsch, who first visited some of the affected communities as a young ethnographer in 1987, became involved in the class-action lawsuit brought against the company and helped villagers participate in the 1996 legal settlement. "I put my career on hold while being an activist," he says.

He subsequently published several papers related to his work with the Yonggom people as they fought for recognition and compensation from mine operators—scholarship that helped him win tenure this year—and he remains involved with the network of activists and academics who follow mining and its impact on undeveloped communities around the world. . . .

The company's practices polluted the Ok Tedi and Fly Rivers and caused thousands of people to leave their homes because the mining-induced flooding made it impossible for them to grow food to feed themselves, says Mr. Kirsch.

BHP Billiton, based in Australia, later acknowledged that the mine was "not compatible with our environmental values," and spun it off to an independent company that pays all of its mining royalties to the government of Papua New Guinea.

But Mr. Kirsch says that in doing so, the company skirted responsibility for ameliorating the damage it caused. BHP Billiton says it would have preferred to close the mine, but the Papua New Guinea government, in need of the mine revenues, pressed to keep it open. The deal freed BHP Billiton from any future liabilities for environmental damage.

"They didn't clean it up; they didn't take responsibility for the damage they had done," Mr. Kirsch says of the company. With that record, "it's supposed to provide education to the University of Michigan?". . . .

Illtud Harri, a BHP Billiton spokesman, says the company regrets its past with Ok Tedi but considers its pullout from the mine "a responsible exit" that left in place a system that supports educational, agricultural, and social programs for the people of the community.

He says the company also aims for the most ethical standards in its projects. The company mines only when it can fully comply with the host country's environmental laws. In places where those regulatory requirements fall below the company's, "we will always be guided by our higher standards," he says.

Mr. Talbot, the interim director of the two-year-old sustainability institute, says . . . "We intentionally selected a cross-sector group of organizations" for the advisory board from a list of about 140 nominees, . . . and several companies that "weren't making any serious efforts" toward sustainability were rejected. . . .

BHP Billiton, a company formed from the 2001 merger of the Australian mining enterprise Broken Hill Proprietary Company with London-based Billiton, is now the world's largest mining company, with more than 100 operations in 25 countries. . . .

The BHP Billiton charter includes a statement that the company has "an overriding commitment to health, safety, environmental responsibility, and sustainable development." But its critics say the company continues to play a key role in mining projects with questionable records on environmental and human rights, even though in many of those cases, it is not directly responsible. . . .

Mr. Kirsch, who is now on leave from Michigan to write a book, says he is planning to press for an open forum at the university that includes environmental scientists, indigenous people affected by the Ok Tedi mine, and company officials themselves.

BHP Billiton has the resources to present itself as the "golden boy," but, says Mr. Kirsch, "it's much harder to see the people on the Ok Tedi and Fly rivers."

A forum could help to right that imbalance, he says. "Let the students and faculty decide whether this is an appropriate company to advise the University of Michigan," says Mr. Kirsch. "It would be an educational process for everyone involved."

Source: Goldie Blumenstyk, "Mining Company Involved in Environmental Disaster Now Advises Sustainability Institute at U. of Michigan," *Chronicle of Higher Education,* December 7, 2007. Copyright © 2007, The Chronicle of Higher Education. Reprinted with permission.

Summary

1. Local societies increasingly participate in wider systems—regional, national, and global. The capitalist world economy depends on production for sale, with the goal of maximizing profits. The key claim of world-system theory is that an identifiable social system, based on wealth and power differentials, extends beyond individual countries. That system is formed by a set of economic and political relations that has characterized much of the globe since the 16th century. World capitalism has political and economic specialization at the core, semiperiphery, and periphery.

2. Columbus's voyages opened the way for a major exchange between the Old and New Worlds. Seventeenth-century plantation economies in the Caribbean and Brazil were based on sugar. In the 18th century, plantation economies based on cotton arose in the southeastern United States.

3. The Industrial Revolution began in England around 1760. Transoceanic commerce supplied capital for industrial investment. Industrialization hastened the separation of workers from the means of production. Marx saw a sharp division between the bourgeoisie and the proletariat. Class consciousness was a key feature of Marx's view of this stratification. Weber believed that social solidarity based on ethnicity, religion, race, or nationality could take priority over class. Today's capitalist world economy maintains the contrast between those who own the means of production and those who don't, but the division is now worldwide. There is a substantial contrast between not only capitalists but workers in the core nations and workers on the periphery.

4. Imperialism is the policy of extending the rule of a nation or empire over other nations and of taking and holding foreign colonies. Colonialism is the domination of a territory and its people by a foreign power for an extended time. European colonialism had two main phases. The first started in 1492 and lasted through 1825. For Britain this phase ended with the American Revolution. For France it ended when Britain won the Seven Years' War, forcing the French to abandon Canada and India. For Spain, it ended with Latin American independence. The second phase of European colonialism extended approximately from 1850 to 1950. The British and French empires were at their height around 1914, when European empires controlled 85 percent of the world. Britain and France had colonies in Africa, Asia, Oceania, and the New World.

5. Many geopolitical labels and identities were created under colonialism that had little or nothing to do with existing social demarcations. The new ethnic or national divisions were colonial inventions, sometimes aggravating conflicts.

6. Like colonialism, economic development has an intervention philosophy that provides a justification for outsiders to guide native peoples toward particular goals. Development usually is justified by the idea that industrialization and modernization are desirable evolutionary advances. Neoliberalism revives and extends classic economic liberalism: the idea that governments should not regulate private enterprise and that free market forces should rule. This intervention philosophy currently dominates aid agreements with postsocialist and developing nations.

7. Spelled with a lowercase *c*, communism describes a social system in which property is owned by the community and in which people work for the common good. Spelled with an uppercase *C*, Communism indicates a political movement and doctrine seeking to overthrow capitalism and to establish a form of communism such as that which prevailed in the Soviet Union from 1917 to 1991. The heyday of Communism was between 1949 and 1989. The fall of Communism can be traced to 1989–1990 in eastern Europe and 1991 in the Soviet Union. Postsocialist states have followed the neoliberal agenda, through privatization, deregulation, and democratization.

8. By 1900 the United States had become a core nation. Mass production gave rise to a culture that valued acquisitiveness and conspicuous consumption. One effect of industrialization has been the destruction of indigenous economies, ecologies, and populations. Another has been the accelerated rate of resource depletion.

Key Terms

bourgeoisie (p. 216)

capital (p. 211)

capitalist world economy (p. 211)

colonialism (p. 219)

communism (p. 225)

Communism (p. 225)

core (p. 212)

imperialism (p. 218)

indigenous peoples (p. 228)

Industrial Revolution (p. 214)

intervention philosophy (p. 223)

neoliberalism (p. 224)

periphery (p. 213)

postcolonial (p. 224)

semiperiphery (p. 212)

working class, or proletariat (p. 216)

world-system theory (p. 212)

Go to our Online Learning Center website at **www.mhhe.com/kottak** for Internet resources directly related to the content of this chapter.

Ethnicity and Race

Ethnicity is based on cultural similarities and differences in a society or nation. The similarities are with members of the same ethnic group; the differences are between that group and others. Ethnic groups must deal with other such groups in the nation or region they inhabit, so that interethnic relations are important in the study of that nation or region. (Table 11.1 lists American ethnic groups, based on 2007 figures.)

Ethnic Groups and Ethnicity

As with any culture, members of an **ethnic group** *share* certain beliefs, values, habits, customs, and norms because of their common background. They define themselves as different and special because of cultural features. This distinction may arise from language, religion, historical experience, geographic placement, kinship, or "race" (see Spickard, ed. 2004). Markers of an ethnic group may include a collective name, belief in common descent, a sense of solidarity, and an association with a specific territory, which the group may or may not hold (Ryan 1990, pp. xiii, xiv).

According to Fredrik Barth (1969), ethnicity can be said to exist when people claim a certain ethnic identity for themselves and are defined by others as having that identity. **Ethnicity** means identification with, and feeling part of, an ethnic group and exclusion from certain other groups because of this affiliation. Ethnic feelings and associated behavior vary in intensity within ethnic groups and countries and over time. A change in the degree of importance attached to an ethnic identity may reflect

TABLE 11.1

Racial/Ethnic Identification in the United States, 2007 (estimated by U.S. Census Bureau)

Claimed Identity	Number (millions)	Percentage
White (non-Hispanic)	199.1	66.1
Hispanic	45.4	15.1
Black	38.8	12.9
Asian	13.4	4.5
American Indian	2.9	1.0
Pacific Islander	.5	.2
Total population	301.1	99.8

SOURCE: Statistical Abstract of the United States, 2009, Table 6, p. 9.

political changes (Soviet rule ends—ethnic feeling rises) or individual life-cycle changes (young people relinquish, or old people reclaim, an ethnic background).

Cultural differences may be associated with ethnicity, class, region, or religion. Individuals often have more than one group identity. People may be loyal (depending on circumstances) to their neighborhood, school, town, state or province, region, nation, continent, religion, ethnic group, or interest group (Ryan 1990, p. xxii). In a complex society such as the United States or Canada, people constantly negotiate their social identities. All of us "wear different hats," presenting ourselves sometimes as one thing, sometimes as another.

Status Shifting

Sometimes our identities (aka social statuses) are mutually exclusive. It's hard to be both black and white or male and female. Sometimes, assuming an identity or joining a group requires a conversion experience, acquiring a new and overwhelming primary identity, such as becoming a "born again" Christian.

Some statuses aren't mutually exclusive, but contextual. People can be both black and Hispanic or both a mother and a senator. One identity is used in certain settings, another in different ones. We call this the *situational negotiation of social identity* (Leman 2001). Hispanics, for example, may shift ethnic affiliations as they negotiate their identities. "Hispanic" is a category based mainly on language. It includes whites, blacks, and "racially" mixed Spanish speakers and their ethnically conscious descendants. (There also are Native American and even Asian Hispanics.) "Hispanics," the fastest-growing ethnic group in the United States, lumps together people of diverse geographic origin—Puerto Rico, Mexico, Cuba, El Salvador, Guatemala, the Dominican Republic, and other Spanish-speaking countries of Central and South America and the Caribbean. "Latino" is a broader category, which also can include Brazilians (who speak Portuguese). The national origins of American Hispanics/Latinos (excluding Brazilians) in 2007 are shown in Table 11.2.

TABLE 11.2

American Hispanics, Latinos, 2007

National Origin	Percentage
Mexican American	64.3%
Puerto Rican	9.1
Cuban	3.5
Central & South American	13.3
Other Hispanic/Latino origin	9.8
Total	100.0%

SOURCE: Pew Hispanic Center, Statistical Portrait of Hispanics in the United States, 2007, Table 5: Detailed Hispanic Origin. http://pewhispanic.org/files/factsheets/hispanics2007/Table-5.pdf.

Mexican Americans (Chicanos), Cuban Americans, and Puerto Ricans may mobilize to promote general Hispanic issues (e.g., opposition to "English-only" laws) but act as three separate interest groups in other contexts. Cuban Americans are richer on average than Chicanos and Puerto Ricans are, and their class interests and voting patterns differ. Cubans often vote Republican, but Puerto Ricans and Chicanos are more likely to favor Democrats. Some Mexican Americans whose families have lived in the United States for generations have little in common with new Hispanic immigrants, such as those from Central America. Many Americans (especially those fluent in English) claim Hispanic ethnicity in some contexts but shift to a general "American" identity in others.

In many societies a racial, ethnic, or caste status is associated with a position in the social–political hierarchy. Certain groups, called **minority groups,** are subordinate. They have inferior power and less secure access to resources than do **majority groups** (which are superordinate, dominant, or controlling). Often ethnic groups are minorities. When an ethnic group is assumed to have a biological basis (distinctively shared "blood" or genes), it is called a **race.** Discrimination against such a group is called **racism** (Cohen 1998; Montagu 1997; Scupin 2003; Shanklin 1995; Wade 2002).

Race and Ethnicity

Race, like ethnicity in general, is a cultural category rather than a biological reality. That is, ethnic groups, including "races," derive from contrasts perceived and perpetuated in particular societies, rather than from scientific classifications based on common genes (see Wade 2002).

It is not possible to define human races biologically. Only cultural constructions of race are possible—even though the average person conceptualizes "race" in biological terms (see Mukhopadhyay, Heuze, and Moses 2007). The belief that human races exist and are important is much more common among the public than it is among scientists. Most Americans, for example, believe that their population includes biologically based races to which various labels have been applied. These labels

The ethnic label "Hispanic" lumps together millions of people of diverse racial types and countries of origin. People of diverse national backgrounds may mobilize to promote general Hispanic issues (such as opposition to "English-only" laws), but act as separate interest groups in other contexts. Shown here are Salvadorians in downtown Los Angeles watching a Central American Independence Day parade on September 19, 2004.

include "white," "black," "yellow," "red," "Caucasoid," "Negroid," "Mongoloid," "Amerindian," "Euro-American," "African American," "Asian American," and "Native American."

We hear the words *ethnicity* and *race* frequently, but American culture doesn't draw a very clear line between them. As illustration, consider two articles in *The New York Times* of May 29, 1992. One, discussing the changing ethnic composition of the United States, explains (correctly) that Hispanics "can be of any race" (Barringer 1992, p. A12). In other words, "Hispanic" is an ethnic category that cross-cuts racial contrasts such as that between "black" and "white." The other article reports that during the Los Angeles riots of spring 1992, "hundreds of Hispanic residents were interrogated about their immigration status on the basis of their *race* alone [emphasis added]" (Mydans 1992*a*, p. A8). Use of "race" here seems inappropriate because "Hispanic" usually is perceived as referring to a linguistically based (Spanish-speaking) ethnic group, rather than a biologically based race. Since these Los Angeles residents were being interrogated because they were Hispanic, the article is actually reporting on ethnic, not racial, discrimination. However, given the lack of a precise distinction between race and ethnicity, it is probably better to use the term "ethnic group" instead of "race" to describe *any* such social group, for example, African Americans, Asian Americans, Irish Americans, Anglo Americans, or Hispanics.

The Social Construction of Race

Races are ethnic groups assumed (by members of a particular culture) to have a biological basis, but actually race is socially constructed. The "races" we hear about every day are cultural, or social, rather than biological categories. Many Americans mistakenly assume that whites and blacks, for example, are biologically distinct and that these terms stand for discrete races. But these labels, like racial terms used in other societies, really designate culturally perceived rather than biologically based groups.

Hypodescent: Race in the United States

How is race culturally constructed in the United States? In American culture, one acquires his or her racial identity at birth, as an ascribed status, but race isn't based on biology or on simple ancestry. Take the case of the child of a "racially mixed" marriage involving one black and one white parent. We know that 50 percent of the child's genes come from one parent and 50 percent from the other. Still, American culture overlooks heredity and classifies this child as black. This rule is arbitrary. On the basis of genotype (genetic composition), it would be just as logical to classify the child as white.

American rules for assigning racial status can be even more arbitrary. In some states, anyone known to have any black ancestor, no matter how remote, is classified as a member of the black race. This is a rule of **descent** (it assigns social identity on the basis of ancestry), but of a sort that is rare outside the contemporary United States. It is called **hypodescent** (Harris and Kottak 1963) because it automatically places the children of a union between members of different groups in the minority group (*hypo* means "lower"). Hypodescent divides American society into groups that have been unequal in their access to wealth, power, and prestige.

The following case from Louisiana is an excellent illustration of the arbitrariness of the hypodescent rule and of the role that governments (federal or, in this case, state) play in legalizing, inventing, or eradicating race and ethnicity (B. Williams 1989). Susie Guillory Phipps, a light-skinned woman with Caucasian features and straight black hair, discovered as an adult that she was black. When Phipps ordered a copy of her birth certificate, she found her race listed as "colored." Since she had been "brought up white and married white twice," Phipps challenged a 1970 Louisiana law declaring anyone with at least one-thirty-second "Negro blood" to be legally black. Although the state's lawyer admitted that Phipps "looks like a white person," the state of Louisiana insisted that her racial classification was proper (Yetman, ed. 1991, pp. 3–4).

Cases like Phipps's are rare because racial identity usually is ascribed at birth and doesn't change. The rule of hypodescent affects blacks, Asians, Native Americans, and Hispanics differently (see Hunter 2005). It's easier to negotiate Indian or Hispanic identity than black identity. The ascription rule isn't as definite, and the assumption of a biological basis isn't as strong.

To be considered Native American, one ancestor out of eight (great-grandparents) or out of four (grandparents) may suffice. This depends on whether the assignment is by federal or state law or by an Indian tribal council. The child of a Hispanic may (or may not, depending on context) claim Hispanic identity. Many Americans with an Indian or Latino grandparent consider themselves white and lay no claim to minority group status.

Race in the Census

The U.S. Census Bureau has gathered data by race since 1790. Initially this was done because the Constitution specified that a slave counted as three-fifths of a white person, and because Indians were not taxed. The racial categories included in the 1990 census were "White," "Black or Negro," "Indian (American)," "Eskimo," "Aleut or Pacific Islander," and "Other." A separate question was asked about Spanish–Hispanic heritage. Check out Figure 11.1 for the racial categories in the 2000 census.

Attempts by social scientists and interested citizens to add a "multiracial" census category have been opposed by the National Association for the Advancement of Colored People (NAACP) and the National Council of La Raza (a Hispanic advocacy group). Racial classification is a political issue (Goldberg 2002) involving access to resources, including jobs, voting districts, and federal funding of programs aimed at minorities. The hypodescent rule results in all the population growth being attributed to the minority category. Minorities fear their political clout will decline if their numbers go down.

But things are changing. Choice of "some other race" in the U.S. Census more than doubled from 1980 (6.8 million) to 2000 (over 15 million)—suggesting imprecision in and dissatisfaction with the existing categories (Mar 1997). In the 2000 census, 2.4 percent of Americans, or 6.8 million people, chose a first-ever option of identifying themselves as belonging to more than one race. The number of interracial marriages and children is increasing, with implications for the traditional system of American racial classification. "Interracial," "biracial," or "multiracial" children who grow up with both parents undoubtedly identify with particular qualities of either parent. It is troubling for many of them to have so important an identity as race dictated by the arbitrary rule of hypodescent. It may be especially discordant when racial identity doesn't parallel gender identity, for instance, a boy with a white father and a black mother, or a girl with a white mother and a black father.

How does the Canadian census compare with the American census in its treatment of race? Rather than race, the Canadian census asks about "visible

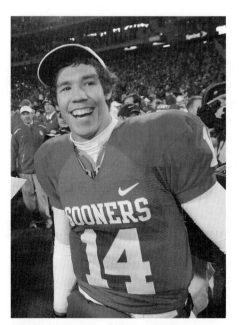

Sooner quarterback and Heisman winner Sam Bradford is a registered Cherokee Indian, but with significant non-Indian ancestry. What's Sam's race?

→ **NOTE: Please answer BOTH Questions 5 and 6.**

5. **Is this person Spanish/Hispanic/Latino?** *Mark* ☒ the
   "No" box if ***not*** *Spanish/Hispanic/Latino.*
   ☐ **No,** not Spanish/Hispanic/Latino   ☐ Yes, Puerto Rican
   ☐ Yes, Mexican, Mexican Am., Chicano   ☐ Yes, Cuban
   ☐ Yes, other Spanish/Hispanic/Latino —*Print group.* ↗

   [write-in grid]

6. **What is this person's race?** *Mark* ☒ ***one or more races*** *to*
   indicate what this person considers himself/herself to be.
   ☐ White
   ☐ Black, African Am., or Negro
   ☐ American Indian or Alaska Native —*Print name of enrolled or principal tribe.* ↗

   [write-in grid]

   ☐ Asian Indian ☐ Japanese   ☐ Native Hawaiian
   ☐ Chinese   ☐ Korean   ☐ Guamanian or Chamorro
   ☐ Filipino   ☐ Vietnamese ☐ Samoan
   ☐ Other Asian —*Print race.* ↗ ☐ Other Pacific Islander —*Print race.* ↗

   [write-in grid]

   ☐ Some other race —*Print race.* ↗

   [write-in grid]

FIGURE 11.1 *Reproduction of Questions on Race and Hispanic Origin from Census 2000*

SOURCE: U.S. Census Bureau, Census 2000 questionnaire.

minorities." That country's Employment Equity Act defines such groups as "persons, other than Aboriginal peoples [aka First Nations in Canada, Native Americans in the United States], who are non-Caucasian in race or non-white in colour" (Statistics Canada 2001a). Table 11.3 shows that "South Asian" and "Chinese" are Canada's largest visible minorities. Note that Canada's total visible minority population of 16.2 percent (up from 11.2 percent in 1996) contrasts with a figure of about 25 percent for the United States in the 2000 census and over 33 percent in 2007. In particular, Canada's black population of 2.5 percent contrasts with the American figure of 12.9 percent (2007) for African Americans, while Canada's Asian population is significantly higher than the U.S. figure of 4.5 percent (2007) on a percentage basis. Only a tiny fraction of the Canadian population (0.4 percent) claimed multiple visible minority affiliation, compared with 2.4 percent claiming "more than one race" in the United States in 2000.

Canada's visible minority population has been increasing steadily. In 1981, 1.1 million visible minorities accounted for 4.7 percent of the total population, versus 16.2 percent today. Visible minorities are growing much faster than is Canada's total population. Between 2001 and 2006, the total population increased 5 percent, while visible minorities rose 27 percent. If recent immigration trends continue, by 2016, visible minorities will account for 20 percent of the Canadian population.

TABLE 11.3

Visible Minority Population of Canada, 2006 Census

	Number	Percent
Total Population	**31,241,030**	**100.0**
Total visible minority population	5,068,090	16.2
South Asian	1,262,865	4.0
Chinese	1,216,515	3.9
Black	783,795	2.5
Filipino	410,695	1.3
Arab/West Asian	374,835	1.2
Latin American	304,245	1.0
Southeast Asian	239,935	0.8
Korean	141,890	0.5
Japanese	83,300	0.3
Other visible minority	116,895	0.4
Multiple visible minority	133,120	0.4
Nonvisible minority	26,172,940	83.8

SOURCE: From Statistics Canada, 2006 Census, http://www12.statcan.ca/english/census06/data/highlights/ethnic.

Not Us: Race in Japan

American culture ignores considerable diversity in biology, language, and geographic origin as it socially constructs race in the United States. North Americans also over-look diversity by seeing Japan as a nation that is homogeneous in race, ethnicity, language, and culture—an image the Japanese themselves cultivate. Thus in 1986 former Prime Minister Nakasone created an international furor by contrasting his country's supposed homogeneity (responsible, he suggested, for Japan's success at that time in international business) with the ethnically mixed United States.

Japan is hardly the uniform entity Nakasone described. Scholars estimate that 10 percent of Japan's national population are minorities of various sorts. These include aboriginal Ainu, annexed Okinawans, outcast *burakumin,* children of mixed marriages, and immigrant nationalities, especially Koreans, who number more than 700,000 (De Vos, Wetherall, and Stearman 1983; Lie 2001).

To describe racial attitudes in Japan, Jennifer Robertson (1992) uses Kwame Anthony Appiah's (1990) term "intrinsic racism"—the belief that a (perceived) racial difference is a sufficient reason to value one person less than another. In Japan the valued group is majority ("pure") Japanese, who are believed to share "the same blood." Thus, the caption to a printed photo of a Japanese American model reads: "She was born in Japan but raised in Hawaii. Her nationality is American but no foreign blood flows in her veins" (Robertson 1992, p. 5). Something like hypodescent also operates in Japan, but less precisely than in the United States, where mixed offspring automatically become members of the minority group. The children of mixed marriages between majority Japanese and others (including Euro-Americans) may not get the same "racial" label as their minority parent, but they are still stigmatized for their non-Japanese ancestry (De Vos and Wagatsuma 1966).

How is race culturally constructed in Japan? The (majority) Japanese define themselves by opposition to others, whether minority groups in their own nation or outsiders—anyone who is "not us." The "not us" should stay that way; assimilation generally is discouraged. Cultural mechanisms, especially residential segregation and taboos on "interracial" marriage, work to keep minorities "in their place."

In its construction of race, Japanese culture regards certain ethnic groups as having a biological basis, when there is no evidence that they do. The best example is the *burakumin,* a stigmatized group of at least 4 million outcasts, sometimes compared to India's untouchables. The burakumin are physically and genetically indistinguishable from other Japanese. Many of them "pass" as (and marry) majority Japanese, but a deceptive marriage can end in divorce if burakumin identity is discovered (Aoki and Dardess, eds. 1981).

Burakumin are perceived as standing apart from majority Japanese. Through ancestry, descent (and thus, it is assumed, "blood," or genetics) burakumin are "not us." Majority Japanese try to keep their lineage pure by discouraging mixing. The burakumin are residentially segregated in neighborhoods (rural or urban) called *buraku,* from which the racial label is derived. Compared with majority Japanese, the burakumin are less likely to attend high school and college. When burakumin attend the same schools as majority Japanese, they face discrimination. Majority children and teachers may refuse to eat with them because burakumin are considered unclean.

In applying for university admission or a job and in dealing with the government, Japanese must list their address, which becomes part of a household or family registry. This list makes residence in a buraku, and likely burakumin social status, evident. Schools and companies use this information to discriminate. (The best way to pass is to move so often that the buraku address eventually disappears from the registry.) Majority Japanese also limit "race" mixture by hiring marriage mediators to check out the family histories of prospective spouses. They are especially careful to check for burakumin ancestry (De Vos et al. 1983).

The origin of the burakumin lies in a historical tiered system of stratification (from the Tokugawa period—1603–1868). The top four ranked categories were warrior-administrators (*samurai*), farmers, artisans, and merchants. The ancestors of the burakumin were below this hierarchy, an outcast group who did unclean jobs such as animal slaughter and disposal of the dead. Burakumin still do similar jobs, including work with leather and other animal products. The burakumin are more likely than majority Japanese to do manual labor (including farm work) and to belong to the national lower class. Burakumin and other Japanese minorities also are more likely to have careers in crime, prostitution, entertainment, and sports (De Vos et al. 1983).

Like blacks in the United States, the burakumin are class-stratified. Because certain jobs are reserved for the burakumin, people who are successful in those occupations (e.g., shoe factory owners) can be wealthy. Burakumin also have found jobs as government bureaucrats. Financially successful burakumin can temporarily escape their stigmatized status by travel, including foreign travel.

Japan's stigmatized burakumin are physically and genetically indistinguishable from other Japanese. In response to burakumin political mobilization, Japan has dismantled the legal structure of discrimination against burakumin. This Sports Day for burakumin children is one kind of mobilization.

Discrimination against the burakumin is strikingly like the discrimination that blacks have experienced in the United States. The burakumin often live in villages and neighborhoods with poor housing and sanitation. They have limited access to education, jobs, amenities, and health facilities. In response to burakumin political mobilization, Japan has dismantled the legal structure of discrimination against burakumin and has worked to improve conditions in the buraku. (The Web site http://blhrri. org/index_e.htm is sponsored by the Buraku Liberation and Human Rights Research Institute and includes the most recent information about the Buraku liberation movement.) Still Japan has yet to institute American-style affirmative action programs for education and jobs. Discrimination against nonmajority Japanese is still the rule in companies. Some employers say that hiring burakumin would give their company an unclean image and thus create a disadvantage in competing with other businesses (De Vos et al. 1983).

Phenotype and Fluidity: Race in Brazil

There are more flexible, less exclusionary ways of constructing social race than those used in the United States and Japan. Along with the rest of Latin America, Brazil has less exclusionary categories, which permit individuals to change their racial classification. Brazil shares a history of slavery with the United States, but it lacks the hypo-descent rule. Nor does Brazil have racial aversion of the sort found in Japan.

These photos, taken in Brazil by the author in 2003 and 2004, give just a glimpse of the spectrum of phenotypical diversity encountered among contemporary Brazilians.

Brazilians use many more racial labels—over 500 were once reported (Harris 1970)—than Americans or Japanese do. In northeastern Brazil, I found 40 different racial terms in use in Arembepe, a village of only 750 people (Kottak 2006). Through their traditional classification system Brazilians recognize and attempt to describe the physical variation that exists in their population. The system used in the United States, by recognizing only three or four races, blinds Americans to an equivalent range of evident physical contrasts. The system Brazilians use to construct social race has other special features. In the United States one's race is an ascribed status; it is assigned automatically by hypodescent and usually doesn't change. In Brazil racial identity is more flexible, more of an achieved status. Brazilian racial classification pays attention to phenotype. As discussed, **phenotype** refers to an organism's evident traits, its "manifest biology"—physiology and anatomy, including skin color, hair form, facial features, and eye color. A Brazilian's phenotype and racial label may change because of environmental factors, such as the tanning rays of the sun or the effects of humidity on the hair.

As physical characteristics change (sunlight alters skin color, humidity affects hair form), so do racial terms. Furthermore, racial differences may be so insignificant in structuring community life that people may forget the terms they have applied to others. Sometimes they even forget the ones they've used for themselves. In Arembepe, I made it a habit to ask the same person on different days to tell me the races of others in the village (and my own). In the United States I am always "white" or "Euro-American," but in Arembepe I got lots of terms besides *branco* ("white"). I could be *claro* ("light"), *louro* ("blond"), *sarará* ("light-skinned redhead"), *mulato claro* ("light mulatto"), or *mulato* ("mulatto"). The racial term used to describe me or anyone else varied from person to person, week to week, even day to day. My best informant, a man with very dark skin color, changed the term he used for himself all the time—from *escuro* ("dark") to *preto* ("black") to *moreno escuro* ("dark brunet").

The American and Japanese racial systems are creations of particular cultures, rather than scientific—or even accurate—descriptions of human biological differences. Brazilian racial classification also is a cultural construction, but Brazilians have developed a way of describing human biological diversity that is more detailed, fluid, and flexible than the systems used in most cultures. Brazil lacks Japan's racial aversion, and it also lacks a rule of descent like that which ascribes racial status in the United States (Degler 1970; Harris 1964).

For centuries the United States and Brazil have had mixed populations, with ancestors from Native America, Europe, Africa, and Asia. Although races have mixed in both countries, Brazilian and American cultures have constructed the results differently. The historical reasons for this contrast lie mainly in the different characteristics of the settlers of the two countries. The mainly English early settlers of the United States came as women, men, and families, but Brazil's Portuguese colonizers were mainly men—merchants and adventurers. Many of these Portuguese men married Native American women and recognized their racially mixed children as their heirs. Like their North American counterparts, Brazilian plantation owners had sexual relations with their slaves. But the Brazilian landlords more often freed the children that resulted—for demographic and economic reasons. (Sometimes these were their only children.) Freed offspring of master and slave became plantation overseers and foremen and filled many intermediate positions in the emerging Brazilian economy. They were not classed with the slaves, but were allowed to join a new intermediate category. No hypodescent rule developed in Brazil to ensure that whites and blacks remained separate (see Degler 1970; Harris 1964).

Ethnic Groups, Nations, and Nationalities

The term **nation** once was synonymous with *tribe* or *ethnic group*. All three of these terms have been used to refer to a single culture sharing a single language, religion, history, territory, ancestry, and kinship. Thus one could speak interchangeably of the Seneca (American Indian) nation, tribe, or ethnic group. Now *nation* has come to mean state—an independent, centrally organized political unit, or a government. *Nation* and *state* have become synonymous. Combined in **nation-state** they refer to an autonomous political entity, a country—like the United States, "one nation, indivisible" (see Farner, ed. 2004; Gellner 1997; Hastings 1997).

Because of migration, conquest, and colonialism, most nation-states are not ethnically homogeneous. Of 132 nation-states existing in 1971, Connor (1972) found just 12 (9 percent) to be ethnically homogeneous. In another 25 (19 percent) a single ethnic group accounted for more than 90 percent of the population. Forty percent of the countries contained more than five significant ethnic groups. In a later study, Nielsson (1985) found that in only 45 of 164 states did one ethnic group account for more than 95 percent of the population.

Nationalities and Imagined Communities

Ethnic groups that once had, or wish to have or regain, autonomous political status (their own country) are called **nationalities.** In the words of Benedict Anderson (1991), they are "imagined communities." Even when they become nation-states, they remain imagined communities because most of their members, though feeling comradeship, will never meet (Anderson 1991, pp. 6–10). They can only imagine they all participate in the same unit.

Anderson traces Western European nationalism, which arose in imperial powers such as England, France, and Spain, back to the 18th century. He stresses that language and print played a crucial role in the growth of European national consciousness. The novel and the newspaper were "two forms of imagining" communities (consisting of all the people who read the same sources and thus witnessed the same events) that flowered in the 18th century (Anderson 1991, pp. 24–25).

Over time, political upheavals, wars, and migration have divided many imagined national communities that arose in the 18th and 19th centuries. The German and Korean homelands were artificially divided after wars, according to communist and capitalist ideologies. World War I split the Kurds, who remain an imagined community, forming a majority in no state. Kurds are a minority group in Turkey, Iran, Iraq, and Syria.

In creating multitribal and multiethnic states, colonialism often erected boundaries that corresponded poorly with preexisting cultural divisions. But colonial institutions also helped created new "imagined communities" beyond nations. A good example is the idea of *négritude* ("Black identity") developed by African intellectuals in Francophone (French-speaking) West Africa. Négritude can be traced to the association and common experience in colonial times of youths from Guinea, Mali, the Ivory Coast, and Senegal at the William Ponty school in Dakar, Senegal (Anderson 1991, pp. 123–124).

Ethnic Tolerance and Accommodation

Ethnic diversity may be associated with positive group interaction and coexistence or with conflict (discussed shortly). There are nation-states in which multiple cultural groups live together in reasonable harmony, including some less developed countries.

Assimilation

Assimilation describes the process of change that a minority ethnic group may experience when it moves to a country where another culture dominates. By assimilating, the minority adopts the patterns and norms of its host culture. It is incorporated into the dominant culture to the point that it no longer exists as a separate cultural unit. Some countries, such as Brazil, are more assimilationist than others. Germans, Italians, Japanese, Middle Easterners, and East Europeans started migrating to Brazil late in the 19th century. These immigrants have assimilated to a common Brazilian culture, which has Portuguese, African, and Native American roots. The descendants of these immigrants speak the national language (Portuguese) and participate in the national culture. (During World War II, Brazil, which was on the Allied side, forced assimilation by banning instruction in any language other than Portuguese—especially in German.)

The Plural Society

Assimilation isn't inevitable, and there can be ethnic harmony without it. Ethnic distinctions can persist despite generations of interethnic contact. Through a study of three ethnic groups in Swat, Pakistan, Fredrik Barth (1958/1968) challenged an old idea that interaction always leads to assimilation. He showed that ethnic groups can be in contact for generations without assimilating and can live in peaceful coexistence.

Barth (1958/1968, p. 324) defines **plural society** (an idea he extended from Pakistan to the entire Middle East) as a society combining ethnic contrasts, ecological specialization (i.e., use of different environmental resources by each ethnic group), and the economic interdependence of those groups. Consider his description of the Middle East (in the 1950s): "The 'environment' of any one ethnic group is not only defined by natural conditions, but also by the presence and activities of the other ethnic groups on which it depends. Each group exploits only part of the total environment, and leaves large parts of it open for other groups to exploit." The ecological interdependence (or, at least, the lack of competition) between ethnic groups may be based on different activities in the same region or on long-term occupation of different regions in the same nation-state.

In Barth's view, ethnic boundaries are most stable and enduring when the groups occupy different ecological niches. That is, they make their living in different ways and don't compete. Ideally, they should depend on each other's activities and exchange with one another. When different ethnic groups exploit the *same* ecological niche, the militarily more powerful group will normally replace the weaker one. If they exploit more or less the same niche, but the weaker group is better able to use marginal environments, they also may coexist (Barth 1958/1968, p. 331). Given niche specialization, ethnic boundaries and interdependence can be maintained, although the specific cultural features of each group may change. By shifting the analytic focus from individual cultures or ethnic groups to *relationships* between cultures or ethnic groups, Barth (1958/1968, 1969) has made important contributions to ethnic studies.

Multiculturalism and Ethnic Identity

The view of cultural diversity in a country as something good and desirable is called **multiculturalism** (see Kottak and Kozaitis 2008). The multicultural model is the opposite of the assimilationist model, in which minorities are expected to abandon their cultural traditions and values, replacing them with those of the majority population. The multicultural view encourages the practice of cultural–ethnic traditions. A multicultural society socializes individuals not only into the dominant (national) culture but also into an ethnic culture. Thus in the United States millions of people speak both English and another language, eat both "American" (apple pie, steak, hamburgers) and "ethnic" foods, and celebrate both national (July 4, Thanksgiving) and ethnic–religious holidays.

In the United States and Canada multiculturalism is of growing importance. This reflects an awareness that the number and size of ethnic groups have grown dramatically in recent years. If this trend continues, the ethnic composition of the United States will change dramatically. (See Figure 11.2.)

Even now, because of immigration and differential population growth, whites are outnumbered by minorities in many urban areas. For example, of the 8,274,527 people living in New York City in 2007, 25 percent were black, 27 percent Hispanic, 12 percent Asian, and 36 percent other—including non-Hispanic whites. The comparable figures for Los Angeles (which had 3,770,590 people in 2007) were 10 percent black, 48 percent Hispanic, 11 percent Asian, and 31 percent other, including non-Hispanic whites (U.S. Census Bureau 2008, 2009).

In October 2006, the population of the United States reached 300 million people, just 39 years after reaching 200 million and 91 years after reaching the 100 million mark (in 1915). The country's ethnic composition has changed dramatically in the past 40 years. The 1970 census, the first to attempt an official count of Hispanics, found they represented no more than 4.7 percent of the American population, compared with 15.1 percent in 2007. The number of African Americans increased from 11.1 percent in 1967 to 12.9 percent in 2007, while (non-Hispanic) whites ("Anglos") declined from 83 to 66.1 percent. In 1967 fewer than 10 million people in the United States (5 percent

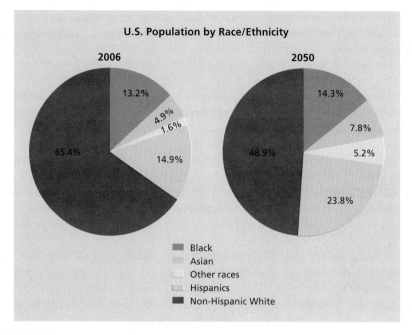

FIGURE 11.2 *Ethnic Composition of the United States* The proportion of the American population that is white and non-Hispanic is declining. The projection for 2050 shown here comes from a U.S. Census Bureau report issued in March 2004. Note especially the dramatic rise in the Hispanic portion of the American population between 2006 and 2050.

SOURCE: Based on data from U.S. Census Bureau, International Data Base, Table 094, http://www.census.gov/ipc/ www.idbprint.html; Files 2005 and http://www.census.gov/Press-Release/www/releases/archives/population/010048.html.

of the population) had been born elsewhere, compared with more than 36 million immigrants (12 percent) today (Ohlemacher 2006).

In 1973, 78 percent of the students in American public schools were white, and 22 percent were minorities: blacks, Hispanics, Asians, Pacific Islanders, and "others." By 2004, only 57 percent of public school students were white, and 43 percent were minorities. If current trends continue, minority students will outnumber (non-Hispanic) white students by 2015. They already do in California, Hawaii, Mississippi, New Mexico, and Texas (Dillon 2006).

Immigration, mainly from southern and eastern Europe, had a similar effect on classroom diversity, at least in the largest American cities, a century ago. A study of American public schools in 1908–09 found that only 42 percent of those urban students were native-born, while 58 percent were immigrants. In a very different (multicultural now versus assimilationist then) context, today's American classrooms have regained the ethnic diversity they demonstrated in the early 1900s, when this author's German-speaking Austro-Hungarian-born father and grandparents immigrated to the United States.

One response to ethnic diversification and awareness has been for many whites to reclaim ethnic identities (Italian, Albanian, Serbian, Lithuanian, etc.) and to joint ethnic associations (clubs, gangs). Some such groups are new. Others have existed for decades, although they lost members during the assimilationist years of the 1920s through the 1950s.

Multiculturalism seeks ways for people to understand and interact that don't depend on sameness but rather on respect for differences. Multiculturalism stresses the interaction of ethnic groups and their contribution to the country. It assumes that each group has something to offer to and learn from the others. Several forces have propelled North America away from the assimilationist model toward multiculturalism. First, multiculturalism reflects the fact of recent large-scale migration, particularly from the "less developed countries" to the "developed" nations of North America and Western Europe. The global scale of modern migration introduces unparalleled ethnic variety to host nations. Multiculturalism is related to globalization: People use modern means of transportation to migrate to nations whose lifestyles they learn about through the media and from tourists who increasingly visit their own countries (see Inda and Rosaldo, eds. 2008).

Migration also is fueled by rapid population growth, coupled with insufficient jobs (both for educated and uneducated people), in the less developed countries. As traditional rural economies decline or mechanize, displaced farmers move to cities, where they and their children often are unable to find jobs. As people in the less developed countries get better educations, they seek more skilled employment. They hope to partake of an international culture of consumption that includes such modern amenities as refrigerators, televisions, and automobiles (Ahmed 2004).

In a world with growing rural–urban and transnational migration, ethnic identities are used increasingly to form self-help organizations focused mainly on enhancing the group's economic competitiveness (Williams 1989). People claim and express ethnic identities for political and economic reasons. Michel Laguerre's (1984, 1998) studies of Haitian immigrants in the United States show that they mobilize to deal with the discriminatory structure (racist in this case, since Haitians tend to be black) of American society. Ethnicity (their common Haitian creole language and cultural background) is a basis for their mobilization. Haitian ethnicity helps distinguish them from African Americans and other ethnic groups.

In the face of globalization, much of the world, including the entire "democratic West," is experiencing an "ethnic revival." The new assertiveness of long-resident ethnic groups extends to the Basques and Catalans in Spain, the Bretons and Corsicans in France, and the Welsh and Scots in the United Kingdom. The United States and Canada are becoming increasingly multicultural, focusing on their internal diversity (see Laguerre 1999). "Melting pots" no longer, they are better described as ethnic "salads" (each ingredient remains distinct, although in the same bowl, with the same dressing).

Roots of Ethnic Conflict

Ethnicity, based on perceived cultural similarities and differences in a society or nation, can be expressed in peaceful multiculturalism or in discrimination or violent interethnic confrontation. The roots of ethnic differentiation—and therefore, potentially, of ethnic conflict—can be political, economic, religious, linguistic, cultural, or racial (see Kuper 2006). Why do ethnic differences often lead to conflict and violence? The causes include a sense of injustice because of resource distribution, economic or political competition, and reaction to discrimination, prejudice, and other expressions of devalued identity (see Friedman 2003; Ryan 1990, p. xxvii).

In Iraq, under the dictator Saddam Hussein, there was discrimination by one Muslim group (Sunnis) against others (Shiites and Kurds). Sunnis, although a numeric minority within Iraq's population, enjoyed privileged access to power, prestige, and position. After the elections of 2005, which many Sunnis chose to boycott, Shiites gained political control. A civil war developed out of "sectarian violence" (conflicts among sects of the same religion) as Sunnis (and their foreign supporters) fueled an insurgency against the new government and its foreign supporters, including the United States. Shiites retaliated against Sunni attacks and a history of Sunni privilege and perceived discrimination against Shiites, as Shiite militias engaged in ethnic (sectarian) cleansing of their own.

Prejudice and Discrimination

Ethnic conflict often arises in reaction to prejudice (attitudes and judgments) or discrimination (action). **Prejudice** means devaluing (looking down on) a group because of its assumed behavior, values, capabilities, or attributes. People are prejudiced when they hold stereotypes about groups and apply them to individuals. (**Stereotypes** are fixed ideas—often unfavorable—about what the members of a group are like.) Prejudiced people assume that members of the group will act as they are "supposed to act" (according to the stereotype) and interpret a wide range of individual behaviors as evidence of the stereotype. They use this behavior to confirm their stereotype (and low opinion) of the group.

Discrimination refers to policies and practices that harm a group and its members. Discrimination may be *de facto* (practiced, but not legally sanctioned) or *de jure* (part of the law). An example of de facto discrimination is the harsher treatment that American minorities (compared with other Americans) tend to get from the police and the judicial system. This unequal treatment isn't legal, but it happens anyway. Segregation in the southern United States and *apartheid* in South Africa provide two examples of de jure discrimination, which no longer are in existence. In both systems, by law, blacks and whites had different rights and privileges. Their social interaction ("mixing") was legally curtailed.

Chips in the Mosaic

Although the multicultural model is increasingly prominent in North America, ethnic competition and conflict also are evident. There is conflict between newer arrivals, for instance, Central Americans and Koreans, and longer-established ethnic groups, such as African Americans. Ethnic antagonism flared in South-Central Los Angeles in spring 1992 in rioting that followed the acquittal of four white police officers who were tried for the videotaped beating of Rodney King (see Abelmann and Lie 1995).

Angry blacks attacked whites, Koreans, and Latinos. This violence expressed frustration by African Americans about their prospects in an increasingly multicultural society. A *New York Times* CBS News Poll conducted just after the Los Angeles riots, found that blacks had a bleaker outlook than whites about the effects of immigration on their lives. Only 23 percent of the blacks felt they had more opportunities than recent immigrants, compared with twice that many whites (Toner 1992).

Korean stores were hard hit during the 1992 riots, and more than a third of the businesses destroyed were Latino-owned. A third of those who died in the riots were Latinos. These mainly recent migrants lacked deep roots to the neighborhood and, as Spanish speakers, faced language barriers (Newman 1992). Many Koreans also had trouble with English.

Koreans interviewed on ABC's *Nightline* on May 6, 1992, recognized that blacks resented them and considered them unfriendly. One man explained, "It's not part of our culture to smile." African Americans interviewed on the same program did complain about Korean unfriendliness. "They come into our neighborhoods and treat us like dirt." These comments suggest a shortcoming of the multicultural perspective: Ethnic groups (blacks here) expect other ethnic groups in the same nation-state to assimilate to some extent to a shared (national) culture. The African Americans' comments invoked a general American value system that includes friendliness, openness, mutual respect, community participation, and "fair play." Los Angeles blacks wanted their Korean neighbors to act more like generalized Americans—and good neighbors.

Aftermaths of Oppression

Fueling ethnic conflict are such forms of discrimination as genocide, forced assimilation, ethnocide, and cultural colonialism. The most extreme form of ethnic discrimination is **genocide,** the deliberate elimination of a group (such as Jews in Nazi Germany, Muslims in Bosnia, or Tutsi in Rwanda) through mass murder. A dominant group may try to destroy the cultures of certain ethnic groups (**ethnocide**) or force them to adopt the dominant culture (*forced assimilation*). Many countries have penalized or banned the language and customs of an ethnic group (including its religious observances). One example of forced assimilation is the anti-Basque campaign that the dictator Francisco Franco (who ruled between 1939 and 1975) waged in Spain. Franco banned Basque books, journals, newspapers, signs, sermons, and tombstones and imposed fines for using the Basque language in schools (Ryan 1990). His policies led to the formation of a Basque terrorist group and spurred strong nationalist sentiment in the Basque region (see "Anthropology Today" which follows).

A policy of *ethnic expulsion* aims at removing groups who are culturally different from a country. There are many examples, including Bosnia-Herzegovina in the 1990s. Uganda expelled 74,000 Asians in 1972. The neofascist parties of contemporary Western Europe advocate repatriation (expulsion) of immigrant workers (West Indians in England, Algerians in France, and Turks in Germany) (see Friedman 2003; Ryan 1990, p. 9). A policy of expulsion may create **refugees**—people who have been forced (involuntary refugees) or who have chosen (voluntary refugees) to flee a country, to escape persecution or war.

Two faces of ethnic difference in the former Soviet empire. A propaganda poster depicts a happy mix of nationalities that make up the population of Kyrgyzstan, Central Asia (top). In August 2008, ethnic Georgians in a refugee camp near Tblisi, Georgia (bottom). They fled Georgia's breakaway province, the self-proclaimed new republic of South Ossetia, where Russians were fighting the Georgian army. A cease-fire did not end the tension; Georgia still views South Ossetia as a Russian-occupied territory.

In many countries, colonial nation-building left ethnic strife in its wake. Thus, over a million Hindus and Muslims were killed in the violence that accompanied the division of the Indian subcontinent into India and Pakistan. Problems between Arabs and Jews in Palestine began during the British mandate period.

Multiculturalism may be growing in the United States and Canada, but the opposite is happening in the former Soviet Union, where ethnic groups (nationalities) want their own nation-states. The flowering of ethnic feeling and conflict as the Soviet empire disintegrated illustrates that years of political repression and ideology provide insufficient common ground for lasting unity. **Cultural colonialism** refers to internal domination—by one group and its culture or ideology over others. One example is the domination over the former Soviet empire by Russian people, language, and culture, and by communist ideology. The dominant culture makes itself the official culture. This is reflected in schools, the media, and public interaction. Under Soviet

ANTHROPOLOGY TODAY

The Basques

Having maintained a strong ethnic identity, perhaps for millennia, the Basques of France and Spain are linguistically unique; their language is unrelated to any other known language. Their homeland lies in the western Pyrenees Mountains, straddling the French–Spanish border (Figure 11.3). Of the seven Basque provinces, three are in France and four are in Spain. Although these provinces have not been unified politically for nearly a millennium, the Basques remain one of Europe's most distinctive ethnic groups.

The French Revolution of 1789 ended the political autonomy of the three Basque provinces in France. During the 19th century in Spain the Basques fought on the losing side in two internal wars, yielding much of their political autonomy in defeat. When the Spanish Civil War broke out in 1936, the Basques remained loyal to the republic, opposing the Spanish dictator Francisco Franco, who eventually defeated them. Under Franco's rule (1936–1975), Basques were executed, imprisoned, and exiled, and Basque culture was systematically repressed.

In the late 1950s disaffected Basque youths founded ETA (*Euskadi Ta Azkatasuna,*

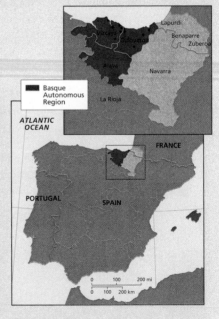

FIGURE 11.3 *Location of the Basque homeland*

or "Basque Country and Freedom"). Its goal was complete independence from Spain (Zulaika 1988). The ETA's opposition to Franco escalated into violence,

rule ethnic minorities had very limited self-rule in republics and regions controlled by Moscow. All the republics and their peoples were to be united by the oneness of "socialist internationalism." One common technique in cultural colonialism is to flood ethnic areas with members of the dominant ethnic group. Thus, in the former Soviet Union, ethnic Russian colonists were sent to many areas, to diminish the cohesion and clout of the local people.

The Commonwealth of Independent States (CIS), founded in 1991 and head-quartered in Minsk, Belarus, is what remains of the once-powerful Soviet Union (see Yurchak 2005). In Russia and other formerly Soviet nations, ethnic groups (nation-alities) have sought, and continue to seek, to forge separate and viable nation-states based on cultural boundaries. This celebration of ethnic autonomy is part of an ethnic florescence that—as surely as globalization and transnationalism—is a trend of the late 20th and early 21st centuries.

which continued thereafter, diminishing in recent years. The group continues its quest for full Basque independence.

Franco's death in 1975 had ushered in an era of democracy in Spain. Mainline Basque nationalists collaborated in framing a new constitution, which gave considerable autonomy to the Basque regions (Trask 1996).

Since 1979 three Spanish Basque provinces have been united as the more or less self-governing Basque Autonomous Region. The Basque language is co-official with Spanish in this territory. Spain's fourth Basque province, Navarra, formed its own autonomous region, where the Basque lan-guage has a degree of official standing. In France, like other regional languages, Basque has been victimized for centuries by laws hostile to languages other than French (Trask 1996). After generations of decline, the number of Basque speakers is increasing today. Much education, publish-ing, and broadcasting now proceed in Basque in the Autonomous Region. Still, Basque faces the same pressures that all other mi-nority languages do: Knowledge of the na-tional language (Spanish or French) is essential, and most education, publishing,

and broadcasting is in the national language (Trask 1996).

How long have the Basques been in their homeland? Archaeological evidence suggests that a single group of people lived in the Basque country continuously from late Paleolithic times through the Bronze Age (about 3,000 years ago). There is no evidence to suggest that any new population entered the area after that (La Fraugh n.d.).

Historically the Basques have been farmers, herders, and fishers. (Today most of them work in business and industry.) The Basque *basseria* (family farm) once thrived as a mixed-farming unit emphasizing self-sufficiency. The farm family grew wheat, corn, vegetables, fruits, and nuts and raised poultry, rabbits, pigs, cows, and sheep. Sub-sistence pursuits increasingly have been commercialized, with the production of vegetables, dairy products, and fish aimed at urban markets (Greenwood 1976).

Basque immigrants originally entered North America as either Spanish or French nationals. Basque Americans, numbering some 50,000, now invoke Basqueness as their primary ethnic identity. They are con-centrated in California, Idaho, and Nevada. First-generation immigrants usually are

Continued

fluent in Basque. They are more likely to be bilingual in Basque and English than to have their parents' fluency in Spanish or French (Douglass 1992).

Building on a traditional occupation in Basque country, Basques in the United States are notable for their identification with sheepherding (see Ott 1981). Most of them settled and worked in the open-range livestock districts of the 13 states of the American West. Basques were among the Spanish soldiers, explorers, missionaries, and administrators in the American Southwest and Spanish California. More Basques came during the California gold rush, many from southern South America, where they were established sheepherders (Douglass 1992).

Restrictive immigration laws enacted in the 1920s, which had an anti-southern European bias, limited Basque immigration to the United States. During World War II, with the country in need of shepherds, the U.S. government exempted Basque herders from immigration quotas. Between 1950 and 1975, several thousand Basques entered the United States on three-year contracts. Later, the decline of the U.S. sheep industry would slow Basque immigration dramatically (Douglass 1992).

Catering to Basque sheepherders, western towns had one or more Basque boardinghouses. The typical one had a bar and a dining room, where meals were served family-style at long tables. A second floor of sleeping rooms was reserved for permanent boarders. Also lodged were herders in town for a brief visit, vacation, or employment layoff or in transit to an employer (Echeverria 1999).

Initially, few Basques came to the United States intending to stay. Most early immigrants were young, unmarried men. Their herding pattern, with solitary summers in the mountains, did not fit well with family life. Eventually, Basque men came with the intent to stay. They either sent back or went back to Europe for brides (few married non-Basques). Many brides, of the "mail order" sort, were sisters or cousins of an acquaintance made in the United States. Basque boardinghouses also became a source of spouses. The boardinghouse owners sent back to Europe for women willing to come to America as domestics. Few remained single for long (Douglass 1992). In these ways Basque Americans drew on their homeland society and culture in establishing the basis of their family and community life in North America.

Basques have not escaped discrimination in the United States. In the American West, sheepherding is an occupation that carries some stigma. Mobile sheepherders competed with settled livestock interests for access to the range. These were some of the sources of anti-Basque sentiment and even legislation. More recently, newspaper coverage of enduring conflict in the Basque country, particularly the activities of the ETA, has made Basque Americans sensitive to the possible charge of being terrorist sympathizers (Douglass 1992; see also Zulaika 1988).

Summary

1. An ethnic group refers to members of a particular culture in a nation or region that contains others. Ethnicity is based on actual, perceived, or assumed cultural similarities (among members of the same ethnic group) and differences (between

that group and others). Ethnic distinctions can be based on language, religion, history, geography, kinship, or race. A race is an ethnic group assumed to have a biological basis. Usually race and ethnicity are ascribed statuses; people are born members of a group and remain so all their lives.

2. Human races are cultural rather than biological categories. Such races derive from contrasts perceived in particular societies, rather than from scientific classifications based on common genes. In the United States, racial labels such as "white" and "black" designate socially constructed categories defined by American culture. American racial classification, governed by the rule of hypodescent, is based neither on phenotype nor on genes. Children of mixed unions, no matter what their appearance, are classified with the minority group parent.

3. Racial attitudes in Japan illustrate intrinsic racism—the belief that a perceived racial difference is a sufficient reason to value one person less than another. The valued group is majority (pure) Japanese, who are believed to share the same blood. Majority Japanese define themselves by opposition to others, such as Koreans and burakumin. These may be minority groups in Japan or outsiders—anyone who is "not us."

4. Such exclusionary racial systems are not inevitable. Although Brazil shares a history of slavery with the United States, it lacks the hypodescent rule. Brazilian racial identity is more of an achieved status. It can change during someone's lifetime, reflecting phenotypical changes.

5. The term *nation* once was synonymous with *ethnic group*. Now nation has come to mean a state—a centrally organized political unit. Because of migration, conquest, and colonialism, most nation-states are not ethnically homogeneous. Ethnic groups that seek autonomous political status (their own country) are nationalities. Political upheavals, wars, and migrations have divided many imagined national communities.

6. Assimilation describes the process of change an ethnic group may experience when it moves to a country where another culture dominates. By assimilating, the minority adopts the patterns and norms of its host culture. Assimilation isn't inevitable, and there can be ethnic harmony without it. A plural society combines ethnic contrasts and economic interdependence between ethnic groups. The view of cultural diversity in a nation-state as good and desirable is multiculturalism. A multicultural society socializes individuals not only into the dominant (national) culture but also into an ethnic one.

7. Ethnicity can be expressed in peaceful multiculturalism, or in discrimination or violent confrontation. Ethnic conflict often arises in reaction to prejudice (attitudes and judgments) or discrimination (action). The most extreme form of ethnic discrimination is genocide, the deliberate elimination of a group through mass murder. A dominant group may try to destroy certain ethnic practices (ethnocide), or to force ethnic group members to adopt the dominant culture (forced assimilation). A policy of ethnic expulsion may create refugees. Cultural colonialism refers to internal domination—by one group and its culture or ideology over others.

Key Terms

assimilation (p. 247)

cultural colonialism (p. 254)

descent (p. 238)

discrimination (p. 251)

ethnic group (p. 234)

ethnicity (p. 234)

ethnocide (p. 252)

genocide (p. 252)

hypodescent (p. 238)

majority groups (p. 236)

minority groups (p. 236)

multiculturalism (p. 248)

nation (p. 246)

nation-state (p. 246)

nationalities (p. 246)

phenotype (p. 245)

plural society (p. 247)

prejudice (p. 251)

race (p. 236)

racism (p. 236)

refugees (p. 252)

stereotypes (p. 251)

 Go to our Online Learning Center website at **www.mhhe.com/kottak** for Internet resources directly related to the content of this chapter.

Applying Anthropology

Applied **anthropology** is one of two dimensions of anthropology, the other being theoretical/academic anthropology. Applied, or *practical,* anthropology is the use of anthropological data, perspectives, theory, and methods to identify, assess, and solve contemporary problems involving human behavior and social and cultural forces, conditions, and contexts (see Ervin 2005). For example, medical anthropologists have worked as cultural interpreters in public health programs, so as to facilitate their fit into local culture. Many applied anthropologists have worked for or with international development agencies, such as the World Bank and the U.S. Agency for International Development (USAID). In North America, garbologists help the Environmental Protection Agency, the paper industry, and packaging and trade associations. Archaeology is applied as well in cultural resource management and historic preservation. Biological anthropologists work in public health, nutrition, genetic counseling, substance abuse, epidemiology, aging, and mental illness. Forensic anthropologists work with the police, medical examiners, the courts, and international organizations to identify victims of crimes, accidents, wars, and terrorism. Linguistic anthropologists study physician–patient interactions and show how dialect differences influence classroom learning. The goal of most applied anthropologists is to find humane and effective ways of helping local people.

One of the most valuable tools in applying anthropology is the ethnographic method. Ethnographers study societies firsthand, living with and learning from ordinary people. Ethnographers are participant observers, taking part in the events they study in order to understand local thought and behavior. Applied anthropologists use ethnographic techniques in both foreign and domestic settings. Other "expert" participants in social-change programs may be content to converse with officials, read reports, and copy statistics. However, the applied anthropologist's likely early request is some variant of "take me to the local people." We know that people must play an active role in the changes that affect them and that "the people" have information "the experts" lack.

Anthropological theory, the body of findings and generalizations of the four subfields, also guides applied anthropology. Anthropology's holistic perspective—its interest in biology, society, culture, and language—permits the evaluation of many issues that affect people. Theory aids practice, and application fuels theory. As we compare social-change policy and programs, our understanding of cause and effect increases. We add new generalizations about culture change to those discovered in traditional and ancient cultures.

The Role of the Applied Anthropologist

Early Applications

Application was a central concern of early anthropology in Great Britain (in the context of colonialism) and the United States (in the context of Native American policy). Before turning to the new, we should consider some dangers of the old. For the British empire, specifically its African colonies, Malinowski (1929) proposed that "practical anthropology" (his term for colonial applied anthropology) should focus on westernization, the diffusion of European culture into tribal societies. Malinowski questioned neither the legitimacy of colonialism nor the anthropologist's role in making it work. He saw nothing wrong with aiding colonial regimes by studying land tenure and land use, to recommend how much of their land local people should be allowed to keep and how much Europeans should get. Malinowski's views exemplify a historical association between early anthropology, particularly in Europe, and colonialism (Maquet 1964).

During World War II, American anthropologists studied Japanese and German "culture at a distance" in an attempt to predict the behavior of the enemies of the United States. After that war, applied anthropologists worked on Pacific islands to promote local-level cooperation with American policies in various trust territories.

Academic and Applied Anthropology

Applied anthropology did not disappear during the 1950s and 1960s, but academic anthropology did most of the growing after World War II. The baby boom, which began in 1946 and peaked in 1957, fueled expansion of the American educational system and thus of academic jobs. New junior, community, and four-year colleges opened, and anthropology became a standard part of the college curriculum. During the 1950s and 1960s, most American anthropologists were college professors, although some still worked in agencies and museums.

This era of academic anthropology continued through the early 1970s. Especially during the Vietnam War, undergraduates flocked to anthropology classes to learn about other cultures. Students were especially interested in Southeast Asia, whose indigenous societies were being disrupted by war. Many anthropologists protested the superpowers' apparent disregard for non-Western lives, values, customs, and social systems.

During the 1970s, and increasingly thereafter, although most anthropologists still worked in academia, others found jobs with international organizations, government, business, hospitals, and schools. This shift toward application, though only partial, has benefited the profession. It has forced anthropologists to consider the wider social value and implications of their research.

Applied Anthropology Today

Today, most applied anthropologists see their work as radically removed from the colonial perspective. Modern applied anthropology usually is seen as a helping profession, devoted to assisting local people, as anthropologists speak up for the disenfranchised in the international political arena. However, applied anthropologists also solve problems for clients who are neither poor nor powerless. Applied anthropologists working for businesses try to solve the problem of expanding profits for their employer or client. In market research, ethical issues may arise as anthropologists attempt to help companies operate more efficiently and profitably. Ethical ambiguities are present as well in cultural resource management (CRM), in deciding how to preserve significant remains and information when sites are threatened by development or public works. A CRM firm typically is hired by someone seeking to build a road or a factory. In such cases, the client may have a strong interest in an outcome in which no sites are found that need protecting. Contemporary applied anthropologists still face ethical questions: To whom does the researcher owe loyalty? What problems are involved in holding firm to the truth? What happens when applied anthropologists don't make the policies they have to implement? How does one criticize programs in which one has participated (see Escobar 1991, 1994)? Anthropology's professional organizations have addressed such questions by establishing codes of ethics and ethics committees. See http://www.aaanet.org for the Code of Ethics of the AAA. As Tice (1997) notes, attention to ethical issues is paramount in the teaching of applied anthropology today.

By instilling an appreciation for human diversity, the entire field of anthropology combats *ethnocentrism*—the tendency to view one's own culture as superior and to use one's own cultural values in judging the behavior and beliefs of people raised in other societies. This broadening, educational role affects the knowledge, values, and attitudes of people exposed to anthropology. This chapter focuses specifically on this question: What specific contributions can anthropology make in identifying and solving problems stirred up by contemporary currents of economic, social, and cultural change, including globalization?

Because anthropologists are experts on human problems and social change and because they study, understand, and respect cultural values, they are highly qualified to suggest, plan, and implement policy affecting people. Proper roles for applied anthropologists include (1) identifying needs for change that local people perceive, (2) working with those people to design culturally appropriate and socially sensitive change, and (3) protecting local people from harmful policies and projects that may threaten them.

Anthropology's systemic perspective recognizes that changes don't occur in a vacuum. A program or project always has multiple effects, some of which are unforeseen. In an American example of unintended consequences, a program aimed at enhancing teachers' appreciation of cultural differences led to ethnic stereotyping (Kleinfield 1975). Specifically, Native American students did not welcome teachers' frequent comments about their Indian heritage. The students felt set apart from their classmates and saw this attention to their ethnicity as patronizing and demeaning. Internationally, dozens of economic development projects intended to increase productivity through irrigation have worsened public health by creating waterways where diseases thrive.

Development Anthropology

Development anthropology is the branch of applied anthropology that focuses on social issues in, and the cultural dimension of, economic development. Development anthropologists do not just carry out development policies planned by others; they also plan and guide policy. (For more detailed discussions of issues in development anthropology, see Edelman and Haugerud 2004; Escobar 1995; Ferguson 1995; Nolan 2002; and Robertson 1995.)

However, ethical dilemmas often confront development anthropologists (Escobar 1991, 1995). Our respect for cultural diversity often is offended because efforts to extend industry and technology may entail profound cultural changes. Foreign aid usually doesn't go where need and suffering are greatest. It is spent on political, economic, and strategic priorities as international donors, political leaders and powerful interest groups perceive them. Planners' interests don't always coincide with the best interests of the local people. Although the aim of most development projects is to enhance the quality of life, living standards often decline in the target area (Bodley, ed. 1988).

Equity

A commonly stated goal of recent development policy is to promote equity. **Increased equity** means reduced poverty and a more even distribution of wealth. However, if projects are to increase equity, they must have the support of reform-minded governments. Wealthy and powerful people typically resist projects that threaten their vested interests.

Some types of development projects, particularly irrigation schemes, are more likely than others to widen wealth disparities, that is, to have a negative equity impact. An initial uneven distribution of resources (particularly land) often becomes the basis for greater skewing after the project. The social impact of new technology tends to be more severe, contributing negatively to quality of life and to equity, when inputs are channeled to or through the rich.

Many fisheries projects also have had negative equity results (see Durrenberger and King, eds. 2000). In Bahia, Brazil (Kottak 2006), sailboat owners (but not non-owners) got loans to buy motors for their boats. To repay the loans, the owners increased the percentage of the catch they took from the men who fished in their boats. Over the years, they used their rising profits to buy larger and more expensive boats. The result was stratification—the creation of a group of wealthy people within a formerly egalitarian community. These events hampered individual initiative and interfered with further development of the fishing industry. With new boats so expensive, ambitious young men who once would have sought careers in fishing no longer had any way to obtain their own boats. They sought wage labor on land instead. To avoid such results, credit-granting agencies must seek out enterprising young fishers rather than giving loans only to owners and established businesspeople.

Strategies for Innovation

Development anthropologists, who are concerned with social issues in, and the cultural dimension of, economic development, must work closely with local people to assess and help them realize their own wishes and needs for change. Too many true local needs cry out for a solution to waste money funding development projects in area A that are inappropriate there but needed in area B, or that are unnecessary anywhere. Development anthropology can help sort out the needs of the As and Bs and fit projects accordingly. Projects that put people first by consulting with them and responding to their expressed needs must be identified (Cernea, ed. 1991). Thereafter, development anthropologists can work to ensure socially compatible ways of implementing a good project.

In a comparative study of 68 rural development projects from all around the world, I found the *culturally compatible* economic development projects to be twice as successful financially as the incompatible ones (Kottak 1990*b*, 1991). This finding shows that using anthropological expertise in planning to ensure cultural compatibility is cost effective. To maximize social and economic benefits, projects must (1) be culturally compatible, (2) respond to locally perceived needs, (3) involve men and women in planning and carrying out the changes that affect them, (4) harness traditional organizations, and (5) be flexible.

Overinnovation

In my comparative study, the compatible and successful projects avoided the fallacy of **overinnovation** (too much change). We would expect people to resist development projects that require major changes in their daily lives. People usually want to change just enough to keep what they have. Motives for modifying behavior come from the traditional culture and the small concerns of ordinary life. Peasants' values are not such abstract ones as "learning a better way," "progressing," "increasing technical know-how," "improving efficiency," or "adopting modern techniques." (Those phrases exemplify intervention philosophy.)

Instead, their objectives are down-to-earth and specific ones. People want to improve yields in a rice field, amass resources for a ceremony, get a child through school, or have enough cash to pay the tax bill. The goals and values of subsistence producers differ from those of people who produce for cash, just as they differ from the intervention philosophy of development planners. Different value systems must be considered during planning.

In the comparative study, the projects that failed were usually both economically and culturally incompatible. For example, one South Asian project promoted the

To maximize benefits, development projects should respond to locally perceived needs. Shown here (foreground) is the president of a Nicaraguan cooperative that makes and markets hammocks. This cooperative has been assisted by an NGO whose goals include increasing the benefits that women derive from economic development. What's an NGO?

cultivation of onions and peppers, expecting this practice to fit into a preexisting labor-intensive system of rice-growing. Cultivation of these cash crops wasn't traditional in the area. It conflicted with existing crop priorities and other interests of farmers. Also, the labor peaks for pepper and onion production coincided with those for rice, to which the farmers gave priority.

Throughout the world, project problems have arisen from inadequate attention to, and consequent lack of fit with, local culture. Another naive and incompatible project was an overinnovative scheme in Ethiopia. Its major fallacy was to try to convert nomadic herders into sedentary cultivators. It ignored traditional land rights. Outsiders—commercial farmers—were to get much of the herders' territory. The pastoralists were expected to settle down and start farming. This project helped wealthy outsiders instead of the local people. The planners naively expected free-ranging herders to give up a generations-old way of life to work three times harder growing rice and picking cotton for bosses.

Underdifferentiation

The fallacy of **underdifferentiation** is the tendency to view "the less-developed countries" as more alike than they are. Development agencies have often ignored cultural diversity (e.g., between Brazil and Burundi) and adopted a uniform approach to deal with very different sets of people. Neglecting cultural diversity, many projects also have tried to impose incompatible property notions and social units. Most often, the faulty social design assumes either (1) individualistic productive units that are privately owned by an individual or couple and worked by a nuclear family or (2) cooperatives that are at least partially based on models from the former Eastern bloc and Socialist countries.

One example of faulty Euro-American models (the individual and the nuclear family) was a West African project designed for an area where the extended family was the basic social unit. The project succeeded despite its faulty social design because the participants used their traditional extended family networks to attract additional settlers. Eventually, twice as many people as planned benefited as extended family members flocked to the project area. Here, settlers modified the project design that had been imposed on them by following the principles of their traditional society.

The second dubious foreign social model that is common in development strategy is the cooperative. In the comparative study of rural development projects, new cooperatives fared badly. Cooperatives succeeded only when they harnessed preexisting local-level communal institutions. This is a corollary of a more general rule: Participants' groups are most effective when they are based on traditional social organization or on a socioeconomic similarity among members.

Neither foreign social model—the nuclear family farm nor the cooperative—has an unblemished record in development. An alternative is needed: greater use of indigenous social models in economic development. These are traditional social units, such as the clans, lineages, and other extended kin groups of Africa, Oceania, and many other nations, with their communally held estates and resources. The most humane and productive strategy for change is to base the social design for innovation on traditional social forms in each target area.

Indigenous Models

Many governments are not genuinely, or realistically, committed to improving the lives of their citizens. Interference by major powers also has kept governments from enacting needed reforms. In some nations, however, the government acts more as an agent of the people. Madagascar provides an example. The people of Madagascar, the Malagasy, had been organized into descent groups before the origin of the state. The Merina, creators of the major precolonial state of Madagascar, wove descent groups into its structure, making members of important groups advisers to the king and thus giving them authority in government. The Merina state made provisions for the people it ruled. It collected taxes and organized labor for public works projects. In return, it redistributed resources to peasants in need. It also granted them some protection against war and slave raids and allowed them to cultivate their rice fields in peace. The government maintained the water works for rice cultivation. It opened to ambitious peasant boys the chance of becoming, through hard work and study, state bureaucrats.

Throughout the history of the Merina state—and continuing in modern Madagascar—there have been strong relationships between the individual, the descent group, and the state. Local Malagasy communities, where residence is based on descent, are more cohesive and homogeneous than are communities in Latin America or North America. Madagascar gained political independence from France in 1960. Although it still was economically dependent on France when I first did research there in 1966–1967, the new government had an economic development policy aimed at increasing the ability of the Malagasy to feed themselves. Government policy emphasized increased production of rice, a subsistence crop, rather than cash crops. Furthermore, local communities, with their traditional cooperative patterns and solidarity based on kinship and descent, were treated as partners in, not obstacles to, the development process.

In a sense, the descent group is preadapted to equitable national development. In Madagascar, members of local descent groups have customarily pooled their resources to educate their ambitious members. Once educated, these men and women gain economically secure positions in the nation. They then share the advantages of their new positions with their kin. For example, they give room and board to rural cousins attending school and help them find jobs.

Malagasy administrations appear generally to have shared a commitment to democratic economic development. Perhaps this is because government officials are of the peasantry or have strong personal ties to it. By contrast, in Latin American countries, the elites and the lower class have different origins and no strong connections through kinship, descent, or marriage.

Furthermore, societies with descent-group organization contradict an assumption that many social scientists and economists seem to make. It is not inevitable that as nations become more tied to the world capitalist economy, indigenous forms of social organization will break down into nuclear family organization, impersonality, and alienation. Descent groups, with their traditional communalism and corporate solidarity, have important roles to play in economic development.

Realistic development promotes change but not overinnovation. Many changes are possible if the aim is to preserve local systems while making them work better. Successful economic development projects respect, or at least don't attack, local cultural patterns. Effective development draws on indigenous cultural practices and social structures.

Anthropology and Education

Attention to culture also is fundamental to **anthropology and education,** involving research that extends from classrooms into homes, neighborhoods, and communities (see Spindler, ed. 2000, 2005). In classrooms, anthropologists have observed interactions among teachers, students, parents, and visitors. Jules Henry's classic account of the American elementary school classroom (1955) shows how students learn to conform to and compete with their peers. Anthropologists view children as total cultural creatures whose enculturation and attitudes toward education belong to a context that includes family and peers.

Sociolinguists and cultural anthropologists work side by side in education research. For example, in a study of Puerto Rican seventh-graders in the urban Midwest (Hill-Burnett 1978), anthropologists uncovered some misconceptions held by teachers.

On February 7, 2009, Afghan girls attend a lesson at the secondary school in Sarkani village, Kunar Province, eastern Afghanistan. What do you see here that differs from classrooms in your country?

The teachers mistakenly had assumed that Puerto Rican parents valued education less than did non-Hispanics, but in-depth interviews revealed that the Puerto Rican parents valued it more.

The anthropologists also found that certain practices were preventing Hispanics from being adequately educated. For example, the teachers' union and the board of education had agreed to teach "English as a foreign language." However, they had provided no bilingual teachers to work with Spanish-speaking students. The school was assigning all students (including non-Hispanics) with low reading scores and behavior problems to the English-as-a-foreign-language classroom. This educational disaster brought together in the classroom a teacher who spoke no Spanish, children who barely spoke English, and a group of English-speaking students with reading and behavior problems. The Spanish speakers were falling behind not just in reading but in all subjects. They could at least have kept up in the other subjects if a Spanish speaker had been teaching them science, social studies, and math until they were ready for English-language instruction in those areas.

Urban Anthropology

Alan and Josephine Smart (2003) note that cities have long been influenced by global forces, including world capitalism and colonialism. However, the roles of cities in the world system have changed recently as a result of the time-space compression made possible by modern transportation and communication systems. That is, everything appears closer today because contact and movement are so much easier.

One-sixth of the Earth's population lives in urban slums. Roçinha (shown here) is a populous shantytown city within the city of Rio de Janeiro, Brazil. How might anthropologists study slums?

In the context of contemporary globalization, the mass media can become as important as local factors in guiding daily routines, dreams, and aspirations. People live in particular places, but their imaginations and attachments don't have to be locally confined (Appadurai 1996). People migrate to cities partly for economic reasons, but also to be where the action is. Rural Brazilians routinely cite *movimento,* urban movement and excitement, as something to be valued. International migrants tend to settle in the largest cities, where the most is happening. For example, in Canada, which, after Australia, has the highest percentage of foreign-born population, 71.2 percent of immigrants settled in Toronto, Vancouver, or Montreal. Nearly half of Toronto's citizens were born outside Canada (Smart and Smart 2003).

The proportion of the world's population living in cities has been increasing ever since the Industrial Revolution. Only about 3 percent of people were city dwellers in 1800, compared with 13 percent in 1900, over 40 percent in 1980, and about 50 percent today (see Smart and Smart 2003). The More Developed Countries (MDCs) were 76 percent urbanized in 1999, compared with 39 percent for the Less Developed Countries (LDCs). However, the urbanization growth rate is much faster in the LDCs (Smart and Smart 2003). The world had only 16 cities with more than a million people in 1900, but there were 314 such cities in 2005. By 2025, 60 percent of the global population will be urban (Butler 2005; Stevens 1992).

About 1 billion people, one-sixth of Earth's population, live in urban slums, mostly without water, sanitation, public services, and legal security (Vidal 2003). If current trends continue, urban population increase and the concentration of people in slums will be accompanied by rising rates of crime, along with water, air, and noise pollution. These problems will be most severe in the LDCs.

As industrialization and urbanization spread globally, anthropologists increasingly study these processes and the social problems they create. **Urban anthropology,** which has theoretical (basic research) and applied dimensions, is the cross-cultural and ethnographic study of global urbanization and life in cities (see Aoyagi, Nas, and Traphagan, eds. 1998; Gmelch and Zenner, eds. 2002; Smart and Smart 2003; Stevenson 2003). The United States and Canada have become popular arenas for urban anthropological research on topics such as immigration, ethnicity, poverty, class, and urban violence (Mullings, ed. 1987; Vigil 2003).

Urban versus Rural

Recognizing that a city is a social context that is very different from a tribal or peasant village, an early student of urbanization, the anthropologist Robert Redfield, focused on contrasts between rural and urban life. He contrasted rural communities, whose social relations are on a face-to-face basis, with cities, where impersonality characterizes many aspects of life. Redfield (1941) proposed that urbanization be studied along a rural–urban continuum. He described differences in values and social relations in four sites that spanned such a continuum. In Mexico's Yucatán peninsula, Redfield compared an isolated Maya-speaking Indian community, a rural peasant village, a small provincial city, and a large capital. Several studies in Africa (Little 1971) and Asia were influenced by Redfield's view that cities are centers through which cultural innovations spread to rural and tribal areas.

In any nation, urban and rural represent different social systems. However, cultural diffusion or borrowing occurs as people, products, images, and messages move from one to the other. Migrants bring rural practices and beliefs to cities and take urban patterns back home. The experiences and social forms of the rural area affect adaptation to city life. City folk also develop new institutions to meet specific urban needs (Mitchell 1966).

An applied anthropology approach to urban planning would start by identifying key social groups in the urban context. After identifying those groups, the anthropologist might elicit their wishes for change, convey those needs to funding agencies, and work with agencies and local people to realize those goals. In Africa relevant groups might include ethnic associations, occupational groups, social clubs, religious groups, and burial societies. Through membership in such groups, urban Africans maintain wide networks of personal contacts and support (Banton 1957; Little 1965). These groups also have links with, and provide cash support and urban lodging for, their rural relatives. Sometimes such groups think of themselves as a gigantic kin group, a clan that includes urban and rural members. Members may call one another "brother" and "sister." As in an extended family, rich members help their poor relatives. A member's improper behavior can lead to expulsion—an unhappy fate for a migrant in a large ethnically heterogeneous city.

One role for the urban applied anthropologist is to help relevant social groups deal with urban institutions, such as legal and social services, with which recent migrants may be unfamiliar. In certain North American cities, as in Africa, kin-based ethnic associations are relevant urban groups. One example comes from Los Angeles, which has the largest Samoan immigrant community (over 12,000 people) in the United States. Samoans in Los Angeles draw on their traditional system of *matai* (*matai* means "chief"; the matai system now refers to respect for elders) to deal with modern urban problems. One example: In 1992, a white police officer shot and killed two unarmed Samoan brothers. When a judge dismissed charges against the officer, local leaders used the matai system to calm angry youths (who have formed gangs, like other ethnic groups in the Los Angeles area). Clan leaders and elders organized a well-attended community meeting, in which they urged young members to be patient. The Samoans then used the American judicial system. They brought a civil case against the officer in question and pressed the U.S. Justice Department to initiate a civil rights case in the matter (Mydans 1992*b*). Not all conflicts involving gangs and law enforcement end so peacefully.

James Vigil (2003) examines gang violence in the context of large-scale immigrant adaptation to American cities. He notes that most gangs prior to the 1970s were located in white ethnic enclaves in Eastern and Midwestern cities. Back then, gang incidents typically were brawls involving fists, sticks, and knives. Today, gangs more often are composed of nonwhite ethnic groups, and handguns have replaced the less lethal weapons of the past. Gangs still consist mostly of male adolescents who have grown up together, usually in a low-income neighborhood, where it's estimated that about 10 percent of young men join gangs. Female gang members are much rarer—from 4 to 15 percent of gang members. With gangs organized hierarchically by age, older members push younger ones (usually 14- to 18-year-olds) to carry out violent acts against rivals (Vigil 2003).

The populations that include most of today's gang members settled originally in poorer urban areas. On the East Coast these usually were rundown neighborhoods where a criminal lifestyle already was present. Around Los Angeles, urban migrants created squatterlike settlements in previously empty spaces. Immigrants tend to reside in neighborhoods apart from middle-class people, thus limiting their opportunities for integration. Confined in this manner, and facing residential overcrowding, poor people often experience frustration, which can lead to aggressive acts (Vigil 2003). As well, industries and jobs have moved from inner cities to distant suburbs and foreign nations. Urban minority youth have limited access to entry-level jobs; often they receive harsh treatment from authorities, especially law enforcement. Frustration and competition over resources can spark aggressive incidents, fueling urban violence. For survival, many residents of abandoned neighborhoods have turned to informal and illegal economic arrangements, of which drug trafficking in particular has heightened gang violence (Vigil 2003). How might an applied anthropologist approach the problem of urban violence? Which groups would be need to be involved in the study?

Medical Anthropology

Medical anthropology is both academic/theoretical and applied/practical and includes anthropologists from all four subfields (see Anderson 1996; Briggs 2005; Brown 1998; Dressler et al. 2005; Joralemon 2006; Singer and Baer 2007; Trevathan, Smith, and

McKenna 2007). Medical anthropologists examine such questions as which diseases and health conditions affect particular populations (and why) and how illness is socially constructed, diagnosed, managed, and treated in various societies.

Disease refers to a scientifically identified health threat caused genetically or by a bacterium, virus, fungus, parasite, or other pathogen. **Illness** is a condition of poor health perceived or felt by an individual (Inhorn and Brown 1990). Perceptions of good and bad health, along with health threats and problems, are culturally constructed. Various ethnic groups and cultures recognize different illnesses, symptoms, and causes and have developed different health care systems and treatment strategies.

The incidence and severity of *disease* vary as well (see Barnes 2005; Baer, Singer, and Susser 2003). Group differences are evident in the United States. Keppel, Pearch, and Wagener (2002) examined data between 1990 and 1998 using 10 health status indicators in relation to racial and ethnic categories used in the U.S. census: non-Hispanic white, non-Hispanic black, Hispanic, American Indian or Alaska Native, and Asian or Pacific Islander. Black Americans' rates for six measures (total mortality, heart disease, lung cancer, breast cancer, stroke, and homicide) exceeded those of other groups by a factor ranging from 2.5 to almost 10. Other ethnic groups had higher rates for suicide (white Americans) and motor vehicle accidents (American Indians and Alaskan Natives). Overall, Asians had the longest life spans (see Dressler et al. 2005).

Hurtado and colleagues (2005) note the prevalence of poor health and unusually high rates of early mortality among indigenous populations in South America. Life expectancy at birth is at least 20 years shorter among indigenous groups compared with other South Americans. In 2000, the life expectancy of indigenous peoples in Brazil and Venezuela was lower than that in Sierra Leone, which had the lowest reported national life expectancy in the world (Hurtado et al. 2005).

How can applied anthropologists help ameliorate the large health disparity between indigenous peoples and other populations? Hurtado and colleagues (2005) suggest three steps: (1) Identify the most pressing health problems that indigenous communities face; (2) gather information on solutions to those problems; and (3) implement solutions in partnership with the agencies and organizations that are in charge of public health programs for indigenous populations.

In many areas, the world system and colonialism worsened the health of indigenous peoples by spreading diseases, warfare, servitude, and other stressors. Traditionally and in ancient times, hunter-gatherers, because of their small numbers, mobility, and relative isolation from other groups, lacked most of the epidemic infectious diseases that affect agrarian and urban societies (Cohen and Armelagos, eds. 1984; Inhorn and Brown 1990). Epidemic diseases such as cholera, typhoid, and bubonic plague thrive in dense populations, and thus among farmers and city dwellers. The spread of malaria has been linked to population growth and deforestation associated with food production.

Certain diseases, and physical conditions such as obesity, have spread with economic development and globalization (Ulijaszek and Lofink 2006). *Schistosomiasis* or bilharzia (liver flukes) is probably the fastest-spreading and most dangerous parasitic infection now known. It is propagated by snails that live in ponds, lakes, and waterways, usually ones created by irrigation projects. A study done in a Nile Delta village in Egypt (Farooq 1966) illustrated the role of culture (religion) in the spread of schistosomiasis. The disease was more common among Muslims than among Christians because of an Islamic practice called *wudu*, ritual ablution (bathing) before prayer. The applied anthropology approach to reducing such diseases is to see if local people perceive a connection between the vector (e.g., snails in the water) and the disease. If not, such information may be provided by enlisting active local groups, schools, and the media.

The highest global rates of HIV infection and AIDS-related deaths are in Africa, especially southern Africa. As it kills productive adults, AIDS leaves behind children and seniors who have difficulty replacing the lost labor force (Baro and Deubel 2006). In southern and eastern Africa, AIDS and other sexually transmitted diseases (STDs) have spread along highways, via encounters between male truckers and female prostitutes. STDs also are spread through prostitution, as young men from rural areas seek wage work in cities, labor camps, and mines. When the men return to their natal villages, they infect their wives (Larson 1989; Miller and Rockwell, eds. 1988). Cities also are prime sites of STD transmission in Europe, Asia, and North and South America (see Baer, Singer, and Susser 2003; French 2002). Cultural factors also affect the spread of HIV, which is less likely to be transmitted when men are circumcised than when they are not.

The kinds of and incidence of disease vary among societies, and cultures interpret and treat illness differently. Standards for sick and healthy bodies are cultural constructions that vary in time and space (Martin 1992). Still, all societies have what George Foster and Barbara Anderson call "disease-theory systems" to identify, classify, and explain illness. According to Foster and Anderson (1978), there are three basic theories about the causes of illness: personalistic, naturalistic, and emotionalistic. *Personalistic disease theories* blame illness on agents, such as sorcerers, witches, ghosts, or ancestral spirits. *Naturalistic disease theories* explain illness in impersonal terms. One example is Western medicine or *biomedicine*, which aims to link illness to scientifically demonstrated agents that bear no personal malice toward their victims. Thus Western medicine attributes illness to organisms (e.g., bacteria, viruses, fungi, or parasites), accidents, toxic materials, or genes.

Other naturalistic ethnomedical systems blame poor health on unbalanced body fluids. Many Latin societies classify food, drink, and environmental conditions as "hot" or "cold." People believe their health suffers when they eat or drink hot or cold substances together or under inappropriate conditions. For example, one shouldn't drink something cold after a hot bath or eat a pineapple (a "cold" fruit) when one is menstruating (a "hot" condition).

Emotionalistic disease theories assume that emotional experiences cause illness. For example, Latin Americans may develop *susto*, an illness caused by anxiety or fright (Bolton 1981; Finkler 1985). Its symptoms (lethargy, vagueness, distraction) are similar to those of "soul loss," a diagnosis of similar symptoms made by people in Madagascar. Modern psychoanalysis also focuses on the role of the emotions in physical and psychological well-being.

All societies have **health care systems** consisting of beliefs, customs, specialists, and techniques aimed at ensuring health and at preventing, diagnosing, and curing illness. A society's illness-causation theory is important for treatment. When illness has a

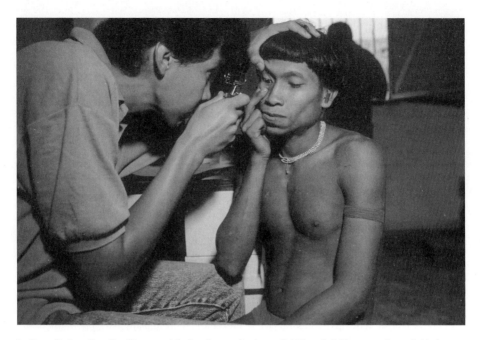

In Serra Parima, Brazil, a Yanomami Indian is examined at a field hospital. Treatment is available here for malaria, which has killed thousands of Yanomami. Such hospitals and clinics provide antibiotics, antimalarials, surgery, and preventive medicine.

personalistic cause, magicoreligious specialists may be good curers. They draw on varied techniques (occult and practical), which comprise their special expertise. A shaman may cure soul loss by enticing the spirit back into the body. Shamans may ease difficult childbirths by asking spirits to travel up the birth canal to guide the baby out (Lévi-Strauss 1967). A shaman may cure a cough by counteracting a curse or removing a substance introduced by a sorcerer.

If there is a "world's oldest profession" besides hunter and gatherer, it is **curer,** often a shaman. The curer's role has some universal features (Foster and Anderson 1978). Thus curers emerge through a culturally defined process of selection (parental prodding, inheritance, visions, dream instructions) and training (apprentice shamanship, medical school). Eventually, the curer is certified by older practitioners and acquires a professional image. Patients believe in the skills of the curer, whom they consult and compensate.

We should not lose sight, ethnocentrically, of the difference between **scientific medicine** and Western medicine per se. Despite advances in technology, genomics, molecular biology, pathology, surgery, diagnostics, and applications, many Western medical procedures have little justification in logic or fact. Overprescription of drugs, unnecessary surgery, and the impersonality and inequality of the physician–patient relationship are questionable features of Western medical systems (see Briggs 2005 for linguistic aspects of this inequality). Also, overuse of antibiotics, not just for people but also in animal feed, seems to be triggering an explosion of resistant microrganisms, which may pose a long-term global public health hazard.

Still, biomedicine surpasses tribal treatment in many ways. Although medicines such as quinine, coca, opium, ephedrine, and rauwolfia were discovered in nonindustrial societies, thousands of effective drugs are available today to treat myriad diseases. Preventive health care improved during the twentieth century. Today's surgical procedures are much safer and more effective than those of traditional societies.

But industrialization and globalization have spawned their own health problems. Modern stressors include poor nutrition, dangerous machinery, impersonal work, isolation, poverty, homelessness, substance abuse, and noise, air, and water pollution (see McElroy and Townsend 2003). Health problems in industrial nations are caused as much by economic, social, political, and cultural factors as by pathogens. In modern North America, for example, poverty contributes to many illnesses, including arthritis, heart conditions, back problems, and hearing and vision impairment (see Bailey 2000). Poverty also is a factor in the differential spread of infectious diseases.

In the United States and other developed countries today, good health has become something of an ethical imperative (Foucault 1990). Individuals are expected to regulate their behavior and shape themselves in keeping with new medical knowledge. Those who do so acquire the status of sanitary citizens—people with modern understanding of the body, health, and illness, who practice hygiene, and depend on doctors and nurses when they are sick. People who act differently (e.g., smokers, overeaters, those who avoid doctors) are stigmatized as unsanitary and blamed for their own health problems (Briggs 2005; Foucault 1990).

Even getting an epidemic disease such as cholera or living in an infected neighborhood may be interpreted today as a moral failure. It's assumed that people who are properly informed and act rationally can avoid such "preventable" diseases. Individuals are expected to follow scientifically based imperatives (e.g., "boil water," "don't smoke"). People (e.g., gay men, Haitians, smokers, veterans) can become objects of avoidance and discrimination simply by belonging to a group seen as having a greater risk of getting a particular disease (Briggs 2005).

Medical anthropologists have served as cultural interpreters in public health programs, which must pay attention to local theories about the nature, causes, and treatment of illness. Health interventions cannot simply be forced on communities. They must fit into local cultures and be accepted by local people. When Western medicine is introduced, people usually retain many of their old methods while also accepting new ones (see Green 1987/1992). Native curers may go on treating certain conditions (spirit possession), whereas doctors may deal with others. If both modern and traditional specialists are consulted and the patient is cured, the native curer may get as much or more credit than the physician.

A more personal treatment of illness that emulates the non-Western curer-patient-community relationship could probably benefit Western systems. Western medicine tends to draw a rigid line between biological and psychological causation. Non-Western theories usually lack this sharp distinction, recognizing that poor health has intertwined physical, emotional, and social causes. The mind–body opposition is part of Western folk taxonomy, not of science (see also Brown 1998; Helman 2001; Joralemon 2006; Strathern and Stewart 1999).

Medical anthropologists increasingly are examining the impact of new scientific and medical techniques on ideas about life, death, and *personhood* (what is and is not a person). For decades, disagreements about personhood—about when life begins and ends—have been part of political and religious discussions of contraception, abortion, assisted suicide, and euthanasia (mercy killing). More recent additions to such discussions include stem cell research, frozen embryos, assisted reproduction, genetic screening, cloning, and life-prolonging medical treatments. Ideas about what it means to be human and to be alive or dead are being reformulated. In the United States, the controversy surrounding the death of Terri Schiavo in 2005 brought such questions into public debate. Kaufman and Morgan (2005) emphasize the contrast between what they call low-tech and high-tech births and deaths in today's world. A desperately poor young mother dies of AIDS in Africa while half a world away an American child of privilege is born as the result of a $50,000 in-vitro fertilization procedure. Medical anthropologists increasingly are concerned with new and contrasting conditions that allow humans to enter, live, and depart life, and with how the boundaries of life and death are being questioned and negotiated in the 21st century.

Anthropology and Business

At a major information technology company, Marietta Baba examines one of the world's fastest supercomputers. She is studying that firm's adaptation to the rise of the service economy. Professor Baba, a prominent applied anthropologist and dean of the College of Social Science at Michigan State University, also has studied Michigan's automobile industry.

Carol Taylor (1987) discusses the value of an "anthropologist-in-residence" in a large, complex organization, such as a hospital or a business. A free-ranging ethnographer can be a perceptive oddball when information and decisions usually move through a rigid hierarchy. If allowed to observe and converse freely with all types and levels of personnel, the anthropologist may acquire a unique perspective on organizational conditions and problems. Also, high-tech companies, such as Xerox, IBM, and Apple, have employed anthropologists in various roles. Closely observing how people actually use computer products, anthropologists work with engineers to design products that are more user-friendly.

For many years anthropologists have used ethnography to study business settings (Arensberg 1987; Jordan 2003). For example, ethnographic research in an auto factory may view workers, managers, and executives as different social categories participating in a common social system. Each group has characteristic attitudes, values, and behavior patterns. These are transmitted through *microenculturation,* the process by which people learn particular roles in a limited social system. The free-ranging nature of ethnography takes the anthropologist back and forth from worker to executive. Each is an individual with a personal viewpoint and a cultural creature whose perspective is, to some extent, shared with other members of a group. Applied anthropologists have acted as "cultural brokers," translating managers' goals or workers' concerns to the other group (see Ferraro 2006).

For business, key features of anthropology include (1) ethnography and observation as ways of gathering data, (2) cross-cultural expertise, and (3) focus on cultural diversity. An important business application of anthropology has to do with knowledge of how consumers use products. Businesses hire anthropologists because of the importance of observation in natural settings and the focus on cultural diversity. Thus, Hallmark Cards has hired anthropologists to observe parties, holidays, and celebrations of ethnic groups to improve its ability to design cards for targeted audiences. Anthropologists go into people's homes to see how they actually use products (see Sunderland and Denny 2007).

Careers and Anthropology

Many college students find anthropology interesting and consider majoring in it. However, their parents or friends may discourage them by asking, "What kind of job are you going to get with an anthropology major?" The first step in answering this question is to consider the more general question, "What do you do with any college major?" The answer is "Not much, without a good bit of effort, thought, and planning." A survey of graduates of the literary college of the University of Michigan showed that few had jobs that were clearly linked to their majors. Medicine, law, and many other professions require advanced degrees. Although many colleges offer bachelor's degrees in engineering, business, accounting, and social work, master's degrees often are needed to get the best jobs in those fields. Anthropologists, too, need an advanced degree, almost always a Ph.D., to find gainful employment in academic, museum, or applied anthropology.

A broad college education, and even a major in anthropology, can be an excellent foundation for success in many fields. A recent survey of women executives showed that most had not majored in business but in the social sciences or humanities. Only after graduating did they study business, obtaining a master's degree in business administration. These executives felt that the breadth of their college educations had contributed to their business careers. Anthropology majors go on to medical, law, and business schools and find success in many professions that often have little explicit connection to anthropology.

Anthropology's breadth provides knowledge and an outlook on the world that are useful in many kinds of work. For example, an anthropology major combined with a master's degree in business is excellent preparation for work in international business. Breadth is anthropology's hallmark. Anthropologists study people biologically, culturally, socially, and linguistically, across time and space, in developed and underdeveloped nations, in simple and complex settings. Most colleges have anthropology courses that compare cultures and others that focus on particular world areas, such as Latin

America, Asia, and Native North America. The knowledge of foreign areas acquired in such courses can be useful in many jobs. Anthropology's comparative outlook, its longstanding Third World focus, and its appreciation of diverse lifestyles combine to provide an excellent foundation for overseas employment (see Omohundro 2001).

Even for work in North America, the focus on culture is valuable. Every day we hear about cultural differences and about social problems whose solutions require a multicultural viewpoint—an ability to recognize and reconcile ethnic differences. Government, schools, and private firms constantly deal with people from different social classes, ethnic groups, and tribal backgrounds. Physicians, attorneys, social workers, police officers, judges, teachers, and students can all do a better job if they understand social differences in a part of the world such as ours that is one of the most ethnically diverse in history.

Knowledge about the traditions and beliefs of the many social groups within a modern nation is important in planning and carrying out programs that affect those groups. Attention to social background and cultural categories helps ensure the welfare of affected ethnic groups, communities, and neighborhoods. Experience in planned social change—whether community organization in North America or economic development overseas—shows that a proper social study should be done before a project or policy is implemented. When local people want the change and it fits their lifestyle and traditions, it will be more successful, beneficial, and cost effective. There will be not only a more humane but also a more economical solution to a real social problem.

People with anthropology backgrounds are doing well in many fields. Even if one's job has little or nothing to do with anthropology in a formal or obvious sense, a background in anthropology provides a useful orientation when we work with our fellow human beings. For most of us, this means every day of our lives.

ANTHROPOLOGY TODAY

Culturally Appropriate Marketing

Innovation succeeds best when it is culturally appropriate. This axiom of applied anthropology could guide the international spread not only of development projects but also of businesses, such as fast food. Each time McDonald's or Burger King expands to a new nation, it must devise a culturally appropriate strategy for fitting into the new setting.

McDonald's has been successful internationally, with more than a quarter of its sales outside the United States. One place where McDonald's is expanding successfully is Brazil, where more than 50 million middle-class people, most living in densely packed cities, provide a concentrated market for a fast-food chain. Still, it took McDonald's some time to find the right marketing strategy for Brazil.

In 1980 when I visited Brazil after a seven-year absence, I first noticed, as a manifestation of Brazil's growing participation in the world economy, the appearance of two McDonald's restaurants in Rio de Janeiro. There wasn't much difference between

Continued

ANTHROPOLOGY TODAY   *Continued*

Brazilian and American McDonald's. The restaurants looked alike. The menus were more or less the same, as was the taste of the quarter-pounders. I picked up an artifact, a white paper bag with yellow lettering, exactly like the take-out bags then used in American McDonald's. An advertising device, it carried several messages about how Brazilians could bring McDonald's into their lives. However, it seemed to me that McDonald's Brazilian ad campaign was missing some important points about how fast food should be marketed in a culture that values large, leisurely lunches.

The bag proclaimed, "You're going to enjoy the [McDonald's] difference," and listed several "favorite places where you can enjoy McDonald's products." This list confirmed that the marketing people were trying to adapt to Brazilian middle-class culture, but they were making some mistakes. "When you go out in the car with the kids" transferred the uniquely developed North American cultural combination of highways, affordable cars, and suburban living to the very different context of urban Brazil. A similar suggestion was "traveling to the country place." Even Brazilians who

owned country places could not find McDonald's, still confined to the cities, on the road. The ad creator had apparently never attempted to drive up to a fast-food restaurant in a neighborhood with no parking spaces.

Several other suggestions pointed customers toward the beach, where *cariocas* (Rio natives) do spend much of their leisure time. One could eat McDonald's products "after a dip in the ocean," "at a picnic at the beach," or "watching the surfers." These suggestions ignored the Brazilian custom of consuming cold things, such as beer, soft drinks, ice cream, and ham and cheese sandwiches, at the beach. Brazilians don't consider a hot, greasy hamburger proper beach food. They view the sea as "cold" and hamburgers as "hot"; they avoid "hot" foods at the beach.

Also culturally dubious was the suggestion to eat McDonald's hamburgers "lunching at the office." Brazilians prefer their main meal at midday, often eating at a leisurely pace with business associates. Many firms serve ample lunches to their employees. Other workers take advantage of a two-hour lunch break to go home to eat

Summary

1. Anthropology has two dimensions: academic and applied. Applied anthropology uses anthropological perspectives, theory, methods, and data to identify, assess, and solve problems. Applied anthropologists have a range of employers. Examples: government agencies; development organizations; NGOs; tribal, ethnic, and interest groups; businesses; social services and educational agencies. Applied anthropologists come from all four subfields. Ethnography is one of applied anthropology's most valuable research tools. A systemic perspective recognizes that changes have multiple consequences, some unintended.

2. Development anthropology focuses on social issues in, and the cultural dimension of, economic development. Development projects typically promote cash

with the spouse and children. Nor did it make sense to suggest that children should eat hamburgers for lunch, since most kids attend school for half-day sessions and have lunch at home. Two other suggestions—"waiting for the bus" and "in the beauty parlor"—did describe common aspects of daily life in a Brazilian city. However, these settings have not proved especially inviting to hamburgers or fish filets.

The homes of Brazilians who can afford McDonald's products have cooks and maids to do many of the things that fast-food restaurants do in the United States. The suggestion that McDonald's products be eaten "while watching your favorite television program" is culturally appropriate, because Brazilians watch TV a lot. However, Brazil's consuming classes can ask the cook to make a snack when hunger strikes. Indeed, much televiewing occurs during the light dinner served when the husband gets home from the office.

Most appropriate to the Brazilian lifestyle was the suggestion to enjoy McDonald's "on the cook's day off." Throughout Brazil, Sunday is that day. The Sunday pattern for middle-class families is a trip to the beach, liters of beer, a full midday meal around 3 P.M., and a light evening snack. McDonald's found its niche in the Sunday evening meal, when families flock to the fast-food restaurant, and it is to this market that its advertising is now appropriately geared.

McDonald's is expanding rapidly in Brazilian cities, and in Brazil as in North America, teenage appetites are fueling the fast-food explosion. As McDonald's outlets appeared in urban neighborhoods, Brazilian teenagers used them for after-school snacks, while families had evening meals there. As an anthropologist could have predicted, the fast-food industry has not revolutionized Brazilian food and meal customs. Rather, McDonald's is succeeding because it has adapted to preexisting Brazilian cultural patterns.

The main contrast with North America is that the Brazilian evening meal is lighter. McDonald's now caters to the evening meal rather than to lunch. Once McDonald's realized that more money could be made by fitting in with, rather than trying to Americanize, Brazilian meal habits, it started aiming its advertising at that goal.

employment and new technology at the expense of subsistence economies. Not all governments seek to increase equality and end poverty. Resistance by elites to reform is typical and hard to combat. At the same time, local people rarely cooperate with projects requiring major and risky changes in their daily lives. Many projects seek to impose inappropriate property notions and incompatible social units on their intended beneficiaries. The best strategy for change is to base the social design for innovation on traditional social forms in each target area.

3. Anthropology and education researchers work in classrooms, homes, and other settings relevant to education. Such studies may lead to policy recommendations. Both academic and applied anthropologists study migration from rural areas to cities and across national boundaries. North America has become a popular arena for urban anthropological research on migration, ethnicity, poverty, and related

topics. Although rural and urban are different social systems, there is cultural diffusion from one to the other.

4. Medical anthropology is the cross-cultural, biocultural study of health problems and conditions, disease, illness, disease theories, and health-care systems. Medical anthropology includes anthropologists from all four subfields and has theoretical (academic) and applied dimensions. In a given setting, the characteristic diseases reflect diet, population density, economy, and social complexity. Native theories of illness may be personalistic, naturalistic, or emotionalistic. In applying anthropology to business, the key features are (1) ethnography and observation as ways of gathering data, (2) cross-cultural expertise, and (3) a focus on cultural diversity.

5. A broad college education, including anthropology and foreign-area courses, offers excellent background for many fields. Anthropology's comparative outlook and cultural relativism provide an excellent basis for overseas employment. Even for work in North America, a focus on culture and cultural diversity is valuable. Anthropology majors attend medical, law, and business schools and succeed in many fields, some of which have little explicit connection with anthropology.

Key Terms

anthropology and education (p. 266)
applied anthropology (p. 259)
curer (p. 273)
development anthropology (p. 262)
disease (p. 271)
equity, increased (p. 262)
health care systems (p. 272)

illness (p. 271)
medical anthropology (p. 270)
overinnovation (p. 263)
scientific medicine (p. 273)
underdifferentiation (p. 264)
urban anthropology (p. 269)

 Go to our Online Learning Center website at **www.mhhe.com/kottak** for Internet resources directly related to the content of this chapter.

Global Issues Today

This chapter applies an anthropological perspective to contemporary global issues, beginning with a discussion of climate change, aka global warming. Next, we return to issues of development, this time alongside an intervention philosophy that seeks to impose global ecological morality without due attention to cultural variation and autonomy. Also considered is the threat that deforestation poses to global biodiversity. The second half of this chapter turns from ecology to the contemporary flows of people, technology, finance, information, images, and ideology that contribute to a global culture of consumption. Globalization promotes intercultural communication, through the media, travel, and migration, which bring people from different societies into direct contact. Finally, we'll consider how such contacts and external linkages influence indigenous peoples, and how those groups have organized to confront and deal with national and global issues, including human, cultural, and political rights.

Global Climate Change

The Earth's surface temperatures have risen about 1.48°F (0.78°C) since the early 20th century. (This chapter's "Anthropology Today" box discusses how this rise has affected an indigenous group in Alaska.) About two-thirds of this increase has been since 1978 (Figure 13.1). Along with rising temperatures, shrinking glaciers and melting polar ice provide additional evidence for global warming. Scientific measurements confirm that global warming is not due to increased solar radiation. The causes are mainly anthropogenic—caused by humans and their activities.

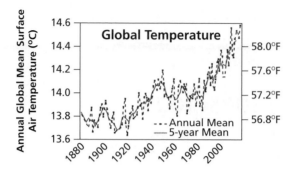

FIGURE 13.1   *Global Temperature Change* Global annual-mean surface air temperature derived from measurements at meteorological stations has increased by 1.4°F (0.7°C) since the early 20th century, with about 0.9°F (0.5°C) of the increase occurring since 1978.

SOURCE: Goddard Institute for Space Studies, from "Understanding and Responding to Climate Change: Highlights of National Academies Reports," http://dels.nas.edu/basc/Climate-HIGH.pdf.

Because our planet's climate is always changing, the key question becomes: How much global warming is due to human activities versus natural climate variability. Most scientists agree that human activities play a major role in global climate change. How can the human factor not be significant given population growth and rapidly increasing use of fossil fuels, which produce greenhouse gases in the atmosphere?

The role of one such gas—carbon dioxide (CO_2)—in warming the Earth's surface has been known for over a century. For hundreds of thousands of years, world temperatures have varied depending on the amount of CO_2 in the atmosphere. The burning of fossil fuels (oil, natural gas, and coal) releases substantial amounts of carbon dioxide. The recent rapid rise in both CO_2 and the Earth's surface temperature is one of the proofs that humans are fueling global warming.

The **greenhouse effect** is a natural phenomenon that keeps the Earth's surface warm. Without greenhouse gases—water vapor (H_2O), carbon dioxide (CO_2), methane (CH_4), nitrous oxide (N_2O), halocarbons, and ozone (O_3)—life as we know it wouldn't exist. Like a greenhouse window, such gases allow sunlight to enter and then prevent heat from escaping the atmosphere. All those gases have increased since the Industrial Revolution. Today, the atmospheric concentration of greenhouse gases has reached its highest level in 400,000 years. It will continue to rise—as will global temperatures—without actions to slow it down (National Academies 2006).

Scientists prefer the term **climate change** to *global warming.* The former term points out that, beyond rising temperatures, there have been changes in sea levels, precipitation, storms, and ecosystem effects. Along with many ordinary people, some scientists see recent weather events as reflecting climate change. Such events include Florida's 2007 worst-in-a-century drought, the 2005 hurricane season featuring Katrina, the first-ever hurricane in the South Atlantic in 2004, and the severe European heat wave of 2003. Although it is difficult to link any one event to climate change, the conjunction of several events may indicate climate change is playing a role.

The precise effects of climate change on regional weather patterns have yet to be determined. Land areas are expected to warm more than oceans, with the greatest warming in higher latitudes, such as Canada, the northern United States, and northern Europe. Global warming may benefit these areas, offering milder winters and extended growing seasons. However, many more people worldwide probably will be harmed. Already we know that in the Arctic, temperatures have risen almost twice as much as the global average. Arctic landscapes and ecosystems are changing rapidly and perceptibly, as "Anthropology Today" illustrates.

The Intergovernmental Panel on Climate Change (IPCC) is composed of hundreds of scientists from the United States and other countries. In 2001 the IPCC predicted that by 2100 average global surface temperatures will rise 2.5 to 10.4°F (1.4 to 5.8°C) above 1990 levels. The IPCC also forecast ocean warming trends—the combined effects of melting glaciers, melting ice caps, and seawater expansion. The global average sea level is projected to rise 4 to 35 inches (0.1 to 0.9 meters) between 1990 and 2100.

Coastal communities can anticipate increased flooding and more severe storms and surges. At risk are people, animals, plants, freshwater supplies, and such industries as tourism and farming. Along with many island nations, Bangladesh, one of the world's poorest countries, is projected to lose a significant portion (17.5 percent) of its land, displacing millions of people (National Academies 2006). Given the political will, developed countries might use science and technology to anticipate and deal with climate impacts and to help less developed countries adapt to climate change.

The U.S. National Academy of Sciences and other national academies have issued several reports on climate change. Citations and highlights of these reports can be found in a brochure titled "Understanding and Responding to Climate Change: Highlights of National Academies Reports" (http://dels.nas.edu/basc/Climate-HIGH.pdf), on which some of this discussion has been based (see also Crate and Nuttall 2008).

Meeting energy needs is the single greatest obstacle to slowing climate change. In the United States, about 80 percent of all energy used comes from fossil fuels. Worldwide, energy use continues to grow with economic and population expansion. China and India in particular are rapidly increasing their use of energy, mainly from fossil fuels, and consequently their emissions of CO_2 (Figure 13.2). These emissions could be reduced by using energy more efficiently or by using renewable sources. One alternative is ethanol, of which the United States is a limited producer. American policy makers give lip service to the value of ethanol, while restricting its inflow from nations, such as Brazil, that produce it most effectively.

Among the alternatives to fossil fuels are nuclear power and such renewable energy technologies as solar, wind, and biomass generators. Replacing coal-fired electric power plants with more efficient natural-gas-fired turbines would reduce carbon emissions. In the United States, these technologies currently are too expensive, or, in the case of nuclear power, they raise environmental or other concerns. This could change with the development and increasing use of new technologies and as the cost of fossil fuels rises.

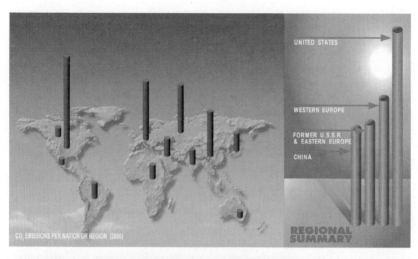

FIGURE 13.2   The panels compare CO_2 emissions per nation in 2000 (top) and projections for 2025 (bottom). In 2000, the largest emitter of CO_2 was the United States, which was responsible for 25 percent of global emissions. In 2025, China and the developing world may significantly increase their CO_2 emissions relative to the United States.

SOURCE: Images courtesy of the Marian Kashland Science Museum of the National Academy of Sciences.

Environmental Anthropology

Anthropology always has been concerned with how environmental forces influence humans and how human activities affect the biosphere and the Earth itself. The 1950s–1970s witnessed the emergence of an area of study known as *cultural ecology* or **ecological anthropology.** That field focused on how cultural beliefs and practices

In the global economy India and China (shown here) in particular have increased their use of fossil fuels, and consequently their emissions of CO_2. This scene, near Beijing, shows the Shougang steel plant, a major source of air pollution in 1997. What's the most polluted place you've ever been?

helped human populations adapt to their environments, and how people used elements of their culture to maintain their ecosystems.

Early ecological anthropologists showed that many indigenous groups did a reasonable job of managing their resources and preserving their ecosystems. Such groups had traditional ways of categorizing resources, regulating their use, and preserving the environment. An **ethnoecology** is any society's set of environmental practices and perceptions—that is, its cultural model of the environment and its relation to people and society. Indigenous ethnoecologies increasingly are being challenged, as migration, media, and commerce spread people, institutions, information, and technology. In the face of national and international incentives to exploit and degrade, ethnoecological systems that once preserved local and regional environments increasingly are ineffective or irrelevant.

Anthropologists routinely witness threats to the people they study and their environments. Among such threats are commercial logging, industrial pollution, and the imposition of external management systems on local ecosystems (see Johnston 2009). Today's ecological anthropology, aka *environmental anthropology,* attempts not only to understand but also to find solutions to environmental problems. Such problems must be tackled at the national and international levels (e.g., global warming). Even in remote places, ecosystem management now involves multiple levels. For example, among the Antankarana of northern Madagascar (Gezon 2006), several levels of authority claim the right to use and regulate natural resources and local ecosystems. Actual or would-be regulators there include local communities, traditional leaders (the regional king or chief), provincial and national governments, and the WWF, the World-wide Fund for Nature (formerly the World Wildlife Fund), an international NGO. Local people, their landscapes, their ideas, their values, and their traditional management systems face attacks from all sides. Outsiders attempt to remake native landscapes and cultures in their own image. The aim of many agricultural development projects, for example, seems to be to make the world as much like a Midwestern American agricultural state as possible. Often there is an attempt to impose mechanized farming and nuclear family ownership, even though these institutions may be inappropriate in areas far removed from the Midwestern United States. Development projects usually fail when they try to replace indigenous institutions with culturally alien concepts (Kottak 1990*b*).

Global Assaults on Local Autonomy

A clash of cultures related to environmental change may occur when development threatens indigenous peoples and their environments. A second clash of cultures related to environmental change may occur when external regulation aimed at conservation confronts indigenous peoples and their ethnoecologies. Like development projects, conservation schemes may ask people to change their ways in order to satisfy planners' goals rather than local goals. In places as different as Madagascar, Brazil, and the Pacific Northwest of the United States, people have been asked, told, or forced to abandon basic economic activities because to do so is good for "nature" or "the globe." "Good for the globe" doesn't play very well in Brazil, whose Amazon is a focus of international environmentalist attention. Brazilians complain that outsiders (e.g., Europeans and North Americans) promote "global needs" and "saving the Amazon" after having destroyed their own forests for economic growth. Well-intentioned conservation plans can be as insensitive as development schemes that promote radical changes without involving local people in planning and carrying out the policies that affect them. When people are asked to give up the basis of their livelihood, they usually resist.

The spread of environmentalism may expose radically different notions about the "rights" and value of plants and animals versus humans. In Madagascar, many intellectuals and officials complain that foreigners seem more concerned about lemurs and other endangered species than about the people of Madagascar (the Malagasy). As a geographer there remarked to me, "The next time you come to Madagascar, there'll be no more Malagasy. All the people will have starved to death, and a lemur will have to meet you at the airport." Most Malagasy perceive human poverty as a more pressing problem than animal and plant survival.

Still, who can doubt that conservation, including the preservation of biodiversity, is a worthy goal? The challenge for applied ecological anthropology is to devise culturally appropriate strategies for achieving biodiversity conservation in the face of unrelenting population growth and commercial expansion. How does one get people to support conservation measures that may, in the short run at least, diminish their access to resources? Like development plans in general, the most effective conservation strategies pay attention to the needs and wishes of the local people.

Deforestation

Deforestation is a global concern. Forest loss can lead to increased greenhouse gas (CO_2) production, which contributes to global warming. The destruction of tropical forests also is a major factor in the loss of global biodiversity, since many species, often of limited distribution and including many primates, live in forests. Tropical forests contain at least half of Earth's species while covering just 6 percent of the planet's land surface. Yet tropical forests are disappearing at the rate of 10 million to 20 million hectares per year (the size of New York State).

Generations of anthropologists have studied how human economic activities (ancient and modern) affect the environment. Anthropologists know that food producers (farmers and herders) typically do more to degrade the environment than foragers do. Population increase and the need to expand farming caused deforestation in many parts of the ancient Middle East and Mesoamerica (see Hornborg and Crumley 2007). Even today, many farmers think of trees as giant weeds to be removed and replaced with productive fields.

Often, deforestation is demographically driven—caused by population pressure. For example, Madagascar's population is growing at a rate of 3 percent annually,

Applied anthropology uses anthropological perspectives to identify and solve contemporary problems that affect humans. Deforestation is one such problem. Here women take part in a reforestation project in coastal Tanzania near Dar es Salaam.

doubling every generation. Population pressure leads to migration, including rural–urban migration. Madagascar's capital, Antananarivo, had just 100,000 people in 1967. The population had risen to about 2 million by 2007.

Urban growth promotes deforestation if city dwellers rely on fuel wood from the countryside, as is true in Madagascar. As forested watersheds disappear, crop productivity declines. Madagascar is known as the "great red island," after the color of its soil. On that island, the effects of soil erosion and water runoff are visible to the naked eye. From the look of its rivers, Madagascar appears to be bleeding to death. Increasing runoff of water no longer trapped by trees causes erosion of low-lying rice fields near swollen rivers as well as siltation in irrigation canals (Kottak 2007).

The global scenarios of deforestation include demographic pressure (from births or immigration) on subsistence economies, commercial logging, road building, cash cropping, fuel wood needs associated with urban expansion, and clearing and burning associated with livestock and grazing. The fact that forest loss has several causes has a policy implication: Different deforestation scenarios require different conservation strategies.

What can be done? On this question applied anthropology weighs in, spurring policy makers to think about new conservation strategies. The traditional approach has been to restrict access to forested areas designated as parks, then employ park guards and punish violators. Modern strategies are more likely to consider the needs, wishes, and abilities of the people (often impoverished) living in and near the forest. Since effective conservation depends on the cooperation of the local people, their concerns must be addressed in devising conservation strategies.

Reasons to change behavior must make sense to local people (see Sillitoe 2007). In Madagascar, the economic value of the forest for agriculture (as an antierosion mechanism and reservoir of potential irrigation water) provides a much more powerful incentive against forest degradation than do such global goals as "preserving biodiversity." Most Malagasy have no idea that lemurs and other endemic species exist only in Madagascar. Nor would such knowledge provide much of an incentive for them to conserve the forests if doing so jeopardized their livelihoods.

To curb the global deforestation threat, we need conservation strategies that work. Laws and enforcement may help reduce commercially driven deforestation caused by burning and clear-cutting. But local people also use and abuse forested lands. A challenge for the environmentally oriented applied anthropologist is to find ways to make forest preservation attractive to local people and ensure their cooperation. Applied anthropologists must work to make "good for the globe" good for the people.

Interethnic Contact

Since at least the 1920s anthropologists have investigated the changes—on both sides—that arise from contact between industrial and nonindustrial societies. Studies of "social change" and "acculturation" are abundant. British and American ethnographers, respectively, have used these terms to describe the same process. *Acculturation* refers to changes that result when groups come into continuous firsthand contact—changes in the cultural patterns of either or both groups (Redfield, Linton, and Herskovits 1936, p. 149).

Acculturation differs from diffusion, or cultural borrowing, which can occur without firsthand contact. For example, most North Americans who eat hot dogs ("frankfurters") have never been to Frankfurt, Germany, nor have most North American Toyota owners or sushi eaters ever visited Japan. Although *acculturation* can be applied to any case of cultural contact and change, the term most often has described **Westernization**—the influence of Western expansion on indigenous peoples and their cultures. Thus, local people who wear store-bought clothes, learn Indo-European languages, and otherwise adopt Western customs are called acculturated. Acculturation may be voluntary or forced, and there may be considerable resistance to the process.

Different degrees of destruction, domination, resistance, survival, adaptation, and modification of native cultures may follow interethnic contact. In the most destructive encounters, native and subordinate cultures face obliteration. In cases where contact between the indigenous societies and more powerful outsiders leads to destruction—a situation that is particularly characteristic of colonialist and expansionist eras—a "shock phase" often follows the initial encounter (Bodley 2008). Outsiders may attack or exploit the native people. Such exploitation may increase mortality, disrupt subsistence, fragment kin groups, damage social support systems, and inspire new religious movements, such as the cargo cults examined in the chapter "Religion" (Bodley 2008). During the shock phase, there may be civil repression backed by military force. Such factors may lead to the group's cultural collapse (*ethnocide*) or physical extinction (*genocide*).

Religious Change

Religious proselytizing can promote ethnocide, as native beliefs and practices are replaced by Western ones. Sometimes a religion and associated customs are replaced by ideology and behavior more compatible with Western culture. One example is the Handsome Lake religion (as described in the chapter on religion), which led the Iroquois to copy European farming techniques, stressing male rather than female labor. The Iroquois also gave up their communal longhouses and matrilineal descent groups for nuclear family households. The teachings of Handsome Lake led to a new church and religion. This revitalization movement helped the Iroquois survive in a drastically modified environment, but much ethnocide was involved.

Handsome Lake was a native who created a new religion, drawing on Western models. More commonly, missionaries and proselytizers representing the major world religions, especially Christianity and Islam, are the proponents of religious change. Protestant and Catholic missionization continues even in remote corners of the world. Evangelical Protestantism, for example, is advancing today in Peru, Brazil, and other parts of Latin America. It challenges an often jaded Catholicism that has too few priests and that is sometimes seen mainly as women's religion.

Sometimes the political ideology of a nation-state is pitted against traditional religion. Officials of the former Soviet empire discouraged Catholicism, Judaism, and

Islam. In Central Asia, Soviet dominators destroyed Muslim mosques and discouraged religious practice. On the other hand, governments often use their power to advance a religion, such as Islam in Iran or Sudan.

A military government seized power in Sudan in 1989. It immediately launched a campaign to change that country of more than 35 million people, where one-quarter were not Muslims, into an Islamic nation. Sudan adopted a policy of religious, linguistic, and cultural imperialism. The government sought to extend Islam and the Arabic language to the non-Muslim south. This was an area of Christianity and tribal religions that had resisted the central government for a decade (Hedges 1992).

This resistance continues and has spilled over into Sudan's drought-stricken and impoverished western province of Darfur. As of this writing, more than 2 million Sudanese are living in camps, having fled years of fighting in the region. Sudan's government and pro-government Arab militias have been accused of war crimes against the region's black African population. The Darfur conflict began early in 2003 as non–Islamic rebels waged attacks against government targets, claiming the government was oppressing black Africans in favor of Arabs. Darfur has faced many years of tension over land and grazing rights between nomadic Arabs and black African farmers. One of the two main rebel groups, the Sudan Liberation Army (SLA), includes Nuer and other Nilotic populations.

Cultural Imperialism

Cultural imperialism refers to the spread or advance of one culture at the expense of others, or its imposition on other cultures, which it modifies, replaces, or destroys—usually because of differential economic or political influence. Thus, children in the French colonial empire learned French history, language, and culture from standard textbooks also used in France. Tahitians, Malagasy, Vietnamese, and Senegalese learned the French language by reciting from books about "our ancestors the Gauls."

To what extent is modern technology, especially the mass media, an agent of cultural imperialism? Some commentators see modern technology as erasing cultural differences, as homogeneous products reach more people worldwide. But others see a role for modern technology in allowing social groups (local cultures) to express themselves and to survive (Marcus and Fischer 1999). Modern radio and TV, for example, constantly bring local happenings (for example, a "chicken festival" in Iowa) to the attention of a larger public. The North American media play a role in stimulating local activities of many sorts. Similarly, in Brazil, local practices, celebrations, and performances are changing in the context of outside forces, including the mass media and tourism.

In the town of Arembepe, Brazil (Kottak 2006), TV coverage has stimulated participation in a traditional annual performance, the *Chegança*. This is a fishermen's danceplay that reenacts the Portuguese discovery of Brazil. Arembepeiros have traveled to the state capital to perform the *Chegança* before television cameras, for a TV program featuring traditional performances from many rural communities.

One national Brazilian Sunday-night variety program (*Fantástico*) is especially popular in rural areas because it shows such local events. In several towns along the Amazon River, annual folk ceremonies are now staged more lavishly for TV cameras. In the Amazon town of Parantíns, for example, boatloads of tourists arriving any time of year are shown a videotape of the town's annual Bumba Meu Boi festival. This is a costumed performance mimicking bullfighting, parts of which have been shown on *Fantástico*. This pattern, in which local communities preserve, revive, and intensify the scale of traditional ceremonies to perform for TV and tourists, is expanding.

Brazilian television also has played a "top-down" role, by spreading the popularity of holidays like Carnaval and Christmas (Kottak 1990*a*). TV has aided the national spread of Carnaval beyond its traditional urban centers. Still, local reactions to the nationwide broadcasting of Carnaval and its trappings (elaborate parades, costumes, and frenzied dancing) are not simple or uniform responses to external stimuli.

Rather than direct adoption of Carnaval, local Brazilians respond in various ways. Often they don't take up Carnaval itself but modify their local festivities to fit Carnaval images. Others actively spurn Carnaval. One example is Arembepe, where Carnaval has never been important, probably because of its calendrical closeness to the main local festival, which is held in February to honor Saint Francis of Assisi. In the past, villagers couldn't afford to celebrate both occasions. Now, not only do the people of Arembepe reject Carnaval; they are also increasingly hostile to their own main festival. Arembepeiros resent the fact that the Saint Francis festival has become "an outsiders' event," because it draws thousands of tourists to Arembepe each February. The villagers think that commercial interests and outsiders have appropriated Saint Francis.

In opposition to these trends, many Arembepeiros now say they like and participate more in the traditional June festivals honoring Saint John, Saint Peter, and Saint Anthony. In the past, these were observed on a much smaller scale than was the festival honoring Saint Francis. Arembepeiros celebrate them now with a new vigor and enthusiasm, as they react to outsiders and their celebrations, real and televised.

Making and Remaking Culture

To understand culture change, it is important to recognize that meaning may be locally manufactured. People assign their own meanings and value to the texts, messages, and products they receive. Those meanings reflect their cultural backgrounds and experiences.

Indigenizing Popular Culture

When forces from world centers enter new societies, they are **indigenized**—modified to fit the local culture. This is true of cultural forces as different as fast food, music, housing styles, science, terrorism, celebrations, and political ideas and institutions (Appadurai 1990). Consider the reception of the movie *Rambo* in Australia as an example of how popular culture may be indigenized. Michaels (1986) found *Rambo* to be very popular among aborigines in the deserts of central Australia, who had manufactured their own meanings from the film. Their "reading" was very different from the one imagined by the movie's creators and by most North Americans. The Native Australians saw Rambo as a representative of the Third World who was engaged in a battle with the white officer class. This reading expressed their negative feelings about white paternalism and about existing race relations. The Native Australians also imagined that there were tribal ties and kin links between Rambo and the prisoners he was rescuing. All this made sense, based on their experience. Native Australians are disproportionately represented in Australian jails. Their most likely liberator would be someone with a personal link to them. These readings of *Rambo* were relevant meanings produced *from* the text, not *by* it (Fiske 1989).

A Global System of Images

All cultures express imagination—in dreams, fantasies, songs, myths, and stories. Today, however, more people in many more places imagine "a wider set of 'possible' lives than they ever did before. One important source of this change is the mass media, which present a rich, ever-changing store of possible lives" (Appadurai 1991, p. 197). The United States as a media center has been joined by Canada, Japan, Western Europe, Brazil, Mexico, Nigeria, Egypt, India, and Hong Kong.

December 26, 2003: Illustrating a process of indigenizing offerings of the modern world system, children dress as Colonel Sanders to promote egg tarts (a local dish now offered by an international restaurant chain) at a KFC store in Shanghai, China.

As print has done for centuries (Anderson 1991), the electronic mass media also can spread, even help create, national and ethnic identities. Like print, television and radio can diffuse the cultures of different countries within their own boundaries, thus enhancing national cultural identity. For example, millions of Brazilians who were formerly cut off (by geographic isolation or illiteracy) from urban and national events and information now participate in a national communication system, through TV networks (Kottak 1990*a*).

Crosscultural studies of television contradict a belief Americans ethnocentrically hold about televiewing in other countries. This misconception is that American programs inevitably triumph over local products. This doesn't happen when there is appealing local competition. In Brazil, for example, the most popular network (TV Globo) relies heavily on native productions, especially *telenovelas*. Globo plays each night to the world's largest and most devoted audience (perhaps 80 million viewers throughout the nation and beyond—via satellite TV). The programs that attract this horde are made by Brazilians, for Brazilians. Thus, it is not North American culture but a new pan-Brazilian national culture that Brazilian TV is propagating. Brazilian productions also compete internationally. They are exported to over 100 countries, spanning Latin America, Europe, Asia, and Africa.

We may generalize that programming that is culturally alien won't do very well anywhere when a quality local choice is available. Confirmation comes from many countries. National productions are highly popular in Japan, Mexico, India, Egypt, and Nigeria. In a survey during the mid-1980s, 75 percent of Nigerian viewers preferred local productions. Only 10 percent favored imports, and the remaining 15 percent liked the two options equally. Local productions are successful in Nigeria because "they are filled with everyday moments that audiences can identify with. These shows are locally produced by Nigerians" (Gray 1986). Thirty million people watched one of the most popular series, *The Village Headmaster,* each week. That program brought rural values to the screens of urbanites who had lost touch with their rural roots (Gray 1986).

The mass media also can play a role in maintaining ethnic and national identities among people who lead transnational lives. Arabic-speaking Muslims, including migrants, in several countries follow the TV network Al Jazeera, based in Qatar, which helps reinforce ethnic and religious identities. As groups move, they can stay linked to each other and to their homeland through the media. Diasporas (people who have spread out from an original, ancestral homeland) have enlarged the markets for media, communication, and travel services targeted at specific ethnic, national, or religious audiences. For a fee, a PBS station in Fairfax, Virginia, offers more than 30 hours a week to immigrant groups in the D.C. area, to make programs in their own languages.

A Global Culture of Consumption

Besides the electronic media, another key transnational force is finance. Multinational corporations and other business interests look beyond national boundaries for places to invest and draw profits. As Arjun Appadurai (1991, p. 194) puts it, "money, commodities, and persons unendingly chase each other around the world." Residents of many Latin American communities now depend on outside cash, remitted from international labor migration. Also, the economy of the United States is increasingly influenced by foreign investment, especially from Britain, China, Canada, Germany, the Netherlands, and Japan (Rouse 1991). The American economy also has increased its dependence on foreign labor—through both the immigration of laborers and the export of jobs.

Contemporary global culture is driven by flows of people, technology, finance, information, images, and ideology (Appadurai 1990, 2001). Business, technology, and the media have increased the craving for commodities and images throughout the world (Gottdiener 2000). This has forced nation-states to open to a global culture of consumption. Almost everyone today participates in this culture. Few people have never seen a T-shirt advertising a Western product. American and English rock stars' recordings blast through the streets of Rio de Janeiro, while taxi drivers from Toronto to Madagascar play Brazilian music tapes. Peasants and tribal people participate in the modern world system not only because they have been hooked on cash, but also because their products and images are appropriated by world capitalism (Root 1996). They are commercialized by others (like the San in the movie *The Gods Must Be Crazy*). Furthermore, indigenous peoples also market their own images and products, through outlets like Cultural Survival (see Mathews 2000).

People in Motion

The linkages in the modern world system have both enlarged and erased old boundaries and distinctions. Arjun Appadurai (1990, p. 1) characterizes today's world as a "translocal" "interactive system" that is "strikingly new." Whether as refugees, migrants, tourists, pilgrims, proselytizers, laborers, businesspeople, development workers, employees of nongovernmental organizations, politicians, terrorists, soldiers, sports figures, or media-borne images, people appear to travel more than ever.

In previous chapters, we saw that foragers and herders are typically seminomadic or nomadic. Today, however, the scale of human movement has expanded dramatically. So important is transnational migration that many Mexican villagers find "their most important kin and friends are as likely to be living hundreds or thousands of miles away as immediately around them" (Rouse 1991). Most migrants maintain their ties with their native land (phoning, e-mailing, visiting, sending money, watching "ethnic TV"). In a sense, they live multilocally—in different places at once. Dominicans in New York City, for example, have been characterized as living "between two islands": Manhattan and the Dominican Republic (Grasmuck and Pessar 1991). Many Dominicans—like migrants from other countries—migrate to the United States temporarily, seeking cash to transform their lifestyles when they return to the Caribbean.

With so many people "in motion," the unit of anthropological study expands from the local community to the **diaspora**—the offspring of an area who have spread to many lands. Anthropologists increasingly follow descendants of the villages we have studied as they move from rural to urban areas and across national boundaries.

With so many people on the move, the unit of anthropological study has expanded from the local community to the diaspora. This refers to the offspring of an area (e.g., South Asia) who have spread to many lands, such as this Indian sweets shop owner on Ealing Road in London, UK.

Postmodernity describes our time and situation: today's world in flux, these people on the move who have learned to manage multiple identities depending on place and context. In its most general sense, **postmodern** refers to the blurring and breakdown of established canons (rules or standards), categories, distinctions, and boundaries. The word is taken from **postmodernism**—a style and movement in architecture that succeeded modernism, beginning in the 1970s. Postmodern architecture rejected the rules, geometric order, and austerity of modernism. Modernist buildings were expected to have a clear and functional design. Postmodern design is "messier" and more playful. It draws on a diversity of styles from different times and places—including popular, ethnic, and non-Western cultures. Postmodernism extends "value" well beyond classic, elite, and Western cultural forms. *Postmodern* is now used to describe comparable developments in music, literature, and visual art. From this origin, *postmodernity* describes a world in which traditional standards, contrasts, groups, boundaries, and identities are opening up, reaching out, and breaking down.

New kinds of political and ethnic units are emerging. In some cases, cultures and ethnic groups have banded together in larger associations. There is a growing pan-Indian identity (Nagel 1996) and an international pantribal movement as well. Thus, in June 1992, the World Conference of Indigenous Peoples met in Rio de Janeiro concurrently with UNCED (the United Nations Conference on the Environment and Development). Along with diplomats, journalists, and environmentalists came 300 representatives of the tribal diversity that survives in the modern world—from Lapland to Mali (Brooke 1992; see also Maybury-Lewis 2002).

Indigenous Peoples

The term *indigenous people* entered international law with the creation in 1982 of the United Nations Working Group on Indigenous Populations (WGIP). This group, which meets annually, has members from six continents. The draft of the Declaration of Indigenous Rights, produced by the WGIP in 1989, was accepted by the UN for discussion in 1993. Convention 169, an ILO (International Labor Organization) document that supports cultural diversity and indigenous empowerment, was approved in 1989. Such documents, along with the work of the WGIP, have influenced governments, NGOs, and international agencies to adopt policies aimed at benefiting indigenous peoples. Social movements worldwide now use the term "indigenous people" as a self-identifying label in their quests for social, cultural, and political rights (de la Peña 2005; Brower and Johnston 2007).

In Spanish-speaking Latin America, social scientists and politicians now favor the term *indígena* (indigenous person) over *indio* (Indian). The latter is a colonial term that European conquerors used for Native Americans, whose situation did not necessarily improve after Latin American nations gained independence from Spain and Portugal, mostly by the 1820s. For the white and *mestizo* (mixed) elites of the

La Paz, Bolivia, May 23, 2005: Bolivians claiming an Indian (indigenous) identity rally for indigenous rights and the nationalization of that country's natural gas resources. In December 2005, Bolivians elected as their president Evo Morales, the candidate of the Indigenous Movement toward Socialism party. The party made further gains in 2006 parliamentary elections.

new nations, *indios* and their lifestyle seemed alien to (European) civilization (de la Peña 2005).

Until the mid- to late 1980s, Latin American public policy emphasized assimilation. Indians were associated with a romanticized past, but marginalized in the present, except for museums, tourism, and folkloric events. Indigenous Bolivians and Peruvians were encouraged to self-identify as *campesinos* (peasants). The past 30 years have witnessed a dramatic shift. The emphasis has shifted from assimilation—*mestizaje*—to cultural difference. In Ecuador groups seen previously as Quichua-speaking peasants are classified now as indigenous communities with their own territories. Brazil has recognized 30 new indigenous communities in the northeast, a region previously seen as having lost its native population. Guatemala, Nicaragua, Brazil, Colombia, Mexico, Paraguay, Ecuador, Argentina, Bolivia, Peru, and Venezuela now are officially multicultural (Jackson and Warren 2005). Several national constitutions recognize the rights of indigenous peoples to cultural distinctiveness and political representation. In Colombia, indigenous territories have the same benefits as any local government (de la Peña 2005).

The indigenous rights movement exists in the context of globalization, including transnational movements focusing on human rights, women's rights, and environmentalism. Transnational organizations have helped indigenous peoples to influence legislation. Since the 1980s there has been a general shift in Latin America from authoritarian to democratic rule. Still, inequality and discrimination persist, and there has been resistance to indigenous mobilization, including assassinations of leaders and their supporters. Guatemala, Peru, and Colombia have witnessed severe repression. There have been thousands of indigenous deaths, refugees, and internally displaced persons (Jackson and Warren 2005).

Ceuppens and Geschiere (2005) explore a recent upsurge, in multiple world areas, of the notion of *autochthony* (being native to, or formed, in the place where found), with an implicit call for excluding strangers. The terms *autochthony* and *indigenous* both go back to classical Greek history, with similar implications. Autochthony refers to self and soil. Indigenous literally means born inside, with the connotation in classical Greek of being born "inside the house." Both notions stress the need to safeguard ancestral lands (patrimony) from strangers, along with the rights of first-comers to special rights and protection versus later immigrants—legal or illegal (Ceuppens and Geschiere 2005).

During the 1990s, autochthony became an issue in many parts of Africa, inspiring violent efforts to exclude (European and Asian) "strangers." Simultaneously, autochthony became a key notion in debates about immigration and multiculturalism in Europe. European majority groups have claimed the label *autochthon*. This term highlights the prominence that the exclusion of strangers has assumed in day-to-day politics worldwide (Ceuppens and Geschiere 2005). One familiar example is the United States, as represented in the congressional debate in 2006–2007, over illegal immigration.

Identity in Indigenous Politics

Essentialism describes the process of viewing an identity as established, real, and frozen, so as to hide the historical processes and politics within which that identity developed. Identities, emphatically, are not fixed. We saw in the chapter "Ethnicity and Race" that identities can be fluid and multiple. People seize on particular, sometimes competing, self-labels and identities. Some Peruvian groups, for instance, self-identify as *mestizos* but still see themselves as indigenous. Identity is a fluid, dynamic process, and there are multiple ways of being indigenous. Neither speaking an indigenous language nor wearing "native" clothing is required. Identities are asserted at particular times and places by particular individuals and groups and after various kinds of negotiations. Indigenous identity coexists with, and must be managed in the context of, other identity components, including religion, race, and gender. Identities always must be seen as (1) potentially plural, (2) emerging through a specific process, (3) ways of being someone or something in particular times and places (Jackson and Warren 2005).

ANTHROPOLOGY TODAY

Engulfed by Climate Change, Town Seeks Lifeline

Globally, climate change is raising questions about how to deal with hurricanes, drought, and other threats that affect millions of people and involve huge sums of money. The people described in this news story are among the first climate change refugees in the United States. Residents of Newtok, Alaska, belong to a federally recognized American Indian tribe. Decades ago, the U.S. government mandated that they and other Alaskan natives abandon a nomadic life based on hunting and fishing for sedentism. They now reside in what used to be a winter camp. What obligations does government have to local people whose lives have been disrupted not only by government decree but also by evident global warming?

NEWTOK, Alaska . . . The earth beneath much of Alaska is not what it used to be. The permanently frozen subsoil, known as permafrost, upon which Newtok and so many other Native Alaskan villages rest is melting, yielding to warming air temperatures and a warming ocean. Sea ice that would normally protect coastal villages is forming later in the year, allowing fall storms to pound away at the shoreline.

Erosion has made Newtok an island, caught between the ever widening Ninglick River and a slough to the north. The village is below sea level, and sinking. Boardwalks squish into the spring muck. Human waste, collected in "honey buckets" that many residents use for toilets, is often dumped within eyeshot in a village where no point is more than a five-minute walk from any other. The ragged wooden houses have to be adjusted regularly to level them on the shifting soil.

Studies say Newtok could be washed away within a decade. Along with the villages of Shishmaref and Kivalina farther to the north, it has been the hardest hit of about 180 Alaska villages that suffer some degree of erosion. Some villages plan to hunker down behind sea walls built or planned by the Army Corps of Engineers, at least for now. Others, like Newtok, have no choice but to abandon their patch of tundra. The corps has estimated that to move Newtok could cost $130 million because of its remoteness, climate and topography. That comes to almost $413,000 for each of the 315 residents. . . .

The Continuance of Diversity

Anthropology has a crucial role to play in promoting a more humanistic vision of social change, one that respects the value of human biological and cultural diversity. The existence of anthropology is itself a tribute to the continuing need to understand similarities and differences among human beings throughout the world. Anthropology teaches us that the adaptive responses of humans can be more flexible than those of other species because our main adaptive means are sociocultural. However, the cultural forms, institutions, values, and customs of the past always influence subsequent adaptation, producing continued diversity and giving a certain uniqueness to the actions and reactions of different groups. With our knowledge and our awareness of our professional responsibilities, let us work to keep anthropology, the study of humankind, the most humanistic of all the sciences.

Newtok's leaders say the corps' relocation estimates are inflated, that they intend to move piecemeal rather than in one collective migration, which they say will save money. But they say government should pay, no matter the cost—if only there were a government agency charged with doing so. There is not a formal process by which a village can apply to the government to relocate.

"They grossly overestimate it, and that's why federal and state agencies are afraid to step in," said Stanley Tom, the current tribal administrator . . . "They don't want to spend that much money." Still, Newtok has made far more progress toward moving than other villages, piecing together its move grant by grant.

Through a land swap with the United States Fish and Wildlife Service, it has secured a new site, on Nelson Island, nine miles south. It is safe from the waves on a windy rise above the Ninglick River. They call it Mertarvik, which means "getting water from the spring." They tell their children they will grow up in a place where E. coli does not thrive in every puddle, the way it does here.

With the help of state agencies, it won a grant of about $1 million to build a barge landing at the new site. Bids go out this summer, and construction could be complete next year, providing a platform to unload equipment for building roads, water and sewer systems, houses and a new landing strip. . . .

[Former] Senator Ted Stevens [served as] the ranking minority member on the Senate's new Disaster Recovery subcommittee. [Stevens, the former lion of Alaska politics,] was instrumental in passing legislation in 2005 that gave the corps broader authority to help [villages like Newtok. . . .]

The administrative leaders of Newtok are mostly men in their 40s, nearly all of them related. They are widely praised by outsiders for their initiative and determination to relocate.

Yet nearly any place would seem an improvement over Newtok as it exists today, and not all of its problems are rooted in climate change. Some are almost universal to Alaskan villages, which have struggled for decades to reconcile their culture of subsistence hunting and fishing with the expectations and temptations of the world outside.

Excrement dumped from honey buckets is piled on the banks of the slow-flowing

Continued

Newtok River, not far from wooden shacks where residents take nightly steam baths. An elderly man drains kerosene into a puddle of snowmelt. Children pedal past a walrus skull left to rot, tusks intact, in the mud beside a boardwalk that serves as a main thoroughfare. There are no cars here, just snow machines, boats and all-terrain vehicles that tear up the tundra. Village elders speak their native Yupik more often than they speak English. They remember when the village was a collection of families who moved with the seasons, making houses from sod, fishing from Nelson Island in the summer, hunting caribou far away in the winter.

Many men still travel with the seasons to hunt and fish. Some will take boats into Bristol Bay this summer to catch salmon alongside commercial fishermen from out of state. But the waterproof jacket sewn from seal gut that Stanley Tom once wore is now stuffed inside a display case at Newtok School next to other relics.

Now Mr. Tom puts on a puffy parka to walk the few hundred feet he travels to work. He checks his e-mail messages to see if there is news from the corps . . . while his brother, Nick, sketches out a budget proposal for a nonprofit corporation to help manage the relocation, presuming the money arrives.

Source: William Yardley, "Engulfed by Climate Change, Town Seeks Lifeline." From *The New York Times,* May 27, 2007. Copyright © 2007 The New York Times. Reprinted by permission.

Summary

1. Fueling global warming are human population growth and use of fossil fuels, which produce greenhouse gases. The atmospheric concentration of those gases has increased since the Industrial Revolution, and especially since 1978. Climate change encompasses global warming along with changing sea levels, precipitation, storms, and ecosystem effects. Coastal communities can anticipate increased flooding and more severe storms and surges. Political will is needed to curb emissions now.

2. Anthropology always has been concerned with how environmental forces influence humans and how human activities affect the biosphere. Many indigenous groups did a reasonable job of preserving their ecosystems. An ethnoecology is any society's set of environmental practices and perceptions— that is, its cultural model of the environment in relation to people and society. Indigenous ethnoecologies increasingly are being challenged by global forces that work to exploit and degrade—and that sometimes aim to protect—the environment. The challenge for applied ecological anthropology is to devise culturally appropriate strategies for conservation in the face of unrelenting population growth and commercial expansion.

3. Deforestation is a major factor in the loss of global biodiversity. The global scenarios of deforestation include demographic pressure (from births or immigration) on subsistence economies, commercial logging, road building, cash cropping, fuel wood needs associated with urban expansion, and clearing and burning associated with livestock and grazing. The fact that forest loss has several causes has a policy implication: Different deforestation scenarios require different conservation strategies. Applied anthropologists must work to make "good for the globe" good for the people.

4. Different degrees of destruction, domination, resistance, survival, and modification of native cultures may follow interethnic contact. This may lead to a tribe's cultural collapse (ethnocide) or its physical extinction (genocide). *Cultural imperialism* refers to the spread of one culture and its imposition on other cultures, which it modifies, replaces, or destroys—usually because of differential economic or political influence. Some worry that modern technology, including the mass media, is destroying traditional cultures. But others see an important role for new technology in allowing local cultures to express themselves.

5. When forces from global centers enter new societies, they are *indigenized*. Like print, the electronic mass media can help diffuse a national culture within its own boundaries. The media also play a role in preserving ethnic and national identities among people who lead transnational lives. Business, technology, and the media have increased the craving for commodities and images throughout the world, creating a global culture of consumption.

6. People travel more than ever. But migrants also maintain ties with home, so they live multilocally. With so many people "in motion," the unit of anthropological study expands from the local community to the diaspora. *Postmodernity* describes this world in flux, such people on the move who manage multiple social identities depending on place and context. New kinds of political and ethnic units are emerging as others break down or disappear.

7. The term and concept *indigenous people* has gained legitimacy within international law. Governments, NGOs, and international agencies have adopted policies designed to recognize and benefit indigenous peoples. Social movements worldwide have adopted this term as a self-identifying and political label based on past oppression but now signaling a search for social, cultural, and political rights.

8. In Latin America, emphasis has shifted from biological and cultural assimilation to identities that value difference. Several national constitutions now recognize the rights of indigenous peoples. Transnational organizations have helped indigenous peoples influence national legislative agendas. Recent use of the notion of *autochthony* (being native to, or formed in, the place where found) includes a call to exclude strangers, such as recent and illegal immigrants. Identity is a fluid, dynamic process, and there are multiple ways of being indigenous. No social movement exists apart from the nation and world that include it.

Key Terms

climate change (p. 282)

cultural imperialism (p. 290)

diaspora (p. 294)

ecological anthropology (p. 284)

essentialism (p. 297)

ethnoecology (p. 285)

greenhouse effect (p. 282)

indigenized (p. 291)

postmodern (p. 295)

postmodernism (p. 295)

postmodernity (p. 295)

Westernization (p. 289)

 Go to our Online Learning Center website at **www.mhhe.com/kottak** for Internet resources directly related to the content of this chapter.

Glossary

A

acculturation   The exchange of cultural features that results when groups come into continuous firsthand contact; the original cultural patterns of either or both groups may be altered, but the groups remain distinct. 39

achieved status   Social status that comes through talents, actions, efforts, activities, and accomplishments, rather than ascription. 122

adaptation   The process by which organisms cope with environmental stresses. 3

age set   Group uniting all men or women (usually men) born during a certain time span; this group controls property and often has political and military functions. 124

agency   The active role that individuals play in interpreting, using, making, and remaking culture. 13

agriculture   Nonindustrial system of plant cultivation characterized by continuous and intensive use of land and labor. 95

animism   Belief in souls or doubles. 191

anthropology   The study of the human species and its immediate ancestors. 2

anthropology and education   Anthropological research in classrooms, homes, and neighborhoods, viewing students as total cultural creatures whose enculturation and attitudes toward education belong to a larger context that includes family, peers, and society. 266

applied anthropology   The application of anthropological data, perspectives, theory, and methods to identify, assess, and solve contemporary social problems. 18, 259

archaeological anthropology   The branch of anthropology that reconstructs, describes, and interprets human behavior and cultural patterns through material remains; best known for the study of prehistory. Also known as "archaeology." 14

ascribed status   Social status (e.g., race or gender) that people have little or no choice about occupying. 122

assimilation   The process of change that a minority group may experience when it moves to a country where another culture dominates; the minority is incorporated into the dominant culture to the point that it no longer exists as a separate cultural unit. 247

B

balanced reciprocity   See *generalized reciprocity*. 106

band   Basic unit of social organization among foragers. A band includes fewer than one hundred people; it often splits up seasonally. 92, 116

big man   Figure often found among tribal horticulturalists and pastoralists. The big man occupies no office but creates his reputation through entrepreneurship and generosity to others. Neither his wealth nor his position passes to his heirs. 121

biological anthropology   The branch of anthropology that studies human biological diversity in time and space—for instance, hominid evolution, human genetics, human biological adaptation; also includes primatology (behavior and evolution of monkeys and apes). Also called *physical anthropology*. 16

Black English Vernacular (BEV)   A rule-governed dialect of American English with roots in southern English. BEV is spoken by

African American youth and by many adults in their casual, intimate speech—sometimes called *ebonics*. 82

biocultural   Referring to the inclusion and combination (to solve a common problem) of both biological and cultural approaches—one of anthropology's hallmarks. 9

bourgeoisie   One of Karl Marx's opposed classes; owners of the means of production (factories, mines, large farms, and other sources of subsistence). 216

bridewealth   A customary gift before, at, or after marriage from the husband and his kin to the wife and her kin; see also *progeny price*. 157

C

call systems   Systems of communication among nonhuman primates, composed of a limited number of sounds that vary in intensity and duration. Tied to environmental stimuli. 65

capital   Wealth or resources invested in business, with the intent of producing a profit. 211

capitalist world economy   The single world system, which emerged in the 16th century, committed to production for sale, with the object of maximizing profits rather than supplying domestic needs. 211

cargo cults   Postcolonial, acculturative, religious movements common in Melanesia that attempt to explain European domination and wealth and to achieve similar success magically by mimicking European behavior. 205

caste system   Closed, hereditary system of stratification, often dictated by religion; hierarchical social status is ascribed at birth, so that people are locked into their parents' social position. 132

chiefdom   Form of sociopolitical organization intermediate between the tribe and the state; kin-based with differential access to resources and a permanent political structure. 116

clan   Unilineal descent group based on stipulated descent. 149

climate change   Global warming, plus changing sea levels, precipitation, storms, and ecosystem effects. 282

colonialism   The political, social, economic, and cultural domination of a territory and its people by a foreign power for an extended time. 219

communal religions   In Wallace's typology, these religions have—in addition to shamanic cults—communal cults in which people organize community rituals such as harvest ceremonies and rites of passage. 201

communism   Spelled with a lowercase *c*, describes a social system in which property is owned by the community and in which people work of the common good. 225

Communism   Spelled with a capital *C*, a political movement and doctrine seeking to overthrow capitalism and to establish a form of communism such as that which prevailed in the Soviet Union (USSR) from 1917 to 1991. 225

communitas   Intense community spirit, a feeling of great social solidarity, equality, and togetherness; characteristic of people experiencing liminality together. 190

complex societies   Nations; large and populous, with social stratification and central governments. 60

conflict resolution   The means by which disputes are socially regulated and settled; found in all societies, but the resolution methods tend to be more formal and effective in states than in nonstates. 118

core   Dominant structural position in the world system; consists of the strongest and most powerful states with advanced systems of production. 212

core values   Key, basic, or central values that integrate a culture and help distinguish it from others. 27

correlation   An association between two or more variables such that when one changes (varies), the other(s) also change(s) (covaries); for example, temperature and sweating. 92

cultural anthropology   The study of human society and culture; describes, analyzes, interprets, and explains social and cultural similarities and differences. 12

cultural colonialism   Within a nation or empire, domination by one ethnic group or nationality and its culture/ ideology over others—e.g., the dominance of Russian people, language, and culture in the former Soviet Union. 254

cultural consultant   Someone the ethnographer gets to know in the field, who teaches him or her about their society and culture, aka *informant*. 53

cultural imperialism   The rapid spread or advance of one culture at the expense of others, or its imposition on other cultures, which it modifies, replaces, or destroys— usually because of differential economic or political influence. 290

cultural relativism   The position that the values and standards of cultures differ and deserve respect. Anthropology is characterized by methodological rather than moral relativism: In order to understand another culture fully, anthropologists try to understand its members' beliefs and motivations. Methodological relativism does not preclude making moral judgments or taking action. 37

cultural resource management (CRM) The branch of applied archaeology aimed at preserving sites threatened by dams, highways, and other projects. 18

cultural rights   Doctrine that certain rights are vested not in individuals but in identifiable groups, such as religious and ethnic minorities and indigenous societies. 38

cultural transmission   A basic feature of language; transmission through learning. 67

culture   Traditions and customs that govern behavior and beliefs; distinctly human; transmitted through learning. 26

curer   Specialized role acquired through a culturally appropriate process of selection, training, certification, and acquisition of a professional image; the curer is consulted by patients, who believe in his or her special powers, and receives some form of special consideration; a cultural universal. 273

D

daughter languages   Languages developing out of the same parent language; for example, French and Spanish are daughter languages of Latin. 83

descent   Rule assigning social identity on the basis of some aspect of one's ancestry. 238

descent group   A permanent social unit whose members claim common ancestry; fundamental to tribal society. 148

descriptive linguistics   The scientific study of a spoken language, including its phonology, morphology, lexicon, and syntax. 70

development anthropology   The branch of applied anthropology that focuses on social issues in, and the cultural dimension of, economic development. 262

diaspora   The offspring of an area who have spread to many lands. 294

differential access   Unequal access to resources; basic attribute of chiefdoms and states. Superordinates have favored access to such resources, while the access of subordinates is limited by superordinates. 130

diffusion   Borrowing between cultures either directly or through intermediaries. 39

diglossia   The existence of "high" (formal) and "low" (familial) dialects of a single language, such as German. 77

discrimination   Policies and practices that harm a group and its members. 251

disease   An etic or scientifically identified health threat caused by a bacterium, virus, fungus, parasite, or other pathogen. 271

displacement   A linguistic capacity that allows humans to talk about things and events that are not present. 68

domestic–public dichotomy   Contrast between women's role in the home and men's role in public life, with a corresponding social devaluation of women's work and worth. 173

dowry   A marital exchange in which the wife's group provides substantial gifts to the husband's family. 157

E

ecological anthropology   Study of cultural adaptations to environments. 284

economy   A population's system of production, distribution, and consumption of resources. 99

emic   The research strategy that focuses on native explanations and criteria of significance. 53

enculturation   The social process by which culture is learned and transmitted across the generations. 23

endogamy   Marriage between people of the same social group. 153

equity, increased   A reduction in absolute poverty and a fairer (more even) distribution of wealth. 262

essentialism   The process of viewing an identity as established, real, and frozen, so as to hide the historical processes and politics within which that identity developed. 297

ethnic group   Group distinguished by cultural similarities (shared among members of that group) and differences (between that group and others); ethnic group members share beliefs, values, habits, customs, and norms, and a common language, religion, history, geography, kinship, and/or race. 234

ethnicity   Identification with, and feeling part of, an ethnic group, and exclusion from certain other groups because of this affiliation. 234

ethnocentrism   The tendency to view one's own culture as best and to judge the behavior and beliefs of culturally different people by one's own standards. 37

ethnocide   Destruction by a dominant group of the culture of an ethnic group. 252

ethnoecology   A culture's set of environmental practices and perceptions. 285

ethnography   Field work in a particular culture. 12

ethnology   The theoretical, comparative study of society and culture; compares cultures in time and space. 13

etic   The research strategy that emphasizes the observer's rather than the natives' explanations, categories, and criteria of significance. 53

exogamy   Mating or marriage outside one's kin group; a cultural universal. 151

extended family household   Expanded household including three or more generations. 143

extradomestic   Outside the home; within or pertaining to the public domain. 178

F

family   A group of people (e.g., parents, children, siblings, grandparents, grandchildren, uncles, aunts, nephews, nieces, cousins, spouses, siblings-in-law, parents-in-law, children-in-law) who are considered to be related in some way, for example, by "blood" (common ancestry or descent) or marriage. 141

family of orientation   Nuclear family in which one is born and grows up. 141

family of procreation   Nuclear family established when one marries and has children. 141

fiscal   Pertaining to finances and taxation. 135

focal vocabulary   A set of words and distinctions that are particularly important to certain groups (those with particular foci of experience or activity), such as types of snow to Eskimos or skiers. 75

food production   Plant cultivation and animal domestication. 4

G

gender roles   The tasks and activities that a culture assigns to each sex. 169

gender stereotypes   Oversimplified but strongly held ideas about the characteristics of males and females. 169

gender stratification   Unequal distribution of rewards (socially valued resources, power, prestige, and personal freedom) between men and women, reflecting their different positions in a social hierarchy. 131, 169

genealogical method   Procedures by which ethnographers discover and record connections of kinship, descent, and marriage, using diagrams and symbols. 52

general anthropology   The field of anthropology as a whole, consisting of cultural, archaeological, biological, and linguistic anthropology. 4

generality   Culture pattern or trait that exists in some but not all societies. 33

generalized reciprocity   Principle that characterizes exchanges between closely related individuals. As social distance increases, reciprocity becomes balanced and finally negative. 106

genitor   Biological father of a child. 151

genocide   Policies aimed at, and/or resulting in, the physical extinction (through mass murder) of a people perceived as a racial group, that is, as sharing defining physical, genetic, or other biological characteristics. 252

globalization   The accelerating interdependence of nations in a world system linked economically and through mass media and modern transportation systems. 40

greenhouse effect   Warming from trapped atmospheric gases. 282

H

head, village   See *village head*. 120

health care systems   Beliefs, customs, and specialists concerned with ensuring health and preventing and curing illness; a cultural universal. 272

historical linguistics   Subdivision of linguistics that studies languages over time. 83

holistic   Interested in the whole of the human condition past, present, and future; biology, society, language, and culture. 2

horticulture   Nonindustrial system of plant cultivation in which plots lie fallow for varying lengths of time. 93

human rights   Doctrine that invokes a realm of justice and morality beyond and superior to particular countries, cultures, and religions. Human rights, usually seen as vested in individuals, would include the right to speak freely, to hold religious beliefs without persecution, and not to be enslaved. 38

hypodescent   A rule that automatically places the children of a union or mating between members of different socioeconomic groups in the less privileged group. 238

I

illness   An emic condition of poor health felt by individual. 271

imperialism   A policy of extending the rule of a nation or empire over foreign nations and of taking and holding foreign colonies. 218

incest   Sexual relations with a close relative. 151

independent invention   Development of the same culture trait or pattern in separate cultures as a result of comparable needs and circumstances. 40

indigenized   Modified to fit the local culture. 291

indigenous peoples   The original inhabitants of particular territories; often descendants of tribespeople who live on as culturally distinct colonized peoples, many of whom aspire to autonomy. 296

Industrial Revolution   The historical transformation (in Europe, after 1750) of "traditional" into "modern" societies through industrialization of the economy. 214

informed consent   An agreement sought by ethnographers from community members to take part in research. 47

intellectual property rights (IPR)   Each society's cultural base—its core beliefs and principles. IPR is claimed as a group right— a cultural right, allowing indigenous groups to control who may know and use their collective knowledge and its applications. 39

international culture   Cultural traditions that extend beyond national boundaries. 36

intervention philosophy   Guiding principle of colonialism, conquest, missionization, or development; an ideological justification for outsiders to guide native peoples in specific directions. 223

interview schedule   Ethnographic tool for structuring a formal interview. A prepared form (usually printed or mimeographed) that guides interviews with households or individuals being compared systematically. Contrasts with a questionnaire because the researcher has personal contact and records people's answers. 51

K

key cultural consultant   An expert on a particular aspect of local life who helps the ethnographer understand that aspect. 52
kinesics   The study of communication through body movements, stances, gestures, and facial expressions. 70

L

law   A legal code, including trial and enforcement; characteristic of state-organized societies. 134
leveling mechanisms   Customs and social actions that operate to reduce differences in wealth and thus to bring standouts in line with community norms. 200
levirate   Custom by which a widow marries the brother of her deceased husband. 159
lexicon   Vocabulary; a dictionary containing all the morphemes in a language and their meaning. 70
life history   Of a cultural consultant; provides a personal cultural portrait of existence or change in a culture. 53
liminality   The critically important marginal or in-between phase of a rite of passage. 195
lineage   Unilineal descent group based on demonstrated descent. 149
linguistic anthropology   The branch of anthropology that studies linguistic variation in time and space, including interrelations between language and culture; includes *historical linguistics* and *sociolinguistics*. 17
longitudinal research   Long-term study of a community, society, culture, or other unit, usually based on repeated visits. 57

M

magic   Use of supernatural techniques to accomplish specific aims. 193

majority groups   Superordinate, dominant, or controlling groups in a social-political hierarchy. 236
mana   Sacred impersonal force in Melanesian and Polynesian religions. 192
market principle   Profit-oriented principle of exchange that dominates in states, particularly industrial states. Goods and services are bought and sold, and values are determined by supply and demand. 104
matrilineal descent   Unilineal descent rule in which people join the mother's group automatically at birth and stay members throughout life. 148
matrilocality   Customary residence with the wife's relatives after marriage, so that children grow up in their mother's community. 150
means (or factors) of production   Land, labor, technology, and capital—major productive resources. 100
medical anthropology   Unites biological and cultural anthropologists in the study of disease, health problems, health care systems, and theories about illness in different cultures and ethnic groups. 270
minority groups   Subordinate groups in a social–political hierarchy, with inferior power and less secure access to resources than majority groups have. 236
mode of production   Way of organizing production—a set of social relations through which labor is deployed to wrest energy from nature by means of tools, skills, and knowledge. 99
monotheism   Worship of an eternal, omniscient, omnipotent, and omnipresent supreme being. 201
morphology   The study of form; used in linguistics (the study of morphemes and word construction) and for form in general—for example, biomorphology relates to physical form. 70
multiculturalism   The view of cultural diversity in a country as something good and desirable; a multicultural society socializes individuals not only into the dominant (national) culture, but also into an ethnic culture. 248

N

nation   Once a synonym for "ethnic group," designating a single culture sharing a language, religion, history, territory, ancestry, and kinship; now usually a synonym for "state" or "nation-state." 246

nation-state   An autonomous political entity, a country like the United States or Canada. 246

national culture   Cultural experiences, beliefs, learned behavior patterns, and values shared by citizens of the same nation. 36

nationalities   Ethnic groups that once had, or wish to have or regain, autonomous political status (their own country). 246

natural selection   Originally formulated by Charles Darwin and Alfred Russel Wallace; the process by which nature selects the forms most fit to survive and reproduce in a given environment, such as the tropics. 10

negative reciprocity   See *generalized reciprocity*. 106

neoliberalism   Revival of Adam Smith's classic economic liberalism, the idea that governments should not regulate private enterprise and that free market forces should rule; a currently dominant intervention philosophy. 224

neolocality   Postmarital residence pattern in which a couple establishes a new place of residence rather than living with or near either set of parents. 143

nomadism, pastoral   Movement throughout the year by the whole pastoral group (men, women, and children) with their animals. More generally, such constant movement in pursuit of strategic resources. 98

O

office   Permanent political position. 128

Olympian religions   In Wallace's typology, develop with state organization; have full-time religious specialists—professional priesthoods. 201

open-class system   Stratification system that facilitates social mobility, with individual achievement and personal merit determining social rank. 132

overinnovation   Characteristic of development projects that require major changes in people's daily lives, especially ones that interfere with customary subsistence pursuits. 263

P

pantribal sodality   A non-kin-based group that exists throughout a tribe, spanning several villages. 124

participant observation   A characteristic ethnographic technique; taking part in the events one is observing, describing, and analyzing. 48

particularity   Distinctive or unique culture trait, pattern, or integration. 33

pastoralists   People who use a food-producing strategy of adaptation based on care of herds of domesticated animals. 97

patriarchy   Political system ruled by men in which women have inferior social and political status, including basic human rights. 179

patrilineal descent   Unilineal descent rule in which people join the father's group automatically at birth and stay members throughout life. 148

patrilineal–patrilocal complex   An interrelated constellation of patrilineality, patrilocality, warfare, and male supremacy. 177

patrilocality   Customary residence with the husband's relatives after marriage, so that children grow up in their father's community. 150

peasant   Small-scale agriculturist living in a state, with rent fund obligations. 104

periphery   Weakest structural position in the world system. 213

phenotype   An organism's evident traits, its "manifest biology"—anatomy and physiology. 6, 245

phoneme   Significant sound contrast in a language that serves to distinguish meaning, as in minimal pairs. 71

phonemics   The study of the sound contrasts (phonemes) of a particular language. 72

phonetics The study of speech sounds in general; what people actually say in various languages. 72

phonology The study of sounds used in speech. 70

physical anthropology See *biological anthropology*.

plural marriage Marriage of a man to two or more women (polygyny) or marriage of a woman to two or more men (polyandry)—at the same time; see also *polygamy*. 158

plural society A society that combines ethnic contrasts, ecological specialization (i.e., use of different environmental resources by each ethnic group), and the economic interdependence of those groups. 247

polyandry Variety of plural marriage in which a woman has more than one husband. 158

polygamy Marriage with three or more spouses, at the same time; see also *plural marriage*. 158

polygyny Variety of plural marriage in which a man has more than one wife. 158

polytheism Belief in several deities who control aspects of nature. 201

postcolonial Referring to interactions between European nations and the societies they colonized (mainly after 1800); more generally, "postcolonial" may be used to signify a position against imperialism and Eurocentrism. 222

postmodern In its most general sense, describes the blurring and breakdown of established canons (rules, standards), categories, distinctions, and boundaries. 295

postmodernism A style and movement in architecture that succeeded modernism. Compared with modernism, postmodernism is less geometric, less functional, less austere, more playful, and more willing to include elements from diverse times and cultures; *post-modern* now describes comparable developments in music, literature, and visual art. 295

postmodernity Condition of a world in flux, with people on-the-move, in which established groups, boundaries, identities, contrasts, and standards are reaching out and breaking down. 295

potlatch Competitive feast among Indians on the North Pacific Coast of North America. 107

power The ability to exercise one's will over others—to do what one wants; the basis of political status. 131

prejudice Devaluing (looking down on) a group because of its assumed behavior, values, capabilities, or attributes. 251

prestige Esteem, respect, or approval for acts, deeds, or qualities considered exemplary. 131

productivity The ability to use the rules of one's language to create new expressions comprehensible to other speakers; a basic feature of language. 67

proletariat See *working class*.

progeny price A gift from the husband and his kin to the wife and her kin before, at, or after marriage; legitimizes children born to the woman as members of the husband's descent group. 157

protolanguage Language ancestral to several daughter languages. 83

R

race An ethnic group assumed to have a biological basis. 236

racial classification The attempt to assign humans to discrete categories (purportedly) based on common ancestry. 6

racism Discrimination against an ethnic group assumed to have a biological basis. 236

random sample A sample in which all members of the population have an equal statistical chance of being included. 60

reciprocity One of the three principles of exchange. Governs exchange between social equals; major exchange mode in band and tribal societies. 105

reciprocity continuum Regarding exchanges, a range running from generalized reciprocity (closely related/deferred return) through balanced reciprocity to negative reciprocity (strangers/immediate return). 105

redistribution   Major exchange mode of chiefdoms, many archaic states, and some states with managed economies. 105

refugees   People who have been forced (involuntary refugees) or who have chosen (voluntary refugees) to flee a country, to escape persecution or war. 252

religion   Beliefs and rituals concerned with supernatural beings, powers, and forces. 190

revitalization movements   Movements that occur in times of change, in which religious leaders emerge and undertake to alter or revitalize a society. 204

rites of passage   Culturally defined activities associated with the transition from one place or stage of life to another. 195

ritual   Behavior that is formal, stylized, repetitive, and stereotyped, performed earnestly as a social act; rituals are held at set times and places and have liturgical orders. 194

S

sample   A smaller study group chosen to represent a larger population. 59

Sapir-Whorf hypothesis   Theory that different languages produce different ways of thinking. 74

science   A systematic field of study or body of knowledge that aims, through experiment, observation, and deduction, to produce reliable explanations of phenomena, with reference to the material and physical world. 17

scientific medicine   As distinguished from Western medicine, a health care system based on scientific knowledge and procedures, encompassing such fields as pathology, microbiology, biochemistry, surgery, diagnostic technology, and applications. 273

semantics   A language's meaning system. 75

semiperiphery   Structural position in the world system intermediate between core and periphery. 212

sexual dimorphism   Marked differences in male and female biology besides the contrasts in breasts and genitals. 167

sexual orientation   A person's habitual sexual attraction to, and activities with

persons of the opposite sex (*heterosexuality*), the same sex (*homosexuality*), or both sexes (*bisexuality*). 184

shaman   A part-time religious practitioner who mediates between ordinary people and supernatural beings and forces. 200

slavery   The most extreme, coercive, abusive, and inhumane form of legalized inequality; people are treated as property. 132

social race   A group assumed to have a biological basis but actually perceived and defined in a social context—by a particular culture rather than by scientific criteria. 245

society   Organized life in groups; typical of humans and other animals. 23

sociolinguistics   Study of relationships between social and linguistic variation; study of language in its social context. 17, 77

sociopolitical typology   Classification scheme based on the scale and complexity of social organization and the effectiveness of political regulation; includes band, tribe, chiefdom, and state. 116

sodality   See *pantribal sodality.*

sororate   Custom by which a widower marries the sister of the deceased wife. 158

state (nation-state)   Complex sociopolitical system that administers a territory and populace with substantial contrasts in occupation, wealth, prestige, and power. An independent, centrally organized political unit, a government. 116

status   Any position that determines where someone fits in society; may be ascribed or achieved. 122

stereotypes   Fixed ideas—often unfavorable—about what members of a group are like. 251

stratification   Characteristic of a system with socioeconomic strata. 131

style shifts   Variations in speech in different contexts. 77

subcultures   Different cultural symbol-based traditions associated with subgroups in the same complex society. 36

subgroups   Languages within a taxonomy of related languages that are most closely related. 83

subordinate   The lower, or underprivileged, group in a stratified system.   132

superordinate   The upper, or privileged, group in a stratified system.   132

survey research   Characteristic research procedure among social scientists other than anthropologists. Studies society through sampling, statistical analysis, and impersonal data collection.   59

symbol   Something, verbal or non-verbal, that arbitrarily and by convention stands for something else, with which it has no necessary or natural connection.   24

syntax   The arrangement and order of words in phrases and sentences.   70

T

taboo   Prohibition backed by supernatural sanctions.   192

text   Something that is creatively "read," interpreted, and assigned meaning by each person who receives it; includes any media-borne image, such as Carnival.   55, 191

transhumance   One of two variants of pastoralism; part of the population moves seasonally with the herds while the other part remains in home villages.   98

tribe   Form of sociopolitical organization usually based on horticulture or pastoralism. Socioeconomic stratification and centralized rule are absent in tribes, and there is no means of enforcing political decisions.   116

tropics   Geographic belt extending about 23 degrees north and south of the equator, between the Tropic of Cancer (north) and the Tropic of Capricorn (south).   10

typology, sociopolitical   See *sociopolitical typology*.

U

underdifferentiation   Planning fallacy of viewing less developed countries as an undifferentiated group; ignoring cultural diversity and adopting a uniform approach (often ethnocentric) for very different types of project beneficiaries.   264

unilineal descent   Matrilineal or patrilineal descent.   149

universal   Something that exists in every culture.   33

urban anthropology   The anthropological study of life in and around world cities, including urban social problems, differences between urban and other environments, and adaptation to city life.   269

V

variables   Attributes (e.g., sex, age, height, weight) that differ from one person or case to the next.   60

vertical mobility   Upward or downward change in a person's social status.   132

village head   Leadership position in a village (as among the Yanomami, where the head is always a man); has limited authority; leads by example and persuasion.   120

W

wealth   All a person's material assets, including income, land, and other types of property; the basis of economic status.   131

Westernization   The acculturative influence of Western expansion on other cultures.   289

working class (or proletariat)   Those who must sell their labor to survive; the antithesis of the bourgeoisie in Marx's class analysis.   216

world-system theory   Argument for the historic and contemporary social, political, and economic significance of an identifiable global system, based on wealth and power differentials, that extends beyond individual countries.   212

Photo Credits

Chapter 1: p. 5: © National Anthropological Archives. Neg.#906-B; p. 7 (top left): © Ed George/National Geographic Image Collection; p. 7 (top right): Darrell Gulin/Corbis; p. 7 (bottom left): © Sabine Vielmo/Argus Fotoarchiv/ Peter Arnold; p. 7 (bottom right): © Penny Tweedie/Woodfin Camp & Associates; p. 10 (left): © Jan Spieczny/Peter Arnold; p. 10 (right): © Digital Vision/Getty Images; p. 14: © Randy Olson/Aurora Photos; p. 19: © AP Images/Obama Presidential Campaign

Chapter 2: p. 28 (top): © William Gottlieb/ Corbis; p. 28 (bottom): © Jamie Rose/ Aurora Photos; p. 31: © OSF/Clive Bromhall/Animals Animals; p. 37: © Joao Silva/Picturenet Africa; p. 40: © Joerg Mueller/Visum/The Image Works

Chapter 3: p. 48: © AP Images; p. 51: © Michael Doolittle/The Image Works; p. 55: © Mary Evans Picture Library/Image Works; p. 58: © Christopher M. O'Leary; p. 61: © Conrad P. Kottak

Chapter 4: p. 67: © Michael Nichols/ Magnum Photos; p. 71: Photos 12/Alamy; p. 74: © Lonny Shavelson; p. 76: Rob Widdis/epa/Corbis; p. 78: © Larry Downing/Reuters/Corbis; p. 81: © Jim Goldberg/Magnum Photos; p. 82: Lawrence Jackson/White House Photo

Chapter 5: p. 94: © D. Halleux/Bios/Peter Arnold; p. 96: Earl & Nazima Kowall/ Corbis; p. 102: Sion Touhig/Corbis; p. 108: Elbridge W. Merrill Collection Photograph Collection./Alaska State Library and Archives [P57-028]; p. 111: © Carl D. Walsh/Aurora Photos

Chapter 6: p. 115: Marilyn Humphries/The Image Works; p. 117: © Joy Tessman/ National Geographic Image Collection; p. 123: © Burt Glinn/Magnum Photos; p. 125: © Douglas Kirkland; p. 129: © John A. Novak/Animals Animals; p. 131: AP Images/Bob Bird

Chapter 7: p. 143: © Brenninger/ Sueddeutsche Zeitung Photo/The Image Works; p. 144: © Najlah Feanny/Stock Boston; p. 155: Marilyn Humphries/The Image Works; p. 162: Henning Christoph/ Peter Arnold Inc.

Chapter 8: p. 168: © Ziva Santop; p. 176: © Lindsay Hebberd/Corbis Images; p. 177: © George Holton/Photo Researchers; p. 181: © National Archives; p. 185: Sinopictures/ Maciej Dakowicz/Peter Arnold Inc.

Chapter 9: p. 194: Tom Dahlin/Getty Images; p. 196 (top): © Thierry Secretan/ COSMOS/Woodfin Camp & Associates; p. 196 (bottom): © Joe McNally/IPNstock. com; p. 203: © R. Giling/Peter Arnold Inc.; p. 206: © Kal Muller/Woodfin Camp & Associates

Chapter 10: p. 212: Maya Barnes Johansen/The Image Works; p. 215: © ARPL/Topham/The Image Works; p. 220: © Hulton Archive/Getty Images; p. 229: Nic Bothma/epa/Corbis

Bibliography

Abelmann, N., and J. Lie 1995. *Blue Dreams: Korean Americans and the Los Angeles Riots.* Cambridge, MA: Harvard University Press.

Adherents.com 2002. Major Religions of the World Ranked by Number of Adherents. http://www.adherents.com/ Religions_By_Adherents.html.

Ahmed, A. S. 1992. *Postmodernism and Islam: Predicament and Promise.* New York: Routledge.

———. 2004. *Postmodernism and Islam: Predicament and Promise,* rev. ed. New York: Routledge.

Amadiume, I. 1987. *Male Daughters, Female Husbands.* Atlantic Highlands, NJ: Zed.

American Anthropological Association *Anthropology Newsletter.* Published 9 times annually by the American Anthropological Association, Washington, DC.

Anderson, B. 1991. *Imagined Communities: Reflections on the Origin and Spread of Nationalism,* rev. ed. London: Verso.

Anderson, R. 1996. *Magic, Science, and Health: The Aims and Achievements of Medical Anthropology.* Fort Worth, TX: Harcourt Brace.

Antoun, R. T. 2008. *Understanding Fundamentalism: Christian, Islamic, and Jewish Movements.* 2nd ed. Lanham, MD: AltaMira.

Aoki, M. Y., and M. B. Dardess, eds. 1981. *As the Japanese See It: Past and Present.* Honolulu: University Press of Hawaii.

Aoyagi, K., P. J. M. Nas, and J. Traphagan, eds. 1998. *Toward Sustainable Cities: Readings in the Anthropology of Urban Environments.* Leiden: Leiden Development Studies, Institute of Cultural and Social Studies, University of Leiden.

Appadurai, A. 1990. Disjuncture and Difference in the Global Cultural Economy. *Public Culture* 2(2):1–24.

———. 1991. Global Ethnoscapes: Notes and Queries for a Transnational Anthropology. In *Recapturing Anthropology: Working in the Present,* R. G. Fox, ed., pp. 191–210. Santa Fe, NM: School of American Research Advanced Seminar Series.

———. 1996. *Modernity at Large. Cultural Dimensions of Globalization.* Minneapolis: University of Minnesota Press.

———. 2001. *Globalization.* Durham, NC: Duke University Press.

Appiah, K. A. 1990. Racisms. In *Anatomy of Racism,* David Theo Goldberg, ed., pp. 3–17. Minneapolis: University of Minnesota Press.

Applebome, P. 1996. English Unique to Blacks Is Officially Recognized. *The New York Times,* December 20, http:// www.nytimes.com.

Arensberg, C. 1987. Theoretical Contributions of Industrial and Development Studies. In *Applied Anthropology in America,* 2nd ed., E. M. Eddy and W. L. Partridge, eds. New York: Columbia University Press.

Arrighi, G. 1994. *The Long Twentieth Century; Money, Power, and the Origins of Our Times.* New York: Verso.

Ashcroft, B., G. Griffiths, and H. Tiffin 1989. *The Empire Writes Back: Theory and Practice in Post-colonial Literatures.* New York: Routledge.

Baer, H., and M. Singer 2008. *Global Warming and the Political Ecology of Health.* Walnut Creek, CA: Left Coast Press.

Baer, H. A., M. Singer, and I. Susser 2003. *Medical Anthropology and the World System.* Westport, CT: Praeger.

Bailey, E. J. 2000. *Medical Anthropology and African American Health.* Westport, CT: Bergin and Garvey.

Bailey, R. C. 1990. *The Behavioral Ecology of Efe Pygmy Men in the Ituri Forest, Zaire.* Ann Arbor: Anthropological Papers, Museum of Anthropology, University of Michigan, no. 86.

Bailey, R. C., G. Head, M. Jenike, B. Owen, R. Rechtman, and E. Zechenter 1989. Hunting and Gathering in Tropical Rain Forests: Is It Possible? *American Anthropologist* 91:59–82.

Banton, M. 1957. *West African City. A Study in Tribal Life in Freetown.* London: Oxford University Press.

Barber, B. R. 1992. Jihad vs. McWorld. *Atlantic Monthly* 269(3):53–65, March 1992.

———. 1995. *Jihad vs. McWorld.* New York: Times Books.

Barker, C. 1997. *Global Television: An Introduction.* Malden, MA: Blackwell.

———. 2003. *Cultural Studies: Theory and Practice.* Thousand Oaks, CA: Sage.

Barnaby, F., ed. 1984. *Future War: Armed Conflict in the Next Decade.* London: M. Joseph.

Barnes, E. 2005. *Diseases and Human Evolution. Albuquerque:* University of New Mexico Press.

Baro, M., and T. F. Deubel 2006. Persistent Hunger: Perspectives on Vulnerability, Famine, and Food Security in Sub-Saharan Africa. *Annual Review of Anthropology* 35:521–538.

Barringer, F. 1992. New Census Data Show More Children Living in Poverty. *The New York Times,* May 29, pp. A1, A12–A13.

Barth, F. 1968. (orig. 1958). Ecologic Relations of Ethnic Groups in Swat, North Pakistan. In *Man in Adaptation: The Cultural Present,* Yehudi Cohen, ed., pp. 324–331. Chicago: Aldine.

———. 1969. *Ethnic Groups and Boundaries: The Social Organization of Cultural Difference.* London: Allen & Unwin.

Beeman, W. 1986. *Language, Status, and Power in Iran.* Bloomington: Indiana University Press.

Behar, R. 1993. *Translated Woman: Crossing the Border with Esperanza's Story.* Boston: Beacon Press.

Bell, W. 1981. Neocolonialism. In *Encyclopedia of Sociology,* p. 193. Guilford, CT: DPG Publishing.

Bellah, R. N. 1978. Religious Evolution. In *Reader in Comparative Religion: An Anthropological Approach,* 4th ed., W. A. Lessa and E. Z. Vogt, eds., pp. 36–50. New York: Harper and Row.

Benedict, R. 1940. *Race, Science and Politics. New York:* Modern Age Books.

Berlin, B., and P. Kay 1992. *Basic Color Terms: Their Universality and Evolution,* 2nd ed. Berkeley: University of California Press.

Bernard, H. R. 2002. *Research Methods in Anthropology: Qualitative and Quantitative Methods,* 3rd ed. Walnut Creek, CA: AltaMira.

———. 2006. *Research Methods in Anthropology: Qualitative and Quantitative Approaches.* 4th ed. Lanham, MD: AltaMira.

Bernard, H. R., ed. 1998. *Handbook of Methods in Cultural Anthropology,* Walnut Creek, CA: AltaMira.

Bicker, A., P. Sillitoe, and J. Pottier 2004. *Investigating Local Knowledge: New Directions, New Approaches.* Burlington, VT: Ashgate.

Bird-David, N. 1992. Beyond "The Original Affluent Society": A Culturalist Reformulation. *Current Anthropology* 33(1):25–47.

Bjuremalm, H. 1997. Rattvisa kan skippas i Rwanda: Folkmordet 1994 gar attt forklara och analysera pa samma satt som forintelsen av judarna. *Dagens Nyheter* [06-03-1997, p. B3].

Blackwood, E., and S. Wieringa, eds. 1999. *Female Desires: Same-Sex Relations and Transgender Practices across Cultures.* New York: Columbia University Press.

Bloch, M., ed. 1975. *Political Language and Oratory in Traditional Societies.* London: Academic Press.

Boas, F. 1966 (orig. 1940). *Race, Language, and Culture.* New York: Free Press.

Bodley, J. H. 2003. *The Power of Scale: A Global History Approach.* Armonk, NY: M. E. Sharpe.

———. 2007. *Anthropology and Contemporary Human Problems,* 5th ed. Lanham, MD: AltaMira.

———. 2008. *Victims of Progress,* 5th ed. Lanham, MD: AltaMira.

Bodley, J. H., ed. 1988. *Tribal Peoples and Development Issues: A Global Overview.* Mountain View, CA: Mayfield.

Boellstorff, T. 2007. Queer Studies in the House of Anthropology. *Annual Review of Anthropology* 36: 375–389.

Bogoras, W. 1904. The Chukchee. In *The Jesup North Pacific Expedition,* F. Boas, ed. New York: Memoir of the American Museum of Natural History.

Bolinger, D., and D. Sears 1981. *Aspects of Language,* 3rd ed. New York: Harcourt Brace Jovanovich.

Bolton, R. 1981. Susto, Hostility, and Hypoglycemia. *Ethnology* 20(4): 227–258.

Bonvillain, N. 2001. *Women and Men: Cultural Constructions of Gender,* 3rd ed. Upper Saddle River, NJ: Prentice Hall.

———. 2008. *Language, Culture, and Communication: The Meaning of Messages,* 5th ed. Upper Saddle River, NJ: Prentice Hall.

Boserup, E. 1970. *Women's Role in Economic Development.* London: Allen and Unwin.

Bourdieu, P. 1977. *Outline of a Theory of Practice.* R. Nice (trans.). Cambridge: Cambridge University Press.

———. 1982. *Ce Que Parler Veut Dire.* Paris: Fayard.

———. 1984. *Distinction: A Social Critique of the Judgment of Taste.* R. Nice (trans.). Cambridge, MA: Harvard University Press.

Bourque, S. C., and K. B. Warren 1987. Technology, Gender and Development. *Daedalus* 116(4): 173–197.

Bowen, J. R. 2008. *Religion in Practice: An Approach to Anthropology of Religion,* 4th ed. Boston: Pearson/Allyn and Bacon.

Bowie, F. 2006. *The Anthropology of Religion: An Introduction.* Malden, MA: Blackwell.

Braudel, F. 1981. *Civilization and Capitalism, 15th–18th Century,* Volume I, *The Structure of Everyday Life: The Limits.* S. Reynolds (trans.). New York: Harper and Row.

———. 1982. *Civilization and Capitalism, 15th–18th Century,* Volume II, *The Wheels of Commerce.* New York: Harper and Row.

———. 1992. *Civilization and Capitalism, 15th–18th Century,* Volume III, *The Perspective of the World.* Berkeley: University of California Press.

Bremen, J. V., and A. Shimizu, eds. 1999. *Anthropology and Colonialism in Asia and Oceania.* London: Curzon.

Brenneis, D. 1988. Language and Disputing. *Annual Review of Anthropology* 17:221–237.

Brettell, C. B., and C. F. Sargent, eds. 2005. *Gender in Cross-Cultural Perspective.* Upper Saddle River, NJ: Pearson/ Prentice Hall.

Briggs, C. L. 2005. Communicability, Racial Discourse, and Disease. *Annual Review of Anthropology* 34:269–291.

Brooke, J. 1992. Rio's New Day in Sun Leaves Laplander Limp. *The New York Times,* June 1, p. A7.

Brower, B., and B. R. Johnston 2007. *Disappearing Peoples?: Indigenous Groups and Ethnic Minorities in South and Central Asia.* Walnut Creek, CA: Left Coast Press.

Brown, A. 2001. Communism. *International Encyclopedia of the Social & Behavioral Sciences*, pp. 2323–2326. New York: Elsevier.

Brown, D. 1991. *Human Universals.* New York: McGraw-Hill.

Brown, P. J. 1998. *Understanding and Applying Medical Anthropology.* Mountain View, CA: Mayfield.

Brown, R. W. 1958. *Words and Things.* Glencoe, IL: Free Press.

Burns, J. F. 1992a. Bosnian Strife Cuts Old Bridges of Trust. *New York Times,* May 22, pp. A1, A6.

———. 1992b. A Serb, Fighting Serbs, Defends Sarajevo. *New York Times,* July 12, sec. 4, p. E3.

———. 1997. A Year of Harsh Islamic Rule Weighs Heavily for Afghans. September 24. www.nytimes.com.

Butler, R. 2005. World's Largest Cities: [Ranked by City Population]. http://www.mongabay.com/cities_pop_01.htm.

Buvinic, M. 1995. The Feminization of Poverty? Research and Policy Needs. In *Reducing Poverty through Labour Market Policies.* Geneva: International Institute for Labour Studies.

Carey, B. 2007. Washoe, a Chimp of Many Words Dies at 42. *New York Times,* November 1. http:// www.nytimes.com.

Carneiro, R. L. 1956. Slash-and-Burn Agriculture: A Closer Look at Its Implications for Settlement Patterns. In *Men and Cultures,* Selected Papers of the Fifth International Congress of Anthropological and Ethnological Sciences, pp. 229–234. Philadelphia: University of Pennsylvania Press.

———. 1968 (orig. 1961). Slash-and-Burn Cultivation among the Kuikuru and Its Implications for Cultural Development in the Amazon Basin. In *Man in Adaptation: The Cultural Present,* Y. A. Cohen, ed., pp. 131–145. Chicago: Aldine.

———. 1970. A Theory of the Origin of the State. *Science* 69:733–738.

Carsten, J. 2004. *After Kinship.* New York: Cambridge University Press.

Carter, J. 1988. Freed from Keepers and Cages, Chimps Come of Age on Baboon Island. *Smithsonian,* June, pp. 36–48.

Cernea, M., ed. 1991. *Putting People First: Sociological Variables in Rural Development,* 2nd ed. New York: Oxford University Press (published for the World Bank).

Ceuppens, B., and P. Geschiere 2005. Autochthony: Local or Global? New Modes in the Struggle over Citizenship and Belonging in Africa and Europe. *Annual Review of Anthropology* 34:385–407.

Chagnon, N. A. 1967. *Yanomamo Warfare: Social Organization and Marriage Alliances.* Ann Arbor, MI: University Microfilms.

———. 1992 (orig. 1983). *Yanomamo: The Fierce People*, 4th ed. New York: Harcourt Brace.

———. 1997. *Yanomamo*, 5th ed. Fort Worth, TX: Harcourt Brace.

Chambers, E. 1987. Applied Anthropology in the Post-Vietnam Era: Anticipations and Ironies. *Annual Review of Anthropology* 16:309–337.

Chatterjee, P. 2004. *The Politics of the Governed: Reflections on Popular Politics in Most of the World.* New York: Columbia University Press.

Chiseri-strater, E., and B. S. Sunstein. 2001. *Fieldworking: Reading and Writing Research,* 2nd ed. Upper Saddle River, NJ: Prentice Hall.

Chomsky, N. 1957. *Syntactic Structures.* The Hague: Mouton.

Christensen, L. 2003. The Politics of Correction. *Rethinking Schools Online.* Fall. http://www.rethinkingschools.org/archive/18_01/corr181.html.

Clifford, J. 1982. *Person and Myth: Maurice Leenhardt in the Melanesian World.* Berkeley: University of California Press.

———. 1988. *The Predicament of Culture: Twentieth-Century Ethnography,*

Literature and Art. Cambridge, MA: Harvard University Press.

Coates, J. 1986. *Women, Men, and Language*. London: Longman.

Cody, D. 1998. British Empire. http://www. stg. brown.edu/projects/hypertext/landow/ victorian/history/Empire.html, May 18.

Cohen, M. 1998. *Culture of Intolerance: Chauvinism, Class, and Racism*. New Haven: Yale University Press.

Cohen, M. N., and Armelagos, G., eds. 1984. *Paleopathology at the Origins of Agriculture*. New York: Academic Press.

Cohen, R. 1967. *The Kanuri of Bornu*. New York: Holt, Rinehart & Winston.

Cohen, Y. 1974. Culture as Adaptation. In *Man in Adaptation: The Cultural Present,* 2nd ed., Y. A. Cohen, ed., pp. 45–68. Chicago: Aldine.

Colson, E., and T. Scudder 1975. New Economic Relationships between the Gwembe Valley and the Line of Rail. In *Town and Country in Central and Eastern Africa,* David Parkin, ed., pp. 190–210. London: Oxford University Press.

———. 1988. *For Prayer and Profit: The Ritual, Economic, and Social Importance of Beer in Gwembe District, Zambia, 1950–1982*. Stanford, CA: Stanford University Press.

Connor, W. 1972. Nation-Building or Nation-Destroying. *World Politics* 24(3).

Cooper, F., and A. L. Stoler, eds. 1997. *Tensions of Empire: Colonial Cultures in a Bourgeois World*. Berkeley: University of California Press.

Council on International and Public Affairs 2006. How Many Dollars at the Top? *Too Much: A Commentary on Excess and Inequality*. New York, April 24, 2006. http://www.toomuchonline.org/ articlenew2006/April24a.html.

Crapo, R. H. 2006. *Anthropology of Religion: The Unity and Diversity of Religions*. Boston: McGraw-Hill.

Crate, S. A., and M. Nuttall 2008. *Anthropology and Climate Change: From Encounters to Actions*. Walnut Creek, CA: Left Coast Press.

Cresswell, T. 2006. *On the Move: Mobility in the Modern West*. New York: Routledge.

Crosby, A. W., Jr. 1986. *Ecological Imperialism: The Biological Expansion of Europe 900–1900*. Cambridge: Cambridge University Press.

———. 2003. *The Columbian Exchange: Biological and Cultural Consequences of 1492*. Westport, CT: Praeger.

Cultural Survival Quarterly. Quarterly Journal. Cambridge, MA: Cultural Survival, Inc.

Cunningham, G. 1999. *Religion and Magic: Approaches and Theories*. New York: New York University Press.

DaMatta, R. 1991. *Carnivals, Rogues, and Heroes: An Interpretation of the Brazilian Dilemma*. Translated from the Portuguese by John Drury. Notre Dame, IN: University of Notre Dame Press.

D'Andrade, R. 1984. Cultural Meaning Systems. In *Culture Theory: Essays on Mind, Self, and Emotion,* R. A. Shweder and R. A. Levine, eds., pp. 88–119. Cambridge: Cambridge University Press.

Das, V., and D. Poole, eds. 2004. *Anthropology in the Margins of the State*. Santa Fe, NM: School of American Research Press.

Degler, C. 1970. *Neither Black nor White: Slavery and Race Relations in Brazil and the United States*. New York: Macmillan.

de la Peña, G. 2005. Social and Cultural Policies toward Indigenous Peoples: Perspectives from Latin America. *Annual Review of Anthropology* 34:717–739.

DeNavas-Walt, C., B. D. Proctor, and C. H. Lee 2006. Income, Poverty, and Health Insurance Coverage in the United States: 2005, U.S. Census Bureau. Current Population Reports, Consumer Income. http://www.census.gov/rpod/2006pubs/ p60-231.pdf

Dentan, R. K. 1979. *The Semai: A Nonviolent People of Malaya,* Fieldwork ed. New York: Harcourt Brace.

De Vos, G. A., and H. Wagatsuma 1966. *Japan's Invisible Race: Caste in Culture and Personality*. Berkeley: University of California Press.

De Vos, G. A., W. O. Wetherall, and K. Stearman 1983. *Japan's Minorities: Burakumin, Koreans, Ainu and Okinawans*. Report no. 3. London: Minority Rights Group.

De Waal, F. B. M. 1997. *Bonobo: The Forgotten Ape*. Berkeley: University of California Press.

Di Leonardo, M., ed. 1991. *Toward a New Anthropology of Gender*. Berkeley: University of California Press.

Diamond, J. M. 1997. *Guns, Germs, and Steel: The Fates of Human Societies*. New York: Norton.

Dillon, S. 2006. In Schools Across U.S., the Melting Pot Overflows. *New York Times,* August 27, http://www.nytimes.com.

Divale, W. T., and M. Harris 1976. Population, Warfare, and the Male Supremacist Complex. *American Anthropologist* 78: 521–538.

Douglass, W. A. 1969. *Death in Murelaga: Funerary Ritual in a Spanish Basque Village*. Seattle: University of Washington Press.

———. 1975. *Echalar and Murelaga: Opportunity and Rural Exodus in Two Spanish Basque Villages*. London: C. Hurst.

———. 1992. Basques. *Encyclopedia of World Cultures*, Vol. 4. Boston: G. K. Hall.

Draper, P. 1975 !Kung Women: Contrasts in Sexual Egalitarianism in Foraging and Sedentary Contexts. In *Toward an Anthropology of Women,* R. Reiter, ed., pp. 77–109. New York: Monthly Review Press.

Dressler, W. W., K. S. Oths, and C. C. Gravlee 2005. Race and Ethnicity in Public Health Research. *Annual Review of Anthropology* 34:231–252.

Durkheim, E. 1951 (orig. 1897). *Suicide: A Study in Sociology*. Glencoe, IL: Free Press.

———. 1961 (orig. 1912). *The Elementary Forms of the Religious Life*. New York: Collier Books.

———. 2001 (orig. 1912). *The Elementary Forms of the Religious Life*. Translated by Carol Cosman. Abridged with an introduction and notes by Mark S. Cladis. New York: Oxford University Press.

Durrenberger, E. P., and T. D. King, eds. 2000. *State and Community in Fisheries Management: Power, Policy, and Practice*. Westport, CT: Bergin and Garvey.

Dwyer, K. 1982. *Moroccan Dialogues: Anthropology in Question*. Baltimore: Johns Hopkins University Press.

Earle, T. K. 1987. Chiefdoms in Archaeological and Ethnohistorical Perspective. *Annual Review of Anthropology* 16:279–308.

———. 1997. *How Chiefs Come to Power: The Political Economy in Prehistory*. Stanford, CA: Stanford University Press.

Eastman, C. M. 1975. *Aspects of Language and Culture*. San Francisco: Chandler and Sharp.

Echeverria, J. 1999. *Home Away from Home: A History of Basque Boardinghouses*. Reno: University of Nevada Press.

Eckert, P. 1989. *Jocks and Burnouts: Social Categories and Identity in the High School*. New York: Teachers College Press, Columbia University.

———. 2000. *Linguistic Variation as Social Practice: The Linguistic Construction of Identity in Belten High*. Malden, MA: Blackwell.

Eckert, P., and S. McConnell-Ginet 2003. *Language and Gender*. New York: Cambridge University Press.

Edelman, M., and A. Haugerud 2004. *The Anthropology of Development and Globalization: From Classical Political Economy to Contemporary Neoliberalism*. Malden, MA: Blackwell.

Escobar, A. 1991. Anthropology and the Development Encounter: The Making and Marketing of Development

Anthropology. *American Ethnologist* 18:658–682.

———. 1994. Welcome to Cyberia: Notes on the Anthropology of Cyberculture. *Current Anthropology* 35(3):211–231.

———. 1995. *Encountering Development: The Making and Unmaking of the Third World*. Princeton, NJ: Princeton University Press.

Eskridge, W. N., Jr. 1996. *The Case for Same-Sex Marriage: From Sexual Liberty to Civilized Commitment*. New York: Free Press.

Evans-Pritchard, E. E. 1970. Sexual Inversion among the Azande. *American Anthropologist* 72:1428–1433.

Fagan, B. M. 1998. *World Prehistory: A Brief Introduction*, 4th ed. New York: Longman.

———. 2002. *World Prehistory: A Brief Introduction*, 5th ed. Upper Saddle River NJ: Prentice Hall.

Farner, R. F., ed. 2004. *Nationalism, Ethnicity, and Identity: Cross-National and Comparative Perspectives*. New Brunswick, NJ: Transaction Publishers.

Farooq, M. 1966. Importance of Determining Transmission Sites in Planning Bilharziasis Control: Field Observations from the Egypt-49 Project Area. *American Journal of Epidemiology* 83:603–612.

Farr, D. M. L. 1980. British Empire. *Academic American Encyclopedia*. Princeton, NJ: Arete, volume 3, pp. 495–496.

Fasold, R. W. 1990. *The Sociolinguistics of Language*. Oxford: Blackwell.

Ferguson, R. B. 1995. *Yanomami Warfare: A Political History*. Santa Fe, NM: School of American Research.

———. 2002. *The State, Identity, and Violence: Political Disintegration in the Post-Cold War Era*. New York: Routledge.

Ferraro, G. 2006. *The Cultural Dimension of International Business,* 5th ed. Upper Saddle River, NJ: Prentice Hall.

Fields, J. M. 2004. America's Families and Living Arrangements: 2003. U.S. Census Bureau. *Current Population Reports*, P20–553, November. http://www.census.gov.

Fields, J. M., and L. M. Casper 2001. America's Families and Living Arrangements: Population Characteristics, 2000. U.S. Census Bureau. *Current Population Reports,* P20–537, June. http://www.census.gov/prod/2001pubs/p20-537.pdf

Files, J. 2005. Report Describes Immigrants as Younger and More Diverse. *The New York Times,* National ed., June 10, p. A11.

Finkler, K. 1985. *Spiritualist Healers in Mexico: Successes and Failures of Alternative Therapeutics*. South Hadley, MA: Bergin and Garvey.

Finnstrom, S. 1997. Postcoloniality and the Postcolony: Theories of the Global and the Local. http://www.stg.brown.edu/projects/hypertext/landow/post/poldiscourse/finnstrom/finnstrom1.html.

Fiske, J. 1989. *Understanding Popular Culture*. Boston: Unwin Hyman.

Fiske, J., and J. Hartley 2003. *Reading Television*. New York: Routledge.

Fleisher, M. L. 2000. *Kuria Cattle Raiders: Violence and Vigilantism on the Tanzania/Kenya Frontier*. Ann Arbor: University of Michigan Press.

Ford, C. S., and F. A. Beach 1951. *Patterns of Sexual Behavior*. New York: Harper Torchbooks.

Fortes, M. 1950. Kinship and Marriage among the Ashanti. In *African Systems of Kinship and Marriage,* A. R. Radcliffe-Brown and D. Forde, eds., pp. 252–284. London: Oxford University Press.

Foster, G. M. 1965. Peasant Society and the Image of Limited Good. *American Anthropologist* 67:293–315.

Foster, G. M., and B. G. Anderson 1978. *Medical Anthropology*. New York: McGraw-Hill.

Foucault, M. 1979. *Discipline and Punish: The Birth of the Prison*. A. Sheridan (trans.). New York: Vintage Books.

———. 1990. *The History of Sexuality,* Volume 2, *The Use of Pleasure.* R Hurley, (trans.). New York: Vintage.

Fouts, R. S. 1997. *Next of Kin: What Chimpanzees Have Taught Me about Who We Are.* New York: William Morrow.

Fouts, R. S., D. H. Fouts, and T. E. Van Cantfort 1989. The Infant Loulis Learns Signs from Cross-Fostered Chimpanzees. In *Teaching Sign Language to Chimpanzees,* R. A. Gardner, B. T. Gardner, and T. E. Van Cantfort, eds., pp. 280–292. Albany: State University of New York Press.

Frake, C. O. 1961. The Diagnosis of Disease among the Subanun of Mindanao. *American Anthropologist* 63:113–132.

Franke, R. 1977. Miracle Seeds and Shattered Dreams in Java. In *Readings in Anthropology,* pp. 197–201. Guilford, CT: Dushkin.

French, H. W. 2002. Whistling Past the Global Graveyard. *New York Times,* July 14, http://www./nytimes.com/2002/01/14.weekinreview/14FREN.html.

Fricke, T. 1994. *Himalayan Households: Tamang Demography and Domestic Processes,* 2nd ed. New York: Columbia University Press.

Fried, M. H. 1960. On the Evolution of Social Stratification and the State. In *Culture in History,* S. Diamond, ed., pp. 713–731. New York: Columbia University Press.

———. 1967. *The Evolution of political Society: An Eassay in Political Anthropology,* New York: McGraw-Hill.

Friedl, E. 1975. *Women and Men: An Anthropologist's View.* New York: Holt, Rinehart & Winston.

Friedman, J., ed. 2003. *Globalization, the State, and Violence.* Walnut Creek, CA: AltaMira.

Friedman, K. E., and J. Friedman 2008. *The Anthropology of Global Systems.* Lanham, MD: AltaMira.

Gal, S. 1989. Language and Political Economy. *Annual Review of Anthropology* 18:345–367.

Gardner, R. A., B. T. Gardner, and T. E. Van Cantfort, eds. 1989. *Teaching Sign Language to Chimpanzees.* Albany: State University of New York Press.

Geertz, C. 1973. *The Interpretation of Cultures.* New York: Basic Books.

Geis, M. L. 1987. *The Language of Politics.* New York: Springer-Verlag.

Gellner, E. 1997. *Nationalism.* New York: New York University Press.

Gezon, L. L. 2006. *Global Visions, Local Landscapes: A Political Ecology of Conservation, Conflict, and Control in Northern Madagascar.* Lanham, MD: AltaMira.

Giddens, A. 1973. *The Class Structure of the Advanced Societies.* New York: Cambridge University Press.

———. 2000. *Runaway World: How Globalization Is Reshaping Our Lives.* New York: Routledge.

Gilmore, D. D. 1987. *Aggression and Community: Paradoxes of Andalusian Culture.* New Haven, CT: Yale University Press.

———. 1991. *Manhood in the Making: Cultural Concepts of Masculinity.* New Haven, CT: Yale University Press.

———. 2001. *Misogyny: The Male Malady.* Philadelphia: University of Pennsylvania Press.

Gledhill, J. 2000. *Power and Its Disguises: Anthropological Perspectives on Politics.* Sterling, VA: Pluto Press.

Gmelch, G. 1978. Baseball Magic. *Human Nature* 1(8):32–40.

———. 2001. *Inside Pitch: Life in Professional Baseball.* Washington, DC: Smithsonian Institution Press.

Gmelch, G., and W. Zenner, eds. 2002. *Urban Life: Readings in the Anthropology of the City.* Prospect Heights, IL: Waveland.

Goldberg, D. T. 2002. *The Racial State.* Malden, MA: Blackwell.

Golden, T. 1997. Oakland Revamps Plan to Teach Black English. *The New York Times,* January 14, http://www.nytimes.com.

Goleman, D. 1992. Anthropology Goes Looking for Love in All the Old Places. *The New York Times,* November 24, 1992, p. B1.

Gottdiener, M., ed. 2000. *New Forms of Consumption: Consumers, Culture, and Commodification*. Lanham, MD: Rowman & Littlefield.

Gough, E. K. 1959. The Nayars and the Definition of Marriage. *Journal of the Royal Anthropological Institute* 89:23–34.

Gramsci, A. 1971. *Selections from the Prison Notebooks*. Q. Hoare and G. N. Smith, ed. and trans. London: Wishart.

Grasmuck, S., and P. Pessar 1991. *Between Two Islands: Dominican International Migration*. Berkeley: University of California Press.

Gray, J. 1986. With a Few Exceptions, Television in Africa Fails to Educate and Enlighten. *Ann Arbor News,* December 8.

Greaves, T. C. 1995. Problems Facing Anthropologists: Cultural Rights and Ethnography. *General Anthropology* 1(2):1, 3–6.

Green, E. C. 1992 (orig. 1987). The Integration of Modern and Traditional Health Sectors in Swaziland. In *Applying Anthropology,* A. Podolefsky and P. J. Brown, eds., pp. 246–251. Mountain View, CA: Mayfield.

Greenwood, D. J. 1976. *Unrewarding Wealth: The Commercialization and Collapse of Agriculture in a Spanish Basque Town*. Cambridge: Cambridge University Press.

Grekova, M. 2001. Postsocialist Societies. *International Encyclopedia of the Social & Behavioral Sciences,* pp. 11877–11881. New York: Elsevier.

Griffin, P. B., and A. Estioko-Griffin, eds. 1985. *The Agta of Northern Luzon: Recent Studies*. Cebu City, Philippines: University of San Carlos.

Gudeman, S., ed. 1999. *Economic Anthropology*. Northhampton, MA: E. Elgar.

Gumperz, J. J., and S. C. Levinson, eds. 1996. *Rethinking Linguistic Relativity*. New York: Cambridge University Press.

Gupta, A., and J. Ferguson 1997a. Culture, Power, Place: Ethnography at the End of an Era. In *Culture, Power, Place: Explorations in Critical Anthropology,* A. Gupta and J. Ferguson, eds., pp. 1–29. Durham, NC: Duke University Press.

———. 1997b. Beyond "Culture": Space, Identity, and the Politics of Difference. In *Culture, Power, Place: Explorations in Critical Anthropology*, A. Gupta and J. Ferguson, eds., pp. 33–51. Durham, NC: Duke University Press.

Gupta, A., and J. Ferguson, eds. 1997c. *Anthropological Locations: Boundaries and Grounds of a Field Science*. Berkeley: University of California Press.

———. 1997d. *Culture, Power, Place: Explorations in Critical Anthropology*. Durham, NC: Duke University Press.

Guyot, J., and C. Hughes 2007. Researchers Find Earliest Evidence for Modern Human Behavior. *Arizona State University Research Magazine.* http://researchmag.asu.edu/2008/02researchers_find_earliest_evid.html.

Hallowell, A. I. 1955. *Culture and Experience*. Philadelphia: University of Pennsylvania Press.

Hansen, K. V. 2004. *Not-So-Nuclear Families: Class, Gender, and Networks of Care*. New Brunswick, NJ: Rutgers University Press.

Hansen, K. V., and A. I. Garey, eds. 1998. *Families in the U.S.: Kinship and Domestic Politics*. Philadelphia: Temple University Press.

Harding, S. 1975. Women and Words in a Spanish Village. In *Toward an Anthropology of Women,* R. Reiter, ed., pp. 283–308. New York: Monthly Review Press.

Harper, J. 2002. *Endangered Species: Health, Illness, and Death among Madagascar's People of the Forest*. Durham, NC: Carolina Academic Press.

Harris, M. 1964. *Patterns of Race in the Americas*. New York: Walker.

———. 1970. Referential Ambiguity in the Calculus of Brazilian Racial Identity. *Southwestern Journal of Anthropology* 26(1):1–14.

———. 1974. *Cows, Pigs, Wars, and Witches: The Riddles of Culture*. New York: Random House.

———. 1978. *Cannibals and Kings*. New York: Vintage Books.

———. 2001 (orig. 1968). *The Rise of Anthropological Theory*. Walnut Creek, CA: AltaMira.

Harris, M., and C. P. Kottak 1963. The Structural Significance of Brazilian Racial Categories. *Sociologia* 25:203–209.

Harrison, G. G., W. L. Rathje, and W. W. Hughes 1994. Food Waste Behavior in an Urban Population. In *Applying Anthropology: An Introductory Reader*, 3rd ed., A. Podolefsky and P. J. Brown, eds., pp. 107–112. Mountain View, CA: Mayfield.

Harrison, K. D. 2007. *When Languages Die: The Extinction of the World's Languages and the Erosion of Human Knowledge*. New York: Oxford University Press.

Hart, C. W. M., A. R. Pilling, and J. C. Goodale 1988. *The Tiwi of North Australia*, 3rd ed. Fort Worth, TX: Harcourt Brace.

Harvey, D. J. 1980. French Empire. *Academic American Encyclopedia*. Princeton, NJ: Arete, volume 8, pp. 309–310.

Hastings, A. 1997. *The Construction of Nationhood: Ethnicity, Religion, and Nationalism*. New York: Cambridge University Press.

Hawkes, K., J. O'connell, and K. Hill 1982. Why Hunters Gather: Optimal Foraging and the Aché of Eastern Paraguay. *American Ethnologist* 9:379–398.

Hedges, C. 1992. Sudan Presses Its Campaign to Impose Islamic Law on Non-Muslims. *The New York Times*, June 1, p. A7.

Helman, C. 2001. *Culture, Health, and Illness: An Introduction for Health Professionals*, 4th ed. Boston: Butterworth-Heinemann.

Henry, J. 1955. Docility, or Giving Teacher What She Wants. *Journal of Social Issues* 2:33–41.

Herdt, G. H. 1981. *Guardians of the Flutes*. New York: McGraw-Hill.

Herdt, G. H., ed. 1984. *Ritualized Homosexuality in Melanesia*. Berkeley: University of California Press.

Hill, J. H. 1978. Apes and Language. *Annual Review of Anthropology* 7:89–112.

Hill, K., H. Kaplan, K. Hawkes, and A. Hurtado 1987. Foraging Decisions among Aché Hunter-gatherers: New Data and Implications for Optimal Foraging Models. *Ethology and Sociobiology* 8:1–36.

Hill-Burnett, J. 1978. Developing Anthropological Knowledge through Application. In *Applied Anthropology in America*, E. M. Eddy and W. L. Partridge, eds., pp. 112–128. New York: Columbia University Press.

Hobhouse, L. T. 1915. *Morals in Evolution*, rev. ed. New York: Holt.

Hoebel, E. A. 1954. *The Law of Primitive Man*. Cambridge, MA: Harvard University Press.

———. 1968 (orig. 1954). The Eskimo: Rudimentary Law in a Primitive Anarchy. In *Studies in Social and Cultural Anthropology*, J. Middleton, ed., pp. 93–127. New York: Crowell.

Hoge, W. 2001. Kautokeino Journal; Reindeer Herders, at Home on a (Very Cold) Range. *The New York Times*, March 26, late ed.—final, sec. A, p. 4.

Holden, A. 2005. *Tourism Studies and the Social Sciences*. New York: Routledge.

Hopkins, T., and I. Wallerstein 1982. Patterns of Development of the Modern World System. In *World System Analysis: Theory and Methodology*, by T. Hopkins, I. Wallerstein, R. Bach, C. Chase-Dunn, and R. Mukherjee, eds., pp. 121–141. Thousand Oaks, CA: Sage.

Hornborg, A., McNeill, J. R., and J. Martinez-Alier 2007. *Rethinking Environmental History: World-System History and Global Environmental Change.* Lanham, MD: AltaMira.

Hornborg, A., and C. L. Crumley, eds. 2007. *The World System and the Earth System: Global Socioenvironmental Change and Sustainability since the Neolithic.* Walnut Creek, CA: Left Coast Press.

Hunt, R. C. 2007. *Beyond Relativism: Comparability in Cultural Anthropology.* Lanham, MD: AltaMira.

Hunter, M. L. 2005. *Race, Gender, and the Politics of Skin Tone.* New York: Routledge.

Hurtado, A. M., C. A. Lambourne, P. James, K. Hill, K. Cheman, and K. Baca 2005. Human Rights, Biomedical Science, and Infectious Diseases among South American Indigenous Groups. *Annual Review of Anthropology* 34:639–665.

Inda, J. X., and R. Rosaldo, eds. 2008. *The Anthropology of Globalization: A Reader.* Malden, MA: Blackwell.

Ingraham, C. 2008. *White Weddings: Romancing Heterosexuality in Popular Culture,* 2nd ed. New York: Routledge.

Inhorn, M. C., and P. J. Brown 1990. The Anthropology of Infectious Disease. *Annual Review of Anthropology* 19:89–117.

Iqbal, S. 2002. A New Light on Skin Color. *National Geographic Online Extra.* http://magma.nationalgeographic.com/ngm/0211/feature2/online_extra.html.

Jablonski, N. G., and Chaplin, G. 2000. The Evolution of Human Skin Coloration. *Journal of Human Evolution* (39):57–106.

Jackson, J., and K. B. Warren 2005. Indigenous Movements in Latin America, 1992–2004: Controversies, Ironies, New Directions. *Annual Review of Anthropology* 34:549–573.

Jenks, C. 2003. *Culture,* 2nd ed. New York: Routledge.

Johansen, B. E. 2003. *Indigenous Peoples and Environmental Issues: An Encyclopedia.* Westport, CT: Greenwood.

Johnson, A. W. 1978. *Quantification in Cultural Anthropology: An Introduction to Research Design.* Stanford, CA: Stanford University Press.

Johnson, A. W., and T. K. Earle 2000. *The Evolution of Human Societies: From Foraging Group to Agrarian State,* 2nd ed. Stanford, CA: Stanford University Press.

Johnston, B. R. 2009. *Life and Death Matters: Human Rights, Environment, and Social Justice,* 2nd ed. Walnut Creek, CA: Left Coast Press.

Jones, D. 1999. Hot Asset in Corporate: Anthropology Degrees. *USA Today,* February 18, p. B1.

Joralemon, D. 2006. *Exploring Medical Anthropology,* 2nd ed. Boston: Pearson.

Jordan, A. 2003. *Business Anthropology.* Prospect Heights, IL: Waveland.

Kan, S. 1986. The 19th-Century Tlingit Potlatch: A New Perspective. *American Ethnologist* 13:191–212.

———. 1989. *Symbolic Immortality: The Tlingit Potlatch of the Nineteenth Century.* Washington, DC: Smithsonian Institution Press.

Kantor, P. 1996. Domestic Violence against Women: A Global Issue. http://metalab.unc.edu/ucis/pubs/Carolina_Papers/Abuse/figure1.html.

Kaufman, S. R., and L. M. Morgan 2005. The Anthropology of the Beginnings and Ends of Life. *Annual Review of Anthropology* 34:317–341.

Kearney, M. 1996. *Reconceptualizing the Peasantry: Anthropology in Global Perspective.* Boulder, CO: West-view Press.

———. 2004. *Changing Fields of Anthropology: From Local to Global.* Lanham, MD: Rowman & Littlefield.

Kelly, R. C. 1976. Witchcraft and Sexual Relations: An Exploration in the Social and Semantic Implications of the Structure of Belief. In *Man and Woman in the New Guinea Highlands,* P. Brown and G. Buchbinder, eds., pp. 36–53. Special Publication no. 8. Washington, DC: American Anthropological Association.

Kelly, R. L. 1995. *The Foraging Spectrum: Diversity in Hunter-Gatherer Lifeways.* Washington, DC: Smithsonian Institution Press.

Kent, S. 1992. The Current Forager Controversy: Real versus Ideal Views of Hunter-gatherers. *Man* 27:45–70.

———. 1996. *Cultural Diversity among Twentieth-Century Foragers: An African Perspective.* New York: Cambridge University Press.

Kent, S., and H. Vierich 1989. The Myth of Ecological Determinism: Anticipated Mobility and Site Organization of Space. In *Farmers as Hunters: The Implications of Sedentism,* S. Kent, ed., pp. 96–130. New York: Cambridge University Press.

Keppel, K. G., J. N. Pearch, and D. K. Wagener 2002. Trends in Racial and Ethnic-Specific Rates for the Health Status Indicators: United States, 1990–98. *Healthy People Statistical Notes No. 23.* Hyattsville, MD: National Center for Health Statistics.

Kerbo, H. R. 2006. World Poverty: *Global Inequality and the Modern World System.* Boston: McGraw-Hill.

Keynes, J. M. 1927. *The End of Laissez-Faire.* London: L and Virginia Woolf.

———. 1936. *General Theory of Employment, Interest, and Money.* New York: Harcourt Brace.

Kimmel, M. S. 2007. *The Gendered Society,* 3rd ed. New York: Oxford University Press.

Kimmel, M. S., and M. A. Messner, eds. 2007. *Men's Lives,* 7th ed. Boston: Pearson.

Kimmel, M. S., and R. Plante 2004. *Sexualities: Identities, Behaviors, and Society.* New York: Oxford University Press.

Kimmel, M. S., J. Hearn, and R. W. Connell 2004. *Handbook of Studies on Men and Masculinities.* Thousand Oaks, CA: Sage.

Kinsey, A. C., W. B. Pomeroy, and C. E. Martin 1948. *Sexual Behavior in the Human Male.* Philadelphia: W. B. Saunders.

Klass, M. 2003. *Mind over Mind: The Anthropology and Psychology of Spirit Possession.* Lanham, MA: Rowman & Littlefield.

Klein, R. G., with B. Edgar 2002. *The Dawn of Human Culture.* New York: Wiley.

Kleinfeld, J. 1975. Positive Stereotyping: The Cultural Relativist in the Classroom. *Human Organization* 34:269–274.

Kluckhohn, C. 1944. *Mirror for Man: A Survey of Human Behavior and Social Attitudes.* Greenwich, CT: Fawcett.

Kottak, C. P. 1980. *The Past in the Present: History, Ecology, and Social Organization in Highland Madagascar.* Ann Arbor: University of Michigan Press.

———. 1990a. Culture and "Economic Development." *American Anthropologist* 93(3):723–731.

———. 1990b. *Prime-Time Society: An Anthropological Analysis of Television and Culture.* Belmont, CA: Wadsworth.

———. 1991. When People Don't Come First: Some Lessons from Completed Projects. In *Putting People First: Sociological Variables in Rural Development,* 2nd ed., M. Cernea, ed., pp. 429–464. New York: Oxford University Press.

———. 2004. An Anthropological Take on Sustainable Development: A Comparative Study of Change. *Human Organization* (63,4): 501–510.

———. 2006. *Assault on Paradise: The Globalization of a Little Community in Brazil,* 4th ed. New York: McGraw-Hill.

———. 2007. Return to Madagascar: A Forty Year Retrospective. *General Anthropology: Bulletin of the General*

Anthropology Division of the American Anthropological Association 14(2):1–10.

Kottak, C. P., and K. A. Kozaitis 2008. *On Being Different: Diversity and Multiculturalism in the North American Mainstream,* 3rd ed. Boston: McGraw-Hill.

Kottak, N. C. 2002. *Stealing the Neighbor's Chicken: Social Control in Northern Mozambique.* Ph.D. dissertation. Department of Anthropology, Emory University, Atlanta, GA.

Kreider, R. M., and J. M. Fields 2002. Number, Timing and Duration of Marriages and Divorces: 1996. U.S. Census Bureau. *Current Population Reports*, P70–80, February. http://www.census.gov/prod/2002pubs/p70–80.pdf.

Kuhn, S. L., M. C. Stiner, and D. S. Reese 2001. Ornaments of the Earliest Upper Paleolithic: New Insights from the Levant. *Proceedings of the National Academy of Sciences of the United States of America* 98(13):7641–7646.

Kulick, D. 1998. *Travesti: Sex, Gender, and Culture among Brazilian Transgendered Prostitutes.* Chicago: University of Chicago Press.

Kuper, L. 2006. *Race, Class, and Power: Ideology and Revolutionary Change in Plural Societies.* New Brunswick, NJ: Transaction Publishers.

Kurtz, D. V. 2001. *Political Anthropology: Power and Paradigms.* Boulder, CO: Westview Press.

Kutsche, P. 1998. *Field Ethnography: A Manual for Doing Cultural Anthropology.* Upper Saddle River, NJ: Prentice Hall.

Labov, W. 1972a. *Language in the Inner City: Studies in the Black English Vernacular.* Philadelphia: University of Pennsylvania Press.

———. 1972b. *Sociolinguistic Patterns.* Philadelphia: University of Pennsylvania Press.

La fraugh, R. J. n.d. Euskara: The History, a True Mystery. The La Fraugh Name History. http://planetrjl.tripod.com/LaFraughName/id5.html.

Laguerre, M. 1984. *American Odyssey: Haitians in New York.* Ithaca, NY: Cornell University Press.

———. 1998. *Diasporic Citizenship: Haitian Americans in Transnational America.* New York: St. Martin's Press.

———. 1999. *The Global Ethnopolis: Chinatown, Japantown, and Manilatown in American Society.* New York: St. Martin's Press.

———. 2001. *Urban Multiculturalism and Globalization in New York City.* New York: Palgrave Macmillan.

Laird, S. A. 2002. *Biodiversity and Traditional Knowledge: Equitable Partnerships in Practice.* Sterling, VA: Earthscan.

Lakoff, R. 2004. *Language and Women's Place: Text and Commentaries,* rev. ed. New York: Oxford University Press.

Lakoff, R. T. 2000. *The Language War.* Berkeley: University of California Press.

———. 2004. *Language and Woman's Place,* rev. ed. New York: Oxford University Press.

Lambek, M. 2008. *A Reader in the Anthropology of Religion.* Malden, MA: Blackwell.

Lancaster, R. N., and M. Di Leonardo, eds. 1997. *The Gender/Sexuality Reader: Culture, History, Political Economy.* New York: Routledge.

Lance, L. M., and E. E. Mckenna 1975. Analysis of Cases Pertaining to the Impact of Western Technology on the Non-Western World. *Human Organization* 34:87–94.

Larson, A. 1989. Social Context of Human Immunodeficiency Virus Transmission in Africa: Historical and Cultural Bases of East and Central African Sexual Relations. *Review of Infectious Diseases* 11:716–731.

Lassiter, L. E. 1998. *The Power of Kiowa Song: A Collaborative Ethnography.* Tucson: University of Arizona Press.

Leach, E. R. 1955. Polyandry, Inheritance and the Definition of Marriage. *Man* 55:182–186.

———. 1961. *Rethinking Anthropology.* London: Athlone Press.

Lee, R. B. 1979. *The !Kung San: Men, Women, and Work in a Foraging Society.* New York: Cambridge University Press.

———. 1984. *The Dobe !Kung.* New York: Harcourt Brace.

———. 1993. *The Dobe Ju/'hoansi,* 2nd ed. Fort Worth, TX: Harcourt Brace.

———. 2003. *The Dobe Ju/'hoansi,* 3rd ed. Belmont, CA: Wadsworth.

Lee, R. B., and R. H. Daly 1999. *The Cambridge Encyclopedia of Hunters and Gatherers.* New York: Cambridge University Press.

Lehmann, A. C., J. E. Meyers, and P. A. Moro, eds. 2005. *Magic, Witchcraft, and Religion: An Anthropological Study of the Supernatural,* 6th ed. Boston: McGraw-Hill.

Leman, J. 2001. *The Dynamics of Emerging Ethnicities: Immigrant and Indigenous Ethnogenesis in Confrontation.* New York: Peter Lang.

Lenski, G. 1966. *Power and Privilege: A Theory of Social Stratification.* New York: McGraw-Hill.

Levine, N. E. 2008. Alternative Kinship, Marriage, and Reproduction. *Annual Review of Anthropology* 37:17–35.

Lèvi-Strauss, C. 1963. *Totemism.* R. Needham (trans.). Boston: Beacon Press.

———. 1967. *Structural Anthropology.* New York: Doubleday.

Levy, J. E., with B. Pepper 1992. *Orayvi Revisited: Social Stratification in an "Egalitarian" Society.* Santa Fe, NM: School of American Research Press, and Seattle: University of Washington Press.

Lewellen, T. C. 2003. *Political Anthropology: An Introduction,* 3rd ed. Westport, CT: Praeger.

Lewis, P. 1992. U.N. Sees a Crisis in Overpopulation. *The New York Times,* p. A6.

Lie, J. 2001. *Multiethnic Japan.* Cambridge, MA: Harvard University Press.

Lieban, R. W. 1977. The Field of Medical Anthropology. In *Culture, Disease, and Healing: Studies in Medical Anthropology,* D. Landy, ed., pp. 13–31. New York: Macmillan.

Lindenbaum, S. 1972. Sorcerers, Ghosts, and Polluting Women: An Analysis of Religious Belief and Population Control. *Ethnology* 11:241–253.

Linton, R. 1943. Nativistic Movements. *American Anthropologist* 45:230–240.

Little, K. 1965. *West African Urbanization: A Study of Voluntary Associations in Social Change.* Cambridge: Cambridge University Press.

———. 1971. Some Aspects of African Urbanization South of the Sahara. Reading, MA: Addison-Wesley, McCaleb Modules in Anthropology.

Lockwood, W. G. 1975. *European Moslems: Economy and Ethnicity in Western Bosnia.* New York: Academic Press.

Lohr, S. 2005. Cutting Here, but Hiring Over There. *The New York Times,* June 24. http://www.nytimes.com.

Lowie, R. H. 1961 (orig. 1920). *Primitive Society.* New York: Harper & Brothers.

Lucentini, J. 2002. Bones Reveal Some Truth in "Noble Savage Myth." *Washington Post,* April 15, p. A09.

Lugaila, T. 1999. Married Adults Still in the Majority, Census Bureau Reports. http://www.census.gov/Press-Release/www/1999/cb99-03.html.

Madra, Y. M. 2004. Karl Polanyi: Freedom in a Complex Society. *Econ-Atrocity Bulletin: In the History of Thought.* http://www.fguide.org/Bulletin/polanyi.htm.

Malinowski, B. 1929. Practical Anthropology. *Africa* 2:23–38.

———. 1961 (orig. 1922). *Argonauts of the Western Pacific.* New York: Dutton.

———. 1978 (orig. 1931). The Role of Magic and Religion. In *Reader in Comparative Religion: An Anthropological Approach,* 4th ed., W. A. Lessa and E. Z. Vogt, eds., pp. 37–46. New York: Harper and Row.

Malkki, Liisa H. 1995. *Purity and Exile: Violence, Memory, and National*

Cosmology among Hutu Refugees in Tanzania. Chicago: University of Chicago Press.

Maquet, J. 1964. Objectivity in Anthropology. *Current Anthropology* 5:47–55.

Mar, M. E. 1997. Secondary Colors: The Multiracial Option. *Harvard Magazine,* May–June, pp. 19–20.

Marcus, G. E., and D. Cushman 1982. Ethnographies as Texts. *Annual Review of Anthropology* 11:25–69.

Marcus, G. E., and F. R. Myers, eds. 1995. *The Traffic in Culture: Refiguring Art and Anthropology.* Berkeley: University of California Press.

Marcus, G. E., and M. M. J. Fischer 1986. *Anthropology as Cultural Critique: An Experimental Moment in the Human Sciences.* Chicago: University of Chicago Press.

———. 1999. *Anthropology as Cultural Critique: An Experimental Moment in the Human Sciences,* 2nd ed. Chicago: University of Chicago Press.

Margolis, M. L. 1984. *Mothers and Such: American Views of Women and How They Changed.* Berkeley: University of California Press.

———. 2000. *True to Her Nature: Changing Advice to American Women.* Prospect Heights, IL: Waveland.

Margolis, M. L. 2003. The Relative Status of Men and Women. In *Encyclopedia of Sex and Gender: Men and Women in the World's Cultures,* C. Ember and M. Ember, eds., pp. 137–145. New York: Kluwer Academic/Plenum.

Martin, E. 1992. The End of the Body? *American Ethnologist* 19:121–140.

Martin, K., and B. Voorhies 1975. *Female of the Species.* New York: Columbia University Press.

Martinez, E., and A. Garcia 2000. What Is "Neo-Liberalism"? A Brief Definition. http://www. globalexchange.org/campaigns/econ101/neoliberalDefined.html.pdf.

Marx, K., and F. Engels 1976 (orig. 1948). *Communist Manifesto.* New York: Pantheon.

Mascia-Lees, F., and N. J. Black 2000. *Gender and Anthropology.* Prospect Heights, IL: Waveland.

Mathews, G. 2000. *Global Culture/Individual Identity: Searching for Home in the Cultural Supermarket.* New York: Routledge.

Maugh, T. H., III 2007. One Language Disappears Every 14 Days; about Half of the World's Distinct Tongues Could Vanish This Century, Researchers Say. *Los Angeles Times,* September 19.

Maybury-Lewis, D. 2002. *Indigenous Peoples, Ethnic Groups, and the State,* 2nd ed. Boston: Allyn & Bacon.

Mayell, H. 2004. Is Bead Find Proof Modern Thought Began in Africa? *National Geographic News,* March 31. http://news.nationalgeographic.com/news/2004/03/0331_040331_ostrichman.html.

McBrearty, S., and A. S. Brooks 2000. The Revolution That Wasn't: A New Interpretation of the Origin of Modern Human Behavior. *Journal of Human Evolution* 39:453–563.

McElroy, A., and P. K. Townsend 2003. *Medical Anthropology in Ecological Perspective,* 4th ed. Boulder, CO: Westview Press.

McKinnon, S. 2005. On Kinship and Marriage: A Critique of the Genetic and Gender Calculus of Evolutionary Psychology. In *Complexities: Beyond Nature and Nurture,* S. McKinnon and S. Silverman, eds., pp. 106–131. Chicago: The University of Chicago Press.

Meigs, A., and K. Barlow 2002. Beyond the Taboo: Imagining Incest. *American Anthropologist* 104(1):38–49.

Merry, S. E. 2006. Anthropology and International Law. *Annual Review of Anthropology* 35:99–116.

Michaels, E. 1986. Aboriginal Content. Paper presented at the meeting of the Australian Screen Studies Association, December, Sydney.

Miles, H. L. 1983. Apes and Language: The Search for Communicative Competence.

In *Language in Primates,* J. de Luce and H. T. Wilder, eds., pp. 43–62. New York: Springer Verlag.

Miller, B. D. 1997. *The Endangered Sex: Neglect of Female Children in Rural North India.* New York: Oxford University Press.

Miller, J. nd. Alaskan Tlingit and Tsimtsian. Seattle: University of Washington Libraries, Digital Collections. http://content.lib.washington.edu/aipnw/miller1.html.

Miller, N., and R. C. Rockwell, eds. 1988. *AIDS in Africa: The Social and Policy Impact.* Lewiston, NY: Edwin Mellen.

Mintz, S. 1985. *Sweetness and Power: The Place of Sugar in Modern History.* New York: Viking Penguin.

Mitchell, J. C. 1966. Theoretical Orientations in African Urban Studies. In *The Social Anthropology of Complex Societies,* M. Banton, ed., pp. 37–68. London: Tavistock.

Moerman, M. 1965. Ethnic Identification in a Complex Civilization: Who Are the Lue? *American Anthropologist* 67(5 Part I):1215–1230.

Montagu, A., ed. 1997. *Man's Most Dangerous Myth: The Fallacy of Race.* Walnut Creek, CA: AltaMira.

Morgen, S., ed. 1989. *Gender and Anthropology: Critical Reviews for Research and Teaching.* Washington, DC: American Anthropological Association.

Motseta, S. 2006. Botswana Gives Bushmen Tough Conditions. *Tulsa World,* December 14.

Mukhopadhyay, C., and P. Higgins 1988. Anthropological Studies of Women's Status Revisited: 1977–1987. *Annual Review of Anthropology* 17:461–495.

Mukhopadhyay, C., R. Henze, and Y. T. Moses 2007. *How Real Is Race? A Sourcebook on Race, Culture, and Biology.* Lanham, MD: AltaMira.

Mullings, L., ed. 1987. *Cities of the United States: Studies in Urban Anthropology.* New York: Columbia University Press.

Murdock, G. P. 1934. *Our Primitive Contemporaries.* New York: Macmillan.

———. 1949. *Social Structure.* New York: Macmillan.

———. 1957. World Ethnographic Sample. *American Anthropologist* 59:664–687.

Murdock, G. P., and C. Provost 1973. Factors in the Division of Labor by Sex: A Cross-Cultural Analysis. *Ethnology* XII(2):203–225.

Murphy, R. F., and L. Kasdan 1959. The Structure of Parallel Cousin Marriage. *American Anthropologist* 61:17–29.

Murray, S. O., and W. Roscoe, eds. 1998. *Boy-wives and Female Husbands: Studies in African Homosexualities.* New York: St. Martin's Press.

Mydans, S. 1992a. Criticism Grows over Aliens Seized during Riots. *The New York Times,* May 29, p. A8.

———. 1992b Judge Dismisses Case in Shooting by Officer. *The New York Times,* June 4, p. A8.

Nagel, J. 1996. *American Indian Ethnic Renewal: Red Power and the Resurgence of Identity and Culture.* New York: Oxford University Press.

Nanda, S. 2000. *Gender Diversity: Crosscultural Variations.* Prospect Heights, IL: Waveland.

National Academies 2007. Understanding and Responding to Climate Change: Highlights of National Academies Reports. http://dels.nas.edu/basc/Climate-HIGH.pdf.

Naylor, L. L. 1996. *Culture and Change: An Introduction.* Westport, CT: Bergin and Garvey.

Nazarea, V. D. 2006. Local Knowledge and Memory in Biodiversity Conservation. *Annual Review of Anthropology* 35:317–335.

Newman, M. 1992. Riots Bring Attention to Growing Hispanic Presence in South-Central Area. *The New York Times,* May 11, p. A10.

Nielsson, G. P. 1985. States and Nation-Groups: A Global Taxonomy. In *New Nationalisms of the Developed World,*

E. A. Tiryakian and R. Rogowski, eds., pp. 27–56. Boston: Allen and Unwin.

Nolan, R. W. 2002. *Development Anthropology: Encounters in the Real World.* Boulder, CO: Westview Press.

———. 2003. *Anthropology in Practice.* Boulder, CO: Lynne Rienner.

Nordstrom, C. 2004. *Shadows of War: Violence, Power, and International Profiteering in the Twenty-First Century.* Berkeley: University of California Press.

Nugent, D., and J. Vincent, eds. 2004. *A Companion to the Anthropology of Politics.* Malden, MA: Blackwell.

O'Leary, C. 2002. *Class Formation, Diet and Economic Transformation in Two Brazilian Fishing Communities.* Unpublished Ph.D. dissertation, University of Michigan, Ann Arbor.

Ohlemacher, S. 2006. 2006: The Year of the 300M Mark: Face of America Changes as Country Grows. *Charleston Post and Courier,* June 26, pp. 1A, 11A.

Omohundro, J. T. 2001. *Careers in Anthropology,* 2nd ed. Boston: McGraw-Hill.

Ong, A. 1987. *Spirits of Resistance and Capitalist Discipline: Factory Women in Malaysia.* Albany: State University of New York Press.

———. 1989. Center, Periphery, and Hierarchy: Gender in Southeast Asia. In *Gender and Anthropology: Critical Reviews for Research and Teaching,* S. Morgen, ed., pp. 294–312. Washington, DC: American Anthropological Association.

Ong, A., and S. J. Collier, eds. 2005. *Global Assemblages: Technology, Politics, and Ethics as Anthropological Problems.* Malden, MA: Blackwell.

Ontario Consultants on Religious Tolerance 1996. Religious Access Dispute Resolved. Internet Mailing List, April 12, http://www.religious tolerance.org/news_694.htm.

———. 2001. Religions of the World: Number of Adherents; Rates of Growth.

http://www.religioustolerance.org/worldrel.htm.

Ortner, S. B. 1984. Theory in Anthropology Since the Sixties. *Comparative Studies in Society and History* 126(1):126–166.

Ott, S. 1981. *The Circle of Mountains: A Basque Shepherding Community.* Oxford: Clarendon Press.

Parkin, R., and L. Stone, eds. 2004. *Kinship and Family: An Anthropological Reader.* Malden, MA: Blackwell.

Patterson, F. 1978. Conversations with a Gorilla. *National Geographic,* October, pp. 438–465.

Paulson, T. E. 2005. Chimp, Human DNA Comparison Finds Vast Similarities, Key Differences. *Seattle Post-Intelligencer Reporter,* September 1, 2005. http://seattlepi.nwsource.com/local/238852_chimp01.html.

Peletz, M. 1988. *A Share of the Harvest: Kinship, Property, and Social History among the Malays of Rembau.* Berkeley: University of California Press.

Pelto, P. 1973. *The Snowmobile Revolution: Technology and Social Change in the Arctic.* Menlo Park, CA: Cummings.

Peplau, L. A., ed. 1999. *Gender, Culture, and Ethnicity: Current Research about Women and Men.* Mountain View, CA: Mayfield.

Peters, J. D. 1997. Seeing Bifocally: Media, Place, Culture. In *Culture, Power, Place: Explorations in Critical Anthropology,* A. Gupta and J. Ferguson, eds., pp. 75–92. Durham, NC: Duke University Press.

Peters-Golden, H. 2006. *Culture Sketches: Case Studies in Anthropology,* 4th ed. New York: McGraw-Hill.

Petraglia-Bahri, D. 1996. Introduction to Postcolonial Studies. http://www.emory.edu/ENGLISH/Bahri/.

Piddington, R. 1960. Action Anthropology. *Journal of the Polynesian Society* 69:199–213.

Piddocke, S. 1969. The Potlatch System of the Southern Kwakiutl: A New Perspective. In *Environment and Cultural Behavior,* A. P. Vayda, ed., pp. 130–156. Garden City, NY: Natural History Press.

Plattner, S., ed. 1989. *Economic Anthropology*. Stanford, CA: Stanford University Press.

Podolefsky, A., and P. J. Brown, eds. 1992. *Applying Anthropology: An Introductory Reader,* 2nd ed. Mountain View, CA: Mayfield.

Polanyi, K. 1968. *Primitive, Archaic and Modern Economies: Essays of Karl Polanyi,* G. Dalton, ed., Garden City, NY: Anchor Books.

Pospisil, L. 1963. *The Kapauku Papuans of West New Guinea*. New York: Holt, Rinehart & Winston.

Potash, B., ed. 1986. *Widows in African Societies: Choices and Constraints*. Stanford, CA: Stanford University Press.

Price, R., ed. 1973. *Maroon Societies*. New York: Anchor Press/Doubleday.

Radcliffe-Brown, A. R. 1965 (orig. 1962). *Structure and Function in Primitive Society*. New York: Free Press.

Ramirez, R. R., and G. P. de la Cruz 2003. The Hispanic Population in the United States. U.S. Census Bureau. *Current Population Reports,* P20–545, March, http://www.census.gov/prod/2003pubs/p20-545.pdf.

Ranger, T. O. 1996. Postscript. In *Postcolonial Identities,* R. Werbner and T. O. Ranger, eds. London: Zed.

Rappaport, R. A. 1974. Obvious Aspects of Ritual. *Cambridge Anthropology* 2: 2–60.

———. 1999. *Holiness and Humanity: Ritual in the Making of Religious Life*. New York: Cambridge University Press.

Rathje, W. L., and C. Murphy 2001. *Rubbish!: The Archaeology of Garbage*. Tucson: University of Arizona Press.

Rathus, S. A., J. S. Nevid, and J. Fichner-Rathus 2008. *Human Sexuality in a World of Diversity,* 7th ed. Boston: Allyn & Bacon.

Redfield, R. 1941. *The Folk Culture of Yucatan*. Chicago: University of Chicago Press.

Redfield, R., R. Linton, and M. Herskovits 1936. Memorandum on the Study of Acculturation. *American Anthropologist* 38:149–152.

Reese, W. L. 1999. *Dictionary of Philosophy and Religion: Eastern and Western Thought*. Amherst, NY: Humanities Books.

Reiter, R. 1975. Men and Women in the South of France: Public and Private Domains. In *Toward an Anthropology of Women,* R. Reiter, ed., pp. 252–282. New York: Monthly Review Press.

Rickford, J. R. 1997. Suite for Ebony and Phonics, *Discover,* December. http://www. stanford.edu/~rickford/papers/SuiteForEbonyAndPhonics.html.

———. 1999. *African American Vernacular English: Features, Evolution, Educational Implications*. Malden, MA: Blackwell.

Rickford, J. R., and R. J. Rickford 2000. *Spoken Soul: The Story of Black English*. New York: Wiley.

Roberts, S., A. Sabar, B. Goodman, and M. Balleza 2007. 51% of Women Are Now Living without Spouse. *New York Times,* January 16. http://www.nytimes.com.

Robertson, A. F. 1995. *The Big Catch: A Practical Introduction to Development*. Boulder, CO: Westview Press.

Robertson, J. 1992. *Koreans in Japan*. Paper presented at the University of Michigan Department of Anthropology, Martin Luther King Jr. Day Panel, January. Ann Arbor: University of Michigan Department of Anthropology (unpublished).

Rodseth, L., R. W. Wrangham, A. M. Harrigan, and B. Smuts 1991. The Human Community as a Primate Society. *Current Anthropology* 32:221–254.

Romaine, S. 1999. *Communicating Gender*. Mahwah, NJ: Erlbaum.

———. 2000. *Language in Society: An Introduction to Sociolinguistics,* 2nd ed. New York: Oxford University Press.

Root, D. 1996. *Cannibal Culture: Art, Appropriation, and the Commodification of Difference*. Boulder, CO: Westview Press.

Rosaldo, M. Z. 1980a. *Knowledge and Passion: Notions of Self and Social Life*. Stanford, CA: Stanford University Press.

———. 1980b. The Use and Abuse of Anthropology: Reflections on Feminism and Cross-Cultural Understanding. *Signs* 5(3):389– 417.

Rouse, R. 1991. Mexican Migration and the Social Space of Postmodernism. *Diaspora* 1(1):8–23.

Royal Anthropological Institute 1951. *Notes and Queries on Anthropology,* 6th ed. London: Routledge and Kegan Paul.

Ryan, S. 1990. *Ethnic Conflict and International Relations*. Brookfield, MA: Dartmouth.

Sahlins, M. D. 1968. *Tribesmen*. Englewood Cliffs, NJ: Prentice Hall.

———. 2004. *Stone Age Economics*. New York: Routledge.

Salzman, P. C. 1974. Political Organization among Nomadic Peoples. In *Man in Adaptation: The Cultural Present*, 2nd ed., Y. A. Cohen, ed., pp. 267–284. Chicago: Aldine.

———. 2004. *Pastoralists: Equality, Hierarchy, and the State*. Boulder, CO: Westview Press.

Salzmann, Z. 2007. *Language, Culture, and Society: An Introduction to Linguistic Anthropology,* 4th ed. Boulder, CO: Westview.

Sanday, P. R. 1974. Female Status in the Public Domain. In *Woman, Culture, and Society*, M. Z. Rosaldo and L. Lamphere, eds., pp. 189–206. Stanford, CA: Stanford University Press.

———. 2002. *Women at the Center: Life in a Modern Matriarchy*. Ithaca, NY: Cornell University Press.

Sapir, E. 1931. Conceptual Categories in Primitive Languages. *Science* 74:578–584.

Scheidel, W. 1997. Brother-Sister Marriage in Roman Egypt. *Journal of Biosocial Science* 29(3):361–371.

Scheinman, M. 1980. Imperialism. *Academic American Encyclopedia*. Princeton, NJ: Arete, volume 11, pp. 61–62.

Schneider, D. M. 1967. Kinship and Culture: Descent and Filiation as Cultural Constructs. *Southwestern Journal of Anthropology* 23:65–73.

Scholte, J. A. 2000. *Globalization: A Critical Introduction*. New York: St. Martin's Press.

Scott, J. C. 1985. *Weapons of the Weak*. New Haven, CT: Yale University Press.

———. 1990. *Domination and the Arts of Resistance*. New Haven, CT: Yale University Press.

Scudder, t., and E. Colson 1980. *Secondary Education and the Formation of an Elite: The Impact of Education on Gwembe District, Zambia*. London: Academic Press.

Scupin, R. 2003. *Race and Ethnicity: An Anthropological Focus on the United States and the World*. Upper Saddle River, NJ: Prentice Hall.

Sebeok, T. A., and J. Umiker-Sebeok, eds. 1980. *Speaking of Apes: A Critical Anthropology of Two-Way Communication with Man*. New York: Plenum.

Service, E. R. 1962. *Primitive Social Organization: An Evolutionary Perspective*. New York: McGraw-Hill.

———. 1966. *The Hunters*. Englewood Cliffs, NJ: Prentice Hall.

Shanklin, E. 1995. *Anthropology and Race*. Belmont, CA: Wadsworth.

Shannon, T. R. 1996. *An Introduction to the World-System Perspective,* 2nd ed. Boulder, CO: Westview Press.

Sharma, A., and A. Gupta, eds. 2006. *The Anthropology of the State: A Reader*. Malden, MA: Blackwell.

Shivaram, C. 1996. Where Women Wore the Crown: Kerala's Dissolving Matriarchies Leave a Rich Legacy of Compassionate Family Culture. *Hinduism Today,* http://www.spiritweb.org/Hinduism Today/96_02_Women_Wore_ Crown.html.

Shostak, M. 1981. *Nisa: The Life and Words of a !Kung Woman*. Cambridge, MA: Harvard University Press.

Silberbauer, G. 1981. *Hunter and Habitat in the Central Kalahari Desert.* New York: Cambridge University Press.

Sillitoe, P., ed. 2007. *Local Science versus Global Science: Approaches to Indigenous Knowledge in International Development.* New York: Berghahn Books.

Singer, M., and H. Bauer 2007. *Introducing Medical Anthropology: A Discipline in Action.* Lanham, MD: AltaMira.

Sinnott, M. J. 2004. *Toms and Dees: Transgender Identity and Female Same-Sex Relationships in Thailand.* Honolulu: University of Hawaii Press.

Slade, M. 1984. Displaying Affection in Public. *The New York Times,* December 17.

Smart, A., and J. Smart 2003. Urbanization and the Global Perspective. *Annual Review of Anthropology* 32:263–285.

Smith, A. T. 2003. *The Political Landscape: Constellations of Authority in Early Complex Polities.* Westport, CT: Praeger.

Smitherman, G. 1986 (orig. 1977). *Talkin and Testifyin: The Language of Black America.* Detroit: Wayne State University Press.

Solway, J., and R. Lee 1990. Foragers, Genuine and Spurious: Situating the Kalahari San in History (with CA treatment). *Current Anthropology* 31(2): 109–146.

Spickard, P., ed. 2004. *Race and Nation: Ethnic Systems in the Modern World.* New York: Routledge.

Spindler, G. D. 2005. *New Horizons in the Anthropology of Education.* Mahwah, NJ: Erlbaum.

———. ed. 2000. *Fifty Years of Anthropology and Education, 1950–2000: A Spindler Anthology.* Mahwah, NJ: Erlbaum.

Srivastava, J., N. J. H. Smith, and D. A. Forno 1998. *Integrating Biodiversity in Agricultural Intensification: Toward Sound Practices.* Washington, DC: World Bank.

Stack, C. B. 1975. *All Our Kin: Strategies for Survival in a Black Community.* New York: Harper Torchbooks.

Statistical Abstract of the United States 1991. 111th ed. Washington, DC: U.S.

Bureau of the Census, U.S.Government Printing Office.

———. 1996. 116th ed. Washington, DC: U.S. Bureau of the Census, U.S.Government Printing Office.

———. 1999. 119th ed. Washington, DC: U.S. Bureau of the Census, U.S.Government Printing Office.

———. 2001. http://www.census.gov/prod/www/statistical-abstract-us.html.

———. 2002. http://www.census.gov/prod/www/statistical-abstract-us.html.

———. 2007. http://www.census.gov/prod/www/statistical-abstract.html.

———.2008. http://www.census.gov/prod/www/statistical-abstract.html.

Statistics Canada 2001a 1996. Census. National Tables. http//www.statcan.ca/english/census96/nation.htm.

———. 2003 Religions in Canada. *2001 Census*—Release 8, May 13, 2003. http://www12.statcan.ca/english/census01/release/index.cfm.

Stein, R. L., and P. L. Stein 2008. *The Anthropology of Religion, Magic, and Witchcraft.* Boston: Pearson.

Stevens, W. K. 1992. Humanity Confronts Its Handiwork: An Altered Planet. *The New York Times,* May 5, pp. B5–B7.

Stevenson, D. 2003. *Cities and Urban Cultures.* Philadelphia, PA: Open University Press.

Stoler, A. 1977. Class Structure and Female Autonomy in Rural Java. *Signs* 3:74–89.

Stone, L. S. 2004. Gay Marriage and Anthropology. *Anthropology News* 45(5). http://www.aaanet.org/press/an/0405ifcomm4.htm.

Strathern, A., and P. J. Stewart 1999. *Curing and Healing: Medical Anthropology in Global Perspective.* Durham, NC: Carolina Academic Press.

Sunderland, P. L., and R. M. Denny 2007. *Doing Anthropology in Consumer Research.* Walnut Creek, CA: Left Coast Press.

Suttles, W. 1960. Affinal Ties, Subsistence, and Prestige among the Coast Salish. *American Anthropologist* 62:296–305.

Swift, M. 1963. Men and Women in Malay Society. In *Women in the New Asia*, B. Ward, ed., pp. 268–286. Paris: UNESCO.

Tanaka, J. 1980. *The San Hunter-Gatherers of the Kalahari*. Tokyo: University of Tokyo Press.

Tannen, D. 1990. *You Just Don't Understand: Women and Men in Conversation*. New York: Ballantine Books.

Tannen, D., ed. 1993. *Gender and Conversational Interaction*. New York: Oxford University Press.

Taylor, C. 1987. Anthropologist-in-Residence. In *Applied Anthropology in America*, 2nd ed., E. M. Eddy and W. L. Partridge, eds. New York: Columbia University Press.

Terrace, H. S. 1979. *Nim*. New York: Knopf.

Thomas, L. 1999. *Language, Society and Power*. New York: Routledge.

Thomas, L., and S. Wareing, eds. 2004. *Language, Society, and Power: An Introduction*. New York: Routledge.

Thompson, W. 1983. Introduction: World System with and without the Hyphen. In *Contending Approaches to World System Analysis*, W. Thompson, ed., pp. 7–26. Thousand Oaks, CA: Sage.

Tice, K. 1997. Reflections on Teaching Anthropology for Use in the Public and Private Sector. In *The Teaching of Anthropology: Problems, Issues, and Decisions*, C. P. Kottak, J. J. White, R. H. Furlow, and P. C. Rice, eds., pp. 273–284. Mountain View, CA: Mayfield.

Tishkov, V. A. 2004. *Chechnya: Life in a War-Torn Society*. Berkeley: University of California Press.

Titiev, M. 1992. *Old Oraibi: A Study of the Hopi Indians of Third Mesa*. Albuquerque: University of New Mexico Press.

Tomlinson, J. 1991. *Cultural Imperialism: A Critical Introduction*. Baltimore: Johns Hopkins University Press.

———. 1999. *Globalization and Culture*. Chicago: University of Chicago Press.

Toner, R. 1992. Los Angeles Riots Are a Warning, Americans Fear. *The New York Times*, May 11, pp. A1, A11.

Trask, L. 1996. FAQs about Basque and the Basques. http://www.cogs.susx.ac.uk/users/larryt/basque.faqs.html.

Trevathan, W. R, Smith, E. O., and McKenna, J., eds. 2007. *Evolutionary Medicine and Health*. New York: Oxford University Press.

Trivedi, B. P. 2001. Scientists Identify a Language Gene. *National Geographic News*, October 4. http://news.nationalgeographic.com/news/2001/10/1004_Tvlanguagegene.html.

Trudgill, P. 2000. *Sociolinguistics: An Introduction to Language and Society*, 4th ed. New York: Penguin Books.

Turnbull, C. 1965. *Wayward Servants: The Two Worlds of the African Pygmies*. Garden City, NY: Natural History Press.

Turner, V. W. 1974 (orig. 1967). *The Ritual Process*. Harmondsworth, England: Penguin Books.

———. 1995 (orig. 1969). *The Ritual Process*. Hawthorne, NY: Aldine de Gruyter.

Tylor, E. B. 1958 (orig. 1871). *Primitive Culture*. New York: Harper Torchbooks.

U.S. Census Bureau 2000. http://www.census.gov.

———. 2004. *Statistical Abstract of the United States, 2003*. Table 688, p. 459. http://www.census.gov/prod/2004pubs/03statab/income.pdf.

———. 2005. *Statistical Abstract of the United States, 2004*. http://www.census.gov/prod/2004pubs/04statab/labor.pdf.

———. 2006. http://quickfacts.census.gov/qfd/index.html.

Ulijaszek, S. J., and H. Lofink 2006. Obesity in Biocultural Perspective. *Annual Review of Anthropology* 35:337–360.

Van Cantfort, T. E., and J. B. Rimpau 1982. Sign Language Studies with Children and Chimpanzees. *Sign Language Studies* 34:15–72.

Van der Elst, D., and P. Bohannan 2003. *Culture as Given, Culture as Choice,* 2nd ed. Prospect Heights, IL: Waveland.

Van Willigen, J. 2002. *Applied Anthropology: An Introduction,* 3rd ed. Westport, CT: Bergin and Garvey.

Vayda, A. P. 1968 (orig. 1961). Economic Systems in Ecological Perspective: The Case of the Northwest Coast. In *Readings in Anthropology,* 2nd ed., volume 2, M. H. Fried, ed., pp. 172–178. New York: Crowell.

Veblen, T. 1934. *The Theory of the Leisure Class: An Economic Study of Institutions.* New York: The Modern Library.

Verdery, K. 2001. Socialist Societies: Anthropological Aspects. *International Encyclopedia of the Social & Behavioral Sciences,* pp. 14496–14500. New York: Elsevier.

Vidal, J. 2003. Every Third Person Will be a Slum Dweller within 30 Years, UN Agency Warns: Biggest Study of World's Cities Finds 940 Million Already Living in Squalor. *The Guardian,* October 4, 2003. http://www.guardian.co.uk/international/story/0,3604,1055785,00.html.

Vigil, J. D. 2003. Urban Violence and Street Gangs. *Annual Review of Anthropology* 32: 225–242.

Viola, H. J., and C. Margolis 1991. *Seeds of Change: Five Hundred Years since Columbus, a Quincentennial Commemoration.* Washington, DC: Smithsonian Institution Press.

Wade, N. 2005. For Gay Men, Different Scent of Attraction. *The New York Times,* Late ed.—Final, May 10, p. A1.

Wade, P. 2002. *Race, Nature, and Culture: An Anthropological Perspective.* Sterling, VA: Pluto Press.

Wagley, C. W. 1968 (orig. 1959). The Concept of Social Race in the Americas. In *The Latin American Tradition,* C. Wagley, ed., pp. 155–174. New York: Columbia University Press.

Wallace, A. F. C. 1956. Revitalization Movements. *American Anthropologist* 58: 264–281.

———. 1966. *Religion: An Anthropological View.* New York: McGraw-Hill.

———. 1969. *The Death and Rebirth of the Seneca.* New York: Knopf.

Wallerstein, I. M. 1982. The Rise and Future Demise of the World Capitalist System: Concepts for Comparative Analysis. In *Introduction to the Sociology of "Developing Societies,"* H. Alavi and T. Shanin, eds., pp. 29–53. New York: Monthly Review Press.

———. 2000. *The Essential Wallerstein.* New York: New Press, Norton.

———. 2004a. *The Decline of American Power: The U.S. in a Chaotic World.* New York: New Press.

———. 2004b. *World-Systems Analysis: An Introduction.* Durham, NC: Duke University Press.

Ward, M. C. 2003. *A World Full of Women,* 3rd ed. Needham Heights, MA: Allyn & Bacon.

Ward, M. C., and M. Edelstein 2008. *A World Full of Women,* 5th ed. Needham Heights, MA: Allyn & Bacon.

Warms, R., J. Garber, and R. J. McGee, eds. 2009. *Sacred Realms: Readings in the Anthropology of Religion,* 2nd ed. New York: Oxford University Press.

Weber, M. 1958 (orig. 1904). *The Protestant Ethic and the Spirit of Capitalism.* New York: Scribner.

———. 1968 (orig. 1922). *Economy and Society.* E. Fischoff et al. (trans.). New York: Bedminster Press.

Webster's New World Encyclopedia 1993. College Edition. Englewood Cliffs, NJ: Prentice Hall.

Wedel, J. 2002. *Blurring the Boundaries of the State-Private Divide: Implications for Corruption.* Paper presented at the European Association of Social Anthropologists (EASA) Conference in Copenhagen, August 14–17, 2002. http://www.anthrobase.com/Txt/W/Wedel_J_01.htm.

Weinberg, D. 1996. Press Briefing on 1995 Income, Poverty, and Health Insurance Estimates. Housing and Household

Economic Statistics Division, U.S. Bureau of the Census. Washington, DC, September 26, http://www.census.gov/Press-Release/speech1.html.

Weise, E. 1999. Anthropologists Adapt Technology to World's Cultures. *USA Today,* May 26. http://www. usatoday. com/life/cyber/tech/ctf256.htm.

Weston, K. 1991. *Families We Choose: Lesbians, Gays, Kinship.* New York: Columbia University Press.

White, L. A. 1959. *The Evolution of Culture: The Development of Civilization to the Fall of Rome.* New York: McGraw-Hill.

Whorf, B. L. 1956. A Linguistic Consideration of Thinking in Primitive Communities. In *Language, Thought, and Reality: Selected Writings of Benjamin Lee Whorf,* J. B. Carroll, ed., pp. 65–86. Cambridge, MA: MIT Press.

Whyte, M. F. 1978. Cross-Cultural Codes Dealing with the Relative Status of Women. *Ethnology* XII(2): 203–225.

Wilford, J. N. 2002. When Humans Became Human. *New York Times,* February 26, late edition—final, sec. F, p. 1, col. 1. http://www.nytimes.com.

Wilk, R. R. 1996. *Economies and Cultures: An Introduction to Economic Anthropology.* Boulder, CO: West-view Press.

Williams, B. 1989. A Class Act: Anthropology and the Race to Nation across Ethnic Terrain. *Annual Review of Anthropology* 18:401–444.

Williams, L. M., and D. Finkelhor 1995. Paternal Caregiving and Incest: Test of a Biosocial Model. *American Journal of Orthopsychiatry* 65(1):101–113.

Willie, C. V. 2003. *A New Look at Black Families.* Walnut Creek, CA: AltaMira.

Wilmsen, E. N. 1989. *Land Filled with Flies: A Political Economy of the Kalahari.* Chicago: University of Chicago Press.

Wilson, R., ed. 1996. *Human Rights: Culture and Context: Anthropological Perspectives.* Chicago: Pluto Press.

Winter, R. 2001. Religions of the World: Number of Adherents; Names of Houses of Worship; Names of Leaders; Rates of Growth. http://www.religioustolerance.org/worldrel.htm.

Winzeler, R. L. 2007. *Anthropology and Religion.* Lanham, MD: AltaMira.

Wolcott, H. F. 2008. *Ethnography: A Way of Seeing,* 2nd ed. Lanham, MD: AltaMira.

Wolf, E. R. 1966. *Peasants.* Englewood Cliffs, NJ: Prentice Hall.

———. 1982. *Europe and the People without History.* Berkeley: University of California Press.

Wolf, E. R., with S. Silverman 2001. *Pathways of Power: Building an Anthropology of the Modern World.* Berkeley: University of California Press.

Worsley, P. 1985 (orig. 1959). Cargo Cults. In *Readings in Anthropology 85/86.* Guilford, CT: Dushkin.

Yetman, N., ed. 1991. *Majority and Minority: The Dynamics of Race and Ethnicity in American Life,* 5th ed. Boston: Allyn & Bacon.

Yurchak, A. 2002. Entrepreneurial Governmentality in Postsocialist Russia. In *The New Entrepreneurs of Europe and Asia*, V. Bonnell and T. Gold, eds., p. 301. Armonk, NY: M. E. Sharpe.

———. 2005. *Everything Was Forever until It Was No More: The Last Soviet Generation.* Princeton, NJ: Princeton University Press.

Zimmer-Tamakoshi, L. 1997. The Last Big Man: Development and Men's Discontents in the Papua New Guinea Highlands. *Oceania* 68(2):107–122

Zou, Y., and E. T. Trueba 2002. *Ethnography and Schools: Qualitative Approaches to the Study of Education.* Lanham, MD: Rowman & Littlefield.

Zulaika, J. 1988. *Basque Violence: Metaphor and Sacrament.* Reno: University of Nevada Press.

Index